Lines of Thought

Lines of Thought

Central Concepts in Cognitive Psychology

LANCE J. RIPS

UNIVERSITY PRESS

2011

OXFORD
UNIVERSITY PRESS

Oxford University Press, Inc., publishes works that further
Oxford University's objective of excellence
in research, scholarship, and education.

Oxford   New York
Auckland   Cape Town   Dar es Salaam   Hong Kong   Karachi
Kuala Lumpur   Madrid   Melbourne   Mexico City   Nairobi
New Delhi   Shanghai   Taipei   Toronto

With offices in
Argentina   Austria   Brazil   Chile   Czech Republic   France   Greece
Guatemala   Hungary   Italy   Japan   Poland   Portugal   Singapore
South Korea   Switzerland   Thailand   Turkey   Ukraine   Vietnam

Copyright © 2011 Oxford University Press

Published by Oxford University Press, Inc.
198 Madison Avenue, New York, New York 10016

Oxford is a registered trademark of Oxford University Press

Library of Congress Cataloging-in-Publication Data
CIP data on file
ISBN 978-0-19-518305-4

For Julie, Barbara, and the Lady Eve

Preface

Much of our thinking is about what might be or must be true, not just about what is actually true. We can think about fictional realms in reading novels or watching movies, think about hypothetical situations in imagining what almost happened to us, and think about ideal states in hoping for a more just or more harmonious life. Not so obviously, our insight into nonfactual states also pervades basic elements of cognition. Our notion of cause and effect is closely linked to our ability to think about whether the effect *would have* occurred if the cause *had not*. Our concepts of numbers depend on the role they play in arithmetic principles that *must* be true. Our ideas about natural categories, such as sparrows and willows, include knowledge of properties these objects *must have* in order to belong to these categories. Even our notion of ordinary physical objects—a particular pen or pet—may rest on causal facts and so on ideas about how things *might have been* in situations that never occurred.

These reflections hint at a perspective on cognition that is quite different from the usual treatment of these topics in experimental psychology. According to standard treatments, ideas about objects, numbers, causes, natural categories, and other targets of cognition are built up empirically from perceptual information. All textbooks on cognition reflect this same organization, beginning with perception and attention, moving to short-term memory, and finally to topics like categorization and inference. Although more progressive (often developmental) theories leave room for some portion of innate knowledge, even these theories typically see this knowledge as something we need to transcend or transform by empirical learning or induction from perceptual experience. This book develops the opposite perspective, one that sees nonperceptual modes of thought as central to very basic cognitive notions. The emphasis here is on what I'll call "modal cognition," in the sense of thought that goes beyond facts about the actual state of affairs. (I wish I had a better word for this concept. Psychologists often use "modal" to mean having to do with the sense modalities, such as vision or audition, but I'm referring here to a type of thought that is distinctly *amodal* on that meaning. Instead, I'm borrowing "modal" in the present sense from modality in logic—a manner of presentation of a thought as necessary, possible, true-in-the-future, believed-by-Obama, known-by-Xavier-Cougat, and so on. Unfortunately, I don't know any other word that does this job.)

I'm hoping this book will be of use to upper-level undergrads, graduate students, and others in the cognitive sciences who are looking for a treatment of what my colleagues call "higher-level cognitive psychology." I currently teach a course on thinking, and the book evolved as I was grappling with ways of providing the class with information that lived up to its title. I once heard a well-known cognitive psychologist say that students in his thinking course complained that although they learned about working memory, semantic memory, text comprehension, decision making, reasoning, and other topics, they never got around to thinking. You could dismiss this as a case of the students failing to see the forest for the trees, but the psychologist was genuinely concerned about his students' complaint, and so am I. It's not that these topics have nothing to do with thinking—quite the contrary—but there does seem to be something missing. In my classes, I've used as texts the superb edited volumes by Posner (1989) and by Smith and Osherson (1995). But as much as I like these collections, students don't always find it satisfying to read a parade of chapters by independent authors, and they're now somewhat out of date.

In an earlier book on deductive reasoning (Rips, 1994), I had claimed that Anderson (e.g., Anderson & Lebiere, 1998) and Newell (1990) were right in supposing that people possess basic rule-like structures that are responsible for performing most cognitive activities, although I argued for greater flexibility in the structure of rules than appears in Anderson's and Newell's production systems. Such systems may provide clues about how to accommodate modal thinking in cognitive theory. For example, the moves that we find most natural in deductive reasoning may be direct reflections of these underlying principles. If both *p and q* are true, then *p* in particular *must* be true; if *p or q* is true and *not-p* is true, then *q must* be true; and so on. These principles help account for our confidence that these transitions in thought are not only correct but are correct in all possible situations.

As I began reviewing my lectures on other topics for my thinking class, I began to see that related structures seem to support similar intuitions within other domains. These domains include mathematics, concepts of causality, and related concepts of physical objects and natural kinds, as I've already hinted. The idea is *not* that specifically logical principles account for our intuitions about how things must be within these domains. However, the present book does explore the way basic cognitive constraints (embodied in cognitive schemas or mental theories) shape modal thinking in these areas. Structural approaches in cognition are, of course, not new, but we can look at them in a new way in the light of current evidence from many of these subfields, since one after another are appealing to related theories.

In line with this theme, my general stance is classically cognitivist. So, on the one hand, you're going to be disappointed if you're hoping for an adaptationist or "embodied" or connectionist or neuropsychological look at these topics. On the other hand, my approach places greater weight on theories from philosophy and linguistics than is usual in cognitive psychology. Many cognitive psychologists look with great suspicion on work from these fields, since they see reliance on such theories as acceptance of a kind of dubious data: the philosophers' or linguists' own intuitions. According to this view, philosophers and linguists do little more than consult their own ideas about mental representations and processes, and relying on their views is like relying on an opinion survey about such topics from a highly biased sample. Practitioners in these fields, this complaint goes, rarely agree about the nature of cognition (or about anything else) and rarely concern themselves with empirical details of cognitive processing or development. In fact, philosophers sometimes voice related complaints about their own enterprise (see, e.g., Alexander & Weinberg, 2007). My guess is, however, that psychologists who take this stance underestimate the role that theories play in their own research programs. Many genuine breakthroughs in scientific disciplines have proceeded from scientists' armchairs. Moreover, the topics covered in this book are closely related to ones to which philosophers have given close attention, and their insights about essentialism, a priori knowledge, foundations of mathematics, persistence over time, deduction, and many other topics are too interestingly and intricately developed to ignore. Ditto for linguists' ideas concerning logical form, semantics, and pragmatics.

You could use this book as a text in an upper-level course on cognition. The chapters are largely independent, so you could also read selectively to catch up on particular topics. I've also tried to avoid technical details in most cases. Some possible exceptions are the use of logic notation in Chapters 2, 3, and 6, and some statistical concepts in the discussion of Bayes nets and other probabilistic models in Chapters 3, 4, and 6. Most undergraduate and graduate students who've concentrated in cognitive science should have little difficulty here. For those looking for background in logic, nearly any introductory textbook should do (e.g., Bergmann, Moor, & Nelson, 2008). For background on Bayes nets, readers might want to review the first part of Gopnik et al. (2004).

However, this book is not a textbook. There are many important topics in higher-level cognitive psychology that I don't cover. One glaring omission is lack of a chapter on space and time. Although such a chapter would fit my emphasis on basic cognitive elements, I haven't tried to tackle it, since there is too much material to cover. And although I review a fair amount of empirical research on object concepts, math, causal cognition, categorization, and reasoning, the idea isn't to cover all earlier work in these areas. Instead, I hope to explore some issues that have received short shrift in these subfields and to fill out our picture of how such cognitive abilities are possible. Even within the topics I have covered, there are many subtopics and points of view that are missing. I provide warnings about some of these within each chapter and apologize in advance for accidental omissions.

Other limitations have to do with the research population. Most of the work I discuss here concerns adults, especially the usual U.S. college freshmen and sophomores who get impressed into psych experiments. Although I mention a bit of newer work on wider samples in connection with natural kinds in Chapter 4, true cross-cultural research in these areas is still fairly limited, and the interpretive problems connected with these results are immense. (For a sample of these controversies, see Nisbett, Peng, Choi, & Narenzayan, 2001, vs. Chan, 2000; Ho, 2000; and Lee, 2000; or Boroditsky, 2001, vs. Chen, 2007, and January & Kako, 2007; or Bloom, 1981, vs. Au, 1983; Cheng, 1985; and Liu, 1985.) Limited sampling restricts the generalizing you can do, but rushing to conclusions from present cross-cultural work also runs its risks. Controversy in cognitive psychology is obviously not confined to cross-cultural studies, and many of the proposals offered in this book are extremely controversial. Still, sorting out the cross-cultural findings calls for linguistic and anthropological acumen that I wish I possessed, but don't. Along similar lines, I concentrate mainly on research with adults, despite the enormous literature on children's thinking. The chapters on objects, causality, and, especially, numbers contain some developmental content, but I haven't tried to present a thorough picture of children's thinking. The emphasis on adults, like the emphasis on Westerners, is unfortunate, but in this case the problem is that there's too much to cover rather than too little. A thorough treatment of cognitive development would easily double the size of this book.

In addition to restrictions in scope, this book probably disqualifies itself as a textbook by its argumentative nature. Textbooks strive to maintain a balanced view by standing back from current debate. But although I've tried to be fair in my assessments, I haven't found it possible to go deeply into these topics without raising issues about some of the experiments and theories. I don't apologize for taking a stance on the issues, but it's fair to warn you that my approach is often a controversial one. (For what it's worth, though, most of the reviewers of this book thought that including some argumentation was okay. What they disliked was the side I come down on. I'm sure we'll be hearing from them again in postpublication reviews.)

This book evolved over a long period, often from lectures and from preliminary chapters and articles that I mention in the endnotes. As such, they have benefited from advice from many editors, reviewers, and colleagues. My coauthors on the earlier articles were Jennifer Asmuth,

Serge Blok, Amber Bloomfield, and George Newman, and they've done much to make the book more veridical. I also owe special thanks to Susan Hespos, Douglas Medin, Daniel Osherson, Aaron Sloman, and Keith Stenning, who each generously read and commented on several chapters. Two anonymous reviewers also provided detailed and helpful comments on the complete manuscript. I'm also grateful to the Fulbright Program and the Guggenheim Foundation for support of sabbatical leaves, during which I wrote parts of this book. The Institute for Education Sciences provided research support during this period.

In the preface to my first book, I mentioned how much I owed my teachers, and, of course, that debt still stands. In writing this book, though, I've been at least equally influenced by my students, especially graduate students in the cognition programs at the University of Chicago and Northwestern. My usual mode of teaching involves assigning each week a set of questions on the readings and asking students to write a few paragraphs on each question. The idea is to use the questions as a basis for discussion, but the questions have become notorious for their complexity, like the items on Professor Kantankerus's nightmare final exam. I don't necessarily recommend this method to others—it probably won't earn you shades on ratemyteacher.com—but it has paid off a surprising number of times with student comments that deepened my own thinking about a topic. I've noted some specific instances in the chapters, but the influence runs throughout the book, and I'm very grateful for the students' help.

I don't know how to thank my family properly for putting up with me while I've been working on these chapters. In an earlier book, I mentioned that I was trying to catch up with their intellectual achievements, but I now realize I've only fallen further behind. I'm still plugging away at a tiny part of cognition, while they've branched out to writing about local history and political philosophy. Not to mention the facts that they're more observant, more sympathetic, and more fun to be around. And one of them *does* have shades on ratemyteacher.com.

Contents

Introduction

These functions of the possible once beheld allured the mind to reconsider them.

Meredith, The Egoist

Suppose you're studying a theorem in elementary mathematics or geometry. You might realize, just in reading it over, that the theorem must be true. Or you might work through a proof of the theorem that convinces you of its truth. As an example, consider Euclid's theorem that there are an infinite number of primes.

Why is Euclid's theorem true? Well, suppose, contrary to the theorem, that there are only finitely many prime numbers, 2, 3, 5, . . ., p_k, where p_k is the largest prime. Now, consider an integer n equal to the product of all these primes plus 1—that is, $n = 2 \cdot 3 \cdot 5 \cdot \ldots \cdot p_k + 1$. Clearly, n can't itself be prime, since that would contradict the hypothesis that p_k is the largest prime; so n is nonprime (composite). By definition, this means that there is a prime number p_j less than n that divides n evenly. This number must be one of 2, 3, 5, . . ., p_k, since our hypothesis is that those are all the primes there are. But p_j can't be 2, since 2 divides $2 \cdot 3 \cdot 5 \cdot \ldots \cdot p_k$ and so could not also divide evenly into $n = 2 \cdot 3 \cdot 5 \cdot \ldots \cdot p_k + 1$. (The first of these numbers has 2 as one of its factors, and this means that 2 divides it evenly. Thus, the first number is even and the second is odd.) Similarly, p_j could not be 3, 5, . . ., or p_k, since no integer greater than 1 can evenly divide both $n - 1$ and n. We've reached a contradiction, since we have just deduced that p_j is not one of 2, 3, 5, . . ., p_k. Thus, our supposition is wrong, and there must be an infinite number of primes.[1]

The truth of Euclid's theorem clearly isn't the usual sort of mundane truth, such as the fact that the Sears Tower is in Chicago. I can see the Sears Tower from where I'm writing, so there is good reason for me to believe that the statement *The Sears Tower is in Chicago* is true as things stand. However, if some cosmic cyclone mixed up the objects in our world, we'd have no assurance that "The Sears Tower theorem" is true, but we would be assured of the truth of Euclid's theorem.[2] We know that Euclid's theorem is true, not just in the current setting, but also in any setting—no matter how the objects and events in the world are arranged. We recognize that the theorem would be true in situations that are not only different from our current one, but that are different from any we ever have or ever will experience. But how can we possibly know what's true in situations with which we have no physical or psychological contact of any kind? Assuming that the proof just sketched convinced you of Euclid's theorem, how did it persuade you of its truth in all settings?

We could also talk about the Euclid example in terms of the concepts of *necessity* and *possibility*: It's necessary that there be an infinity of prime numbers. Necessary truths, unlike mundane truths, tell us about how things have to be and not just how they are. In many philosophical theories, necessity is represented in terms of possible worlds. A possible world is, roughly speaking, a complete catalog of the properties and relations that hold among all objects in a specified domain. Our own, actual world is a possible world, and propositions that are true in the ordinary way—for example, that the Sears Tower is in Chicago—are propositions that are true in this actual world. Necessary truths like Euclid's theorem are true, according to this scheme, in every possible world, and a proposition is a possible truth if it's true in at least one possible world. This way of understanding necessary truths has some big advantages in analyzing statements about necessity, but possible worlds aren't much help in understanding the psychology of necessary truths. For one thing, there are typically an infinite number of possible worlds, so we can't search through them all to see if some statement is necessary. For another, it is far from clear that we have cognitive access to other possible worlds, so it's not clear what it would mean to inspect one. The problem is just the same as it was before: The question "How do we know that some statement is true in all possible worlds?" doesn't have a clearer psychological answer than, "How are we able to recognize that some statement is necessarily true?"

0.1 Modalities and Commonalities

The issue of how we know information about nonactual situations arises clearly in the case of mathematical thinking. But similar problems occur in many other areas of cognitive psychology, as I try to show in the next section of this chapter and in the rest of the book. Yet attempts to explain these abilities on cognitive grounds become stymied, since the abilities seem to demand access to information that is not available either to an individual or to a culture—information about all (or all causally possible) situations or possible worlds or future states. Math and logic seem to demand knowledge of the relations between propositions in all logically possible situations. Induction and causal justification require knowledge of relations between events that go beyond those we have experienced; current and past events can't decide between those explanations we correctly endorse and those we correctly deny. Likewise, beliefs about natural categories depend on knowledge that outstrips anything we might have learned from actual category members. In each case, our beliefs seem to rest on evidence with which, paradoxically, we could not possibly have come in contact. Yet in all these cases, our beliefs conform reasonably well with normative standards, at least within the limits imposed by time, memory, and other constraints on mental resources.

Picking up a term from the Preface, we can use "modal cognition" for thoughts about situations that go beyond our actual one. Modal beliefs are crucial, since they're the foundation for our scientific view of the world and, in part, our commonsense view as well. But they are notoriously difficult to explain on psychological grounds because psychologists' favorite explanatory mechanisms stick quite closely to past experience, especially perceptual experience. For the reasons we're about to review, it is difficult to explain our mathematical and scientific beliefs on the basis of reasoning via prior cases, empirical probabilities, or ordinary learning. Much the same can be said about explanations based on evolution or cultural transmission or the nature of the environment in which we are "embodied," at least if you conceive of these mechanisms as constrained by the historical experience of the individual, species, or culture. The goal of this book is to explore ways of coping with modal (e.g., mathematical, logical, and causal) beliefs that don't trivialize them and that don't resort to implausible psychological models. The tools that I use here are experimental: Studies of people (usually normal adults) solving novel problems can help reveal the cognitive goings on that are responsible for these beliefs.

Having said what the book is about, though, this might be the place to say what it isn't about. The issue addressed here is *not* how psychology can explain why mathematical, logical, or causal statements are true. The truth of causal statements almost certainly rests on facts that are independent of mind, and the same may be true of mathematical and logical theorems. The opposite doctrine—that causal, mathematical, and logical facts are nothing but psychological facts—is a version of *psychologism*, and the odds against it are formidable. Could the nature of matter and energy, sets and number be solely a matter of our conception? There is no pressing reason why psychologists would need or want to take on the project of supporting a "yes" answer, since a psychology that recognizes mind-independent facts is no less viable or interesting than one that doesn't. It is incontestable, however, that we have beliefs about mathematical and causal matters, and these beliefs are bona fide psychological entities. The real cognitive issue, then, is to determine why we place faith in these beliefs and not to determine why the corresponding statements are true. Of course, if psychologism were correct, then this problem would be a lot easier to solve—our beliefs about math and science would be secured by the fact that math and science are themselves psychological. But since psychologism is probably not correct, we have to look around for a different solution.

0.2 Modal Thinking in Cognitive Domains

The psychological problem of modal cognition would be a pressing one if only because it underlies our understanding of mathematics. The issue of how we gain knowledge of mathematics is at center stage in Chapter 2, but although mathematical theorems illustrate the problem of modality in the starkest way, related problems surface in nearly every corner of higher cognitive psychology. It will come as no surprise that similar issues arise in deductive reasoning, given the close connection between deduction and math. However, causal explanation and knowledge of objects and natural categories all present very similar puzzles, since in each of them our understanding seems to outrun our knowledge of what's actual. This theme unfolds in detail in the individual chapters of this book, but it might be helpful at this point to get a preliminary peek at how the issue arises in each of these subfields.

0.2.1 Causal Explanation

Justifications of our beliefs can take several forms. If I ask you why you think capital punishment fails to deter crime, you might cite statistical evidence that bears on your opinion. Perhaps you can show that those states that have imposed capital punishment have obtained no corresponding decrease in capital crimes, or perhaps crime rates are equivalent for states with capital punishment as for states with no capital punishment. Sometimes, however, justifications take the form of hypotheses or opinions for which no strict empirical evidence is available (Brem & Rips, 2000; Kuhn, 1991). Maybe you think capital punishment has the side effect of inciting violent behavior in the general population, even though you currently have no hard evidence to support this position. Although offering this latter sort of unsubstantiated explanation is sometimes counted an error in reasoning, such explanations are an important component in thinking about social and physical events. First, hypotheses like these often form a first step in guiding a search for evidence. You could perform an unlimited number of correlations between capital punishment rates and other variables, but only a few of these would be relevant to establishing the worth of capital punishment. The theoretically interesting ones can't be determined by more correlations; prior theory has to dictate which results are meaningful. Second, as psychologists are fond of asserting, correlation is not the same as causation. No matter how strong or how many correlations there are between two types of events, we can always explain these relations through the influence of third factors or in other ways. Even if we have hard evidence at hand, it's a further step to conclude that a causal link is present. Causal justifications always outrun the merely statistical.

But the fact that causal explanations go beyond statistics means that theories of causal thinking can't get off the ground if they are based entirely on past events. On the one hand, unless we record an event's causal history along with its other properties, then the only way we can derive causal facts from these events is by tabulating them and computing correlations (or using some other method that derives causal from noncausal information). As we have just seen, there is no obvious way to do this. On the other hand, if memory for events includes causal facts, then we're left with the question of where these facts came from.

Chapter 3, as well as parts of Chapters 1 and 6, are devoted to the issue of causal knowledge.

0.2.2 Concepts of Objects and Categories

Our knowledge of people and other objects includes not only facts about their present circumstances, but also beliefs about what would happen to them in situations that are only possible. We can predict what our friends would be likely to do in imaginary settings they have never faced. Similarly, scientific knowledge often allows us to make quite accurate predictions about the behavior of objects, as their path evolves from merely hypothetical initial conditions. Like other forms of causal knowledge, these predictions aren't logically necessary in the way mathematical statements are, but they do go beyond the empirical facts we've witnessed.

Much the same is true of natural categories, such as daisies and antelopes. It seems correct to say that daisies have petals and that antelopes have four legs, despite the fact that, strictly speaking, not all daisies have petals and not all antelopes have four legs. Finding a few daisies whose petals are missing or a few three-legged antelopes wouldn't shake our faith in the truth of the original generalities. In fact, these generalities could even survive the discovery that there are *no* instances that they correctly describe. Belief that a worldwide storm had blown off the petals of all existing daisies would not necessarily cause us to retract the idea that daisies have petals. Whatever lies behind the truth of these category statements, then, must be more than a simple enumeration of examples. Of course, such statements are not immune to revision. We can imagine situations in which genetic mutations cause daisies to become petalless or in which botanists convince us that what we thought were daisy petals are actually leaves of a special sort (compare poinsettias). In these cases, we can say daisies don't have petals, though they formerly did (or we formerly thought they did). Such revisions or disconfirmations, though, depend on more than the simple discovery of isolated daisies that happen to have missing petals. Statements like *Daisies have petals* or *Antelopes have four legs* are causal generalizations. The very same difficulties that we met in Section 0.2.1 beset our ability to explain our knowledge of categories. We pursue the relevant issues about objects in Chapter 1 and about categories in Chapter 4.

We may have mental representations for categories like daisies that allow us to refer to them without committing ourselves to descriptive information, such as the fact that they have white petals or yellow centers. Perhaps these stripped-down mental representations have a better claim to be the concept of daisy than more enriched representations that include the descriptive facts.[3] At some basic level of language comprehension, descriptive facts about categories may play no role. At this level, we may use only the stripped-down representations to construct the meanings of sentences in which the names of these categories figure. Still, the descriptive facts about daisies and other natural categories are important ones, since they comprise much of our knowledge of the natural world. Any psychological theory of categories will eventually have to cope with the problem of what underlies the faith we place in such facts. Chapter 5 looks at the role of both sparse representations and rich representations in the context of categorization and language understanding.

0.2.3 Reasoning

In a deductively correct argument—for example, the argument from the premise *Everyone dislikes iguana pudding* to the conclusion *Calvin dislikes iguana pudding*—the second statement holds in all states of affairs in which the first statement does. People draw simple inferences that echo these arguments, and people recognize their deductive correctness when they read or hear them. It is less clear whether people appreciate deductive correctness as such (see Harman, 1986)—whether they can discriminate arguments that are deductively correct from those in which the premise merely makes the conclusion more probable (e.g., the argument from *Most people dislike iguana pudding* to *Calvin dislikes iguana pudding*). But if they do, they must be able to recognize, at least indirectly, the stability of the premise-conclusion relationship across situations.

Deductive correctness, as it is treated in logic, isn't equivalent to high probability: A deductively correct argument isn't simply one whose premises lend a probability of 1 to the conclusion. The premise *Amber has a backbone* gives the conclusion *Amber has a heart* a probability of 1, since every creature that has a backbone also has a heart.[4] But the corresponding argument is not deductively correct. In some logically possible situations, creatures may exist with backbones but no hearts. It is possible to get from probability to validity (see Field, 1977), but doing so requires generalizing over different probability assignments, which presents much the same problem as generalizing over states of affairs. Chapter 6 explores the relation between deductive correctness and other forms of thought.

Reasoning seems to involve alternative states of affairs, not only indirectly via validity, but more directly in inferences that use modal notions such as necessity or possibility. Even children appreciate that *It is possible that Calvin doesn't like iguana pudding* entails and is entailed by *It's not necessarily true that Calvin likes iguana pudding* (Osherson, 1976). These inferences pose an obvious problem for theories that extract reasoning from the past experiences of the reasoner. Such theories don't seem to have sufficient power to account for our confidence in these inferences. Modal thinking of this sort also occurs in reasoning about time, knowledge, and obligation, so the problems it raises are important and general ones. Although philosophy and artificial intelligence provide numerous formal models of modal reasoning, there are only a few proposals about how to adapt them to human styles of thinking.

As we've already noticed, a related problem is that inferences in both scientific and everyday thinking often involve generalizations that specify how things would be under conditions that go beyond those that currently exist. For example, a generalization like *Humans learn a native language* allows you to predict that if Amber were human, then she would learn her native language. Reasoning to these generalizations is problematic, as Nelson Goodman (1955) pointed out, because past and present instances are equally consistent with many rival generalizations that you would not rely on—for instance, that all humans but Amber learn to speak, that all and only humans born before next month learn to speak, or that all and only humans born within 50,000 miles of Fargo learn to speak. Non-lawlike generalizations—such as *All current residents of Fargo have learned their native language*—do not have these problems, since present instances completely determine their truth or falsity.

0.3 Psychological Approaches to Modal Thinking

When we try to get straight about our conviction in the necessity of Euclid's theorem, we get surprisingly little help from current psychological explanations. Theories based on mental imagery and mental diagrams don't seem powerful enough to establish the generality of such statements. Neither do theories based on heuristics, embodied cognition, probability, or memory for instances. The failure of these and other mechanisms may even lead us to bite the bullet and to conclude that there is no important psychological difference between Euclid's theorem and ordinary empirical statements, such as *The Sears Tower is in Chicago*. Let's take a preliminary look at some difficulties with these approaches, since they also affect the theories' ability to handle the other sorts of information that we reviewed in the previous section—knowledge of objects, natural categories, causality, and reasoned justification.

0.3.1 Mental Imagery

In his work on mathematical discovery, Jacques Hadamard (1945) attempted to describe "what takes place in my own mind when I undertake to build up or to comprehend . . . a mathematical argument" (p. 75). The most detailed of his examples is the proof of Euclid's theorem, which he uses to illustrate the role of "concrete representations," that is, imaginal or diagrammatic representations, rather than words or algebraic symbols. Hadamard's description appears verbatim in Table 0.1, in his own two-column format, which coordinates the proofs steps with his accompanying imagery.

Hadamard's testimony is important, especially because his contribution to the theory of prime numbers is immense (see, e.g., Davis & Hersh, 1980, pp. 209–216). So how should we interpret the mental pictures he describes? Hadamard is clear that "the use of such a strange and cloudy imagery . . . is not meant to remind me of any property of divisibility, prime numbers and so on. This is most important because any such information which it could give me is likely to be more or less inaccurate and to deceive me" (1945, p. 77). This may be so of this very example,

TABLE 0.1   Hadamard's Description of the Steps in the Proof of Euclid's Theorem (1945, pp. 76–77).

STEPS IN THE PROOF	MY MENTAL PICTURES
I consider all primes from 2 to 11, say 2, 3, 5, 7, 11.	I see a confused mass.
I form the product 2 x 3 x 5 x 7 x 11 = N	N being a rather large number, I imagine a point rather remote from the confused mass.
I increase that product by 1, say N + 1.	I see a second point a little beyond the first.
That number, if not a prime, must admit of a prime divisor, which is the required number.	I see a place somewhere between the confused mass and the first point.

Hadamard begins, "We have, for instance, to prove that there is a prime greater than 11."

since, as James Anderson (1998) observes, the value of $N + 1 = 2 \cdot 3 \cdot 5 \cdot 7 \cdot 11 + 1 = 2,311$ in step 3 is prime; so there is no prime divisor in the "place" mentioned in the fourth step of the argument.

Anderson uses Hadamard's example to illustrate the fact that, although "visual images do not prove theorems . . . they can be used to verify the essential insights and to justify the formal arguments" (Anderson, 1998, p. 274). It is fairly clear, however, that this does not represent Hadamard's own view of Table 0.1. If the image does not provide information about "any property of divisibility, prime numbers and so on"—and, especially, if such information is likely to be deceptive—then how could the image be used to justify or verify the argument? Instead, Hadamard's hypothesis seems to be that the image plays an organizing role that pulls together the individual objects in the proof, making their interrelations easier to grasp and to remember (1945, p. 77):

> I need it in order to have a simultaneous view of all elements
> of the argument, to hold them together, to make a whole of
> them—in short, to achieve that synthesis which we spoke of in the
> beginning of this section and give the problem its physiognomy.
> It does not inform me on any link of the argument (i.e., on any

property of divisibility or primes); but it reminds me how these links are to be brought together.

This schematic function of imagery is probably familiar to most college students. If you visit college classrooms at night—after the last class of the day and before the janitorial staff erases the blackboards—you'll find many examples of "strange and cloudy imagery" with arrows, balloons, and labels. These occur, not just in math and science classes, but in all classes in which the instructor wants to tie together a number of considerations in order to present a unified picture—to give students an overview of what's related to what. Instructors don't necessarily intend these diagrams to justify a claim or theory but to provide a capsule framework.

How does Euclid's proof manage to transmit conviction in the necessity of the theorem, if not through this type of imagery? A bit later in his book, Hadamard (1945) remarks, "in our case, we have also a sequel of images developing parallel to thought properly called. Both mental streams, images and reasonings, constantly guide each other though keeping perfectly distinct and even, to a certain extent, independent" (pp. 97–98). Although the images may be important or even essential to understanding the proof, it's these reasonings, then, that must provide the properties of elementary number theory that empower proofs like Euclid's. The issue becomes what such "thought properly called" is like. This isn't to say that diagrams never justify our conviction about necessary truths, but they do possess inherent limitations, which we will explore in Chapter 6. Chapter 3 shows that similar limitations affect diagrammatic representations of causal systems.

0.3.2 Embodiment and Heuristics

A typical reaction to the dilemma we have encountered is to argue that we have not cast our net widely enough. Perhaps if we think of math knowledge (and knowledge of other modal information) as residing in the environment or as transmitted by social practice, then some of these difficulties will go away. Obviously, mathematics does propagate through social channels. Parents introduce children to mathematics, and schools, businesses, and professional groups perpetuate it. Mathematicians communicate their findings to others face-to-face and in journals, books, and conference proceedings, and this communication facilitates mathematical results both historically and concurrently. All these forms of interaction and communication give weight to the claim that the social environment is a source of math knowledge. Although this interaction is an appropriate object of study in its own right, we can wonder how this distribution of information explains people's knowledge of truths like Euclid's theorem.

A social account would be helpful if it explained not just how mathematical information circulates from person to person but also the conviction we attach to it. Social practice can account for the transmission of rumors and superstitions, as well as that of necessary truths. To aid us in understanding mathematical knowledge, social practice also has to explain why we see mathematical statements as conveying only necessarily true or necessarily false information, unlike the statement about the Sears Tower. Could the social practice of mathematics or the environment of mathematicians distinguish math activities from practices in other domains in ways that could account for its special status?

A social approach might take mathematics as the collective practices of those involved in mathematical endeavors. Instead of interpreting this knowledge as a set of mental sentences, rules, or schemas, we could think of it as the practices that people engage in when they do math. One route to this conclusion comes from the ethnographic study of people's math-related activities outside school. Careful observation of grocery shoppers (Lave, 1988), candy sellers (Saxe, 1988), dairy workers (Scribner, 1984), and others suggests that these individuals usually don't apply general-purpose arithmetic algorithms, but instead carry out special-purpose procedures that they tailor tightly to their circumstances. In comparing two varieties of a particular product, for example, grocery shoppers don't always approach the problem in the same way (e.g., they don't always compute unit price) but instead adopt different strategies, depending on their current situation and current goals. This variability has led Lave (1988) to conclude that people don't transfer prestored algorithms, such as school-taught subtraction or division procedures, to problems they encounter, but the problems and their solutions emerge interactively within specific situations. As an example of "the multiple and mutually constitutive character of the problem solving process,"

Lave (1988, p. 165) cites the case of an individual who had been asked to find "three quarters of two-thirds cup of cottage cheese":

> He filled a measuring cup two-thirds full of cottage cheese, dumped it out on a cutting board, patted it into a circle, marked a cross on it, scooped away one quadrant, and served the rest. Thus, "take three-quarters of two-thirds of a cup of cottage cheese" was not just the problem statement but also the solution to the problem and the procedure for solving it. The setting was part of the calculating process and the solution was simply the problem statement, enacted with the setting.

Thus, although "conventional assumptions treat calculation as a cognitive function and its context merely as a stage on which action occurs," in fact "activity-in-setting, seamlessly stretched across persons-acting and setting often turns the latter into a calculating device" (Lave, 1988, p. 154). We can summarize the argument as denying that there is any such thing as "knowing mathematics" if mathematical knowledge is taken as limited either to possessing mental mathematical statements (schemas, rules, models, etc.) or to executing internal procedures involving these statements. This approach does not question the existence of internal mental statements or processes, and in this way, it differs from traditional behaviorism. The claim is rather that, because mathematics depends essentially on external factors, nothing that a cognizer does internally amounts to knowing mathematics. The social and physical arena in which mathematics takes place provides the actual locus of mathematics, according to Lave.

Psychologists should perhaps be grateful to proponents of such approaches for lifting some of the explanatory burden from their shoulders. If mathematics is largely an anthropological or sociological phenomenon, then it may be easier to craft a simple account of the remaining psychological parts. Still, there might be some doubts about whether these theories are explaining mathematical knowledge or are instead refusing to acknowledge part of the issue (see Bloch, 1998, chap. 8, and Sperber, 1985, for similar criticism from the anthropological side). If math is itself a relation or "dialectic" among people and settings, then this simplifies cognitive explanations of episodes like the cottage-cheese calculation by reducing what cognition contributes to the interaction.

In incidents like these, external components decrease the amount of purely mental activity that goes into a mathematical episode, much as calculators or computers do. But an account of math knowledge also has to extend in a natural way to cases in which proportionally more work occurs internally. If we look only at the external relations between an individual and his or her setting, we miss much of the richness of the experience of making mathematical discoveries, such as the realization of why Euclid's theorem is true. It's good to be reminded that mathematics often takes place outside the sphere of professional mathematicians, teachers, and students. Still, theories of mathematics have to scale up to cover their activities, too. Although external interactions among mathematicians and their settings account for part of the nature of mathematics, focusing too narrowly on these relations misses the apparent complexity of the internal steps leading up to mathematical results of even moderate difficulty. At the time of a mathematician's crucial "aha," little in her external circumstances may reflect or support this insight.

Exactly the same is true of the idea that mathematical reasoning is simply a matter of quick and dirty heuristics that have been tuned to human ecology over the course of evolutionary history (Gigerenzer, 2000). The idea is that practical concerns and evolutionary pressures have produced in us simple procedures that not only allow us to get by in our everyday decision-making, but that also define what it means to reason correctly. This approach, however, provides little insight into how people comprehend an interesting piece of mathematics—for example, how people understand Euclid's theorem—since the thinking that goes into this realization is not heuristic in character. We don't understand why Euclid's theorem is true by performing mental shortcuts but by following the steps of Euclid's proof. Of course, evolution has indirectly shaped our ability to do math, since evolution has shaped *us*. But trying to tell a revealing story about how environmental constraints produce mathematical understanding is like trying to tell a revealing story about how subatomic forces do. Although there are connections in both cases—how we think depends on both subatomic structure and evolutionary factors—neither story will help answer our questions about mathematical understanding, since they start at the wrong level of explanation.

A proponent of the heuristics approach could claim that the thinking that goes into Euclid's proof is something virtually no one can do, aside from a few mathematicians, and, in any case, is a skill that is unimportant in human experience. But neither claim is very convincing. Middle school students have little difficulty appreciating Euclid's proof, and the importance of mathematics in science and technology suggests that related mental abilities are crucial in current pursuits. Although we will glimpse some related theories in Chapters 2 and 6, we shouldn't hold much hope that they will shed light on our ability to understand theorems and other necessary truths.

0.3.3 Probabilistic and Instance Theories

Further reactions to the problem of modal information go along with the heuristics theory in denying that we treat such information as qualitatively different from ordinary truths. Maybe the best we can do is to think of such statements as extremely likely, more likely than other statements, such as *The Sears Tower is in Chicago*. According to this *probabilistic* approach, we distribute specific degrees of confidence (subjective probability or some other one-dimensional quantity) to the statements we understand. Mathematical and logical truths (e.g., Euclid's theorem) will garner the maximum amount of confidence; causally necessary statements (e.g., statements of physical laws) will gain a large (but not maximum) amount of confidence; and ordinary empirical statements (e.g., that the Sears Tower is in Chicago) will get lesser (but not minimum) degrees of confidence. The cognitive system treats these statements as quantitatively different but otherwise handles them in exactly the same way. When we learn new information, we update our confidence in our old beliefs to reflect the way the new information supports or fails to support those beliefs. Reasoning similarly consists in adjusting confidence about some beliefs based on confidence in others. Although these adjustments in confidence may not always match what's required by standard probability theory, they come close enough in practice to allow our belief system to function in adequate ways. All thinking, on this view, is the shifting of confidence levels among beliefs.

Another reaction to the problem of modal thinking is based on the idea that all our knowledge derives from specific objects and events that we have encountered and remembered as such. If we must make inferences about situations we have not directly experienced, we do so by calculating the similarity between the new situation and the old, remembered ones. Similarity (or analogical reasoning) carries over some of the properties of the old entities to the new instances, allowing us to make predictions about the unseen circumstances. Such an *instance-based* approach (sometimes called an *exemplar* theory or *case-based* theory) might attempt to account for our knowledge of a mathematical truth or a causal law in terms of the number of remembered instances that support it. Causal generalizations about categories, such as *daisies have petals*, receive support from the number of positive instances so far observed. In the case of Euclid's theorem, an instance theory might claim that if we can find a prime number larger than any in the set of primes that we have encountered and remembered, then it's reasonable to think that there is no largest prime. A weaker, and perhaps more plausible, version of the instance theory might contend that as long as there is a clear mapping between the primes we've encountered and some larger prime, then there is no largest prime.[5]

My guess is that most psychologists hold views that lie in the vicinity of the probabilistic or instance theories, but we might wonder whether they can really explain the facts. In the case of mathematics, we seem to be able to recognize certain statements as being either necessarily true or necessarily false, even when we aren't sure which. Consider twin primes, which are pairs of prime numbers, such as 5 and 7 or 59 and 61, whose difference is 2. No one has yet been able to prove that there are an infinite number of twin primes. We have no theorem for twin primes analogous to Euclid's. Nevertheless, if the proposition is true, it must be necessarily true, and if it is false, it is necessarily false. This suggests that our assessment of the necessity or impossibility of a statement may be independent of our confidence in it. Along the same lines, it might be difficult to explain people's ability to recognize necessarily true mathematical statements if what they are doing is imagining a few situations in which the statement is true and extrapolating to the rest. What makes people so sure that things will turn out the same way in the infinite number of situations that they *haven't* considered? Examining several different prime numbers and noticing that there is a larger one doesn't seem a plausible explanation for why we believe that Euclid's theorem is necessarily true. At the moment that I am writing this introduction, the largest known prime number is "only" $2^{43,112,609} - 1$. What about the instance theory gives us reason to think there is a larger one? Analogizing between old and new primes might be more promising, but what governs the mapping process? The analogy can't rest simply on more instances, but on what, then?

0.4 Summary

The question of how we deal with modal information—mathematical, logical, and causal information that goes beyond actual experiences—is the main puzzle that I want to examine in this book. Of course, people aren't always successful in doing this. Many math theorems are far from obvious on first encounter, and people sometimes make mistakes in understanding and proving them. Similarly, people make errors in understanding complex causal systems, for example, in the context of debugging or troubleshooting. Uncertainties and errors are important to psychologists because they provide some clues about how we reason. But the point here is that, at least sometimes, we do appreciate the theorem-ness of a theorem or the causally necessary relations that govern an object, category, or complex system, and it is equally important to understand how we can do that. On the face of it, it's an utterly mysterious talent.

If there are any jokes left in this book after the copy editor has done with it, they are probably at the expense of instance theories, probabilistic theories, heuristic theories, or the Psychology Department at the University of [name omitted in proofs]. My aim, though, isn't just to poke fun at the opposition. I propose to take it as given that adults have accumulated beliefs about scientific and logical matters (however these beliefs have arrived on the scene), that they hold these beliefs strongly, and that they use them to generate more beliefs of the same kind. The problems, then, are to spell out the more central of these beliefs, why people put faith in them, and how they manage to produce others from this initial stock.

NOTES

[1] This isn't quite the way Euclid's proof is usually presented, but it's close. The usual proof rests on the observation that if p_j evenly divides both $2 \cdot 3 \cdot 5 \cdot \ldots \cdot p_k$ and $2 \cdot 3 \cdot 5 \cdot \ldots \cdot p_k + 1$, then it must also evenly divide 1, which is impossible.

The proof above may be a little more self-explanatory. One reason for using Euclid's theorem as an example is that it has figured in many earlier discussions of the nature of proof. In addition to the works by Anderson and Hadamard cited below, see Resnik (1992).

² In fact, the Sears Tower has recently been renamed the "Willis Tower"; so the Sears Tower is no longer in Chicago, in a certain sense. I'll ignore this factoid, though, in the rest of the Introduction.

³ Like most psychologists, I use the term "concept" to mean a mental representation. I'm tempted by "conception" as a less ambiguous way of referring to the psychologists' "concept," but it sounds too clumsy to me. So I'll continue to use "concept" in its psychological meaning. In naming concepts, I follow the convention of using all capital letters. So FROG refers to the concept (i.e., mental representation) of the category of frogs, and XAVIER COUGAT is the concept of Xavier Cougat.

⁴ I'm assuming here that the probability is determined by the relative frequency of creatures having hearts among (presently existing) creatures having backbones. If probability is defined subjectively, it is possible for someone to give a probability less than 1 to Amber having a heart given that she has a backbone. But the point here is a general one about the relation between high probability and entailment: On a subjective interpretation of probability, too, it is possible for someone to give a conditional probability of 1 to these statements (as you probably do), even though the relation between the statements is not an entailment.

⁵ The probabilistic/instance terminology may call to mind the probabilistic and exemplar models in Smith and Medin's (1981) description of psychological theories of concepts. What I'm calling "instance theories" here are quite similar to exemplar models in assuming that people store all or most of their information about objects and events in the form of descriptions of specific examples rather than in more abstract forms—for example, schemas, frames, prototypes, and other generalities. For more on exemplar approaches, see Chapter 5 of this book. My use of "probabilistic theory," however, is meant more literally than Smith and Medin's and conveys the idea that people remember information along with some indication of its certainty, perhaps in the form of a probability value, amount of activation, or some other continuous measure. (Smith and Medin's probabilistic theories were those in which information about categories took an abstract form that applied to most examples or to best examples of those categories.)

Lines of Thought

I

Individuals

There are convincing arguments that . . . the most important sort of glue that unites
the successive stages of the same persisting thing is causal glue.

David Lewis, *"Zimmerman and the Spinning Sphere"*

About half way through *The Lady Eve*, there is a scene in which the hero,
Charles Pike, is dressing for dinner with the help of his valet, Muggsy.
Charles and Muggsy have just encountered Lady Eve, Countess of
Sidwich. (Production note: "The Lady Eve [wears] a silver lame dress
which I am baffled to describe . . . She looks gorgeous and she knows
it.") Muggsy has noticed a perfect likeness between Eve and an earlier
character, Jean, with whom Charles had fallen in love but whom he had
thrown over after learning that she is a professional card sharp. Here's the
dialog in the dressing scene (Sturges, 1985, pp. 465–468):

MUGGSY: That's the same dame . . . she looks the same, she
walks the same and she's tossing you just like she did
last time.

CHARLES: She doesn't talk the same.

MUGGSY: Anybody can put on an act . . . .

CHARLES: Weren't her eyes a little closer together?

MUGGSY: They were not . . . they were right where they
are . . . on each side of her nose . . . .

CHARLES: They look too much alike.

MUGGSY: You said it. They couldn't be two Janes as . . . .

CHARLES: You don't understand me: They look too much alike
to be the same.

MUGGSY: That's what I been telling you, they . . . hunh?

CHARLES: You see, if she came here with her hair dyed yellow
and her eyebrows different . . . but she *didn't* dye her
hair and she didn't pretend she'd never seen me
before which is the *first thing* anybody would do.
She *says* I look familiar.

MUGGSY: Why shouldn't you?

CHARLES: Because if I did she wouldn't admit it. . . . If she
           didn't look so exactly *like* the other girl I might be
           suspicious, but . . . you see you don't understand
           psychology. If *you* wanted to pretend to be some-
           body else you'd glue a muff on your chin and the
           dog wouldn't even bark at you.

MUGGSY: (Indignantly) You tryin' to tell me this ain't the same
           rib was on the boat? She even wears the same perfume.

CHARLES: (Vacillating) I don't know.

He picks up his dinner jacket and Muggsy helps him on with it.
Charles walks out.

Charles's psychological theory works against him here, since it turns
out that Muggsy's straightforward reaction is correct. The very last line of
the movie belongs to Muggsy: "Positively, the same dame." But is there
anything wrong with Charles's reasoning, aside from the fact that he is up
against a brilliant woman con artist whose own psychological theorizing
is superior to (and able to anticipate) his own? This chapter tries to make
the case that, although Muggsy's intuitive response often delivers the
right verdict about the identity of people and other objects, Charles
is right that identity is a more complicated matter. Our beliefs about
connections that unite the earlier and later stages of an object are a main
part of our concepts of these individuals.

1.1 Object Concepts and Object Identity

A popular genre in recent historical writing relates what might have
happened to important persons but never did. What if Charles I had
died of plague in August 1641 (Rabb, 2001)? What if Pizarro had not
found potatoes in Peru (McNeill, 2001)? What if Woodrow Wilson had
decided not to make public the Zimmerman telegram (Tally, 2000)?
Closer to home, we sometimes contemplate contrary-to-fact scenarios
in which we play our own starring roles, perhaps in order to figure out
what actions might have averted negative events in the past and might
avert them in the future (e.g., Kahneman & Miller, 1986; Roese, 1997).

In these speculative moments, we must be able to follow the individuals in question through circumstances in which they never actually existed. Thinking about the results of Wilson failing to disclose the critical telegram, for example, means imagining Wilson's actions in a situation that never occurred. Thinking about what would have happened if you had decided not to go to college entails tracing your path in a world that is only partly like your own.

In spinning these hypothetical stories, we have to identify people and other objects, not only across time and space, but also across alternative histories. This suggests, at a minimum, that our concepts of individuals have to include information that goes beyond what purely perceptual or attentional mechanisms afford. Although we can imagine seeing Wilson carrying out actions that he never iperformed, the mechanisms responsible for such envisioning can't be purely perceptual, since hypothetical events produce no visual traces. Some alternative scenarios would clearly be impossible for Wilson, even in these contrary-to-fact circumstances. Our concept of Wilson helps us decide how he might have acted, and this concept contributes to the overall plausibility of these imaginary events.

The aim of this book is to examine the nature of concepts that are rich enough to support this type of thinking, and we can begin by concentrating on the individual objects that occur in these beliefs and suppositions. I'll use the term *singular concept* to denote a mental representation of a unique individual, and I'll contrast singular concepts with *general concepts*, which are representations of categories. A representation of the Sears Tower is a singular concept in these terms, but our representation of (the category of) buildings or skyscrapers is a general one. The focus in this chapter is on how singular concepts promote judgments of the identity of objects—on how they determine that an object at one time and situation is the same as an object at another time and situation. I'll return to general concepts in Chapter 4, but for now, the basic form of our question is this:

(1)   Given knowledge about a target individual x_0 in some situation S, how do we decide whether this individual continues to exist in another (possibly hypothetical) situation S', and if so, which of the individuals $x_1, x_2, \ldots, x_n$ in S' is the same as x_0?

In this context, asking whether individual x_i is the same as x_0 means asking whether x_i is *numerically identical* to x_0. This is the equality relation that holds between each specific thing and itself, $x_i = x_0$. Question (1) probes central facts about singular concepts and identity. By comparing potential answers to (1), we can begin to determine which factors are most crucial to our notion of the identity of things.

In deciding among theories of singular concepts, it's helpful to keep the basic properties of the identity relation in mind. According to most treatments, individual identity is reflexive, symmetric, and transitive (e.g., Mendelson, 1964). That is, for any x_i, x_j, and x_k:

(2)   a. $x_i = x_i$ (reflexivity).
       b. If $x_i = x_j$ then $x_j = x_i$ (symmetry).
       c. If $x_i = x_j$ and $x_j = x_k$ then $x_i = x_k$ (transitivity).

People's judgments of identity may sometimes violate these principles, as I discuss later, but the principles provide a starting point for theory development. In order to specify the identity relation more precisely, we can add a fourth principle that is also widely agreed to characterize numerical identity. This principle, sometimes called *Leibniz's Law*, is that if two objects are identical, then any property true of one is also true of the other. This can be expressed as in (3):

(3)   For any property F: If $x_i = x_j$, then Fx_i if and only if Fx_j
       (Leibniz's Law).

Although the principles in (2) and (3) may seem obvious, we will see shortly that it is not always easy to square them with people's judgments about identity.

In the next section of this chapter, I look at earlier cognitive theories of object identity. I argue that these theories are either not powerful enough to explain singular concepts or they rely on overly strong assumptions about the relation between singular and general concepts. I then outline a new theory based on a notion of causal proximity that overcomes some of the earlier theories' difficulties, and I apply it to studies in which participants have to decide whether possible successor objects are identical to an original object. Finally, the last two sections of the chapter discuss how the theory handles problematic cases of identity and compare the model's advantages and disadvantages to those of earlier approaches.

1.2 Theories of Object Concepts

Around Christmas, many of us get cards and accompanying xeroxed letters from friends whom we haven't seen in years. The letters provide news, usually of vacation trips and children's successes, but occasionally of more important life changes, allowing us to keep track of these friends and update our knowledge of them. Our initial encounters with these friends may have given us a rich stock of perceptual information, and this information may survive as part of our mental representation. But unless snapshots come along with these cards, we have to track our friends using nonperceptual facts. Our surviving images may be radically out of date (Bjork, 1978). Still, the Christmas cards may provide enough nonperceptual, descriptive information to allow us to reidentify these people—to determine who in 2011 is the same individual as Aunt Dahlia, whom we last saw in 1970. At a minimum, higher-level information about identity will come into play when perceptual information is absent. Although we sometimes misrecognize people and other objects we know (e.g., Young, Hay, & Ellis, 1985), nevertheless we're often able to keep track of individuals across a night's sleep, lapses of attention, and other perceptual interruptions. Even preschool children can follow individuals over changes in perceptual properties (e.g., Gutheil & Rosengren, 1996; Hall, Lee, & Bélanger, 2001; Hall, Waxman, Brédart, & Nicolay, 2003; Sorrentino, 2001), and they prefer special objects (e.g., their favorite doll or blanket) to perceptually identical duplicates (Hood & Bloom, 2008). We can therefore meaningfully ask what sort of knowledge is relevant to such abilities.

Before introducing a new theory, I outline three earlier ways of looking at this problem of identity of individuals across time. A first possibility makes use of the similarity between object descriptions. An alternative possibility, directed at the identity of concrete, physical objects, depends on the spatial and temporal pathway that an individual follows. According to this proposal, people decide that an individual at an earlier time is the same as one at a later time if and only if a continuous spatiotemporal path connects them. Finally, people's notions of individual identity may depend on knowledge specific to the category in which it belongs. Perhaps people acquire criteria or rules for tracing identity as they learn what kind of thing an individual is. If so, then decisions about identity across time may be domain specific—different for members of different basic-level categories, such as lions or icebergs.

All three earlier proposals have plausible elements, and people may well employ them in some settings to decide questions of identity. However, each has shortcomings that make it unlikely to serve as a general theory. This section discusses their relative merits, concentrating on theoretical strengths and weaknesses. The following section revisits these proposals and considers their ability to predict new psychological data.

1.2.1 Similarity

A simple answer to the question of how we determine that items are identical is that we use our knowledge of their common and distinctive properties. If we can compute a measure of the similarity between the items from these properties, we could then judge the items identical if their similarity exceeds some threshold. This is a proposal we should take seriously for several reasons. For one thing, similarity seems to influence perceptual impressions of identity. When observers are shown two line segments, one after the other, rapidly alternating, they are more likely to see a single line segment "moving" than to see two distinct line segments if the segments have a similar orientation (Ullman, 1979; for related results with polygons, see Farrell & Shepard, 1981). For another, recognition of both individual words (e.g., Anisfeld & Knapp, 1968) and pictures (Bower & Glass, 1976) is sensitive to the similarity between the originally presented items and the test items.[1] Similarity almost inevitably plays a role in judging identity. If a cat runs behind a couch and a very similar looking cat runs out the other side, we take this similarity as indicating a single cat in the absence of information to the contrary (such as the presence of twin cats). This is the instinct that Muggsy goes on.

However, a pure similarity theory runs into some difficulties, and these difficulties provide a secondary theme in this book (see Sloman & Rips, 1998, for the status of similarity in cognitive models). First, properties of the items in question are likely to contribute unequally to judgments of identity. Aunt Dahlia's taste in music and other matters in 1970 (mostly Motown) may be vastly different from her taste in 2011 (mostly Mahler), so that her taste and preferences in 1970 and 2011 may differ in ways irrelevant to her identity. We therefore need a theory about which properties are relevant to judgments of identity—a variation of the question with which we started.

Second, similarity may presuppose identity (as Fodor & Lepore, 1992, argue). If we use properties of $Dahlia_{1970}$ and $Dahlia_{2011}$ to establish the similarity between them, then we must be able to determine that these properties are the same. For example, if near-sightedness is one such property, we need to know that $Dahlia's\text{-}nearsightedness_{1970} = Dahlia's\text{-}nearsightedness_{2011}$. But this shifts the problem from sameness of objects to sameness of properties.

Third, things change. We should expect some of Aunt Dahlia's properties to change in predictable ways over time, and although these changes make for dissimilarities, they should count for, rather than against, the possibility that a later stage belongs to the same individual as her earlier stages (Rosengren, Gelman, Kalish, & McCormick, 1991; Sternberg, 1982). An individual at three years of age would typically be shorter than, not the same size as, the same individual at 23. If the individual x_0 is 3′5″ in 1989 and x_1 is 3′5″ in 2011, that could be evidence they were *not* identical. Along the same lines, people sometimes perceive identity despite radical dissimilarities. In a well-known demonstration by Simons and Levin (1998), an experimenter asked a pedestrian for directions on a university campus. While the pedestrian was engaged in the conversation, confederates barged in front of the pedestrian, carrying a door that momentarily concealed the experimenter. During the concealment, one of the confederates exchanged places with the experimenter, continuing the interaction with the pedestrian. But despite the fact that the two experimenters were not especially similar in appearance, only about half the pedestrian participants noticed the change in identity.

For these reasons, similarity is limited in what it can do as a theory of object identity. Although "identical" twins can be amazingly similar, they can't be truly identical.

1.2.2 *Spatiotemporal Continuity*

According to the continuity view, we judge two individuals identical if we know that these individuals fall on the same unbroken spatiotemporal path. $Dahlia_{1970} = Dahlia_{2011}$, for example, if we can find a continuous path linking the first to the second. This theory is similar to one that is sometimes offered for perceptual tracking (e.g., Spelke, Kestenbaum, Simons, & Wein, 1995). There is also evidence (Stone, 1998) that the spatiotemporal path that an object takes can influence later recognition of that object: Recognition is better if observers see the same path at test than if they see an equally informative alternative path.

Although the continuity theory is more substantial than the similarity proposal, counterexamples suggest it won't work. D. M. Armstrong (1980), Nozick (1981, pp. 655–656), and Shoemaker (1979) provide a thought experiment of this sort:

> *Dual-ing machines*: Imagine two machines: one capable of vaporizing an object and the other capable of materializing an object in an arbitrarily brief interval. Suppose, too, that these machines operate on completely independent schedules so there is no connection between one machine and the other. It is possible to conceive the first machine vaporizing a specific object—say, a chair—and the second machine, by chance, immediately materializing a qualitatively similar but distinct object without a temporal gap and in exactly the same spatial location. Under these circumstances, an observer would notice no change whatever, since nothing about their spatial or temporal position or their qualitative properties would distinguish the vaporized and materialized chairs from a single chair. But in the imagined scenario, although an unbroken spatiotemporal sequence of chair stages exists, there are two chairs in play rather than one.

If this example is correct, people may always be willing to override purely spatiotemporal information if they know enough about the facts of the case. For any imagined spatiotemporal evidence pointing to one object, we can conceive Armstrong-Nozick-Shoemaker machines that substitute multiple objects. The example also shows that any sort of perceptual evidence for identity will also be insufficient.

One reaction to this example is that the machines don't truly preserve spatiotemporal continuity; there must be some break between the two chairs, since they have different material composition or other properties. But although a difference exists between the chairs, it needn't be a *spatial* or *temporal* discontinuity. We can envision the materializing machine outputting the second chair within any temporal interval ε ($\varepsilon > 0$)

following the disappearance of the first chair. If so, this meets the standard definition of continuity. Of course, this example depends on contemplating sci-fi devices that may never actually exist, but the fact that we can make sense of dual-ing machines suggests that we don't conceive of spatiotemporal continuity as guaranteeing identity over time.

Hirsch (1982) provides a second type of counterexample to the idea that spatiotemporal continuity is sufficient for identity. As Hirsch points out, indefinitely many spatially and temporally continuous sequences don't count as a single object. The north half of a cat from 10 to 11 pm is one such nonobject.

To be sure, the dual-ing machine example does not show that all forms of continuity are irrelevant for identity. Intuitively, the reason the example describes two chairs rather than one is that the vaporized chair is not connected to the materialized one in the same way as the successive stages of a single chair. In particular, there is no causal link between the vaporized and the materialized chairs. This intuition leads directly to the theory of identity that I propose later. Incorporating causal relations takes us a significant step beyond spatial and temporal continuity.

It also seems doubtful that spatiotemporal continuity is necessary for identity. We could disassemble a computer into its individual circuit components, store the resulting hundreds or thousands of parts in separate locations, and then reassemble the parts later in yet another location but according to exactly the same pattern. Under these circumstances, the later reconstructed computer would seem to be identical to the earlier intact one. However, no continuous spatiotemporal path links the two halves of the computer's existence. This implies that identity is possible over gaps in time and space (as Hirsch, 1982, argues from a similar example).[2]

The computer example should make us cautious about requiring continuity as a criterion of identity, but the example also hints at another basis for singular concepts. Computers, tables, chairs, cars, and many other artifacts can survive complete disassembly and reassembly, but cats, robins, roses, and many other living things can't survive total dismemberment. Some evidence that older children and adults recognize such a distinction comes from Hall (1998), which I discuss in Section 1.4. Perhaps, then, identity over time is relative to the category to which an object belongs. A common theme in cognitive research on categorization is that knowledge of an object's category can provide theoretical information about the object, information that fuels inference and prediction (see Chapters 4 and 5, in this volume). The theory I'm about to take up extends this idea by supposing that category-level concepts also supply criteria for identifying category members from one moment to the next.

1.2.3 Sortals

Certain concepts may determine rules for individuating and identifying their instances. The concept of cats, for example, may consist in part of rules for differentiating individual cats in a mass of cats-and-other-objects and identifying each cat over time. (Not all psychological theories assume that general concepts contain rules, as we will see in Chapters 4 and 5, but the theory we're about to discuss presupposes them.)

Philosophical work discusses this idea under the heading of *sortals* (Strawson, 1959, p. 168). A sortal is a count noun like *table* that is capable of singling out individual tables. By contrast, an adjective like *black* denotes a property that doesn't by itself distinguish things. We can't count the black stuff that composes a black table, say, since the total is indeterminate: It might be one thing (the table), five (the legs + the top), six (the legs + the top + the table), or more. Nouns like *table*, *leg*, or *top*, however, do provide the resources we need to get a determinate answer. Orthodox sortal theories assert that there are no individuals at all, apart from the sortal concepts that carve them out and establish their beginnings and endings. As Dummett (1973, p. 179) puts it, "[John Stuart] Mill wrote as though the world already came to us sliced up into objects, and all we have to learn is which label to tie on to which object. But it is not so: the proper names which we use, and the corresponding sortal terms, determine principles whereby the slicing up is to be effected, principles which are acquired with the acquisition of the uses of these words." In what follows, I'll use the term *sortal* for linguistic expressions (i.e., for certain count nouns), *sortal concept* to refer to the associated mental representation, and *sortal category* for the referent of the sortal (a set of objects).[3]

The identity conditions that these sortals furnish are necessary and sufficient relations for identifying objects at different times, and they take the form in (4) (see Lowe, 1989):

(4)   If object x at time t_1 and object y at time t_2 are members of sortal category S, then $x = y$ if and only if $R_S(x,y)$.

In this formulation, R_S is an equivalence relation (i.e., it is reflexive, symmetric, and transitive; see (2) above). In addition, R_S must be an informative relation—one that does not merely paraphrase or presuppose identity for S's—in order to avoid trivializing the analysis. The plausibility of sortal theory will, of course, depend on whether a relation exists that can fill R_S's role in (4). In the case of formal or mathematical categories, the relation is sometimes obvious. For example, we can define the identity of two sets in terms of the same-member relation: Sets x and y are identical if and only if x has as its members all and only the members of y. In the case of natural categories, however, the existence of an appropriate R_S might be in doubt, an issue we will return to in Section 1.5.2. Most sortal theories also assume that objects in distinct sortals cannot be identical. In other words:

(5)   If object x at time t_1 is a member of sortal category S and object y at time t_2 is not a member of S, then $x \neq y$.[4]

Some psychologists have enlisted sortals to explain how people trace the history of individuals. An individual object, such as a cat or a table, can undergo a variety of changes without ceasing to exist, whereas other changes are not compatible with its continued existence. By (5), the compatible changes can't take an individual outside its sortal category. An individual x_0 can't persist as an individual x_1 if x_0 is in sortal category S_0 and x_1 is in a different sortal category S_1. Which changes are possible and which impossible vary across types of objects: They are relative to an object's sortal. Some changes—such as total disassembly—may be possible for a table but not for a cat. According to Wiggins (2001), an object's sortal (e.g., *table* or *cat*) is the term that best provides the answer to the question "What is it?" for that object.

One advantage of the sortal theory is that it handles some issues that are problematic for continuity accounts. Consider, for example, a car that loses a hubcap on a bumpy road. Although both the hubcapless car and the carless hubcap are continuous with the original item, the sortal *car* applies to the initial object and dictates that it's the hubcapless car that is identical to the original car. A second advantage is that the sortal theory can help explain the problem with which we started: how we are able to make judgments about object identity even in counterfactual contexts. Because sortals separate possible from impossible changes for the objects they apply to, they rule out some alternative histories for an object. These theoretical advantages suggest that it might be useful to incorporate the sortalist insights in psychological explanations of object identity, so we need to examine carefully some recent attempts of this kind.

1.2.3.1 Sortalist Approaches in Psychological Theories

For researchers who see deficiencies in pure similarity and continuity accounts, sortals fill a gap by providing a source of rules that people can use to keep track of things. In this vein, Macnamara (1986) assumed on theoretical grounds that when children learn a proper name for an object, they interpret the name with the help of the object's sortal concept. The sortal concept—which Macnamara took to be a prototype or perceptual "gestalt" of a category—provides criteria for individuation and identity that support correct use of the proper name. The same considerations apply to the use of personal pronouns, such as *I* and *you* (Oshima-Takane, 1999). Similarly, according to Carey (1995a, p. 108), "To see the logical role sortals play in our thought, first consider that we cannot simply count what is in this room. Before we begin counting, we must be told what to count. We must supply a sortal . . . Next consider whether a given entity is the same one as we saw before. Again, we must be supplied a sortal to trace identity."

Xu and Carey (1996; Xu, Carey, & Quint, 2004) recruit sortals to explain results on the way infants discriminate objects. In these experiments, infants viewed an opaque screen from which objects emerged, either at the right or left. An infant might see, for example, a toy elephant emerge from the right side of the screen and then return behind the screen. A short time later, a cup emerges from the left side of the screen and returns behind the screen. This performance is repeated a number of times with the same two objects. The screen is then removed, revealing either a single object (e.g., the cup) or two objects (cup and elephant). The data from these experiments show that, when the screen is removed, 10-month-old infants look no longer at the scene with one object than at the scene with two (relative to baseline performance). By contrast, 12-month-olds look longer at the one-object tableau, as long as the objects are from different basic-level categories. (If the objects are from the same category—e.g., two cups with different colors—even

12-month-olds fail to look longer at the one-object scenes; see Xu et al., 2004.) Xu and Carey interpret this to mean that the younger infants do not expect to see two objects and so are no more surprised by one than by two in this context. Older infants, however, can use their knowledge of the sortal concepts CUP and ELEPHANT to make the discrimination.[5]

Several factors allow younger infants to anticipate two objects correctly. First, if the 10-month-olds are able to inspect simultaneously the elephant and the cup before the start of the trial, then they do stare longer at the one-object scene (Xu & Carey, 1996). Second, if the experimenter labels the two objects differently ("look a blicket" vs. "look a gax") while they are moving back and forth, 10-month-olds again perform correctly (Xu, 2002). This combination of results suggests, according to Xu and Carey, that younger infants can use spatial or verbal cues to individuate the objects; without these cues, they are unable to anticipate the presence of two objects, since they don't know that elephants don't morph into cups while briefly out of sight.

According to Xu and Carey (1996), the younger infants who fail this is-it-one-or-two task lack knowledge of sortal concepts (e.g., CUP, [toy] ELEPHANT) that would allow them to individuate the objects conceptually. Since this individuating information is supposed to be a crucial part of the meaning of sortals, these infants don't know these meanings; they don't have adult-like concepts for even basic-level categories such as *cup*.[6]

1.2.3.2 Evidence Concerning Sortals

Carey and Xu (2001; Xu, 2003a) maintain that infants acquire the meaning of these sortals at about 12 months of age and that the sortals are responsible for older infants' and adults' correct performance in the is-it-one-or-two task.[7] Is there psychological evidence that *cup, elephant,* and similar count nouns play this identifying role?

One way to investigate this issue takes advantage of Wiggins's (1997, 2001) contention that the sortal for a particular object is the term that answers the question, "What is it?" Brown (1958) and Rosch, Mervis, Gray, Johnson, and Boyes-Braem (1976) have claimed that words for basic-level categories, such as *cup* or *elephant,* usually provide the answer to this question; so we may be able to check whether knowledge of basic-level categories gives people the means to identify objects.[8] In one attempt of this kind, Liittschwager (1995) gave 4-year-old children illustrated stories about people who were magically transformed to different states. The transformations ranged, across trials, from simple within-category changes in properties (e.g., from a clean to a dirty child) to more extreme cross-category changes (e.g., from a girl to a cat or from a woman to rain). For each type of transformation, participants decided whether the transformed object could still be called by the name of the original person—for example, "Do you think that now *this* is Ali?" According to sortal theories, objects cannot maintain their identity across changes in sortal categories (see Principle (5)); so participants should use the same proper name only if the transformation is within the basic-level category person. The results of this study showed that as the transformational distance increased between the original person and the final product, participants were less willing to apply the proper name. However, there was no discernible elbow in this function at the sortal category— the boundary between persons and nonpersons. According to Liittschwager (1995, pp. 33–34), the data "provide little support for Macnamara's (1986) position that proper names should be maintained across changes up to (but not beyond) the basic level."

Sergey Blok, George Newman, and I (Blok, Newman, & Rips, 2005) report a similar finding in an experiment that also employed transformation stories. Participants (college students) read stories about an individual—say, Jim—who has a severe traffic accident in the year 2020 and whose only hope for survival is radical surgery. In the condition most relevant for present purposes, participants learned that Jim's brain was transplanted to a different body. On some trials, scientists placed the brain in "a highly sophisticated cybernetic body," while on others they placed it in a human body that scientists had grown for just such emergencies. In each case, Jim's old body was destroyed. The stories described the operation as successful in allowing the brain to control the new body, but participants also learned either that Jim's memories survived the operation intact or did not survive. After reading the scenario, participants rated on a 0-to-9 scale their agreement with each of two statements: (a) The transplant recipient is Jim after the operation, and (b) the transplant recipient is a person after the operation.[9]

The results from Blok et al. (2005) show a dissociation between identity and category judgments. Figure 1.1 displays the mean agreement ratings as a function of whether the story described the brain transplanted to a robot or to a human body and also whether the memories survived or did not survive the operation. Participants were more likely to agree that the post-op recipient was still Jim (open circles in Figure 1.1) if Jim's memories were preserved. However, there was a much smaller effect of whether these memories were embodied in a human or in a

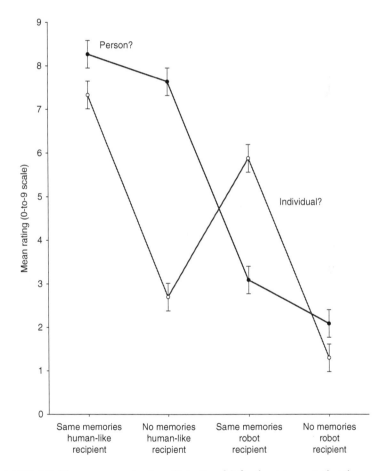

FIGURE 1.1 Mean agreement ratings (0-to-9 scale) for the statements that the transplant recipient is "still Jim" (open circles) and "still a person" (closed circles). The x-axis represents four versions of the accident story. Error bars indicate ±1 standard error of the mean (from Blok et al., 2005).

robot body (see also Nichols & Bruno, 2010). Ratings about whether the recipient was a person (filled circles), however, show the opposite pattern. Participants were more likely to think the transformed object was a person if it had a human rather than a robot body, but they relied less heavily on whether Jim's memories remained intact. This combination of effects produced the finding that when Jim's memories survive in a robotic body, participants were much more likely to think that the transformed individual is Jim than that it (!) is a person.

Psychological versions of sortal theories seem at odds with this outcome. Because these theories subscribe to Principle (5), they assume that an individual can't exist outside the bounds of its sortal. Thus, doubts about whether the transplant recipient is a person should translate into doubts about whether it is Jim. However, when Jim's brain is transplanted to a robot body with his memories intact, participants judge him to have undergone a change incompatible with his sortal (he is no longer a person) while remaining Jim. This contradicts Principle (5) and casts doubt on sortal theories. Of course, the category of persons may be special and perhaps unrepresentative of other kinds of objects (e.g., Bonatti, Frot, Zangl, & Mehler, 2002; Kuhlmeier, Bloom, & Wynn, 2004; Sternberg, Chawarski, & Allbritton, 1998). But similar dissociations appear in experiments using other categories (Blok et al., 2005, Experiment 2; Rhemtulla, 2005; Rhemtulla & Hall, 2009). I report another study of this type in the next section.

Sortal theories capture the intuition that pure spatiotemporal continuity does not suffice for object identity, and they capitalize on the observation that individuals usually don't switch sortal categories in midcareer. It's tempting to assume, then, that sortal concepts furnish identity conditions for category members. The evidence I've just reviewed suggests, however, that if we take the sortal category to be the basic-level category (the category that typically answers the question "What is it?") then identity doesn't always coincide with membership in the sortal. Maybe we've been too quick, though, in taking sortals to be basic-level category terms. Although *dog* and *cat*, for example, are basic-level terms and seem to answer the "What is it?" question, we may establish Rover's or Cat-astrophe's criteria of identity at some other level. Since dogs and cats are similar biologically, their identity may depend on general principles at the level of mammals, vertebrates, or even animals (see Dummett,

1973, p. 76; but also Wiggins, 2001, p. 129, for an explicit denial that *animal* is a sortal). It appears to be a difficult matter to pin down exactly which term is the appropriate sortal, as Mackie (2006) has pointed out. But if we cut the tie to basic-level categories, we seem to be left with a fairly weak hypothesis. A softened version of the sortal theory might claim that for any object there is some count noun or other whose concept provides identity conditions for the object. But all the softened theory does is narrow down the identity conditions to those that a count noun can represent. And this seems little different from the claim that objects have identity conditions.

1.2.4 Summary

Similarity and continuity are often relevant to our decisions about the identity of objects over time. We use them as heuristics, and they often serve us well. However, like other heuristics, they take a backseat when definitive information is available. Even if we are able to observe a spatially and temporally continuous path, our knowledge of the circumstances may convince us that two objects are at hand rather than one (D. M. Armstrong, 1980; Nozick, 1981; Shoemaker, 1979). Likewise, what we perceive to be temporally and spatially discontinuous, like a table before and after its disassembly and reassembly, may turn out to be a single object after all. Our perception in these cases can be perfectly veridical in providing a correct description of whether the material in question is actually continuous in time and space. The problem in determining identity isn't just that perception can be illusory; it's that spatiotemporal continuity isn't necessary or sufficient for identity over time.

People adopt different criteria in judging the identity of different types of things. We're more likely to think that an artifact that is completely taken apart and put back together is the same object than is an organism that receives the same ghoulish treatment (Hall, 1998). Psychological versions of sortal theories are right in stressing this variation in our criteria. Sortal theories also seem correct in asserting that identity over time depends on the kinds of changes that are possible or impossible for an individual. What's more controversial is the source of identity principles. The evidence to date suggests that these principles are not simply inherited from basic-level concepts. Our decisions about whether items are identical depend on induction over a potentially broader knowledge base.

1.3 A Causal Continuer Theory of Object Identity

This section considers a theory of identity judgments that draws on some of the elements of the earlier views just surveyed, but combines them in a new way—one that is consistent with the perspective on general concepts that I develop later in this book (see Chapter 4). The theory attempts to answer the question posed in (1) by describing the cognitive processes people go through when they have to decide whether an individual object, x_0, existing at one time, is identical to one of a set of candidate objects $x_1, x_2, \ldots, x_n$, existing at a later time. The model derives from a proposal by Nozick (1981)—his Closest Continuer theory— but I recast the proposal here as a descriptive psychological account. I intend the model to help explain how people judge object identity, and it may not necessarily give a correct account of the underlying (metaphysical) nature of identity over time. I first describe the theory in outline and then apply it to some experimental data that Blok, Newman, and I have collected to test a quantitative version of this approach.

1.3.1 The Causal Continuer Theory

As its name implies, Nozick's (1981) Closest Continuer theory commits itself to the idea that the object identical to the original x_0 is the one that is, in some sense, "closest." But unlike the similarity approach, discussed in the preceding section, the present theory determines closeness within a framework of causal principles. As a reminder of this restriction (and some additional modifications, mentioned later) I refer to the model proposed here as the *Causal Continuer* theory.

Causality is important in this context, since the theory's chief principle is that the continuer of the original object must be a causal outgrowth of that original. Here's a story to illustrate this idea:

> *The missing chair:* Suppose you own a chair with a distinctive color and shape. One day you regrettably leave the chair in one of the

classrooms in the department, from which it disappears. The
following week you spot two different chairs that are qualitatively
identical to yours. One is sitting in the office of Professor A;
the other in the office of Professor B. Which, if either, of these
chairs is yours? Similarity is clearly unable to decide the case.
Spatiotemporal continuity might be helpful if you could establish
that there is a continuous pathway from the chair in the classroom
to the chair in one of the offices. But suppose that on investigating
you find the case is this: Professor A, who had never seen your
chair, happened to construct one of the same shape and color.
Professor B, however, has disassembled the chair he found in the
classroom, stealthily moved the parts to his office one at a time, and
reassembled the chair. No spatially continuous path connects your
chair to either chair, but there is a clear intuition that the chair
in Professor B's office, and not the one in Professor A's, is yours.
A causal relation links each step in the transition from the chair in
the classroom to the chair in Professor B's office, but no such causal
relation exists between your chair and Professor A's.

The important role that causality plays in the theory goes along with
the idea that causal forces are central in producing an object, maintaining
it through time, and eventually destroying it. In this respect, the Causal
Continuer theory is akin to psychological essentialism (S. A. Gelman,
2003; Medin & Ortony, 1989), which also emphasizes the role of causality in people's thinking about natural kinds (see Chapter 4 in this book
for a discussion of essentialism). It also agrees with some versions of psychological essentialism in supposing that separate causal factors are
responsible for category membership and individual persistence (Gelman,
2003; Gutheil & Rosengren, 1996). However, the present theory takes no
stand on a unique, distinctive cause that would answer to the notion of
an essence. The existence of an object may be a function of many con-
spiring causes, some internal and some external to the object (see Sloman
& Malt, 2003; Strevens, 2000; and Chapter 4 of this book). Moreover,
the causes governing a category member may partially overlap those
governing its category. For example, respiration, circulation, and many
other bodily causal systems may be necessary for the survival of both an
individual organism and the species to which it belongs.

Similarly, the Causal Continuer theory also makes contact with recent models of categories that emphasize the role of causality in category structure (e.g., Ahn, 1998; Rehder & Hastie, 2001). For reasons that I have mentioned in connection with sortals, however, I assume that the causes responsible for an individual's persistence may include not only those associated with its basic-level category, but also the larger set of background causes that governs the environment in which the individual finds itself. Otherwise, it would be difficult to explain the dissociation between Jim's continued existence as Jim and his continued existence as a person in the experiment reported earlier.

A second aspect of the theory is that, in determining a continuer, we cannot select something that is arbitrarily far from the original. In some later situations, *no* object may qualify as identical to the one with which we started. Although later objects may causally stem from the original, the causal connections to those objects may be so attenuated that none can serve as a continuer, and the original object thereby goes out of existence. If a book is ripped apart into its covers and its individual pages (each page separated from the others), then each of the resulting pieces maintains a causal connection to the original, but the connection may not be strong enough to qualify any of the pieces (or their sum) as the book. Similarly, the causal connection between the original object and a later one cannot be too abrupt. Although the dead remains of an animal are causal products of its living state, the transition is not smooth enough to allow the remains to serve as a continuer of the organism.

We can think of these restrictions as imposing a two-step decision process. To determine which of a set of objects at a later time is identical to an original: (a) we consider only those later objects whose connection to the original exceeds some threshold (no other objects can be continuers), and (b) within the range of close-enough objects, we select the closest as the one identical to the original. It may seem natural to assume that people carry out step (a) before step (b), but the opposite ordering is also possible. People may identify the closest object before determining whether that object is close enough to be identical. Note, too, that step (b) allows the decision process to be context sensitive. An item that is closest in one situation may not be closest in another if the second situation contains an even closer object.[10]

In Nozick's (1981) theory, the closest continuer must be closest in an absolute sense—no ties are allowed. For example, if an amoeba x_0 divides in such a way that the two descendants, x_1 and x_2, are equally like their common parent, then the parent cannot be identical to either descendant. The reason for this additional restriction has to do with the transitivity of identity, which we glimpsed in (2c). The two amoeba descendants, x_1 and x_2, aren't equal to each other, since each can go its own way, acquiring different properties after the division that produced it. But then if the parent x_0 is equal to both the descendants, the result is an intransitivity: $x_1 = x_0$ and $x_0 = x_2$, but $x_1 \neq x_2$. However, similar apparent intransitivities arise in certain perceptual situations (Ullman, 1979), and for this reason I leave room for the possibility of ties in judgments about conceptual identity. If such judgments do exist, we can then consider how to interpret them.[11] I'll take up this issue in more detail in Section 1.5.1.

In examining the theory, I concentrate on the basic two-part decision structure just outlined. The rest of this section presents two experiments that carry out such an examination, and the Appendix formulates a quantitative version of the theory that applies to the data.

1.3.2 An Experiment on Individual Persistence

To find out how well the Causal Continuer theory handles people's identity judgments, we need an experimental situation that gives participants a choice between potential continuers and that varies the causal distance between the continuers and the original object. Because the effect of category membership is of interest (as an additional test of sortal theories), the original object must be able to switch categories. These requirements are difficult or impossible to satisfy with everyday objects, but we can approximate such situations in stories about hypothetical transformations, as in much earlier research on concepts and categories (e.g., Blok et al., 2005; S. A. Gelman & Wellman, 1991; C. N. Johnson, 1990; Keil, 1989; Liittschwager, 1995; Rips, 1989). It's good to keep in mind, however, that the Causal Continuer theory applies to everyday identity decisions, as well as to the recherché cases we consider here. The purpose of using hypothetical scenarios is the usual one of achieving experimental control over variables that are confounded in typical situations. Experimental control is nearly always in tension with ecological validity. In Section 1.3.4, however, we will look at an experimental setting that may be closer to the usual contexts in which identity is in question.

The stories I used in this experiment are similar to those in some philosophical discussions (e.g., Lewis, 1983; Nozick, 1981; Parfit, 1984; Perry, 1972) and described a "transporter" that could copy and transfer objects from place to place on a particle-by-particle basis. The copied particles are transmitted to a new location and put back together according to a blueprint of the original. The particles of the original are entirely destroyed in the copying process. Thus, there was no spatiotemporal or material continuity between the original and the copy, but the copy causally stems from the original by means of the duplicating process. (This explicit causal relation distinguishes this set up from the one in the dual-ing machines example.) Each trial of the experiment described a different hypothetical transformation, and participants' task was to make two decisions about the resulting copies: (a) whether the copy is the same object as the original, and (b) whether the copy is in the same category as the original.

The experimental stories included three variations. First, they varied whether there was one copy or two. In one block of trials, the instructions told participants that the transporter had made a single copy of the particles, and the participants decided whether that copy was identical to the original and whether it was in the same category as the original. On a second block of trials, the instructions stated that the transporter constructed two copies. Participants then decided whether one, both, or neither of these copies was identical to the original, and whether one, both, or neither was in the original's category. The second variation among the stories concerned the percentage of copied particles that went into the reconstituted objects. In the one-copy condition, the copy could contain 0, 25, 50, 75, or 100% of the particles copied from the original. The story specified that in the 0, 25, 50, or 75% conditions the remaining particles came from a different object. In the two-copy condition, each copy could independently contain any of the five percentages just mentioned, with the residual particles again coming from a different object. For example, participants might learn that one copy included 50% particles coming from the original object and 50% from a separate object, while the second copy included 75% particles from the original and 25% from the separate object. (The percentage of particles from the original needn't add to 100%, since the transporter was said to have made two complete batches of particles.) In the context of this experiment, the percentage of particles from the original object provides a measure of the causal distance between the original and each of the copies. Finally, the stories also varied whether the residual particles came from a member of the same category as the original or from a member of a different category. In each story, the original item was a lion (named "Fred"), and the residual particles were either from a second lion ("Calvin") or from a tiger ("Joe"). Thus, in the one-copy condition, participants might learn on one trial that the newly constructed creature contained 75% particles from Fred and the remaining 25% from the same-category member, Calvin. On another trial, the creature contained 75% particles from Fred and the remaining 25% from the different-category member, Joe. In the two-copy condition, both copies had residual particles from the second lion or both had residual particles from the tiger.

The instructions explained the workings of the "transporter" in the same way that I described it earlier. In the one-copy condition, the participants (Northwestern University students) received nine scenarios that differed in the percentage of particles coming from the original object and in the source of the remaining particles. (There were nine rather than ten scenarios, since when 100% of particles were from the original, there were no residual particles and thus no possible difference in source.) On each trial, participants made separate decisions about whether the outcome of the transformation was the same individual (they chose between "Is Fred" or "Is not Fred") and whether it was a member of the same category ("Is a lion" or "Is not a lion"). In the two-copy condition, participants received 30 two-copy trials. For each story, they again made an individual decision (they selected one of: "Only Copy A is Fred," "Only Copy B is Fred," "Both copies are Fred," or "Neither copy is Fred") and a category decision ("Only Copy A is a lion," "Only Copy B is a lion," "Both copies are lions," or "Neither copy is a lion").

I focus on the results of the two-copy condition, since they provide the best test of the model, and use the one-copy condition mainly to estimate parameters associated with causal distance between the original object and each alternative (see the Appendix to this chapter). However,

the one-copy data also provide some evidence about which of the
experimental factors affect decisions about individual identity and about
category membership. The results appear in Figure 1.2, and they exhibit
a clear dissociation between these two types of judgments, confirming
the conclusions from Blok et al. (2005) discussed earlier. The x-axis in

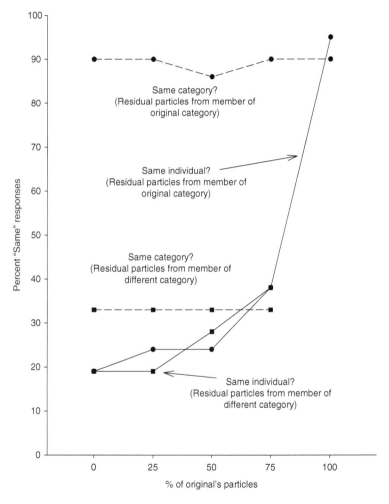

FIGURE 1.2 Percentage of responses indicating that the result of the transformation
was still the same individual (solid lines) and was still a member of the same
category (dashed lines). Lines with circles denote stories in which residual particles
were from a member of the same category. Lines with squares indicate stories
in which residual particles were from a member of a different category.

this figure indicates the percentage of the copy's particles coming from the original object, and the y-axis shows the percentage of trials on which participants agreed that the copy was the same individual as the original object (solid lines) or was in the same category as the original (dashed lines). Lines with circles represent stories in which the residual particles (those not copied from the original object) came from another member of the same species, while lines with squares are stories in which the residual particles come from a member of a different species. (For the two right-most points, all particles came from the original object, and there are no residual particles.)

Figure 1.2 shows that the larger the percentage of particles from the original individual, the more likely participants are to say that the copy is the same individual as the original. In the 0–75% range, the slope is fairly gradual but still amounts to an increase of 19 percentage points. There is no effect, though, of whether the residual particles are from a member of the same category or of a different category. By contrast, judgments of whether the copy is in the same category as the original produce the opposite effects. When the residual particles are from a member of the same category, participants agree that the copy is also a member of that category on 89% of trials. When any of the particles are from a member of a different category, however, agreement falls abruptly to 33% and does not vary with the proportion of particles from that category member.

The results in Figure 1.2 demonstrate that factors affecting category membership don't necessarily affect decisions about individual persistence. Although the source of the residual particles had a strong influence on category judgments, it had almost none on judgments of identity. This finding echoes the one I reported earlier (see Figure 1.1) and presents another puzzle for the view that persistence conditions come from knowledge of sortal membership. Assuming that "lion" is the relevant sortal, factors that cast doubt on whether the copy is a lion should also cast doubt on whether the copy is Fred, contrary to these results.

1.3.3 A Quantitative Version of the Causal Continuer Model

Results from the two-copy condition were similar to those from the one-copy condition in that judgments of individual identity depended on the percentage of particles from the original individual, but not on the source of the remaining particles. Figure 1.3 graphs these results, with solid circles representing cases in which the residual particles were from a member of the same category (a different lion) and open circles representing cases in which the residual particles were from a member of a different category (a tiger). Each of the smaller graphs within Figure 1.3 corresponds to a combination in which one copy contained a given percentage of particles from the original individual (the initial lion) and the other copy contained another (possibly equal) percentage. For example, the graph in the lower left-hand corner represents the case in

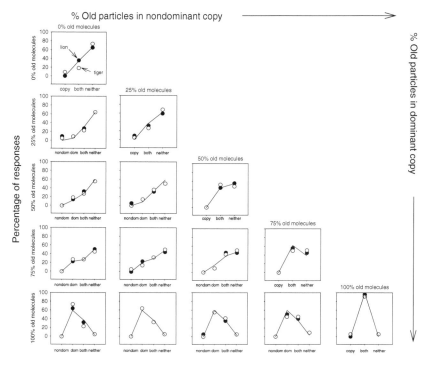

FIGURE 1.3 Percentage of responses that the dominant copy, nondominant copy, both copies, or neither copy was the same individual as the original. The graphs represent combinations in which each copy has either 0, 25, 50, 75, or 100% of its particles from the original object. Filled circles denote stories in which the residual particles were from a member of the same species. Open circles denote stories in which the residual particles were from a member of a different species. Lines are predictions from the Causal Continuer theory.

which one copy had 0% of its particles from the original individual and the other copy had 100% of its particles from the original. The points within each graph show the distribution of participants' responses. From left to right, these are the percentages of trials on which respondents judged: (a) that only the copy with fewer particles from the original (the *nondominant* copy) was identical to that original; (b) that only the copy with more particles from the original (the *dominant* copy) was identical; (c) that both copies were identical; and (d) that neither copy was identical. The graphs along the diagonal from the upper left to the lower right of the figure are cases in which both copies had the same percentage of original particles. In these cases, neither copy was dominant (and there were no other features to distinguish the copies); so I have combined the responses in which participants chose only one of these copies as identical. These responses are labeled *copy* on the *x*-axis. The solid lines in the graphs are the model's predictions, which I describe shortly.

Figure 1.3 highlights several trends in the results. First, the percentage of "dominant copy" or "copy" responses (relative to "both" or "neither" responses) increases from top to bottom, along the columns of graphs. The increase is steep between 75% and 100% of old particles, but is perceivable at lower levels as well. This indicates that as the percentage of original particles in the two copies becomes more dissimilar, participants shift toward thinking that only the dominant copy is identical to the original item. Second, a glance along the diagonal from upper left to lower right shows that the percentage of "both" responses increases (relative to "neither" responses). Both copies have the same proportion of original particles here, and as this proportion rises, participants increasingly believe that both copies are identical. Third, whether the residual particles came from a member of the same category as the original or from a different category has no effect on participants' choices. This finding replicates the results from the one-copy condition, as noted earlier. In applying the Causal Continuer model, I focus on these individual decisions. However, the decisions about category membership in the two-copy condition also replicate the one-copy condition in showing an effect of the residual particles' source, but not of the percentage of particles from the original. This echoes the dissociation in Figure 1.2.

The Causal Continuer approach is consistent with these trends. According to this theory, a participant's response on a particular trial should depend on two decisions. First, she needs to determine whether one of the copies is causally closer than the other. Second, she also needs to know whether either copy is close enough to the original to qualify as identical to it. If the answer to both questions is "yes," she should respond that only the closer copy is identical. If the answer to the first question is "no" but the answer to the second is "yes," she should respond that both are identical. In all other cases (i.e., the answer to the second question is "no"), she should report that neither is identical. The first of these decisions is responsible for the increase in "dominant" responses along the columns of Figure 1.3. The greater the difference between the two copies in the percentage of original particles, the more likely the dominant copy is to be closer than the nondominant copy to the original, and the more likely participants are to make a "dominant" response. The second decision is responsible for the increase in "both" responses along the diagonal, where the two copies have the same percentage of original particles. The larger this percentage, the more likely "both" copies will be close enough, and the more likely participants are to make a "both" response. The lines in the Figure 1.3 graphs show the fit of a simple mathematical model based on combining these two decisions. The Appendix to this chapter contains the details of the model-fitting, but the results confirm the visual impression that the model does quite well, accounting for 96% of the variance with only a single free parameter.

1.3.4 An Experiment on the Effects of Causality and Similarity

It is reasonable to think that similarity between an object and its successor can sometimes provide evidence for identity over time. Similarity between Aunt Dahlia's appearance in 1970 and in 2011 may be enough to lead us to believe that these two manifestations belong to the same person. The Causal Continuer model claims, however, that causal factors can override similarity if the two factors conflict. We judge someone who is merely similar to Aunt Dahlia (but who is not a causal outgrowth of her earlier stages) as nonidentical, perhaps even as an imposter (for historical cases, see Barry, 2003; N. Z. Davis, 1983; Grann, 2008; Munsell, 1854). To see why, imagine an iceberg whose size is 3 x 3 x 3 m at a particular time t_o. Most people probably assume that over time icebergs tend to shrink due to temperature and to splitting (caused by stress from storms and other factors).[12] Thus, at a later time t_1, the original iceberg's continuer would presumably have smaller dimensions rather than larger ones. The similarity of icebergs, however, might be more symmetric. The 3 x 3 x 3 m original might be about equally similar to a 4 x 4 x 4 m iceberg and to a 2 x 2 x 2 m iceberg at t_1, but only the latter is likely to be identical to the original.

To see whether causal beliefs do indeed dominate similarity, I asked participants in a further study to make judgments about icebergs.[13] In the experiment, participants read a scenario in which scientists were studying an iceberg named *Sample* 94, whose dimensions were 3 x 3 x 3 m. During the two parts of the experiment, I gave participants a list of icebergs of varying dimensions (e.g., 4 x 3 x 1 m or 2 x 1 x 1 m) that the instructions described as being found "sometime later" in the same vicinity. Participants rated both how similar each item was to the original Sample 94 and how likely the item *was to be* Sample 94. The goal of the study was to distinguish identity and similarity judgments. If causal mechanisms dominate judgments of identity, we should find that participants give lower identity ratings than similarity ratings to icebergs whose dimensions are greater than the original sample. Similarity and identity judgments may converge for icebergs whose dimensions are smaller than the original.

In their similarity and identity ratings, participants compared the 3 x 3 x 3 m iceberg to each of a set of items formed by combining the dimensions 4 m, 3 m, 2 m, and 1 m in all distinct ways. Thus, one item was 4 x 4 x 4 m, another 4 x 4 x 3 m, and so on. (The instructions told participants that the dimensions were always given with the larger sides first, without regard for the iceberg's orientation. For example, participants rated a 4 x 3 x 1 iceberg but not a 3 x 1 x 4 iceberg, since these would be the same item. Because of this aliasing, there were 20 items in the stimulus set, shown on the x-axis of Figure 1.4, below.) After each item was a rating scale, containing the numbers 0 to 9. I tested 46 Northwestern undergraduates in this experiment. Half these participants rated similarity first; half rated identity first.

When comparing the standard iceberg (3 x 3 x 3 m) to one with a larger dimension (e.g., 4 x 3 x 3 m), participants should see the second as potentially similar to the first but not identical to it. Because icebergs tend to shrink over time, a comparison iceberg with a larger dimension can be similar but not identical to the standard. The mean ratings appear in Figure 1.4, and they confirm this prediction. Filled circles in the figure are mean identity ratings, and open circles mean similarity ratings. The *x*-axis lists the individual iceberg dimensions, with the vertical dashed line separating icebergs whose dimensions are all less than or equal to the standard from those icebergs containing one or more larger dimensions. When the comparison iceberg has a larger dimension (right side of the figure), its mean similarity rating is always higher than its identity rating, but when the comparison iceberg's dimensions are smaller or equal to those of the standard (left side of the figure), the ratings are more nearly equivalent.

As Figure 1.4 suggests, there is a significant interaction between type of judgment (similarity versus identity) and whether the iceberg has a dimension greater than that of the standard. We can get a more revealing

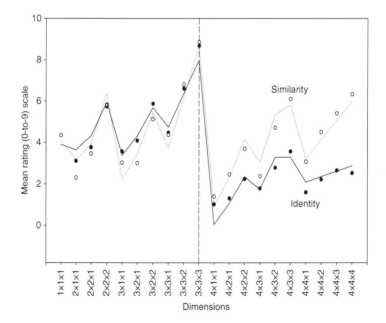

FIGURE 1.4 Mean ratings (0-to-9 scale) of similarity (open circles) and identity (filled circles) between icebergs of varying sizes (*x*-axis) and a 3 x 3 x 3 standard. The dashed line shows predictions for similarity ratings from a regression model; the solid line shows predictions for identity ratings (see text for a description of these models).

picture, though, by examining variables that may have contributed to participants' reasoning about these judgments. Figure 1.4 shows peaks in the ratings when the icebergs were cubical (e.g., 2 x 2 x 2 or 4 x 4 x 4) or nearly so (e.g., 3 x 2 x 2 or 4 x 3 x 3), suggesting that participants were taking into account the iceberg's shape. Because the standard iceberg was itself cubical, participants may have given the comparison iceberg higher ratings if it too had approximately the same shape. In addition, participants considered overall size, giving higher ratings when the size of the comparison iceberg was nearly that of the standard. Initial analyses hinted that participants might have compared the icebergs in terms of the sum of their dimensions rather than their product, possibly for computational ease. Icebergs whose dimensions summed to a total near 9, the sum of the dimensions of the 3 x 3 x 3 standard, got higher identity and similarity ratings than the others. Compare, for example, the ratings of the 4 x 3 x 2 item (dimension sum = 9) to the 4 x 2 x 1 item (dimension sum = 7) in Figure 1.4.

To see how well these factors predicted the mean ratings, I applied two regression equations to the Figure 1.4 data, one for the similarity and the other for the identity judgments. Both equations contained three terms: The first captured departure from cubical shape in terms of the standard deviation of the iceberg's three dimensions. The second term measured the overall difference in size between the standard and comparison iceberg, using the sum of the dimensions, as just discussed. That is, if d_1, d_2, and d_3 are the dimensions of the comparison iceberg, then the value of this term was $| \ d_1 + d_2 + d_3 - 9 \ |$. The final term was a binary indicator of whether any of the iceberg's dimensions was greater than that of the standard (1 if one or more of the dimensions was 4 m, and 0 otherwise). I expected this last term to discriminate the identity ratings from the similarity ratings. Predictions from these two regression equations appear in Figure 1.4: The solid line corresponds to the identity predictions and accounts for 95.4% of the variance among the means. All three terms produced statistically significant coefficients. Figure 1.4 shows the predictions for the similarity ratings as the dotted line, and these predictions account for 92.6% of the data. The shape and size terms were significant in this analysis, but as we would expect, there was no effect on the similarity ratings of whether the comparison iceberg contained a dimension larger than those of the standard.

When one of the comparison iceberg's dimensions exceeded the standard's, participants discounted the possibility that it could *be* the standard but not the possibility that it could be similar to it. Thus, people's judgments of an object's identity are not simply a matter of similarity. They involve the causal trajectory of the item as it evolves—in this case, shrinking rather than stretching over time.[14]

1.4 Fission and Fusion

Although I believe that the Causal Continuer model has advantages over earlier approaches, we've considered so far only a fairly narrow range of identity judgments. I've focused on situations that are difficult for other theories to explain—ones that deliberately eliminate spatiotemporal continuity (destroying the particles of the original object in the lion scenarios) and that dissociate identity from basic-level category membership and similarity. We should also ask, however, whether the model can deal with other identity issues. In this section, I consider two further examples of identity questions from previous research.

1.4.1 The Ship of Theseus

One famous test case for theories of identity is due to Thomas Hobbes (1838–1845) and is the subject of some recent research in developmental psychology (Hall, 1998; Noles & Bloom, 2006).

> *The Ship of Theseus:* A wooden ship was repaired over a long interval by removing individual planks one-at-a-time and replacing them at each step with new ones. This process continued until none of the old planks remained, and the ship consisted entirely of new planks. However, the old planks were stored and then reassembled exactly as before. Two ships exist at this later point, each of which could claim to be the original ship: the one with old planks and the one with new planks. Which, if either, is Theseus's ship?

The Causal Continuer model can afford to be neutral with respect to this question (see Nozick, 1981). Both resulting ships—call them *Old Parts* and *New Parts*—are causal outgrowths of the original. This is a case of fission, in which an initial object gives rise to two possible successors. In this case, New Parts enjoys closer temporal continuity with the original, while Old Parts has greater overlap in material composition. Whether we deem Old Parts, New Parts, both, or neither as Theseus's ship will then depend on how we weigh these two factors. The model does not make an a priori decision among the options, but it does explain the uncertainty we feel about the choice. Both composition and temporal overlap are typically important and perfectly confounded in identity judgments about ordinary ships. Both are diagnostic of the causal forces that support a ship's existence. Hobbes's story separates these factors, forcing us to consider them independently, and this demand for independent weighting creates the puzzle. In the same manner, the model accounts for the intuition that either Old Parts *or* New Parts would unambiguously be Theseus's ship if the other were out of the picture. For example, if the original ship were simply disassembled and reassembled, we probably wouldn't hesitate to identify it with the ship of Theseus. Similarly, if the parts of the original were gradually replaced with no reassembly of the old parts, the ship of Theseus would be the repaired ship. What creates indecision in Hobbes's problem is the competition between Old Parts and New Parts for being the closest or best option. The same factor produced the equivalent effect in the multiple-copy experiment I described earlier.

A study by Hall (1998) provides some evidence about children's and adults' preferences in a closely related problem. In Hall's version, participants heard stories and saw pictures of a star-shaped object, called "Sam's quiggle," which the stories described as an artifact (a kind of paperweight) in one condition and as a natural object (a jungle animal) in another. This object loses its old parts and gains new ones until it is composed entirely of new parts. In some stories, a person performs this substitution; in others, no agent is specified (the change "simply happens"). Someone then reassembles the old parts as before. The participants had to choose whether Old Parts or New Parts was Sam's quiggle. The results showed that adults tended to choose New Parts when the object was an animal that lost and gained parts spontaneously, and they chose Old Parts when the original object was an artifact that a human revamped. In the two remaining cases (animal that a human revamps and artifact that changes spontaneously), adults split their vote. Five year-olds favored Old Parts in all conditions, with seven year-olds showing a pattern intermediate between that of younger children and adults.

We can't directly apply the Causal Continuer theory to Hall's results because we don't have an independent measure of the causal closeness of the original to the two resulting objects. The theory is consistent with the pattern of data, however, given two reasonable assumptions. The first of these concerns adults' biological knowledge about the transformations. Adults know that living things, unlike artifacts, rarely survive complete disassembly. In operating on a live animal, for example, a surgeon must be careful to keep most of the animal intact if it is to survive the operation. By contrast, persistence over complete disassembly and reassembly is much more plausible in the case of an artifact. Disassembling a multipart paperweight and putting it back together can produce a perfectly good paperweight. This distinction between natural objects and artifacts would tend to shift adult responses toward New Parts in the natural-object condition, since Old Parts would no longer be a living creature. Younger children may lack such information and may therefore treat natural objects like artifacts in this respect.

Biological knowledge, however, is not sufficient to explain all facets of the data. For example, when the object was an artifact and a person replaced each part to create New Parts, both adults and children overwhelmingly favored Old Parts. This condition is the one most similar to the standard Ship-of-Theseus puzzle, where opinion seems more evenly divided between the two contenders. Why then did participants in Hall's study regard Old Parts as the identical item? One possibility concerns the details of the change. When an agent performed the substitution creating New Parts, the stories described the change as occurring over a several week period, with the agent replacing one part per week. This discontinuous change may have weakened the causal link between the original object and New Parts, causing participants to choose Old Parts instead in both the artifact and natural object conditions. The pictures illustrating the individual steps may have abetted the feeling of discontinuity by showing stages in which parts were missing from the object that was eventually to become New Parts. By contrast, when there was no human agent responsible for the change, participants probably saw the transformation that produced New Parts as more continuous (e.g., a kind of molting), as Hall (1998) suggests.

Taken together, these assumptions explain the results in terms that are congenial to the Causal Continuer model. Although the assumptions are obviously after-the-fact, they seem plausible and provide a bridge between Ship-of-Theseus cases and the new results described here.

1.4.2 Fission and Fusion in Memory

Our concept of an individual object can sometimes undergo fission or fusion, even when the object itself is unchanged. I had read from time to time about a remarkable British polymath, Sir William Hamilton, who, among other accomplishments, was a mathematician (W. R. Hamilton, 1866/1969), astronomer, expert on volcanoes (the subject of Susan Sontag's, 1992, novel, *The Volcano Lover*), diplomat, collector of antiquities, and philosopher (the target of Mill's, 1868, *Examination of Sir William Hamilton's Philosophy*). I took a surprisingly long time to realize that this individual was really three different people—an astronomer-mathematician, a volcanologist-diplomat-collector, and a philosopher—each named "Sir William Hamilton." This discovery meant creating new singular concepts and reassigning the properties of the old merged Hamilton concept to its fissioned counterparts.

The opposite process, conceptual fusion, sometimes also occurs in revising our knowledge of people. I might have learned about Art Jones, the softball coach, in one context, and Arthur P. Jones, the Chevy salesman, in another, and only later determined that these two Joneses were the same. Fusion cases like this are analogous to the problem originally described by Frege (1892/1952) for the meaning of identity statements—for example, the Morning Star is identical to the Evening Star. To put this issue in a more contemporary light, suppose the meaning of a singular concept like ARTHUR JONES is a particular individual, Jones himself. Many philosophers currently believe that this meaning is fixed by a causal-historical connection that runs from the denoted individual (Jones) to the person who possesses the concept (me). But since only one Arthur Jones exists, who is both the softball coach and the Chevy salesman, my ARTHUR JONES concepts must have referred to him all along.

So how can it be a surprise for me to discover that only one individual is involved rather than two? (See Jeshion, 2010; Lawlor, 2001; and Perry, 2001, for recent philosophical treatments of this issue.)

John Anderson (1977; J. R. Anderson & Hastie, 1974) has studied the fusion case by presenting participants with identity information before or after they had learned separate facts about individuals. In one condition, for example, participants first learned *James Bartlett played the banjo* and *The lawyer sold the boat* (among other unrelated sentences) and then learned *James Bartlett is the lawyer.* Response times to verify directly stated information (*Bartlett played the banjo*) versus inferred information (*Bartlett sold the boat*) suggested that participants transferred the predicates originally associated with the proper name to the concept associated with the description. For example, the predicate *played the banjo* would come to be directly associated with the concept THE LAWYER and the concept BARTLETT would be abandoned (J. R. Anderson, 1977).

Anderson (1977) suggests that which concept is retained and which abandoned might depend on the relative amount of information connected to the two. We're more likely to retain a concept that is associated with more information, since less work is then required in revising memory. According to the present perspective, however, the revision process might also depend on relations between the old concepts and the revised ones. In fusion cases like Anderson's, we might prefer to keep the concept of the person that we can most easily imagine becoming the merged individual, the person who could more readily acquire the properties of the other. This may be the individual who already has more properties, in line with Anderson's hypothesis, but may also be the one whose properties are less malleable, more reliable, or fixed over a longer interval. In these cases, a causal transition to a merged state is easier to envision. Although I know of no direct test of this hypothesis, it seems consistent with other examples of imagined change (see, e.g., Kahneman & Miller, 1986, and the discussion of counterfactuals in Chapter 3 of this book).

In the case of conceptual fission, like the initial Hamilton example, the Causal Continuer approach likewise suggests that the conceptual change may be similar to what would happen if actual fission were to take place. I had to create new representations for some of the new people that I discovered in order to have separate concepts for each of the Hamiltons. One possibility is to abandon completely the old Hamilton concept and create three new ones for each of the "descendents." This is analogous to a "neither" response in the lion experiment, and it might occur if none of the true Hamiltons is more closely related than the others to the old false concept. But an alternative is to retain a version of the old merged concept, editing it to represent one of the final individuals, and then construct just two new representations for the others. This is analogous to choosing one of the potential continuers as identical to the original in actual fission cases. If we can easily imagine a causal transition from the merged individual to one of the final people, then we might reasonably choose to modify the old concept to represent him, constructing new representations for the others. For example, if we can conceive the old merged Hamilton shedding some of his properties to become the diplomat-volcanologist-collector, then it might be easiest to modify the original concept to represent that person and create new concepts for the mathematician-astronomer and for the philosopher.

Conceptual versions of causal-continuer effects may also influence the ease with which people can track characters in stories or assign referents to anaphoric expressions, such as pronouns or definite noun phrases. (See, e.g., Caramazza, Grober, Garvey, & Yates, 1977, for evidence of effects of causal prominence on pronoun assignment, and Rudolph & Försterling, 1997, for a review.)

1.5 Extensions and Limitations

The Causal Continuer approach contends that a later manifestation of a single object must causally stem from earlier ones, so that causality takes precedence over qualitative overlap in properties, spatiotemporal continuity, or sortal membership. Similarity, continuity, and other properties can come into play, however, if direct causal information is absent or ambiguous. The model makes its identity judgments on the basis of two interrelated decisions: An object x_0 is identical to another x_1 if x_1 is causally close enough to be the continuation of x_0 and if x_1 is the closest of all the close-enough competitors. This is the answer the model gives to our opening question in (1). Evidence for this approach comes from the study in Section 1.3.2, which manipulated the closeness of an original object to each of two possible continuers. The model succeeded in predicting participants' decisions about which continuer was identical to the original in a setting where there was no spatial continuity between the items. The same study showed a dissociation between these identity judgments and judgments of basic-level category membership. The study in Section 1.3.4 tested the model's prediction that people rely on causal continuity over similarity when these two factors are at odds.

The model appears to describe participants' responses in these experiments, but some of the model's principles may seem puzzling for theoretical reasons. First, the model goes along with judgments that a single object can divide into two and remain identical to both descendants. Such judgments seem to imply that object identity is intransitive, contrary to property (2c), and they raise issues about whether the model's (and the participants') concept of identity is coherent. Second, the model maintains that object identity is not necessarily tied to the category-level concepts to which the object belongs. However, there are some presumptive reasons to think that categories must be involved in any identity decision. The rest of this chapter considers ways to resolve these two problems.

1.5.1 *Transitivity of Identity*

Although the Causal Continuer model provides a good account of the data from the dual copy experiment, this accomplishment depends on its liberal policy with respect to the "both" responses. The model produces these responses when the difference between the possible continuers is small enough to be ignored. In this case, if either copy is close enough to be identical, then both must be identical; otherwise, neither is identical. This assumption is consistent with participants' responses: In the case in which both contenders consisted only of particles copied from the original, nearly all participants made a "both" response (see the bottom right graph in Figure 1.3). The trouble is that these responses appear to violate the transitivity property of identity in (2c). How could both copies be identical to the original while not being identical to each other?

We could view these responses as mistakes in participants' thinking about identity. Perhaps participants' identity decisions reflect a simple heuristic rather than a considered, normatively appropriate procedure. For example, they may have used the causal distance between the original item and the copies, without concerning themselves with the extra constraints that identity imposes. This behavior might be the result of the relatively greater importance of causal continuity over strict identity in dealing with issues of survival and persistence (as Parfit, 1984, argues; see also Bartels & Rips, 2010, for evidence supporting Parfit's position). According to this approach, the responses are much like intransitivities in the preference judgments of decision makers (Tversky, 1969): Sometimes people prefer option A over option B and B over C, yet prefer C over A.

Alternatively, we could interpret the experimental findings in a way that brings the "both" responses in line with transitivity. We have been assuming that participants believe the two copies in the experiment are distinct individuals, and this assumption leads to intransitivity when both copies are also identical to the original. But another way of viewing the situation is that the transporter produces, not two independent objects, but two parts of a single temporally branching one (this is one of the individuals or "lifetimes" that Perry, 1972, describes in fission cases). Figure 1.5a schematically illustrates this approach. The diagram indicates

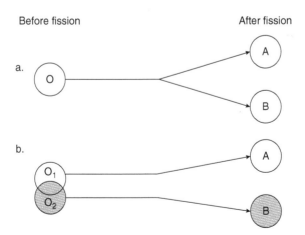

FIGURE 1.5 Two ways of interpreting fission examples. (a) The original and the copies are temporal and spatial parts of a single branching object, and (b) each copy is a distinct object that overlaps with the other spatially during the initial stage of its life and diverges thereafter.

the temporal sequence of events in the life of the lion, from its birth at the left-hand side, to the point at which it is copied, to its end state at the right. According to this way of thinking, the duplicated lion in the stimulus stories exists after division in something like the way that a tree exists spatially in its multiple branches. Just as the branches are parts of the same tree, the multiple copies are parts of the same creature. No intransitivity appears on this interpretation: Copy A, copy B, and the original object, O, are all the same individual.

A possible problem for this solution, however, is that it is difficult to shake the idea that the two copies must be nonidentical, since each can presumably function on its own, develop distinct properties, and appear and behave just like two ordinary objects, despite their common origin. According to this counterargument, the copies are more like identical twins (or embryonic clones) than like a single temporally branching object. Although they have a common origin, identical twins count as two people in a census, have two votes in an election, and so on.

A second way of salvaging transitivity is to construe the two copies as distinct objects, but ones that existed all along, sharing the spatial parts of the original (Lewis, 1983). Figure 1.5b illustrates this reinterpretation. Copy A begins life when the original does, surviving the division and continuing on its own way. Copy B does the same. What's unusual about these individuals is that they are indistinguishable during the pre-fission part of their existence: What seemed to be a single original object turns out to be two cohabitors. Intransitivities also disappear on this interpretation, as they did with branching objects: When participants say that copy A is still Fred (the original lion in the experiment), they mean that he is still $Fred_1$, one of the two co-embodied creatures, and when they say that copy B is still Fred, they mean he is still $Fred_2$, the other co-embodied one. Copy A = $Fred_1$, Copy B = $Fred_2$, but since these two are distinct individuals, the judgments do not violate transitivity. The difficulty with this interpretation (as Lewis acknowledges) is that it seems to produce a population overcount before fission. Contrary to the co-embodiment idea, if the individuals were people, we would probably refuse to count the pre-fission stage twice in a census, would deny it two votes in an election, and so on. Moreover, although this alternative keeps participants' judgments from being inconsistent with the identity axioms, it does so at the cost of positing a hidden ambiguity in the proper name for the original object in the two-copy condition (*Fred* can refer to either Fred$_1$ or Fred$_2$), where no such ambiguity was present in the one-copy condition.

Both these solutions to the transitivity problem come at a high price. Positing co-embodied individuals appears to produce too many pre-fission objects, while positing branching individuals produces too few post-fission ones. Although there are ways of reconciling these solutions with our instinctive ways of counting, they require adjustments to our counting strategies (e.g., counting object stages rather than objects, as in Lewis, 1983). Still, these distinct ways of interpreting fission cases stand as alternatives to the view that participants were committing a performance error or making a mistake in judgment. "Both" responses rule out some ways of construing the two-copy condition; they eliminate the possibility that the initial object has gone out of existence and two new ones have appeared. Nonetheless, they leave open other possibilities that could be explored, such as branching or co-embodiment. Which interpretation is correct is an issue that must remain open here.

In some respects, the participants' situation parallels that of observers in certain types of apparent motion experiments (Ullman, 1979). Figure 1.6 illustrates the simplest situation of this type. An observer sees a central dot, x_0, in an initial display. This dot disappears, and then two dots, x_1 and x_2, appear in a second display, with x_1 and x_2 located on either side of, and equally distant from, the position x_0 had occupied. If the interstimulus interval is appropriate and the observer fixates x_0, then he or she sees simultaneous movement toward both x_1 and x_2, as the arrows indicate in Figure 1.6. However, on the assumption that motion correspondence implies identity (Kahneman, Treisman, & Gibbs, 1992), we get a potential

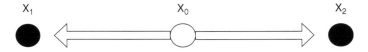

FIGURE I.6 A situation in which apparent motion leads to perceived fission of an object. A display containing dot x_0 is presented first. This dot disappears and is followed by a second display containing x_1 and x_2 at the locations shown. In this case, x_0 appears to move simultaneously to both x_1 and x_2. (Arrows show the direction of motion but do not appear in the display.)

violation of the transitivity relation in (2c). If $x_1 = x_0$ and $x_0 = x_2$, then transitivity yields $x_1 = x_2$. But it appears that $x_1 \neq x_2$ since these two dots are in separate locations in the second display. However, are observers who report motion in opposite directions committing a performance error? Committing themselves to the idea that identity is intransitive? We can only interpret the report as an intransitivity error if we reject alternative interpretations of these judgments, such as branching.

1.5.2 Relations to Earlier Theories

The Causal Continuer approach seems capable of handling many of the issues that created obstacles for earlier theories. Because the model subordinates similarity judgments to causal continuity, it explains why similarity can function as evidence for identity in some situations but as evidence against it in others. For example, a difference in size (a dissimilarity) may support the hypothesis that the flower you perceive now is the same one you planted earlier, but contradict the hypothesis that the cup you perceive now is the same one you washed earlier.

Along the same lines, although knowledge of spatiotemporal continuity is an important clue to sameness, it need not be decisive. In the vicinity of a dual-ing machine, for example, causal facts about the device blocks the inference from continuity to the conclusion that the later object is a causal outgrowth of the earlier. We needn't resort to any kind of spatiotemporal continuity if we already know the causal facts.

The Causal Continuer theory assumes that (people believe that) causal forces (and the objects they create) exist in their own right, independent of language and thought. In particular, physical objects don't depend on the concepts or categories to which these objects belong. Of course, different kinds of causes may support the existence of different kinds of objects. The physiological causes that determine the life course of cats or canaries differ from the physical-mechanical causes that determine the life course of bridges or buildings. But it doesn't follow from this difference in type of cause that objects inherit their identity conditions from their sortal categories.

All theories of identity must acknowledge that objects vary in their behavior in ways that are important for identity and persistence. Dropping a wine glass on a slate floor from a height of 3 ft. will probably cause it to shatter and go out of existence, whereas dropping a cat on the same floor from the same height will probably leave it unscathed. But this domain specificity does not distinguish between the sortal and the Causal Continuer approaches. What does distinguish the theories is the explanation for such differences. In the case of the sortal view, the source of the differences is the meaning of the sortal terms that describe the objects. Part of the meaning of (*wine*) *glass*, for example, is an identity condition (see (4) above) that stipulates that nothing following a shattering event can be identical to the original glass. By contrast, the Causal Continuer theory accounts for the difference in terms of the kinds of causes responsible for maintaining the integrity of the object in question. It is an empirical fact, and not part of the meaning of *glass* or *cat*, that some of the causes that disrupt a glass's existence do no damage to a cat.[15]

An analogy may make this distinction clearer. The internal temperature of objects varies by domain, with some types of objects having systematically higher temperature than do others. The body temperature of birds, for example, tends to be higher than that of humans under normal conditions. In a sense, then, body temperature could be said to be "sortal relative." But no one would suppose that the meanings of the terms *bird* and *human* include "temperature conditions" that specify the allowable range of body temperatures in these species. Instead, the temperature of different creatures is the result of mechanisms of thermal regulation, among other causal factors. In a parallel way, the Causal Continuer theory claims that domain differences in identity are due to differences in the kinds of causal mechanisms that maintain an object during its career rather than to differences in the meaning of expressions for these objects.

To see that sortals are not necessary, notice that examples of sortal-relative identity conditions are in short supply. Sortal theories need these conditions to specify the R_S relations in (4). But no clear examples of identity conditions exist for everyday sortals such as *cats* or *trucks*, with the possible exception of (much disputed) criteria for *persons*. What are the necessary and sufficient conditions that cat x at t_1 and cat y at t_2 must possess in order for x to be identical to y [i.e., what is $R_{CAT}(x,y)$], and how do they differ from those conditions for dogs [$R_{DOG}(x,y)$]? (See Mackie, 2006, for similar complaints.) The difficulties for sortal theories of singular concepts parallel the well-known difficulties for classical theories of category-level concepts (see Murphy, 2002; E. E. Smith & Medin, 1981). There are few convincing examples of necessary and sufficient properties for membership in everyday categories, and most cognitive psychologists have given up hope of uncovering them. We suspect that in the case of sortal theories, too, the shortage of plausible examples is due to the fact that people simply do not know sortal-relative conditions of identity for everyday categories.[16] If so, and if sortals are count nouns that furnish identity conditions, then there are few or no sortals.

1.5.3 Identity and Modal Thinking

I mentioned at the beginning of this chapter that our concepts of people and other things must be rich enough to support conjectures about what might have happened to these individuals in situations that are possible but never actually take place. The concept of my friend Georgine, for example, informs my guesses about how she will behave in settings she hasn't yet, and perhaps never will, experience. The same goes for predictions about political figures or celebrities whose dispositions I think I know. In the realm of inanimate objects, predictions about location and change have the warrant of well-established physical principles, even when the predictions' initial conditions never occur. What give us the ability to make these counterfactual judgments are the same causal relations that, according to the Causal Continuer theory, govern our ability to trace these individuals in the real world. As many theorists have argued, causal relations yield law-like generalizations that support our theorizing.

To see the similarity between counterfactual judgments and judgments of identity, consider the relation between an ordinary historical narrative and a historical fiction. Both stories might begin with the same set of events—for example, the actual events that have occurred during the life of Georgine from her birth in 1950 to her 30th birthday in 1980. The straight historical account would continue to follow the actual causal stream from 1980 to the present, but the historical fiction might diverge from the true state of affairs, perhaps beginning with a fictitious chance event that Georgine is said to experience in 1980. The author of the historical fiction could then elaborate the counterfactual post-1980 story by spinning out the causal consequences that follow the fictitious event and the actual Georgine events that preceded it. This elaboration might require adjusting these actual events in order to accommodate the fictitious ones. "Minor miracles" may be necessary to explain the divergence (Lewis, 1979), but a plausible story would make such adjustments in a way that minimizes changes to the facts. However, both the factual and fictional narratives make use of most of the same causal principles that get Georgine from one moment on her time line to the next. When we try to imagine what Georgine would be like if such and such a counterfactual event had taken place, these principles organize our projections.

Category-level concepts display many of these same normative features. We can reason about what will happen to categories under unknown or counterfactual conditions, drawing out the consequences, for example, of supposing that poodles can bite through wire (e.g., Osherson, Smith, Shafir, Gualtierotti, & Biolsi, 1995) or that furniture is eaten at the end of a meal (Sternberg & Gastel, 1989). We can also state generalizations about these categories (e.g., that lions have manes) that withstand numerous exceptions (female or immature lions). It seems likely that causal knowledge about these categories is again responsible for these abilities. These facts raise issues about people's ability to represent causal relations and about the difference between relations that sustain individuals and those that sustain categories. Chapters 3 and 4 in this book are devoted to these questions, but before tackling them, I'd like to consider some further questions about identity and individuation that arise in mathematical contexts.

Appendix

A Mathematical Version of the Causal Continuer Theory

To fit the Causal Continuer model to the data in Figure 1.3, we can assume that causal closeness in this experiment depends on the percentage of the copy's particles that derives from the original. In the stories, the "transporter" is the causal mechanism that produces closeness by copying particles and transmitting them. We might therefore represent the probability that the dominant copy, d, is closer than the nondominant copy, n, in terms of the ratio in (A1), when the proportion of original particles in n is less than 1:

$(A1)$ $\Pr(d \ closer) =$

$$\frac{k \cdot (proportion\ original\ particles\ in\ d - proportion\ original\ particles\ in\ n)}{1 - proportion\ original\ particles\ in\ n}$$

When the proportion of original particles in n is 1, we can define $\Pr(d \ closer) = 0$. In Equation (A1), k is a free parameter representing the maximum probability that d can attain. Even if copy d has all its particles from the original and n has none, some participants might still feel that there is not enough difference between them for d to be causally closer than n. We can also assume that if d is not closer (with probability $1 - \Pr(d \ closer)$), then we have a tie (i.e., n can never be closer than d).

To predict the data, we must also determine whether either copy is close enough to be potentially identical to the original item. Since the same participants made identity judgments for each copy separately in the one-copy condition, we can use these decisions to estimate empirically the likelihood of a "yes" answer to this question. During one of the two-copy trials, for example, participants learned that one copy contains 75% of its particles from the original and the second copy contains 25%. Participants had judged that a copy with 75% original particles was identical to the original on .38 of trials and that a copy with 25% original particles was identical on .21 of the trials in the one-copy condition. We can then estimate the likelihood that one or the other is causally close enough to be identical as $1 - (1 - .38)*(1 - .21) = .51$. The general relationship is that in (A2):

$(A2)$ $\Pr(d \text{ or } n \text{ close enough})$ $= 1 - (1 - \Pr(d \text{ close enough})) \cdot$
$$(1 - \Pr(n \text{ close enough})).$$

Combining Equations (A1) and (A2) gives us the predictions for the two-copy condition in Figure 1.3. For example, $\Pr(d \text{ closer}) \cdot \Pr(d \text{ or } n \text{ close enough})$ is the probability that participants should identify only the dominant copy as identical to the original. Similarly, $(1 - \Pr(d \text{ closer})) \cdot \Pr(d \text{ or } n \text{ close enough})$ is the probability of a "both" response. To evaluate the model, I fit these equations to the data in Figure 1.3, using nonlinear least-squares approximation. Since there is no apparent difference between cases in which the residual particles were from the same or different species, I collapsed the data from these two conditions before fitting the model. As noted earlier, the model predicts that participants should never respond that only the nondominant copy is identical to the original. Figure 1.3 shows that this is approximately true, but I omitted these points in fitting in order to obtain a more conservative view of the model's accuracy. The model was therefore fit to 45 data points: the "dominant only," "both," and "neither" responses in the 15 graphs in Figure 1.3. The resulting predictions appear as the lines in the figure, and the overall fit of the model is quite good. The root mean square deviation ($RMSD$) for the 45 critical observations is only 5.1 percentage points, and $R^2 = .957$. The value of the single free parameter, k, from Equation (A1) is 0.62.

Another way to evaluate the model is to compare it to a simpler variant. Suppose, for example, that participants make their decisions based on their separate judgments of whether the dominant copy is identical and whether the nondominant copy is identical. This procedure differs from the Causal Continuer idea in that there is no explicit comparison for closeness of the sort embodied in Equation (A1). If we represent the probability that the dominant copy is close enough to be identical as Pr(d close enough) and the probability that the nondominant copy is close enough as Pr(n close enough), as we did in (A2), then the probability that both are identical should be Pr(d close enough)·Pr(n close enough), assuming independence between the decision. Similarly, the probability that only the dominant copy is identical is Pr(d close enough)·(1 - Pr(n close enough)), and so on. Estimating the component probabilities from the one-choice data, as we did earlier, allows us to fit this simpler model directly with no free parameters. This model does considerably less well than the one I have just described (*RMSD* = 16.1 percentage points and R^2 = .618). The discrepancy is especially marked for "both" responses when the proportion of original particles is the same in the two copies, since the simpler model greatly underpredicts these proportions. In this model, a "both" response depends on both copies being independently close enough to be identical, as just noted. In the full model, however, there is no relevant difference between the two copies (the value of Pr(d closer) = 0 in Equation (A1)); so a "both" response depends on whether *either* copy could be considered close enough, as given by Equation (A2). This is typically a much larger value, in accord with the data. A likelihood ratio test (Bates & Watts, 1988) shows that the Causal Continuer model significantly improves on the simpler model, taking into account the former model's extra parameter.

NOTES

This chapter is based on an earlier article with Sergey Blok and George Newman (Rips, Blok, & Newman, 2006). I've also taken some material from Blok, Newman, and Rips (2007). In addition to Serge and George, I thank Jennifer Asmuth, Dan Bartels, Jennifer Behr, Amber Bloomfield, Aveen Farooq, Robert Goldstone, Gabe Greenberg, Douglas Medin, Ariela Lazar, Beth Lynch, Jeff Pasch, Andrea Proctor, Eyal Sagi, Steven Sloman, Elizabeth Spelke, Edward Smith, and Sandra Waxman for their help on the earlier versions of this chapter. Some of the ideas developed in classes on object identity at Northwestern University, and I thank the students in these classes for their suggestions.

1. The relation between object identity and traditional recognition memory may not be straightforward. The standard recognition task is in some ways more about categorization than about object identity. If you were presented with the word *eggplant* and are now asked whether it was on an earlier list, the correct answer is "yes" even if the word now appears in a different font, color, or modality. The correct answer depends on whether the original word and the current word are tokens of the same type, but as I have already indicated, identity judgments are decisions about whether two appearances belong to the same token (i.e., are numerically identical). The relationship between perceptual object recognition and judgments of identity is potentially much closer. But even here, much of the research on object recognition is devoted to how people recognize objects as members of categories (e.g., horses) rather than on how they identify individuals (see Peterson, 2001, for a review of theories of object recognition). For example, the announced goal of Biederman's (1987) recognition-by-components theory is "to account for the initial categorization of isolated objects. Often, but not always, this categorization will be at a basic level, for example, when we know that a given object is a typewriter, a banana, or a giraffe." This is not to say that recognition is irrelevant to judgments of object identity, but only that the relationships need to be carefully worked out.

2. It is possible to debate whether the computer exists during the time at which it is disassembled. Whether people view a disassembled object as the same individual may depend on the extent of the transformation (e.g., the number of resulting pieces or the size of these pieces). For instance, people may be more likely to believe that a scattered collection consisting of the disassembled top and legs of a table is still the same individual than a scattered collection consisting of the zillions of disassembled circuit components of a computer (see Gutheil, Bloom, Valderrama, & Freedman, 2004, for relevant evidence). If the computer does not exist when its components are disassembled (as seems likely), then the example shows that objects can survive gaps in time. But even if the computer continues to exist during its disassembled phase, it clearly doesn't exist as a spatially continuous entity. Therefore, transformations can preserve identity across (at least) spatial discontinuity.

3. The term *sortal* is due to Locke (1690/1975, p. 417) in the same famous passage in which he distinguishes real and nominal essences. Wiggins (2001) points out that Locke's, Strawson's, and his own use of *sortal* derive from Aristotle's distinction between categories of substance and qualities.

4. Sortal theories in psychology appeal almost exclusively to principle (5), as we will see later in this chapter, but it is very difficult to state this

principle adequately. The main problem is that some sortal theories allow sortal categories to be nested. According to Xu (1997), for example, both *dog* and *physical object* are sortals with distinct identity conditions, R_{DOG} and R_{OBJECT}. Hence, Fido can go from being a dog to being a non-dog as long as he is covered by the sortal *physical object*. If we can always appeal to *physical object* as a sortal, however, then ordinary objects cannot go out of existence without somehow becoming nonphysical. This is inconsistent with the intuition that a chair that is splintered by an axe ceases to exist rather than continues to exist as a pile of wood scraps. I'm unsure whether there is a way to formulate (5) that is not question-begging, but we can safely leave this problem for proponents of sortal theories.

5. As mentioned in the Introduction to this book, I follow the usual convention of spelling names for concepts in all caps and names for linguistic entities (e.g., words or sentences) in italics or quotation marks.

6. One possible issue, and a source of conflict with sortal theories in philosophy (e.g., Wiggins, 2001), is that sortals like *cup* or *elephant* should also be necessary in order to individuate objects that appear together in the perceptual field. The evidence from Xu and Carey's experiments (Xu & Carey, 1995; Xu et al., 2004), however, is that younger infants do perform correctly when they have the advantage of previewing the objects. To explain this difference in performance, Xu and Carey argue that even the younger infants have a high-level sortal concept, equivalent to the concept PHYSICAL OBJECT, that Spelke has posited to explain infants' object tracking (e.g., Spelke, 1990; Spelke, Gutheil, & Van de Walle, 1995). This concept provides the sortal information that infants use in the preview condition. As Xu (1997, p. 369) states, "for both adults and young infants, there is nonetheless a sortal *physical object*, which is more general than *person, car,* or *tree*. A physical object is defined as any three-dimensional, bounded entity that moves on a spatiotemporally continuous path" (see also, Carey, 1995a; Carey & Xu, 1999). But sortal theories in philosophy typically hold that terms like *thing, object, physical object, space-occupier, entity,* and so on, are not sortals, despite their count-noun syntax, since they don't provide identity conditions (e.g., Hirsch, 1982, p. 38; Wiggins, 1980, p. 63; 1997, p. 418). Just as we can't count the black stuff that constitutes a black table, we can't count the physical objects that constitute it; the number could again be one (the table), five (the legs and top), six (the legs, top, and the table), and so on.

One way to square sortals with Spelke's physical objects is to note that Spelke's object concept is more specific than the ordinary notion of a physical object. Many things that we single out as objects don't move independently and aren't spatially separated from their backgrounds (as Hirsch, 1997, and Wiggins, 1997, have pointed out). Trees, mountains, houses, fences, fire hydrants, and sidewalks, among many other things, are typically fixed in place and would fail to trigger an object concept that is sensitive only to movement and spatial isolation. Similarly, nonmoving parts of larger wholes often qualify as objects in the everyday sense, but not in the sense of independently moving, spatially separated entities. We speak of legs of tables, fenders of cars, handles of mugs, organs of animals, and other parts as objects in their own right, despite the fact that they usually occupy a fixed position with respect to the relevant larger entity. A Spelke-type object concept can't pick out such objects, and for this reason, it seems best to regard this concept as corresponding to a kind of primitive or proto-object (sometimes called a *Spelke-object*). Could *proto-object* be a sortal? Because the parts of a table, for example, aren't proto-objects (since they usually don't move on their own), counting the proto-objects that constitute a table doesn't pose the problem that counting physical objects does (Carey & Xu, 1999; Xu, 1997). A table is a single proto-object. (For arguments against the idea that *proto-object* is a sortal, see Ayers, 1997; Hirsch, 1997; and Wiggins, 1997.) However, the idea that both *proto-object* and lower-level terms like *cup* simultaneously function as sortals still conflicts with strong sortal theories (e.g., Wiggins, 2001) in which only a single sortal captures all the identity conditions for a particular object. See also Note 4 of this chapter for further difficulties with the idea of multiple sortals for single objects.

7. Experiments following Xu and Carey (1996) have found cases in which infants younger than 10 months are able to perform correctly in simplified versions of the is-it-one-or-two task (e.g., Wilcox & Baillargeon, 1998; Xu & Baker, 2005). The exact age at which infants succeed at such tasks is not of central interest here; however, some of the explanations for this early success do bear on the question of what knowledge they draw on when they anticipate two versus one object. Carey and Xu (2001, p. 194) argue that "when spatiotemporal evidence does not favor one solution over another, infants can use featural differences for object individuation" (see also Xu, 2003a). Thus, in Xu and Carey's original (1996) task, spatiotemporal information from the moving objects (the fact that the elephant and cup fall on the same trajectory) overrides featural differences that would otherwise serve to distinguish the objects, causing errors for the younger infants. Older infants are able to marshal sortals that, in turn, overcome the misleading spatiotemporal facts. However, featural differences (e.g., shape and size changes) are precisely the kinds of properties that *don't* individuate objects, according to the philosophical theories of sortals described earlier (e.g., Strawson, 1959). To the extent that infants can use properties (without the support of underlying sortals) to distinguish the items in these experiments, the very difference between sortal and nonsortal predicates is placed in doubt (see Blok, Newman, & Rips, 2007, and Section 1.4.2 for further discussion).

8. Basic-level categories are sets like apples or chairs that are at a middle level of abstractness. They contrast with subordinate categories (such as Winesap

apples or Eames chairs), and superordinate categories (such as fruit or furniture). Rosch et al. (1976) provided evidence that basic-level categories possess advantages over subordinates and superordinates in a variety of cognitive tasks. Since Rosch et al.'s classic paper, investigators have raised questions about the stability of the basic level across tasks and amounts of expertise (see Murphy, 2002, for a discussion and defense of the basic-level notion). The present point, however, is simply that terms for basic-level categories tend to be those people favor in naming individual objects. Asked *What is it?* of a particular Winesap apple, people usually say *apple,* not *Winesap* or *fruit.*

9. We assume, along with Liittschwager and others, that proper names like *Jim* are rigid designators that always refer to the same individual across situations or possible worlds; see Kripke (1972). Participants who state that the transplant recipient is no longer Jim are therefore affirming that the recipient is no longer the same individual.

10. Criticism of the Closest Continuer theory has focused on this context sensitivity (e.g., Noonan, 1985; Williams, 1982). According to these criticisms, the question of whether x_0 is identical to x_1 cannot depend on the presence of individuals $x_2, x_3, \ldots$ that may also exist at the same time as x_1. The appeal of this idea (sometimes called the *only-x-and-y* principle) arises from the intuition that the identity of an individual is a relation between the individual and itself, and therefore cannot be affected by the presence of other things. But whether or not this is a correct metaphysical rule (Nozick, 1981, argues against it), considering alternatives seems an inevitable part of *recognizing* the identity of objects, which is the process in (1) that I hope to clarify. This context sensitivity is on a par with similar effects in judgments of similarity (e.g., Tversky, 1977) and choice (e.g., Shafir, Simonson, & Tversky, 1993).

11. Although Nozick's model blocks intransitivities of the sort just described, there is another way in which both Nozick's model and my own allow for intransitivities. Suppose object x_0 exists at time t_0, x_1 at t_1, and x_2 and x_2' at t_2. Then x_1 might be the closest continuer of x_0, and x_2 the closest continuer of x_1, but x_2' might be the closest continuer of x_0. In the experiments to be reported here, however, I consider only situations involving two time points; so no evidence exists on whether people produce this type of intransitivity.

12. This assumption is also factually correct. Although it might seem icebergs would have to grow before they can shrink, in fact icebergs are created when they break off from ice shelves in Arctic or Antarctic regions.

13. I thank Douglas Medin for suggesting this idea.

14. This experiment also contained a second part in which participants judged which of two icebergs later found in the same vicinity was Sample 94. Like

the two-choice condition in the first experiment, this was intended to test the quantitative version of the Causal Continuer theory. In general, the results were again favorable to the model; for details, see Rips, Blok, and Newman (2006).

15. It is possible to object that "causal integrity" itself presupposes sortal information, since what's integral in one domain may not be in another. But we are not taking causal integrity as the basic explanatory concept here. What *is* basic is the Causal Continuer model's evaluation of identity based on causal factors, and our use of "causal integrity" is meant as a stand-in for this evaluation. Since the model appears to account for identity judgments in domains as diverse as animals and icebergs, there is evidence that it applies successfully in a domain-general way. See Blok et al. (2005, 2007) for further discussion.

16. Psychological essentialists believe that, although people don't know the essential properties for a category, they nevertheless believe there are some (S. A. Gelman, 2003; Medin & Ortony, 1989). See Chapter 4 of this book for a discussion. But the same tactic will not work for psychological sortalists. In order to identify objects over time, it is usually not enough for people to believe that a category has some identity conditions or other (i.e., to have a placeholder for these conditions); they have to know exactly what the conditions are in order to identify the objects via principle (4).

2

Numbers

D.S. Age:	6 years, 2 months:
D.S.:	The numbers only go to million and ninety-nine.
Experimenter:	What happens after million and ninety-nine?
D.S.:	You go back to zero.
E:	I start all over again? So, the numbers do have an end? Or do the numbers go on and on?
D.S.:	Well, everybody says numbers go on and on because you start over again with million and ninety-nine.
E:	. . . you start all over again.
D.S:	Yeah, you go zero, one, two, three, four—all the way up to million and ninety-nine, and then you start all over again.
E:	How about if I tell you that there is a number after that? A million one hundred.
D.S:	Well, I wish there was a million and one hundred, but there isn't.

Hartnett (1991, pp. 115–116)

On the face of it, the objects of mathematics—numbers, angles, sets, functions—are unlike the physical objects of Chapter 1 in that we can have no direct contact with them. Although we can perceive and manipulate representations of these objects—for example, numerals such as "2" or "II" that denote the number 2—we don't have empirical access to the numbers themselves. According to the usual assumption, numbers are inherently abstract entities. Because knowledge of objects typically depends on causal links between people's mental states and the objects these states are about, we seem to be left without an explanation of how knowledge of math is possible or in what this knowledge consists (as Benacerraf, 1973, has argued). In this chapter, I canvas proposed connections between minds and numbers that might make knowledge of mathematics possible. The goal will be to determine whether any promising leads are available in accounting for people's ability to represent math objects.

In the introduction to this book, I used the example of Euclid's theorem to illustrate how our knowledge of mathematical propositions, such as *There are an infinite number of prime numbers*, outruns ordinary empirical experience. Much the same is true of our knowledge of the mathematical objects, such as prime numbers, these propositions are about. As just mentioned, the usual perceptual mechanisms that put us in contact with everyday physical objects don't directly supply information about mathematical ones. It's true that many psychologists and philosophers view natural numbers as based on sets of physical objects. According to these theories, children learn the meaning of the numeral "2" by counting sets of two objects, and "2" may refer to the set of all sets containing exactly two objects. In this chapter, however, I argue for a different basis for number learning and number meaning.

One of the themes of the chapter is that attempts to explain mathematical objects in terms of physical ones are bound to fail. Nevertheless, a common psychological treatment for physical and math objects will emerge at a more general level of description. We have certain primitive concepts (e.g., CAUSE in the case of physical objects, UNIQUENESS in the case of mathematical ones) and certain primitive operations (instantiation, recursion, and other procedures specialized for concept combination) that allow us to form schemas or theories for both physical and mathematical domains. We may then posit that the best of these theories are true—that they correctly describe the nature of our world—and that the objects they describe are elements of that world. The final part of this chapter suggests that such a schema-based approach has advantages over most current theories of mathematical knowledge.

I focus on natural numbers here because of their central role in psychological studies. Natural numbers are the familiar positive whole numbers: 1, 2, 3, . . . (or, on some treatments, the nonnegative whole numbers: 0, 1, 2, 3, . . .), and they clearly play an essential part in many mathematical activities, for example, counting and arithmetic. In addition to their practical role, natural numbers also have a central place in mathematical theory. Texts on set theory prove that the natural numbers can be used to construct more complicated number systems: the integers, rationals, reals, complex numbers (e.g., Enderton, 1977; A. G. Hamilton, 1982), even the surreal numbers (Knuth, 1974). For example, we can represent the integers (positive, negative, and zero) as the difference between pairs of natural numbers (e.g., -7 = 2 − 9). Similarly, we can represent the rationals as the ratio of two integers (-7/9) and, thus, as the ratio of the differences between two natural numbers (e.g., (2 − 9) / (9 − 0)). Children may not necessarily learn the integers, rationals, or (especially) reals in terms of natural numbers, but the availability of these constructions is an important unifying step in the development of mathematical theory, testifying to natural numbers' central foundational role. Entities like functions and sets present many of the same psychological questions as natural numbers, but we know much less about the way people represent them. Geometric objects like lines and angles may have a claim to universality that numbers don't (see, e.g., Dehaene, Izard, Pica, & Spelke, 2006, vs. Pica, Lemer, Izard, & Dehaene, 2004), but they raise special questions because of their possible ties to perceptual space. Numbers are mathematical objects, pure, if not simple.

Adults have access to some basic mathematical facts about numbers—for example, facts of elementary arithmetic—and are in a position to learn others. The question is how this is possible, given mathematical entities' apparently abstract nature and people's more concrete abilities. In exploring this issue, we will need to look at developmental issues, since the story about how math is possible might be quite different depending on whether nativists or nonnativists are right about where mathematics comes from. I will be less concerned, however, about the exact age at which children acquire particular math skills (e.g., when they first understand zero or fractions) except as this impinges on our basic issue. Similarly, I will not be dealing with those topic areas in math cognition, such as adults' mental arithmetic, whose findings and controversies don't bear directly on questions of knowledge of math objects. Our concern is with an issue common to all rival models of these topics: how they are able to capture properties of seemingly abstract entities such as numbers.

I start by considering the question of whether innate or early-acquired skills provide any evidence on how knowledge of numbers is possible. After some stage setting in Section 2.1, I attempt to describe in Section 2.2 what I think is the currently most plausible view of these numerical skills, based on previous data and theory. These results suggest, however, that we can explain the numerical abilities of preschool children in developmental experiments without supposing that they have *any* concept of numbers, as I argue in Section 2.3. Better evidence for number concepts comes from school-aged children, who are able to deal with arithmetic generalizations, which are overtly about all numbers. Section 2.4 examines data from studies of how children learn one such generalization, additive commutativity—the principle that $a + b = b + a$. Nearly all psychological theories of how we acquire such generalizations assume they are the result of a mapping process—for example, mapping from children's experience in grouping physical objects. Section 2.4 surveys the difficulties these approaches face. I won't be offering a fully formed theory of my own to counter the mapping views, but Section 2.5 sketches what I believe is a more promising theory-based route to such an account.

I think there is no way to get from early quantitative representations, as current theories describe them, to mature number concepts, and because of this assessment, this chapter will be more negative in its implications than are most other chapters of this book. But you shouldn't confuse this assessment with more sweeping or dismissive ones. First, I won't be claiming that current theories are mistaken in the way they account for infants' quantitative abilities. Section 2.2 outlines some of the careful experimental work that has greatly increased our knowledge of infants' sensitivity to the number of objects they perceive. Although current theories may not be telling us everything we want to know about infants' number concepts, they may well be right about how infants perform the tasks that developmentalists have set. A summary of the current theories for these tasks appears later on in Figure 2.3, and I am not disputing either the findings or their explanation. Second, I will not be claiming that early quantitative representations are unimportant or irrelevant to later adult performance. There is evidence, for example, that magnitude representations, which many psychologists believe underlie infants' quantitative abilities (see Section 2.3), also play a role in adults' mathematics. My concern here is solely with whether psychological research is on the right track in its search for the cognitive origins of natural number, since I believe there's a good chance that it is not.

2.1 Words and Numbers

In exploring numerical cognition, we'll find it helpful to stick to a few terminological restrictions, since the uses of key terms such as "number" and "counting" are far from uniform in everyday language. First, I'll refer to the number of elements in a set as the set's cardinality, which can be finite or infinite. (Other authors use the terms "numerosity" or "set size" for the same concept.) Second, as already hinted, I will follow the trend in psychology of using *natural numbers* for the positive integers (1, 2, 3, . . .). In most formal treatments, the natural numbers start with 0, rather than 1, but for psychological purposes, it is useful to think of 1 as the first natural number, since children may not initially view 0 as part of this sequence (see Section 2.5.3.1 for further discussion). In any case, we can eliminate from consideration as the natural numbers any sequence that fails to have:

(1)   a. a unique first element (e.g., 1);
       b. a unique immediate successor for each element in the sequence (e.g., 905 is the one and only immediate successor of 904);
       c. a unique immediate predecessor for each element except the first (e.g., 904 is the one and only immediate predecessor of 905);
       d. the property of (second-order) mathematical induction.

The latter property prohibits any element from being a natural number unless it is the initial number or the successor (. . . of the successor) of the initial number. I discuss these requirements in more detail in Section 2.5. It might be reasonable to place further restrictions on the natural numbers, but systems that fail to observe the requirements in (1) are simply too remote from standard usage in mathematics to be on topic.

Finally, counting. The term "counting" has an intransitive use ("Calvin counted to ten") and a transitive one ("Martha counted the cats"). In this chapter, I reserve the term for the intransitive meaning and distinguish two forms of counting in this sense. One form, which I'll call *simple counting*, consists of just reciting the number sequence to some fixed numeral, for example, "ten" or "one hundred." The second form, *advanced counting*, is the ability to get from any numeral "n" to its successor "$n + 1$" in some system of numerals for the natural numbers. Thus, an advanced counter who is given the English term "one million ninety-nine" could supply the successor "one million one hundred," and an advanced counter with Arabic numerals who is given "1,000,099" could supply "1,000,100." Advanced counting, but not simple counting, implies knowledge of the full system of numerals for the natural numbers. (For studies of numerical notation, such as the Arabic or Roman numerals, see Chrisomalis, 2004, and Zhang & Norman, 1995; for studies of number terms in natural languages, see Hurford, 1975, and the contributions to Gvozdanović, 1992.)

For clarity, I'll use the term "enumerating" for the transitive meaning of counting—determining the cardinality of a collection. It is enumerating that is the focus of much developmental research on the origins of mathematics, notably R. Gelman and Gallistel's (1978) landmark book. Enumerating typically involves pairing verbal numerals with objects to reach a determinable total, but research has also considered forms of nonverbal enumeration. In some theories, for example, an internal continuous quantity (e.g., activation strength) is adjusted, either over time (serially) or simultaneously (in parallel), to achieve a measure of a set's cardinality. We can use the term "mental magnitude" (or "magnitude" for short) to denote such a continuous mental representation, and we can contrast this with countable representations, such as the numerals in standard systems (e.g., Arabic numerals or natural-language terms for natural numbers).[1] Mental magnitudes could, of course, represent many different properties, such as duration, length, or volume, but unless I indicate otherwise, the mental magnitudes at issue will be representations of cardinality.

Psychologists have almost universally assumed that numbers are cardinalities and that cardinalities have to do with physical objects. For example, "two" might refer to the set of all sets containing exactly two physical objects. This assumption has led, in turn, to the idea that people understand number terms by connecting them to objects through enumeration. I believe these assumptions are responsible for many of the difficulties in current research that this chapter outlines. I'll argue in Section 2.5 that we can make more progress by adopting a concept of number more in line with current structuralist theories in the philosophy of mathematics (e.g., Resnik, 1997; Shapiro, 1997). But for now (in Sections 2.2-2.4), let's temporarily go along with the ideas that numbers are essentially cardinalities and that cardinalities are sets of sets of objects in order to see where these notions lead.

2.2 Possible Precursors of Natural Numbers

Children's skill in enumerating objects depends on observing adults' demonstrations and on practicing this technique on their own. But in order for the demonstrations to take or the practice to be effective, the child must already have an appreciation of some of the components (R. Gelman & Gallistel, 1978). Children may repeat the number sequence as ritual recitation or as part of a game (Hurford, 1987), but in order to use it to determine cardinality, they must at least have a concept of a delimited collection of separate objects with a determinable total, based on the kinds of skills outlined in Chapter 1. One issue is, therefore, whether we shouldn't also credit children with the concept of number itself. Perhaps children have an innate natural-number concept that training in counting grafts onto. But even if natural numbers aren't themselves innate, we must still identify the concepts children have in place that allow them to conceive of numbers when they are prepared to learn them.

2.2.1 Innate Natural Number Concepts

Infants might start with prespecified number concepts that represent individual cardinalities, one concept representing all sets with one element, a second representing all sets with two elements, and so on. A simple mental system of this sort might be one in which each concept is diagrammatic, with a symbol such as "■" standing for all one-item sets, "■■" standing for all two-item sets, and continuing with a new item added to the previous one to form the next number symbol.[2] Of course, such a system could never represent each of the infinitely many cardinalities by storing separate concepts for each. Any system for representing the complete set of natural numbers must be generative: It must have the potential or capacity to produce a representation of an arbitrary natural number from a finite base of information. In the case of the sequence of squares, a simple generative rule might derive new symbols from old ones (by adding a "■" to form the successor), allowing the infant to represent in a potential way all cardinalities that the natural numbers can. Section 2.3 contains a grammar for one such system. A system of this kind is consistent with Chomsky's (1988, p. 169) suggestion that "we might think of the human number faculty as essentially an 'abstraction' from human language, preserving the mechanism of discrete infinity and eliminating the other special features of language."

An infant could use such a diagrammatic system for enumerating things and for simple arithmetic operations. For example, they could add two numbers by concatenating symbols for each of the addends (■■ + ■■■ = ■■■■■). Older children's reflections on the system could lead them to an understanding of other mathematical domains (e.g., the positive and negative integers or the rational numbers). A recent proposal along similar lines by A. M. Leslie, Gallistel, and Gelman (2007) contends that there is an innately given internal symbol for the integer value 1 and an innate successor function that generates the remaining positive integers (subject to some further psychological refinements).

But although evidence exists that infants have an early appreciation of cardinality (as we will see in the next subsection), several investigators have argued against innate number concepts based on "discrete" (i.e., countable) representations. For example, Wynn (1992a) concludes on the basis of a longitudinal study of 2- and 3-year-olds that there is a phase in which children interpret "two," "three," and higher terms in their own counting sequence to stand for some cardinality or other without knowing which specific cardinality is correct. They may know, for instance, that "three" represents the size of a set containing either two elements or a set containing three elements, and so on. However, they may not be able to carry out the command to point to the picture with three dogs when confronted by a pair of pictures, one with two dogs and the other with three. These children can, of course, perceptually discriminate the pictures; their difficulty lies in understanding the meaning of "three" in this context.

Wynn's (1992a) evidence is that children in this dilemma can already perform simple counting—for example, they can recite the number terms "one" through "nine." And they already understand that "one" refers to sets containing just one object. They also know that "one" contrasts in meaning with "two" and other elements in their list of count terms. The argument is that if children already had a countable internal representation of the natural numbers, there should not be a delay between the time they understand "one" and the time they understand "two" (and between the time they understand "two" and "three") in such tasks. But because a lag does, in fact, occur, younger children must represent cardinality by means of a system that differs from that of the natural numbers. Wynn opts for a representation in which mental magnitudes (degrees of a continuous or analog medium) represent cardinality.

One point worth noting is that Wynn's argument was not directed against innate natural numbers in general, but against a more specific proposal attributed to Gelman and Gallistel (1978). This proposal included not only a countable representation but also a set of innate principles for using the representation to enumerate sets of objects. Wynn's argument is that if children already have (a) an innate countable representation for natural numbers, (b) an algorithm for applying it to enumerate sets, (c) knowledge of the initial portion of the numeral sequence in their native language (e.g., "one," "two," . . ., "nine"), and (d) knowledge that the first term of the natural-language sequence ("one") maps onto the first term of their innate representation, then it is difficult to see why they don't immediately know which cardinality "two" ("three," . . ., "nine") denotes. The evidence tells against (a)–(d), considered jointly. But children's delay between understanding "one dog" and "two dogs" may be due to incomplete knowledge of the principles for enumerating sets (Le Corre, Van de Walle, Brannon, & Carey, 2006) or to processing difficulties in applying the principles to larger sets (Cordes & Gelman, 2005), rather than to lack of a countable representation of natural numbers.

We shouldn't dismiss too quickly the possibility of an innate system for the natural numbers. Such a theory, though, is clearly out of favor among psychologists (though see A. M. Leslie et al., 2007, for a reappraisal). According to many current views, children build the natural-number concept from preliminary representations, and the transition between these preliminary representations and the mature ones creates the theoretical gap with which I'm concerned.

2.2.2 Magnitudes and Object Individuation

Many current theories in cognitive development argue that people's understanding of number derives from concepts that are strikingly unlike those of the natural numbers. Some claim that numerical ability in infants depends on internal magnitudes—perhaps some type of continuous strength or activation—that nonhuman vertebrates also use for similar purposes (Dehaene, 1997; Gallistel & Gelman, 1992; Gallistel, Gelman, & Cordes, 2006; Wynn, 1992b). Others believe that infants' math-like skills also draw on discrete representations, but ones limited to integer values less than four (Carey, 2001; Spelke, 2000). Both approaches require some account of how children arrive at natural numbers from these beginnings.

2.2.2.1 Experimental Evidence on Infants' Numerical Abilities

Infants are sensitive to quantitative information in their surroundings. For example, 10- to 12-month-old infants demonstrate their awareness of quantity in *addition-subtraction tasks:* An infant might see an experimenter hide two ping-pong balls in an opaque box. The infant is then allowed to reach into the box and remove one of the balls, as shown in Figure 2.1, panels 1–3. The experiment secretly hides the remaining ball, timing how long the baby spends searching for it inside the box (Figure 2.1, panel 4). Finally, the experimenter removes the remaining ball in the baby's sight and again times the baby's search (Figure 2.1, panels 5–6). The search times show that infants hunt longer in the box when one ball remains than when no balls remain (e.g., Feigenson & Carey, 2003, 2005; Van de Walle, Carey, & Prevor, 2000). That is, search time is longer during step 4 of the Figure 2.1 procedure than during step 6. This suggests that the babies appreciate that two balls minus one leaves one, but two balls minus two leaves none. This difference is not due to the baby's fatigue: In a control condition, infants see just one ball placed in the box, and they then remove it. Search time after the removal is about the same as in the final step of the experimental condition, just described.

Similarly, in *habituation experiments,* infants see a sequence of displays one-at-a-time, each display containing a fixed number of dots in varying configurations. One group of infants, for example, might see the sequence of 8-dot displays at the left side of Figure 2.2, and a second group, the set of 16-dot displays at the right side. After the infants habituate—that is, begin to ignore the displays by looking away—they see a new test array containing either the same number of dots (8 if the infants habituated to

1) Box is placed on table.

2) Experimenter places 2 balls on box,
   then hides them inside.

3) Infant allowed to retrieve 1 ball.
   Experimenter surreptitiously removes 2nd ball.

4) 2-Objects (More Remaining) trial: Infant's
   searching is measured. 1 ball expected inside.   *Measurement
                                                                    period

5) Experimenter "finds" 2nd ball.

6) 2-Objects (Box Empty) trial: Infant's
   searching is measured. Box expected empty.   *Measurement
                                                                    period

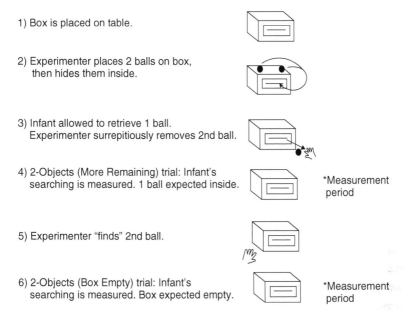

FIGURE 2.1 An example of the experimental procedure for an addition-and-subtraction task: (1) Babies see an opaque box with a flexible slit; (2) the experimenter places two ping-pong balls on the box and then puts them inside; (3) the baby is allowed to remove one of the balls from the box; (4) the experimenter covertly hides the second ball while the baby searches for it, and the baby's search time is measured; (5) the experimenter removes the second ball from the box; and (6) the baby's search time is again measured (from Feigenson & Carey, 2005).

8 or 16 if they habituated to 16) or a novel number (8 if the infants habituated to 16 or 16 if they had habituated to 8). Under these conditions (and with the overall surface area of the dots controlled), infants as young as 6 months look longer at the novel number of items, as long as the ratio of dots in the two kinds of display exceeds some critical value (e.g., Xu, 2003b; Xu & Spelke, 2000; Xu, Spelke, & Goddard, 2005).

Controversy surrounds the reason for the infants' success. Wynn (1992b) argued that infants keep track of the number of objects in the addition-subtraction task by means of internal continuous magnitudes, using the magnitudes to predict what they will find. A magnitude representation of this sort has also the advantage of accounting for the results from animal studies of cardinality detection (see Gallistel et al., 2006,

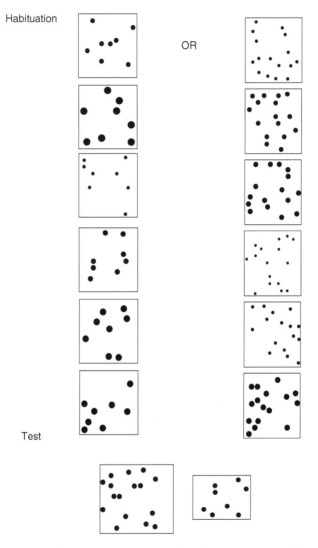

FIGURE 2.2 Displays from an experiment on infants' ability to distinguish large numbers of dots. Infants habituate to either the 8-dot displays (column at left) or the 16-dot displays (column at right). They are then tested on new displays of either 8 or 16 dots, shown at bottom (from Xu & Spelke, 2000).

for a review) and for experiments on number comparison by adults (e.g., Banks, Fujii, & Kayra-Stuart, 1976; Buckley & Gillman, 1974; Moyer & Landauer, 1967; Parkman, 1971). In the latter studies, participants see a pair of single-digit numerals (e.g., 8 and 2) on each trial, one digit on the left and the other on the right of a screen. They must then choose the numeral that represents the larger number, pressing a button on the left if the left-hand numeral is larger or a button on the right if the right-hand numeral is larger. Participants are cautioned to make their response as quickly as possible, but without making mistakes. Under these conditions, mean response times are faster the larger the absolute difference between the digits. For example, participants take less time to compare 8 and 2 than 4 and 2. This symbolic distance effect is what we should expect if participants make their judgment by comparing two internal magnitudes, one for each digit. If the magnitudes include some amount of noise, then the larger the absolute difference between the digits, the more clear-cut the comparison and the faster the response times. The mental-magnitude idea also accords with people's ability to provide rough estimates of cardinality in situations where an exact count is difficult or impossible (e.g., Conrad, Brown, & Cashman, 1998).

People may produce these magnitude representations in an iterative way by successively incrementing a summed magnitude for each item to be counted (an *accumulator* mechanism), but they could also produce a magnitude representation in parallel as a global impression of a total (for details of this issue, see Barth, La Mont, Lipton, & Spelke, 2006; Cordes, Gelman, Gallistel, & Whalen, 2001; Whalen, Gallistel, & Gelman, 1999; and Wood & Spelke, 2005). I'll use the term *single-mechanism theory* for all such models in which magnitudes are infants' sole means of keeping track of quantity.

Carey (2001, 2004), Spelke (2000, 2003), and their colleagues, however, have argued that infants' ability to predict the total number of objects in small sets (less than 4) depends not on internal magnitudes but on attentional or short-term memory mechanisms that represent individual objects as distinct entities (see, also, Scholl & Leslie, 1999). A baby maintains one such representation for each object within a four-object capacity limit. Infants seem unable to anticipate the correct number of objects in addition-subtraction tasks for cardinalities of four or more (Feigenson, Carey, & Hauser, 2002; Feigenson & Carey, 2003), even though they can discriminate much larger arrays of items (e.g., 8 vs. 16 dots) in habituation tasks (Xu, 2003b; Xu & Spelke, 2000; Xu et al., 2005). Carey and Spelke therefore argue that infants' failure in the former tasks is due to the infants' tendency to engage object representations (rather than magnitudes) for small numbers of items. In the original formulation, these were preconceptual object-tracking devices—called *object files* or *visual indexes*—that record objects' spatial position and perhaps other properties (Kahneman, Treisman, & Gibbs, 1992; Pylyshyn, 2001). In more recent formulations (Le Corre & Carey, 2007), the representations exist in working memory. Success with larger arrays depends instead on a magnitude mechanism that correctly distinguishes sets only if the sets' ratio is large enough (e.g., 3:2 or greater for older infants; Lipton & Spelke, 2003; Xu & Arriaga, 2007). I'll call this account the *dual mechanism* view (see Feigenson, Dehaene, & Spelke, 2004).

2.2.2.2 A Summary of Infants' Numerical Abilities

Should we conclude, then, that infants' knowledge of number is built on magnitude information alone, on magnitude information in combination with discrete object-based representations, or on some other basis?

One issue concerns small numbers of objects. Recent addition-subtraction and habituation experiments with two or three visually presented objects have also controlled for total surface area, contour length (i.e., sum of object perimeters), and other continuous variables. Some of these studies have found that infants respond to the continuous variables rather than to cardinality (Clearfield & Mix, 1999; Feigenson, Carey, & Spelke, 2002; Xu et al., 2005). According to the dual-mechanism explanation, small numbers of objects selectively engage infants' discrete object-representing process, and this process operates correctly in this range. So why don't the infants attend to cardinality? Feigenson, Carey, and Spelke (2002; and Feigenson et al., 2004) suggest that infants do employ discrete object representations in this situation but attend to the continuous properties of the tracked objects when these objects are not distinctive—for example, qualitatively similar dolls. When the objects do have distinctive properties (Feigenson, 2005) or when the infants have to reach for particular toys (Feigenson & Carey, 2003), the individuality of the items becomes important, and the infants respond to cardinality.

This suggests a three-way distinction among infants' quantitative abilities: (a) With small sets of distinctive objects, infants use discrete representations to discriminate the objects and to maintain a trace of each. (b) With small sets of nondistinctive items, however, infants feed some continuous property from the representation (e.g., surface area) into a mental magnitude and remember the total magnitude (total surface area). (c) With large sets of objects, infants form a magnitude for the total number. According to (b), infants should fail in discriminating small numbers of nondistinctive objects (e.g., 1 vs. 2 dots) under conditions that control for continuous variables, since they are relying on an irrelevant magnitude, such as total area. But by (c), they should succeed with larger numbers (e.g., 4 vs. 8 dots) under controlled conditions, since they are using a relevant magnitude (total number of items). In fact, there is evidence that this prediction is correct (Xu, 2003b).[3]

A second issue has to do with large numbers of objects. People's ability to respond to the cardinality of large sets, as well as small sets, depends on individuating the items in the set, barring the kinds of confounds just discussed. This follows from the very concept of cardinality (as Schwartz, 1995, has argued). Even a magnitude representation for the total number of objects in a collection must be sensitive to the individual objects; else it is not measuring cardinality but some other variable. Individuating objects, in the sense I use here, means determining, for the parts of an array, which parts belong to the same object. Thus, individuation is the basis for deciding when we are dealing with a single object and when we are dealing with more. Of course, people don't have to recognize each object overtly in order to appreciate the set's cardinality. It's enough that some level of the perceptual system segregates the set into its individual items. But this segregation must occur before any true enumeration of the items is possible.

Investigators in this area have concluded that object files or working-memory representations can't be the only means infants have to individuate objects. If they were, then the limitations of these mechanisms would appear in experiments with larger sets of nondistinctive objects (Barth, Kanwisher, & Spelke, 2003; Barth et al., 2006; Wood & Spelke, 2005; Xu, 2003b; Xu & Arriaga, 2007; Xu & Spelke, 2000; Xu et al., 2005). If these object representations simply output information about some continuous variable such as surface area (as they do for small numbers of nondistinctive items), then infants should also fail to distinguish the number of items in large sets in studies that implement appropriate controls (see Mix, Huttenlocher, & Levine, 2002a, and Xu et al., 2005, for debate about the controls' appropriateness). Moreover, current experiments with both infants (Wood & Spelke, 2005) and adults (Barth et al., 2003) find that increasing the cardinality of large arrays does not necessarily increase the time required for discriminating the arrays, provided that the sets to be compared maintain the same ratio (e.g., 2:1). This would be impossible if object files, with their three-item limit, had to be applied sequentially in order to individuate all the elements of the large arrays.

In order to handle the problem of dealing with large sets, we apparently need a mechanism for individuating items, but one that is not subject to the capacity limits of working memory or object files. One possibility is that some perceptual mechanism is able to individuate relatively large numbers of items in parallel, with the output of this analysis fed to a magnitude indicator. Dehaene and Changeux (1993) propose a parallel analysis of this sort, and parallel individuation is also consistent with estimates that adults can attentionally discriminate at least 60 nondistinctive items in the visual field (Intriligator & Cavanagh, 2001).[4]

The model in Figure 2.3 provides a summary of infants' quantitative abilities based on this account. According to this model, infants first segregate items in the visual field by means of a parallel attentive mechanism, similar to that discussed by Intriligator and Cavanagh (2001) or Dehaene and Changeux (1993). Infants will quickly forget the results of this analysis once the physical display is no longer in view. But while the display is visible, infants assign a more permanent object representation to each item if the total number of items is less than four. If the number of items is four or more, however, infants cannot employ object representations, but may instead use the output from the initial parallel analysis to produce a single measure of approximate cardinality. Thus, the lower track accords with Barth et al.'s (2003) and Wood and Spelke's (2005) findings of constant time to discriminate large displays with equal ratios. The model assumes ad hoc that object representations take precedence over the global cardinality measure for small arrays. But perhaps an explanation for this co-opting behavior could be framed in terms of the functional importance of keeping track of individual objects

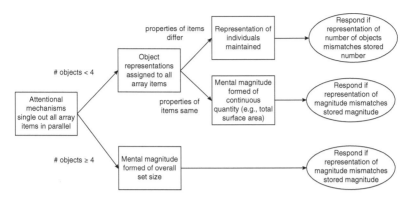

FIGURE 2.3 A model for infants' quantitative abilities. Response rules in ovals indicate conditions under which infants look longer in addition-subtraction or habituation tasks. They are not meant to exhaust possible uses of these representations.

compared to treating them as a lump sum. The contexts for tracing object identity that we examined in Chapter 1 may provide a motive for such attention.[5]

I don't mean to suggest that the tracks in Figure 2.3 are the only quantitative processes that people (especially adults) can apply to an array of items. While the display is visible, adults can obviously enumerate the elements verbally. Similarly, children and adults may use a nonverbal, serial enumeration mechanism similar to that described by Cordes et al. (2001), Gallistel et al. (2006), and Whalen et al. (1999) in some conditions. Which strategies people deploy may depend on properties of the display, task demands, and other factors, and I have not tried to capture this interaction in the figure. I should add that the model in Figure 2.3 is an attempt to understand current empirical results within the dual-mechanism framework, and it may not be an accurate depiction of the views of specific dual-mechanism theorists. The aim is to clarify the implications of such theories rather than to provide an exact account of a particular version of the model.

Although many uncertainties surround the Figure 2.3 model, I use it here as a convenient way of summarizing the findings on preverbal quantitative skills and not as a final account of these abilities. The issue is this: Many psychologists believe that people's mathematical thinking originates from roughly the components in Figure 2.3. But if the picture in Figure 2.3 is even approximately correct, it presents some extremely difficult problems for how children acquire the concept of natural number. These problems are next on the agenda.

2.3 The Route to Concepts of Number

Let's suppose the Figure 2.3 model or some close relative correctly captures infants' sensitivity to cardinality. Should we then say that they have concepts of natural numbers? Dual-mechanism theorists tend to answer "no" (Carey, 2004, 2009, and Carey & Sarnecka, 2006, are explicit on this point). Neither magnitudes nor short-term representations of individual objects have the properties of the natural numbers; hence, according to these theories, children's quantitative concepts have to undergo conceptual change in order to qualify as true number representations. The task for these theorists is then to specify the nature of this change. Some single-mechanism accounts claim that although magnitudes don't represent natural numbers, they do represent continuous quantity, perhaps even the real numbers (Gallistel et al., 2006). The route to natural numbers in this case involves transforming a continuous representation into a countable one. In this section, I extend dual theorists' skepticism about the relation between natural number concepts, on the one hand, and object files, magnitudes, and similar representations, on the other. Not only do the latter representations fail to qualify as representations of numbers in their own right, there is no straightforward way for them to provide a foundation for number concepts.

In examining proposals about the acquisition of natural number (and related arithmetic principles in Section 2.4), I repeatedly use a simple methodological rule that it might be worth describing in advance. In explaining how a person acquires some idea Q, cognitive scientists often claim that people make an inductive inference to Q from some body of information P, which these people already possess. If people already know P and if the inference from P to Q is plausible to them, then the inference is a potential explanation of how they acquire Q. However, rival inferences can undercut such an explanation. Suppose there is also a body of information P' (possibly equal to P) and an inference from P' to a contrary idea *non-Q*. Then if P' is as believable and as salient as P and if the inference from P' to *non-Q* is as plausible as the one from P to Q, then the inference from P to Q fails to explain Q adequately. I call this rule, the *no competing inference* test for psychological explanations. To make this more concrete with a nonmathematical example, suppose we want to explain people's belief that their deity is omnipotent. We might hypothesize that this idea comes from previous knowledge of a powerful parent, plus a conscious or unconscious inference from the parent to the deity. But although this may be the right account, we should also consider possible competing inferences. In everyday experience, we encounter only individuals (even parents) with limited power. So why don't people draw the inference from a person with limited power to a deity who is nonomnipotent? Of course, there could be considerations that favor the first inference over the second. For example, Freud (1927/1961) believed that people's fear and need for protection from hostile forces motivates the inference to an omnipotent deity. However, unless we can supply such a reason—a reason why the selected inference is more convincing than potential competing ones— the initial explanation is incomplete.

It is understandable why theories sometimes violate the no-competing-inference test. Because we ordinarily know the final knowledge state Q that we want to explain, we naturally look for antecedents P that would lead people to Q. Because we're not trying to explain *non-Q*, we don't seek out antecedents for these rivals. Cognitive scientists who work on mathematical thinking are no more prone than others are to violating the no-competing-inference principle. Still, I find this principle helpful in evaluating the strengths and weaknesses of existing theories in this domain.

2.3.1 Numerical Concepts Versus Concepts of Numbers

As dual-mechanism theorists have pointed out, analog magnitudes are too coarse to provide the precision associated with specific natural numbers (Carey, 2004, 2009; Carey & Sarnecka, 2006; Spelke, 2000, 2003). The magnitude representation of 157 would barely differ from that of 158 (if a magnitude device could represent them at all), so their properties would not have the specificity of a unique natural number and its successor. Short-term object representations do have the discreteness of natural numbers, but they aren't unitary representations. Without further apparatus, having one, two, or three such active representations doesn't amount to a representation of oneness, twoness, or threeness. If a child is tracking three objects, he or she has one object representation per object but nothing that represents the (cardinality of the) set of three. Unless such representations build in the concept of a unified set of individuated elements, there is nothing here to represent number. Moreover, any representation of the natural numbers must be generative. As mentioned earlier (Section 2.2.1), people could not possibly represent them all simultaneously using single mental symbols for each. However, generative capacity is a problem for object files because of the strict limit on the number of available files. According to the dual-mechanism story, then, only when children learn to count and to combine the precursor representations do they attain true concepts of natural numbers.

Some single-mechanism theorists credit infants (and nonhuman animals) with more mathematical sophistication. For example, Gallistel et al. (2006, p. 247) assert that "when we refer to 'mental magnitudes' we are referring to a real number system in the brain." Although we tend to think of real numbers as more advanced concepts than natural numbers, this may reverse the true developmental progression. The reals may be the innate system, with natural numbers emerging later as the result of counting or through other means.

However, some of the criticisms that dual-mechanism theorists level against magnitudes as representations of natural numbers also apply to magnitudes as representations of the reals. Because the mental magnitudes become increasingly noisy and imprecise as the size of the number increases, larger numbers are less discriminable than smaller ones. For example, if we consider 157 and 158 as real numbers (i.e., as 157.000 ... and 158.000 ...), they will be much less discriminable than two smaller but equally spaced numbers, such as 3 and 4 (3.000 ... and 4.000 ...). In Gallistel et al.'s view, this imprecision is the result of the way people retrieve mental magnitudes rather than a property of the magnitudes themselves. But this is of no comfort to the idea that infants can represent real numbers. If cognitive access to this representation is always noisy or approximate, how could the system attribute the correct real-number properties to the representation, without some independent concept of the reals? People can't skirt the retrieval step since, as Gallistel et al.

consistently emphasize, the representation of a number can't be inert but has to play a role in arithmetic reasoning. An analogy may be helpful on this point. Suppose you have access to some continuously varying quantity, such as the level of water in a tub, and suppose, too, that the viewing conditions are such that the higher the level of water, the greater the perceived level randomly deviates from the true level. Could you use such a device to represent the real numbers and to perform real-number arithmetic? Although you could combine two quantities of water to get a bigger one, the representation of the sum would be even fuzzier than that of the original quantities (Barth et al., 2006) and has few of the properties of real-number arithmetic. For example, real-number addition is a function that takes two reals as inputs and yields a unique real as output. But addition with noisy magnitudes is not a function at all: For any two real input values, it can yield any value within a range as a possible output. Of course, if you already knew some statistics, you might be able to use this tool to compensate for the deviations, but this depends on a preexisting grasp of real-number properties.[6]

These considerations suggest that if prelinguistic infants start from the components in Figure 2.3, then there is no reason to think that they have concepts of either the natural or the real numbers. Many theorists believe, however, that once children have learned language or, at least, language-based counting, they're in a position to attain true concepts of natural numbers and that they've acquired these concepts when they're able to perform tasks like enumerating the items in an array or carrying out simple commands (e.g., "Give me six balloons"). In what follows, I suggest that neither of these ideas stands up to scrutiny. Language is unable to transform magnitudes or object representations to true number concepts, and tests involving small numbers of objects don't necessarily tap concepts of natural number.

2.3.2 The Role of Language and Verbal Counting

I have mentioned Chomsky's (1988) hypothesis that mathematics piggybacks on language, making use of the ability of syntax to generate countably infinite sequences. In more recent work, Hauser, Chomsky, and Fitch (2002) take what seems a different view of the relation between language and mathematics, one in which both systems spring from an underlying ability to perform recursive computations. We will return to this idea in Section 2.5. However, many theorists continue to see language as necessary in shaping a true understanding of the natural numbers. Considering this issue draws us back into an arena of active controversy.

2.3.2.1 Language as Sufficient for Number Concepts

There are several reasons why the language-to-math hypothesis is attractive. First, natural languages possess properties that are also crucial in mathematics and that are difficult to obtain from experience with everyday objects and actions. The grammatical resources of language can easily generate the type of countably infinite sequence that can represent the natural numbers. For example, the nearly trivial grammar in (2) produces the "square language" I introduced earlier:

(2) $S \rightarrow \blacksquare + F$
       $F \rightarrow \blacksquare + F$
       $F \rightarrow \varnothing$

I originally used this language in Section 2.2.1 to represent cardinality, but it will also serve more generally as a system of numerals. As an example, these phrase-structure rules generate the following tree structure as the representation of three:

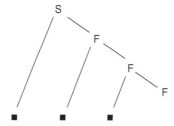

The role of the F symbol in this grammar illustrates the way recursion is useful in generating the natural numbers. The symbol F can be embedded as many times as necessary in order to produce the correct number of squares. What makes this representation a representation of three is in part that it occupies the third position in the sequence of such strings that the grammar in (2) generates. Of course, I am not proposing the square language as a cognitively plausible representation but only as a simple illustration of the generative capacity that such representations would require; I consider other ways to formulate the natural numbers in Section 2.5.

The tie to language would clearly be helpful in accounting for math properties that depend on the infinite size of the natural numbers (see Section 2.4). Along similar lines, Pollmann (2003) and Wiese (2003) have pointed out that the natural numbers, like certain parts of language, are an inherently relational system in which the meaning of any numeral depends on its position in the system as a whole. Language furnishes a type of relationally determined meaning in which a sentence, for example, depends on the grammatical relations among its constituents. *The financier dazzled the actress* differs in meaning from *The actress dazzled the financier.* Thus, language can set the stage for understanding mathematics. Moreover, the linguistic structure of a language's count terms can affect children's ability to learn this sequence. K. F. Miller and Stigler (1987) found that English-speaking children have more difficulty learning the natural-language terms for 11–19 than do Chinese-speaking children, whose terms for those numbers have a morphology more regular than that of English. (A literal translation of the Chinese term for "eleven" would be "ten-one," "twelve" would be "ten-two," etc.)

A strong version of the language-to-mathematics hypothesis might claim that possessing a natural language is not only necessary but also sufficient for the development of concepts of natural numbers. According to this type of theory, language is the sole source of number concepts. Psychologists who see a role for language in acquiring number concepts have more often taken the "catalyst" view that I will describe momentarily, but the stronger position may be implicit in the idea that "the human number faculty [is] essentially an 'abstraction' from human language" (Chomsky, 1988, p. 169).

Evidence against this possibility comes from recent studies of native Brazilian peoples, the Mundurukú and the Pirahã, who appear to lack concepts for exact numbers greater than four (Gordon, 2004; Pica et al., 2004). These people have no number terms that distinguish between, for example, six and seven, using words like "many" for larger numbers of items. In tasks that require knowledge of approximate quantity, members of these cultures perform in a way that's comparable to Americans or

Europeans. Pica et al. (2004) report that the Mundurukú are able to point to the larger of two sets of 20–80 dots with accuracy that is nearly the same as French participants. However, in tasks that require exact enumeration, accuracy is relatively low. If the Mundurukú see a number of objects placed in a container and then see a subset of the objects withdrawn, they have difficulty predicting how many (Pica et al., 2004)—or whether any (Gordon, 2004)—objects remain. These experiments suggest that the Mundurukú and Pirahã peoples use a system for dealing with cardinality roughly similar to that of Figure 2.3. They treat large cardinalities (and, perhaps, small cardinalities, as well) as approximate quantities. As in the case of findings with Western infants, we could question the link between knowledge of number and knowledge of cardinality (see Sections 2.2 and 2.3.3). But in this case, it's difficult to argue for knowledge of natural number in the absence of evidence for more than four discrete representations for numerical properties. R. Gelman and Butterworth (2005) suggest that such counterevidence might be obtainable. But taking the Brazilian results at face value, we need to explain why natural language shows up in such cultures but natural numbers don't, if there is an innate linguistic basis for a countable number system.[7,8]

The idea on the table is that natural language is a sufficient basis for the concept of natural number. The Brazilian evidence casts doubt on this idea, but, of course, it doesn't rule out the possibility that language affects numerical abilities. Many numerical tasks require people to use natural-language count terms. For example, we might be required to comprehend a math problem couched in natural language, or we might be required to count aloud to answer an arithmetic problem using a particular language's numerals. If so, the linguistic properties of the count terms might affect performance, as in K. F. Miller and Stigler's (1987) studies. These properties could even influence the way we solve problems that aren't overtly language-based if the problems involve remembering numbers, since natural-language terms may provide a convenient means of encoding these numbers. Results of this sort show that language provides a tool for communicating and remembering numbers, just as it provides a tool for communicating and remembering information from many other domains of knowledge. What such results don't show, however, is that language is causally sufficient for producing number concepts. Language is also useful for communicating and remembering information about hiking, auto mechanics, dark energy, reality TV, and barbeque, but it isn't sufficient for creating concepts of these items.

2.3.2.2 Language as a Catalyst for Number Concepts

A weaker, and more plausible, hypothesis is that the natural-number concept requires not language in general but some type of language-based technique for enumeration. A possible explanation for why the Munduruku and Piraha don't keep track of the exact number of objects in large sets is that they lack a verbal procedure for tallying these objects. Similarly, in the case of prelinguistic children. When children eventually begin verbally enumerating items, they do so by means of simple counting: They match a small fixed list of numerals to the elements of a collection (see Section 2.1 for the distinction between simple and advanced counting). Perhaps some procedure of this sort is necessary in order for them to attain the natural numbers.

Adults in nonnative cultures can, of course, enumerate by advanced counting, and advanced counting could, no doubt, be helpful in conveying the concept of natural numbers. Once children have mastered advanced counting, they have a model of the natural numbers that is much closer than anything in the world of (finite) physical experience. This is because the elements of advanced counting (the numerals of the counting system) are in a one-to-one correspondence with the natural numbers—a correspondence that preserves the successor relation. (That is, the successor relation on the numerals corresponds to that on the natural numbers.) I am not claiming that children attain the concept of natural number by learning advanced counting: I think it more likely that children learn an underlying set of principles that facilitates both advanced counting and the concept of natural number (see Section 2.5). However, advanced counting, not simple counting, provides the numerals that are the obvious counterpart of the natural numbers.

Most psychologists believe, nevertheless, that children acquire the natural number concepts long before they master advanced counting in either natural language or in explicit mathematical notation. Thus, if language-based counting plays a role in forming these concepts, simple counting and associated enumerating must be responsible. How are they able to produce this effect? Some recent dual theories of a counting-to-number link suggest that enumerating items with natural-language count terms provides a conceptual bridge between magnitudes and object representations, giving rise to a new sort of mental representation (Spelke, 2000, 2003; Spelke & Tsivkin, 2001). Magnitudes bring to this marriage the concept of a set, object representations bring the concept of an individual, and the offspring is the concept of cardinality as a set of distinct individuals:

> To learn the full meaning of *two*, however, children must combine their representations of individuals and sets: they must learn that *two* applies just in case the array contains a set composed of an individual, of another, numerically distinct individual, and of no further individuals . . . . The lexical item *two* is learned slowly, on this view, because it must be mapped simultaneously to representations from two distinct core domains (Spelke, 2003, p. 301).

But it is difficult to understand how conjoining these systems could transform number representations in the desired way (see R. Gelman & Butterworth, 2005, and Laurence & Margolis, 2005, for related criticism). Suppose the meaning of a number word like *two* connects to both a fuzzy magnitude and two object files. According to this theory, magnitude information must transform the representation of two separate objects into a representation of a single set of two. But why doesn't the fuzziness of the magnitudes lead the children to believe that two means approximately two individuals (or a few)? Why do magnitudes lead to sets rather than some other form of composite, such as a part-whole grouping? Why is language necessary if even infants can treat individual items as parts of chunks (Feigenson & Halberda, 2004; Wynn, Bloom, & Chiang, 2002)? Unless we can somehow answer these questions, the explanation trips over what I called the no-competing-inference rule.

We might do better to discard magnitudes and to think of the resulting representations as drawing on some other form of set-like grouping. Along these lines, Carey and colleagues (2004, 2009; Carey & Sarnecka, 2006; Le Corre & Carey, 2007) propose that children use natural-language quantifiers to combine object representations into sets, so that children come to represent one as {a}, two as {a, b}, and so on—representations which I'll refer to as "internal sets." "It is language that spurs the creation of an internal symbol whose meaning is *that which is common to all situations where a pair of individuals are being tracked at the same time*. Associating linguistic markers with unique states of the parallel individuation system is only possible for up to three objects, because the parallel individuation system can only keep track of up to three individuals at once" (Carey & Sarnecka, 2006, p. 490).

Some single-mechanism theories describe infants as already having true natural number concepts for smaller numbers; so the role of counting is more plausibly confined to extending these concepts to the rest of the integers (Bloom, 2000; see, also, Hurford, 1987, for a related account). According to Bloom (2000, p. 215), for example, "Long before language learning, . . . [babies] have the main prerequisite for learning the smaller number words: they have the concepts of oneness, twoness, and threeness. Their problem is simply figuring out the names that go with these concepts."

The crucial question for both single-mechanism and dual-mechanism theories is whether simple counting and enumerating allow children to extend their knowledge of number beyond these first three to a full concept of natural number. Suppose, in other words, that at a critical stage, children have worked out facts like those in (3):

(3)   "one" represents one.
       "two" represents two.
       "three" represents three.

According to the assumptions I've temporarily adopted, words occupy the left-hand side of these relations, and cardinalities occupy the right-hand sides (e.g., "one" represents the size of singleton sets, "two" the size of two-member sets, etc.). The concepts that mediate the relations in (3) depend on the theory in question. For single-mechanism theories, internal magnitudes underlie these associations; for example, "two" denotes two because children learn that "two" represents what the corresponding internal magnitude does. For dual-mechanism theories, the associations depend on preliminary combinations of object representations and magnitudes (Spelke, 2003) or object representations and set-like groupings (Carey, 2004, 2009; Carey & Sarnecka, 2006; Le Corre & Carey, 2007).

In all cases, though, the outcome of these linkages is that children acquire the denotations in (3). Then, by correlating the sequence of words in the count series with the regular increase in cardinality, the children arrive at something like the generalization in (4):

(4)   For any count word "n," the next count word "$s(n)$" in the count sequence refers to the cardinality (n+1) obtained by adding one element to collections whose cardinality is denoted by "n."

Carey (2004, 2009) and Hurford (1987) have detailed formulations along these lines. Similar suggestions appear in Bloom (1994) and Schaeffer, Eggleston, and Scott (1974). According to Carey and Sarnecka (2006, p. 490), "This idea (one word forward [in the count list] equals one more individual) captures the successor principle." Notice, though, that (4) depends on the concept of the next count word, which I've referred to as "$s(n)$," for any count term "n." (If "n" is "five," "$s(n)$" is "six"; if "n" is "ninety," "$s(n)$" is "ninety-one"; etc.) For these purposes, simple counting will not do as a guide to "$s(n)$", since simple counting uses a finite list of elements. For example, if a child's count list stops at "nine," then (4) can extend the numeral-cardinality connection through nine. But in order to capture all the natural numbers, (4) requires advanced counting: an appreciation of the full numeral system.

At this point, though, the trouble with the counting hypothesis comes clearly into view, for at the point at which children are supposed to infer (4)—at a little over 4 years of age—they have not yet mastered advanced counting. Nothing determines for such a number learner which function or sequence specifies the natural number words (i.e., the function that appears as "$s(n)$" in (4)).

In learning ordinary correlations or functions, children induce a relation between two preexisting concepts, for example, degree of hunger and time since lunch. By contrast, what lies behind the proposal that children induce (4) from (3) is the bootstrapping hypothesis that they are simultaneously learning advanced counting along with (and because of) the correlation with cardinality. But it's unclear how this is possible in the case of natural numbers (see Rips, Asmuth, & Bloomfield, 2006, 2008). Suppose, for example, that the count system the child is learning is not one for the natural numbers but instead for arithmetic modulo 10, so that adding 1 to 0 produces 1, adding 1 to 1 produces 2, . . . , and adding 1 to 8 produces 9, but adding 1 to 9 produces 0, and so on in a cyclical pattern. In this case, (4) is still a valid generalization of (3) if we interpret

"$s(n)$" as the next numeral in the modular cycle, but then what's been learned isn't the natural numbers.

The generalization in (4) can seduce you if you think of the child as interpreting it (after a year of struggle) as "Aha, I finally get it! The next number in the count sequence denotes the size of sets that have one more thing." But "next number in the count sequence" isn't an innocent expression since the issue is, in part, how children figure out from (3) that the next number is given by the successor function for natural numbers and not by, say, the successor function for addition $\mod_{10}$ or $\mod_{38}$ or $\mod_{983}$. You might be tempted to reply that this problem isn't any different from other cases of (empirical) induction, where normally an infinite choice of potential extrapolations exists. Some constraints on induction are necessary in order to make learning humanly possible (Chomsky, 1965). But although this is true, the problem with the inference from (3) to (4) is not that it opts for one possible continuation over a set of rivals. Instead, the problem is that the conclusion in (4) is completely vague about the continuation, because the function "next count word" (i.e., "$s(n)$") is undefined for children at this stage beyond the small count list they've memorized. Also unclear is what general constraints could steer (4) toward the natural numbers, especially because the function successor-mod-10 and many others seem less complicated than the successor function for natural numbers, with its infinite domain. (See Rips et al., 2006, for a discussion of the relation between the bootstrapping problem and more general problems of induction and meaning.)[9]

I have been concentrating on the relation between numerals and cardinalities, since the issues are clearest in this context, but the same difficulties appear if we look at acquisition of number meanings from the perspective of the mental representations that support them. The theories in question suppose that the mental representations are latched to external cardinalities, so that larger internal magnitudes or larger internal sets always correlate with larger external cardinalities. Using this assumption, if we are learning the standard system for natural numbers, "nine" will come to be associated with a single magnitude or internal set, whereas if we are learning the $\mod_{10}$ system, "nine" will be associated with a collection of internal magnitudes or sets. Principle (4) doesn't tell us which of these connections is correct.

Some theorists may understand Principle (4) as a way of transcending, rather than extending, the initial representations. On this understanding, children no longer need mental magnitudes or internal sets once they arrive at this principle. If this is not the case, however, properties of the initial representations will bring additional difficulties to number concepts. If we start with a magnitude representation for (3) and extend it by (4), we get increasingly noisy representations as we go to higher numbers. Nothing about the representation gives us the ingredients we need to formulate the correct hypothesis of a countable sequence (as A. M. Leslie et al., 2007, point out). If we start with a set-like representation for (3) and try to extend it by (4), we run into the problem that we can't possibly represent in this way more than a small initial segment of the natural numbers. Our ability to represent individual sets (e.g., {a}, {a, b}) must quickly end because of memory limits, but the natural numbers keep going. To take up the slack, the concepts have to go generative, like the grammar in (2). But because the right generative principle is not supposed to be available beforehand, we have no guarantee that the structure will continue infinitely. To represent the natural numbers, though, we need a representation for a sequence that is both countable and infinite.

This isn't to say that the generalization in (4) is false or that it is unhelpful to number learners. Principle (4) can help children get from the meanings of "one" through "three" to the meanings of the rest of the terms in their current count list (e.g., "four" through "nine"), and we shouldn't disparage children's achievement in getting to "nine" (or developmentalists' achievement in explaining how they do it). Still, this leaves unanswered our original question of how children learn the concept of the natural numbers. The generalization in (4) is true, but it doesn't serve to fix the meaning of the numerals for the child because the child doesn't know what function "$s(n)$" is. For this reason, (4) can't tell them what the natural numbers are; (4) is indeterminate for them. For practical purposes of enumerating objects, of course, children need to realize that some systematic relation holds between the numeral sequence and the cardinalities, and (4) could mark this recognition. But realizing that such a link exists doesn't fully specify it. Theories of number acquisition rely on (4) both because they take the meaning of a numeral to be a cardinality and because they suppose (4) specifies this meaning for the natural numbers. However, (4) is incapable of performing this function, since (4) presupposes knowledge of the very structure it is intended to create. This suggests that enumerating might be less crucial to the development of natural number than might first appear. Enumerating—pairing numerals to cardinalities—can't create the natural numbers, since many forms of enumerating that are consistent with (4) lead to nonstandard systems (see Section 2.5.3.4).

2.3.3 Do Tests of "How Many Objects?" Require Concepts of Number?

Suppose, though, that the child finally succeeds in the standard tests of number comprehension, performing correctly when asked to "Point to the picture with six dogs" or "Give me six balloons." Should we now say that he or she has concepts of natural numbers? The answer seems to be "no," when we're dealing with the small collections that these experiments employ. A textbook exercise in first-order logic asks students to paraphrase sentences like *There are (exactly) two dogs* or *There are (exactly) three hats.*[10] An answer to the first of these exercises appears in (5):

(5) $(\exists x)(\exists y)(x$ is a dog$) \& (y$ is a dog$) \& (x \neq y)$
    $\& (\forall z)(z$ is a dog $\supset ((z = x) \vee (z = y)))$

Sentences like this one don't contain references to numbers or any other mathematical objects but get along with concrete objects, such as dogs. The quantifiers and variables in (5) make clear its commitments about the existence of objects: (5) is committed to dogs but not to numbers (see Hodes, 1984; C. Parsons, 2008; and Quine, 1974). Internal magnitudes and sets, as representations of two dogs, aren't as explicit, but they presumably are no more committed to numbers than is (5).

To be sure, children's quantitative abilities extend beyond concrete physical objects like dogs. Even infants are sensitive to the number of tones in a sequence (e.g., Lipton & Spelke, 2003) and to the number of jumps of a puppet (Wynn, 1996). They also keep track of sums of entities appearing in different modalities—for example, visual objects plus tones—provided they have previously witnessed the tones paired with the objects (Kobayashi, Hiraki, Mugitani, & Hasegawa, 2004). In this respect, the infants' numerical skills are more abstract than what is required to enumerate visually presented items. But this type of abstractness does not affect the present argument, since the infants can accomplish all these tasks by representing objects, tones, or jumps (or combinations of them) rather than number.[11]

2.3.4 Summary of Children's Concept of Natural Number

As I mentioned in the introduction to this chapter, the goal is to find out how people are able to represent mathematical objects—in particular, the natural numbers. To summarize our interim conclusions about this, let's consider hypothetical children who have made the inference to Principle (4) and can correctly understand requests, such as "Give me *n* balloons," for "*n*" up to "nine" (or the last of the children's current set of count terms). I think I see a number of hands raised:

> *Do such children have the concept NATURAL NUMBER?*
> No, since many definitional properties of the natural numbers are unknown to them (e.g., that the numbers do not loop around).
>
> *Could the children have partial knowledge of NATURAL NUMBER?*
> Yes, in that they could know some properties of this concept.
> There is no reason to think that knowledge of natural numbers
> is all or none. Although children must have a certain body of
> information to be said to have the natural number concept, such as
> those in (1), they may assemble the components of this information
> over an extended period of time.
>
> *Do such children have the concept of ONE (or TWO or . . . or NINE)?*
> Not that we can discern from the results of tests such as "Give me
> *n*." Although children may have such concepts, the range of tasks
> we have reviewed does not reveal their presence. To put this in a
> slightly different way, the developmental studies may have revealed
> numerical concepts but not concepts of numbers. It may be only
> when children make mathematical judgments *about numbers* (rather
> than about objects) that we can study the nature of these concepts.
> For example, although we can express the idea that there are two
> dogs by means of (5) without using concepts of numbers, we'll
> have more difficulty avoiding such concepts in expressing the ideas
> that one is the first number, one is less than two, for any number
> there is a larger one, and so on.[12]

To forestall a possible misunderstanding, I am *not* asking whether children have conscious access to the principles governing the natural number system or other mathematical domains, and I am not asking when (or if) children are able to behave like "little mathematicians" in explicitly wielding such principles in reasoning or computation. Of course, a child's explicit formulation of such principles would be evidence that he or she had concepts of natural numbers, and it would place an upper bound on when he or she had acquired these concepts. But the child could also display evidence of such concepts indirectly— for example, evidence of a correct understanding of the sentence "Three is less than four." R. Gelman and Greeno (1989) have clarified this point concerning mathematical principles, and the analogous point about linguistic rules is well known. What I am interested in probing is whether children have any concept whatsoever of numbers, implicit or explicit, and our review of research on infants and preschool children has turned up no evidence that allows us to decide this issue. This is due to limitations in the nature of the experimental tasks. To find such evidence, then, we need to look at how children make mathematical judgments that have a more complex structure, as we do in the following section.

Another hand goes up:

> Early quantitative abilities can't be disconnected from true
> concepts of number, since evidence for these precursors appears
> even in adults' mathematics. For example, adults' judgments of
> which of two digits is larger yield distance effects on reaction
> times (see the studies cited in Section 2.2.2). Assuming that a
> magnitude representation is responsible for this effect, magnitude
> must be part of adults' natural-number concept. For this reason,
> some proposals about number representation in adults have
> included these magnitudes, along with other ingredients
> (e.g., J. A. Anderson, 1998; McCloskey & Lindemann, 1992).

Adults might well find magnitude representations useful, for example, in carrying out tasks that call for estimation of quantity or amounts. But the fact that adults associate number terms with magnitudes doesn't imply that magnitudes are responsible for number concepts. There may be a sense of "concept" in psychology in which anything can be part of a concept, as long as a corresponding expression reminds us of it (see Chapter 5 of this book). But what proponents of magnitudes-as-precursors-of-natural-numbers have to claim is not just that magnitude is associated with natural number (in the way, e.g., that BREAD is associated with JAM). They also have to claim that magnitudes play a causal role in children's acquisition of this concept—that NATURAL NUMBER is built on a foundation of magnitude—and we've seen no reason for believing this is true. NATURAL NUMBER includes the notion that each such number has a unique successor. But magnitudes can't enforce this idea (since magnitudes don't have successors), and there is no obvious way for magnitudes to be conjoined with this idea to produce the adult concept of natural number.

Here's a related objection:

> Some of the components of Figure 2.3 seem likely to be part of
> adults' ability to enumerate objects using advanced counting. For
> example, they must use object individuation to discriminate the
> to-be-enumerated items, and they may need object representations
> or magnitudes as well. Granted: these resources are not sufficient for
> adults' (or even children's) object enumeration, as this requires
> further knowledge, such as the knowledge that the last element of
> the count sequence represents the cardinality of a collection
> (Gelman & Gallistel's cardinal principle). Nevertheless, some of the
> Figure 2.3 processes are surely part of the story of adult enumeration
> and, hence, must be part of adults' concept of natural number.

This objection is initially tempting because of the assumptions that we have temporarily adopted: that numbers are cardinalities and that cardinalities are sets of sets of physical objects. The components of Figure 2.3 that determine object representations no doubt carry over to adult performance in enumerating objects (i.e., determining the cardinality of groups of objects), but this only makes the difficulties we have just identified seem more acute. The lack of a plausible story about how children graduate from the representations and processes of Figure 2.3 to an adult concept of natural number suggests that the assumptions themselves are incorrect. As in the case of the previous objection, this one works only if you assume that adults' concept NATURAL NUMBER is necessarily linked to the ability to enumerate physical objects. What I suggest in Section 2.5 is that the natural number concept, and even concepts of particular numbers such as TEN, may not necessarily depend on enumeration, either definitionally or empirically. Before exploring this idea, however, we first examine a different route from objects to number.

2.4 Knowledge of Mathematical Principles

The ability to perform simple counting and estimating probably won't suffice as evidence of concepts of numbers for the reasons we have just seen. Even early arithmetic may be too restricted a skill to demand number concepts. A child's first taste of arithmetic may involve object tracking, mental manipulation of images of objects, counting strategies, or mental look up of sums that don't require the numerals to refer to numbers. This may seem to raise the issue of whether even adults have or use the concept of natural number outside very special contexts, such as mathematics classes. Certainly, older children and adults continue to use number words in phrases such as "three stooges" for which no concepts of number may be in play. However, older children and adults also appear to have a range of knowledge about numbers, which they can use in nontrivial arithmetic, numerical problem solving, and other tasks, and a look at this knowledge may give us some ideas about how the natural number concept first appears.

One place to search for evidence of concepts of numbers is knowledge of general statements that hold for infinitely many numbers. Understanding generalizations of the form "for any number x, $F(x)$" forces people to deal with concepts that carry a commitment to numbers rather than to physical objects, since these generalizations are overtly about numbers. Statements of this kind include those that define the numbers (e.g., every natural number has just one immediate successor) and those that state arithmetic principles that adults can express with algebraic variables (e.g., additive commutativity: $a + b = b + a$; the additive inverse principle: $a + b - b = a$). Statements of the first sort have an especially important role here, since they bear on the issue of when people can be said to have the concept NATURAL NUMBER, and we return to them in Section 2.5. General arithmetic principles, though, are also of interest because their infinite scope makes it difficult to paraphrase them purely in terms of statements about physical objects (at least not without additional mathematical apparatus). Children's knowledge of these principles can provide evidence that they have a concept of number, whether or not this exactly coincides with the natural numbers. In this section, I consider as an example the additive commutativity principle because there is a substantial body of research devoted to how children acquire it. (I also consider briefly the additive inverse principle in Note 13.) Bear in mind, though, that many other principles could serve the same purpose.

I am not requiring that children be able to compute the answers to specific arithmetic problems in order to demonstrate their understanding of math principles. It's enough that they recognize the necessity of the rule itself. Although children would, of course, have to possess the notion of addition in order for them to recognize that $a + b = b + a$, we needn't require them to be able to compute correctly, say, $946 + 285 = 1,231$ and $285 + 946 = 1,231$. What's crucial is that they understand that, *for all natural numbers*, reversing the order of the numbers in addition doesn't change the sum.

2.4.1 Acquisition of Commutativity

Commutativity appears to be one of the few general relations to attract researchers' attention, probably because of its close ties to children's early addition strategies. It may also be one of the first general properties of addition that children acquire (Canobi, Reeve, & Pattison, 2002; see Baroody, Wilkins, & Tiilikainen, 2003, for an extensive review of children's concept of commutativity).

Evidence on commutativity suggests that most 5-year-olds know that the left-to-right order of two groups of objects is irrelevant to their total. Three ducks on the right and two ducks on the left have the same sum as two on the right and three on the left. Children recognize the truth of this relation even when they can't count the number of items in one or both groups—for example, because the experimenter has concealed them (Canobi et al., 2002; Cowan & Renton, 1996; Ioakimidou, 1998, as cited in Cowan, 2003; Sophian, Harley, & Manos Martin, 1995). Of course, children do not read any mathematical notation in these studies; they merely make same/different judgments about the total number of objects. Hence, any potential difficulties in coping with explicit mathematical variables do not come into play in the way they might for beginning algebra students

(MacGregor & Stacey, 1997; Matz, 1982). However, the lack of explicit mathematical connections raises an issue about the children's knowledge. Do their judgments about the spatial or temporal order of the combination reflect the same notion of commutativity as their later understanding that $a + b = b + a$? Children who succeed in these grouping tasks have apparently understood the idea that for two disjoint collections of concrete objects, A and B, certain spatial or temporal rearrangements don't change the cardinality of their union. But commutativity of addition is the proposition that for any two *numbers, a* and *b,* the number produced by adding a to b is the same as that produced by adding b to a.

This difference between generalizing over objects and over numbers doesn't imply that knowledge of the spatial or temporal commutativity of objects is irrelevant in learning the commutativity of addition. In working out the relation between them, however, keep in mind that not all binary mathematical operations are commutative. For example, subtraction, division, and matrix multiplication are not; even addition of ordinal numbers is not commutative (A. G. Hamilton, 1982, p. 216). Similarly, not all physical grouping operations are commutative for cardinality. The total number of objects in a pile may depend on whether fragile objects are put on before or after heavy ones. This suggests that any transfer of commutativity from physical to mathematical operations must be selective rather than automatic. In making this transition, children would have to hedge the initial discovery in ways that might be difficult to anticipate before they had some knowledge of addition itself, and they would have to transfer the properties to some mathematical operations but not to others.

This difference between commutativity in the physical and mathematical domains helps account for some empirical findings. Many children are able to pass a commutativity test involving sums of hidden objects, as in the experiments cited earlier, before they are able to solve simple addition problems (Ioakimidou, 1998, as cited in Cowan, 2003). Once they've learned addition, however, they don't automatically recognize the commutativity of specific totals (e.g., that $2 + 5 = 5 + 2$). This is true even when the addition strategies they use presuppose commutativity. For example, some children solve addition problems by finding the larger of the two addends and then counting upward by the smaller addend: These children solve both $2 + 5$ and $5 + 2$ by starting with 5 and counting up two more units to 7. But children who use this strategy of counting-on-from-the-larger-addend don't always see that addition is commutative when directly faced with this problem. Although they may use counting-from-the-larger-addend to solve both 2 + 5 and 5 + 2, they may not be able to affirm that 2 + 5 = 5 + 2 without performing the two addition operations separately and comparing them (Baroody & Gannon, 1984). In fact, some children seem to discover the commutativity of addition only after noticing that these paired sums turn out to be the same over a range of problems (Baroody et al., 2003).

I argued in Section 2.3 that no evidence exists from studies of infants that they possess concepts of numbers. Even tasks with older children that require them to determine the cardinality associated with specific number words don't necessarily reveal their presence. Of course, pre-school children may actually have such concepts. The available experimental techniques may simply not be the right ones to detect them. The studies on commutativity of addition are of interest in this respect because this principle *does* seem to require concepts of numbers in order for children to appreciate the principle's generality. The results of these studies suggest, however, that children don't automatically recognize the validity of the principle when they first confront it.[13]

We are about to explore the issue of where such principles come from. But the findings about additive commutativity already suggest that people's understanding of mathematical properties can't be completely explained by their nonmathematical experience. This partial independence is in line with the relative certainty we attach to mathematical versus nonmathematical versions of these properties. We conceive of the commutativity of addition for natural numbers as true in all possible worlds, but not the commutativity of physical grouping operations.

2.4.2 Mapping of Mathematical Principles from Physical Experience

Most psychological theories of math principles (e.g., commutativity) portray them as based on knowledge of physical objects or actions. In this respect, these theories follow Mill's assertion that:

> the fundamental truths of [the science of Number] all rest on
> the evidence of sense; they are proved by showing to our eyes
> and fingers that any given number of objects—ten balls, for

example—may by separation and re-arrangement exhibit to the senses all the different sets of numbers the sum of which is equal to ten. (Mill, 1874, p. 190)

Of course, nearly all contemporary theories in this area credit children with some innate knowledge of numerical concepts (e.g., magnitudes), as we have seen in Section 2.2. Unlike Mill's proposal, these theories do not try to reduce all mathematical knowledge to perceptual knowledge. Nevertheless, all theories of how children acquire arithmetic principles, such as the commutativity or the additive-inverse principle, view these principles as based, at least in part, on physical object grouping. In the case of the commutativity of addition, these theories typically see spatial-temporal commutativity for sums of objects as a precursor, though they may also acknowledge the role of other psychological components, such as experience with computation (e.g., R. Gelman & Gallistel, 1978, p. 191; Lakoff & Núñez, 2000, p. 58; Piaget, 1970, pp. 16–17; Resnick, 1992, pp. 407–408). Theories of this sort must then explain the transition from knowledge of the object domain to the mathematical domain. An account of the empirical-to-mathematical transition is pressing in view of the evidence that this transition is not automatic. How does this transformation take place?

According to Lakoff and Núñez (2000), general properties of arithmetic depend on mappings from everyday experience. These mappings begin with simple correlations between a child's perceptual-motor activities and a set of innate, but limited, arithmetic operations (roughly the ones covered by the Figure 2.3 model). The child experiences the grouping of physical objects simultaneously with the addition or subtraction of small numbers. This correlation is supposed to produce neural connections between cortical sensory-motor areas and areas specialized for arithmetic, and these connections then support mapping of properties from object grouping to arithmetic. Lakoff and Núñez call such a mapping a *conceptual metaphor*—in this case, the Arithmetic is Object Collection metaphor. This metaphor transfers inferences from the domain of object collections to that of arithmetic, including some inferences that don't hold of the innate part of arithmetic. For example, closure of addition—the principle that adding any two natural numbers produces a natural number—does not hold in innate arithmetic, according to Lakoff and Núñez, because innate arithmetic is limited to numbers less than four. The metaphor Arithmetic is Object Collection, however, allows children to transfer closure from the object to the number domain, expanding the nature of arithmetic:

> The metaphor [Arithmetic is Object Collection] will also extend innate arithmetic, adding properties that the innate arithmetic of numbers 1 through 4 does not have, because of its limited range—namely, *closure* (e.g., under addition) and what follows from closure . . . . The metaphor will map these properties from the domain of object collections to the expanded domain of number. The result is the elementary arithmetic of addition and subtraction for natural numbers, *which goes beyond innate arithmetic* (Lakoff & Núñez, 2000, p. 60, emphasis in original).

A key issue for the theory, though, is that everyday experience with physical objects, which provides the source domain for the metaphors, doesn't always exhibit the properties that these metaphors are supposed to supply. Closure under addition, for example, doesn't always hold for physical objects, since obvious restrictions limit our ability to collect objects together. The mappings in question are unconscious ones, according to Lakoff and Núñez: They don't require deliberative reasoning about object collections or mathematics, and they are not posited specifically for arithmetic. Still, given everyday limits on the disposition of objects, why don't people acquire the opposite "nonclosure" property—that collections of objects *cannot* always be grouped together—and project it to numbers? Acquiring the closure property can't rest on a child's experience that it is always possible "in principle" to add another object, since it is exactly this principle that the theory must explain. The theory seems to run up against the no-competing-inference test that I outlined at the beginning of Section 2.3.

The Lakoff-Núñez theory also contains a metaphor that produces the concept of infinity from experience with physical processes: The Basic Metaphor of Infinity. This metaphor projects the notion of an infinite entity (e.g., an infinite set) from experience with repeated physical processes, such as repeated jumping. The repeated process is conceived in the metaphor as unending and yet as having not only intermediate states but also a final resultant state. Mapping this conception to a mathematical operation yields the idea of an infinitely repeated process (e.g., adding items to a set) and an infinite resulting entity (e.g., an infinite set). Lakoff and Núñez do not invoke the Basic Metaphor of Infinity in their initial explanation of closure under addition (pp. 56–60), perhaps because closure does not necessarily require an infinite set (e.g., modular arithmetic is closed under addition, even though only a finite set of elements is involved). But they do use this metaphor later in dealing with what they call "generative closure" (pp. 176–178). Closure of addition over the natural numbers does involve an infinite set; so the Basic Metaphor of Infinity may be needed in this context. However, this additional apparatus encounters the same difficulty from the no-competing-inference test as does their earlier explanation. Although a metaphorical mapping may exist from iterated physical processes to infinite sets of numbers, we can as easily imagine other mappings from iterated processes to finite sets. Why would people follow the first type of inference rather than the second?

Lakoff and Núñez's theory is part of the more encompassing framework of cognitive semantics and embodied cognition (see Lakoff & Núñez, 2000, for references to this literature), and it includes many more conceptual metaphors. But nothing about this background seems to resolve this issue. Of course, the presence of competing metaphors doesn't mean that such mappings are worthless. Math teachers can exploit them to motivate complex ideas by emphasizing certain metaphors over their rivals ("Don't think about limits that way, think about them this way"). But without some method for making rival inferences less plausible than the chosen one, the mappings don't explain acquisition.

The principles that make trouble for mapping theories are precisely the ones that are of central interest for our purposes: They are generalizations over all numbers within some math domain. To see that these principles are true, people can't simply enumerate instances but must grasp, at least implicitly, general properties of the number system. Because the domain of ordinary physical objects and actions contains no counterpart to these principles, people can't automatically transfer them from that domain. Perhaps cognitive theories could get around these difficulties by envisioning a different kind of relation between the physical and mathematical realms. In particular, ideas about mathematical objects may be the result of idealizing or theorizing about concrete experience, a view that goes along with certain strains in the philosophy of mathematics (e.g., Quine, 1960; Putnam, 1971). But it isn't easy to get a clear picture of how a psychological abstraction process works. How can such a theory compensate for the messiness of object grouping to obtain the crisp properties of addition (commutativity, additive closure, and so on) that allow mathematical reasoning to proceed? Some versions of the abstraction idea in psychology depend on postulating a metacognitive process that allows people to reflect on lower-level mental representations and to create a new higher-level representation that generalizes their properties (e.g., Beth & Piaget, 1966; Resnick, 1992). However, once the abstracting begins, how does this system know which features to preserve, which to regularize or idealize, and which to discard?

In this section, we have been exploring possible ways for children to arrive at math generalizations. This is because these generalizations provide evidence that children have concepts of number. If our present considerations are correct, however, children cannot reach such generalizations by induction over physical objects, and we should therefore consider direct ways of reaching them. Many of these same concerns also apply to theories in which abstracting over physical objects yields not mathematical principles like commutativity but the numbers themselves. Suppose that children initially notice that two similar sets of objects—for example, two sets of three toy cars—can be matched one-to-one. At a later stage, they may extend this matching to successively less similar objects—three toy cars matched to three toy drivers—and eventually to one-to-one matching for any sets of three items. This process could yield the general concept of sets that can be matched one-to-one to a target set of three objects—a possible representation for three itself. In this way, learning the number three could be seen as a concept forming process similar to, but more abstract than, the formation of other natural language concepts (see Mix, Huttenlocher, & Levine, 2002b). But even if it is possible to learn the concepts of small natural numbers (e.g., THREE) in this way, this abstraction process is clearly not sufficient for learning all natural numbers, since children can't learn them one by one.

2.5 Math Schemas

I suggested that early quantitative skills may reveal more about object concepts than about math concepts, and I also suggested that children can't bootstrap their way from these beginnings to true math concepts by means of empirical induction. For this reason, we looked at beliefs that are more directly about numbers and other math entities. Principles such as the commutativity of addition fit this bill, as do others that generalize over all numbers in some infinite domain. Most psychological theories of math suppose that people acquire such generalizations from their experience with physical objects (with the aid of innate numerical concepts, such as magnitudes), but an inspection of these theories revealed gaps in their explanations. These theoretical problems go hand in hand with psychological evidence that questions the possibility of abstracting math from everyday experience. What's left as an account of concepts of number?

2.5.1 An Alternative View of Number Knowledge

A better explanation of how people understand math takes a top-down approach. Instead of attempting to project the natural numbers from knowledge of physical objects or from partial knowledge of the numerals and cardinality, children form a schema for the numbers that specifies their structure as a countably infinite sequence. Once the schema is in place, they can use it to reorganize and to extend their fragmentary knowledge. The schema furnishes them with a representation for the natural numbers because the elements of the structure play just such a role. (By *schema* I mean an organized chunk of mental representations about a common topic, as in classical schema theory in cognitive science. See Bobrow & Winograd, 1977; Brachman & Schmolze, 1985; Minsky, 1975; Rumelhart, 1975; Rumelhart & Norman, 1988, for examples. I also assume, as in these theories, that schemas express generalities by means of variables. In later chapters, I sometimes use *theory* or *minitheory* instead of schema when I want to emphasize the content of these representations.)

This view contrasts with the bottom-up approaches that we have canvassed in Sections 2.3 and 2.4. These approaches assert that children achieve knowledge of the natural number concept by extrapolating from their early skills in enumerating or manipulating objects. Some form of inductive inference transforms these skills into a full-fledged grasp of the natural numbers. Our review turned up no plausible proposals about the crucial inference, and our suspicion is that this gap is a principled one. Children's simple counting and enumerating do not provide rich enough constraints to formulate the right hypothesis about the natural numbers (Rips et al., 2006, 2008). Investigators could agree, of course, that a pure bottom-up approach cannot be the whole story and that early numerical concepts have to be supplemented with further constraints in order for children to converge on the correct concept. But although this hybrid idea might be right, the missing constraints, which I discuss in this section, are themselves sufficient to determine the correct structure. Why not suppose, then, that children build a schema for the natural numbers from these constraints and then instantiate the schema to their preliminary number knowledge?

What's distinctive to the approach I am exploring is the idea that children understand the natural number schema as being about numbers and arithmetic operations rather than about objects and physical operations, such as enumerating or grouping. According to the present view, it's no use trying to reduce number talk to object talk, or number thought to object thought. Of course, early numerical concepts could help motivate children to search for math schemas as a way of dealing with their experience. In the present view, however, although these concepts may play a motivational role, they don't provide direct input to schema construction, and they don't play a role in framing hypotheses about the concept NATURAL NUMBER. A kind of caricaturized version of the present theory is that children learn axioms for math domains, having come equipped with enough math concepts to be able to express these axioms and with enough deductive machinery to draw out some of their consequences. I don't have a full theory at this point, since not enough evidence is available about the key principles. But in what follows, I consider in a tentative and speculative way what some of the components of such a theory might be, attempting to fill in enough gaps to make it seem less like a caricature. In Section 2.4, we looked at principles that refer to numbers in general, exploring proposals about where these concepts come from. In this section, the focus narrows to principles that define the concept NATURAL NUMBER.

2.5.2 Starting Points

A first approximation is to think of a knowledge schema for a mathematical domain as knowledge of its definitions or axioms, plus inference rules for applying them. Of course, in the case of knowledge of the natural numbers, we don't introduce children to the topic by giving them axioms, definitions, and inference rules. What are the starting points for learning this information if they are not the quantitative abilities discussed in Sections 2.2–2.4? I assume that children have an innate grasp of concepts that allow them to express the notions of uniqueness (*there is one and only one P such that . . .*) and mapping (*for every P there is a Q such that . . .*). These resources would allow children to formulate the idea of a function (*for every P, there is one and only one Q such that . . .*) and a function that is one-to-one. It is important for our purposes that these representations contain variables for individuals and predicates, since it is in this sense that the representations are schematic.

I also assume that children have innate processing abilities for combining and applying these representations. The crucial built-in operation for math is recursion: A particular token operation may need to carry out other tokens of the same operation in the course of its execution. The system must maintain procedures that keep track of potential levels of embedding, so that execution of the highest-level operation can continue when the second-level finishes after the third level finishes . . . after the lowest-level finishes. The same operations can also be used to perform simple iterative tasks. The importance of recursion for understanding natural numbers comes from its close relation to the successor function, as we noticed in connection with the grammar for the square language for natural numbers in (2). The proposal by Hauser et al. (2002) is that natural language, mathematics, and navigation all draw on a more basic recursive capacity, and this proposal is consistent with the present suggestions. Of course, recursion alone is not sufficient for producing the natural numbers, but it may well be a necessary part of people's ability to use these structures.

Like all theories that include an innate component, this one has to deal with the fact that children tend to develop mathematics relatively late and in a relatively variable way, compared to skills like comprehending their native language. In addition to the built-in aspects, however, children must still assemble the schematic or structural information that is specific to a domain of mathematics (see the following subsection). We typically expect children to acquire abilities like these in a measured way that depends in part on their exposure to the key information. I take no position on the exact relationship between language learning and mathematics learning; but from the point of view of Hauser et al. (2002), in which language and mathematics both draw on the same recursive resources, the issue isn't why mathematics is slow and effortful but why language is fast and easy.

2.5.3 Math Principles

What information must children include in their math schema to possess the concept of a natural number? As mentioned earlier, it's hard to escape the conclusion that they need to understand that a unique initial number exists (0 or 1); that each number has a unique successor; that each number (but the first) has a unique predecessor; and that nothing else (nothing other than the initial number and its successors) can be a natural number. These are the ideas that the Dedekind-Peano axioms for the natural numbers codify (Dedekind, 1888/1963), and my top-down approach suggests that these principles (or logically equivalent ones) are acquired as such—that is, as generalizations—rather than being induced from facts about physical objects. But children need not be consciously aware of these ideas, to have them in a formalized language, to cite them explicitly in reasoning, or to come upon them all at once. People also supplement these basic ideas with many elaborations rather than deriving all their number knowledge from basic principles. Without something like a tacit grasp of these ideas, though, children's concept of natural number is simply unclear or incomplete, and this conclusion makes it odd how little research has been devoted to these principles. Here I summarize the state of knowledge of such principles, partly to identify where gaps exist in research.

2.5.3.1 The First Number

Children may appreciate quite early in their mathematical career that the unique starting number is one. By the time they are three years old, they can recite short counting sequences beginning with *one*, and they are able to understand phrases like *one dog* (Fuson, 1988; Wynn, 1992a). As I've emphasized, though, these abilities do not necessarily indicate that children think of one as a number. The functions *one* performs in sentences such as *Give me one balloon* are similar to those of determiners like *a* (*Give me a balloon*), which are not numbers (e.g., Carey, 2004, 2009; Carey & Sarnecka, 2006). Evidence seems to be lacking about when children use number terms in expressions such as *One is the first number* or *One is less than two*, that are prima facie about numbers rather than about (physical) objects. Even when children are able to affirm that one is a number, it is unclear at what point they've distinguished numbers from the numerals they see in picture books, puzzles, and games. In ordinary talk, number terms are ambiguous in this respect (*The number one is to the left of the number two* refers to numerals, but *The number one is less than the number two* refers to numbers).

Although most psychological theories consider "one" to be the first number term because of its position in the standard sequence of count terms and because of its role in enumerating, it is not completely clear that this should rule out zero as a possible initial number for children. On the one hand, zero seems to present some conceptual difficulties for children (Wellman & Miller, 1986). On the other hand, children have an early understanding of quantifiers such as *none* or *no* (as in *There are no cookies*) that express a cardinality of 0 items (Hanlon, 1988). The theory that numbers are cardinalities (and that numbers derive from natural language quantifiers) makes mysterious why zero should be so difficult. You can't locate the source of this difficulty in problems children have recognizing when zero items are in question. That hypothesis would predict that they would have the same problems realizing that there are no cookies on the plate or no toys in the living room, contrary to the results from Hanlon.

2.5.3.2 The Successor Function Is One-to-One

The one-to-one nature of the successor function (together with the uniqueness of the starting point) makes the natural numbers unending. Children must learn that each natural number has just one successor (so the successor relation is a function) and that each natural number except 1 has just a single predecessor (so the successor function is one-to-one). If 1 (or 0) cannot be a successor and if the successor function is one-to-one, then the sequence of natural numbers can't stop or double back. Evidence concerning children's appreciation of these facts suggests that they appear rather late (Hartnett, 1991). Although children in kindergarten are often able to affirm that you can keep on counting or adding 1 to numbers, it takes them awhile—perhaps as long as another year or two—to work out the fact that this implies that no largest number exists. Counting skill is not a good predictor of the ability to understand the successor function, although knowledge of numbers larger than 100 does seem predictive. It may be, as Hartnett suggests, that children who can grapple with larger numbers have learned enough about the generative rules of the numeral sequence (i.e., advanced counting) to understand their implications about the infinity of the numbers. We should expect a relation between knowledge of advanced counting and knowledge of the successor function, but the exact form of this interaction can't be determined from present evidence.

2.5.3.3 Math Induction

In its usual formal presentations, this closure principle takes the form: "For all properties P: if $P(1)$ and if $P(k)$ implies $P(k + 1)$ for an arbitrary natural number k, then for all natural numbers n, $P(n)$." For example, high school students learn to prove that the sum of the first n odd numbers is n^2 using mathematical induction. Here, $P(1)$ is the property 1 has if the "sum" of first odd number (just the single number 1) is equal to $1^2 = 1$. $P(k)$ is the property k has if the sum of the first k odd numbers $(1 + 3 + \ldots + [2k - 1])$ has a sum equal to k^2. However, the role math induction plays in the definition of natural number is not so much that of a proof rule but as a principle ensuring that the natural numbers are limited to those including just 1, the successor of 1, the successor of the successor of 1, and so on.

The importance of mathematical induction makes it odd that psychologists have given this principle so little attention. Only one recent study appears to investigate children's understanding of mathematical induction (L. Smith, 2002), but unfortunately it actually examines a quite different logical principle—universal generalization—as I have argued elsewhere (Rips & Asmuth, 2007). Some may find it strange even to suppose that children just learning the natural numbers could cope with a principle as complex as math induction. But math induction is equivalent to the following idea (the Least Number Principle), given other facts about the natural numbers (Kaye, 1991): For all properties P: If $P(n)$, then there is a smallest number m such that $P(m)$. The Least Number Principle does not seem out of reach of children.

2.5.3.4 Other Principles?

Mention of the Least Number Principle should make it clear that I am not claiming that the Dedekind-Peano axioms are the only ones that are sufficient for producing the natural numbers or that they are the most cognitively plausible for the job. But I don't know of systematic attempts to find substitutes in the psychological literature. You might suggest that R. Gelman and Gallistel's (1978) How-to-Count principles define a successor relation and that research in this area has concentrated on these principles for just this reason. Here's an informal statement of these principles:

(6)   a. One-One Principle: Each to-be-counted item must be
          paired one-one with an element from the count list.
      b. Stable-Order Principle: Elements from the count list must
          be in a stable (repeatable) sequence.
      c. Cardinal Principle: The element from the count list that is
          paired with the final item in the to-be-counted set
          represents the cardinality of the set.

The counting principles, of course, are crucial in understanding children's ability to enumerate objects and are a worthy subject of investigation in their own right. But as a definition of the successor relation for natural numbers, their status is similar to the rule in (4) and subject to the same argument that appears in Section 2.3.2.2. The principles map the terms in a count list onto the cardinalities they denote, so the next term in the count list comes to be connected with a cardinality that has one more element than the last. This induces a function on the cardinalities. Moreover, Gelman and Gallistel's One-One principle (6a) would prohibit sequences that violate the successor function by looping around. For example, the One-One principle would prevent counting sequences such as "one, two, three, one, two, three, . . . " instead of "one, two, three, four, five, six, . . . " (though R. Gelman & Gallistel 1978, p. 132, do report children's occasional use of such sequences). Does this yield the structure of the natural numbers? Not necessarily, as we have no guarantee that the sequence will continue indefinitely. R. Gelman and Gallistel's (1978) original treatment may have assumed an innate sequence of mental count terms ("numerons") that do have the structure of the natural numbers and will therefore produce the correct successor function. But in that case, the structure of the numerons (along with the counting principles) is responsible for the natural number concept, not the How-to-Count principles alone.[14] This again goes along with the hunch that advanced counting, but not enumerating, is closely linked with knowledge of the natural numbers.

2.5.4 Competition among Schemas

The natural numbers are, of course, not the only structures that children are learning at this age. They must also cope with linear but finite sequences (e.g., the letters of the alphabet), circular structures (e.g., the days of the week or the hours of the day), partial orders (e.g., object tax-onomies or part-whole relations), and many others. In top-down learn-ing of the structure of the natural numbers, children must decide which of these schemas is the right one. Their preliminary numerical concepts cannot decide this, since simple counting and enumerating small, finite sets are compatible with several distinct structures. Finite linear lists and circular structures are both consistent with their experience, provided the number of elements in these structures is greater than the number they have so far encountered. For this reason, I suspect that external clues are probably necessary to determine the right alternative. We can expect children to be undecided about whether there is a last number or whether numbers circle back and to experiment with different schemas, as they sometimes do (Hartnett, 1991). What decides them in favor of a count-ably infinite sequence may be hints from parents or teachers (e.g., that there is no end to the numbers) or more implicit clues about the numer-als or arithmetic. Children are able to absorb this information because they already have access to schemas that are potentially relevant.

Once children know the right schema, they are in a position to make inferences about the natural numbers that would have seemed unwar-ranted earlier. These include the kinds of generalizations that we encoun-tered in Section 2.4: closure under addition, the property that any two numbers can be ordered under ≤, and many others. Likewise, they can infer new facts about the numerals, such as the existence of numerals beyond those in their current count list. There should be a burst of such inferences following children's discovery of the natural number schema, but current data about such properties are too thin to trace this time course.

What we do know is that adults have reliable intuitions about the structure of number systems. In a recent study, I presented to 36 college students the "number lines" in Figure 2.4a and asked them to rate the extent to which each could represent a possible number system. (Participants did not receive a definition of number system, but the instructions reminded them that they already knew number systems, such as the natural, real, and complex numbers.) The number lines varied in their structure and were simple lines (first row in Figure 2.4a), double lines (second row), forward-branching trees (third row), or backward-branching trees (fourth row). We told participants that numbers on parallel lines or branches could not be compared to each other but that numbers on the branches of the trees could be compared to numbers on their "trunks." The instructions also mentioned that if a line intersected the right side of the frame, the numbers continued indefinitely in the positive direction, and if it intersected the left side of the frame, the numbers continued indefinitely in the negative direction. Thus, the numbers could be unbounded (first column of Figure 2.4a), bounded below (second column), bounded above (third column), bounded in both directions (fourth column), or circular (fifth column).

The second part of the figure shows the mean ratings of these structures as possible number systems. The ratings (points in the figure) were significantly higher for the linear than for the bilinear structure, and higher for the bilinear structure than for either of the trees. Circular patterns produced lower ratings than other forms of bounding. To predict these results, we also collected participants' judgments about a group of mathematical properties that might be true of number systems. These included relational properties (associativity, commutativity, closure, density, and others, which we defined for the participants), the presence of particular arithmetic operations over the numbers (e.g., addition, multiplication, subtraction), and the presence of specific numbers (0, 1, positives, negatives, additive and multiplicative inverses). We asked participants to decide whether each property was true of each of the number lines

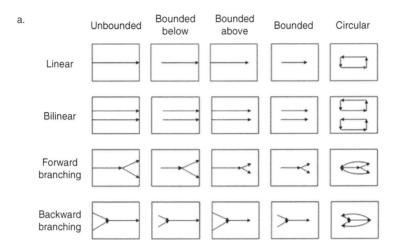

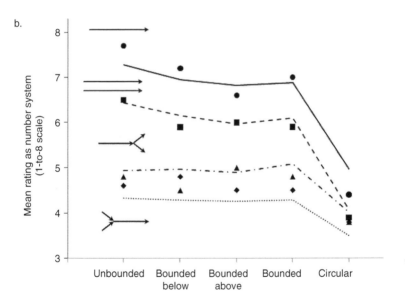

FIGURE 2.4 a. "Number lines" used as stimuli in a study of adults' intuitions about what constitutes a number system. b. Mean ratings of the extent to which each of the lines in Panel a could be number systems. The points indicate means from 36 participants. The lines are predictions from a regression model, including as predictors: whether the line supports commutativity, whether the line supports closure of arithmetic operations, and the perceptual complexity of the line. Circles and solid lines represent linear diagrams, squares and dashed lines represent bilinear diagrams, triangles and dashed-and-dotted lines represent forward branching diagrams, and diamonds and dotted lines backward branching diagrams.

and to rate the importance of the property in defining number systems. We also asked an independent group of participants to rate the perceptual complexity of the number lines. (These latter participants were not told that the lines represented numbers; they merely viewed the diagrams and rated their complexity.)

The results showed that some of the relational math properties did a very good job of predicting ratings of whether the lines could be number systems. To test the correlations, we multiplied the rated importance of a property by +1 if a participant said the property applied to a diagram, and we multiplied the importance by -1 if the participant said the property did not apply. In terms of these signed ratings, commutativity correlated highly (r = .95) with the ratings of the number lines, as did closure (r = .76).[15] As you might expect, perceptual complexity also correlated with the number-line ratings (r = .84). However, a regression containing commutativity, closure, and complexity as predictors found significant coefficients for only the first two. The predicted values from this regression appear as the lines in Figure 2.4b, and the model accounts for 94% of the variance among the means.

Participants are sensitive to the diagrams' implications for relational math properties, such as commutativity and closure. If a diagram is ambiguous about whether such an arithmetic property holds, participants give the diagram a low rating as a potential number system. This tends to favor linear and bilinear diagrams over branching or circular ones. Adding or subtracting on trees may lead to uncertainty about which branch to take, and adding or subtracting on circular structures may lead to uncertainty about what happens if the result loops around. Of course, these participants were college students and well-practiced in math with standard number systems, and we don't know when or how their intuitions emerge. But perhaps we can adapt diagrams like these to study children's thinking about numbers in a way that supplements research on enumerating and estimating. (See Siegler & Ramani, 2009, for recent work in this direction.)

2.5.5 Positing Numbers

As I mentioned at the beginning of this chapter, mathematical entities pose a special problem for psychology, because, on a realist theory, mathematical entities are abstract objects with no causal links to humans. We can't gain access to them through the usual sensory channels, since math entities produce no detectable traces.

Realism, however, is not an insurmountable obstacle for cognitive approaches. People may posit the existence of mathematical structures in much the same way they posit the existence of scientific but unobservable entities, such as black holes or 300-dimensional meaning spaces (Resnik, 1997). In fact, this type of positing with respect to mathematics arises in a natural way from math schemas. A schema for any nontrivial mathematical domain will not represent explicitly each of the infinitely many objects that the schema entails. Yet the way in which the schema presupposes the full set seems to invite exactly the kind of positing I am suggesting here. Positing, of course, does not bring such structures into existence (assuming that realism is true). There's no question, though, that people can make these posits, since many philosophers of mathematics have done so explicitly. It may or may not be revealing to describe nonspecialists as committing themselves to independent mathematical entities in the same way. The present point is simply that the possibility of realism for these entities is not inconsistent with (and in some ways goes hand in hand with) the type of approach I am sketching.

2.6 Concluding Comments

Thanks to analytic work by Dedekind (1888/1963), Frege (1884/1974), and others, we have a firm idea about the constituents of natural-number concepts. Psychological research on number, however, hasn't always taken advantage of these leads. I hope to refocus effort in this area by outlining a framework that can accommodate research on such issues. The math schema idea obviously doesn't amount to a full-fledged theory of people's knowledge of natural numbers, much less a theory for all mathematics, but I hope it points to the kind of information we need to fill in.

If this picture is roughly correct, though, it may have some radical consequences for current cognitive theory.[16] How does the number concept depend on object files, internal magnitudes, experience with concrete objects, and mental models or internal sets of such objects? A potential answer that I believe is consistent with the evidence is that there is no dependency whatever. The early representations may simply not be causally responsible for, or part of the meaning of, the adult concept of natural number.

You might view as a paradoxical consequence of this position that it cuts off some everyday numerical activities from the concept of number. Activities such as estimating the number of objects in a collection or even exactly enumerating these objects may proceed without drawing on natural number concepts. Number concepts may come into play only at a more abstract level—for example, in arithmetic—where the focus is on the numbers themselves rather than on physical objects. However, this means no more than that people can bring to bear different analyses in numerical contexts. Moreover, we need not view such a consequence as belittling either sort of activity or the research that targets them. Estimating and enumerating objects are well worth studying, even if they do not directly support number concepts. Number concepts are worth studying because of their role in mathematical reasoning, even if mathematical reasoning is not the whole of numerical cognition. Separating these forms of thinking clarifies their origins and interrelations. In particular, understanding the natural number concept may allow us to avoid trying to derive it from unwieldy raw material from which no such derivation is possible.

NOTES

The chapter originated from an earlier paper that I wrote with Amber Bloomfield and Jennifer Asmuth (Rips, Bloomfield, & Asmuth, 2008). I thank Susan Carey, Stella Christie, Lisa Feigenson, Dedre Gentner, Rochel Gelman, Susan Hespos, George Lakoff, Jeffrey Lidz, and Douglas Medin for their comments on earlier versions of this chapter. I also thank the Fulbright Foundation for providing the time during which this chapter was written and to the Psychology Department, Katholieke Universiteit Leuven, and its chairman, Paul De Boeck, for providing the space.

1. A representation is countable if its elements are either finite or can be paired one-to-one with the natural numbers. In the present chapter, the countable representations at issue will usually be infinite rather than finite.

2. Hilbert (1922/1996; 1926/1983) introduced strings of symbols like these as a basis for all mathematics. The strings were supposed to be "extralogical concrete objects which are intuited as directly experienced prior to all thinking" (1926/1983, p. 192). Because these strings are concrete and easily surveyable, Hilbert believed they provided a better foundation for numbers than more abstract items, such as sets. See, also, Resnik (1997, chap. 11) for a "quasi-historical" account of the development of Greek mathematics using strings of this kind.

3. According to this theory, liquids and other noncohesive items, such as sand, will not engage object files. Hence, infants will not treat puddles of water or piles of sand as individual objects, and they should not be surprised in addition-subtraction experiments if the wrong number of puddles or piles appears after the operations (Huntley-Fenner, Carey, & Solimando, 2002; Rosenberg & Carey, 2009). It seems possible that a magnitude mechanism could apply directly to the piles or puddles to keep track of the total amount of water or sand. If so, infants should be surprised by the wrong *amount* of stuff in these experiments, even if they aren't surprised by the wrong *number* of objects. However, current evidence appears to be inconsistent on this point. On the one hand, Hespos, Dora, Rips, and Christie (in press), Gao, Levine, and Huttenlocher (2000) and vanMarle (2004) provide evidence for infants' sensitivity to continuous amounts of substance, and vanMarle, Aw, McKrink, and Santos (2006) and Wood, Hauser, Glynn, and Barner (2008) report related findings for monkeys. On the other, Huntley-Fenner et al. (2002) and Rosenberg and Carey (2009) find no such evidence. (I'm grateful to Kaitlin Ainsworth and Rumen Iliev for pointing out this issue.)

4. Wood and Spelke (2005) point out, however, that such a device has difficulty explaining on its own why infants are unable to discriminate small numbers of nondistinctive items in addition-subtraction and habituation tasks. A parallel individuating process should presumably work as well or better in dealing with 1 versus 2 objects than in dealing with 8 versus 16.

Barth et al. (2003) and Wood and Spelke (2005) suggest instead that the number of objects (e.g., dots) in a large array is computed from the array's global properties, such as its area and density. Although some studies control both density (e.g., dots per square inch) and area (e.g., total number of square inches in the array), observers might compute the product of these quantities, which is a measure of the total number of dots. The issue here, however, rearises in the way in which observers calculate density. Observers could unconsciously count the number of dots and divide by the area to determine density and then use density in further computations, but this would beg the question of how they determine their initial count. However, if observers determine density by a truly global property—a sense of visual crowding in the display—then there is no reason to think that the proposed calculation could yield anything like a veridical measure of cardinality. The same sense of perceptual crowding that arises from a set of 40 dots in an area of 150 cm² could also come from one irregularly shaped strand, weaving back and forth within the same area. Although the magnitude system may deliver approximate measures of cardinality, it cannot deliver arbitrary measures. If the density that is input to the computation is based on visual crowding and is the same for a one-item strand as for a 40-dot array, then the output of the computation will be unable to distinguish one item from 40.

A third alternative for computing density is sampling. If the items to be enumerated were evenly spaced (e.g., dots on a line at equal intervals), then density could be calculated from a single interval between an item and its neighbor. (Church & Broadbent, 1990, suggest such an algorithm for evenly spaced tones.) In experiments with large numbers of visual elements, however, the displays randomly distribute the elements. Using a fixed number of elements to calculate density would, in general, lead to widely varying estimates of the same cardinality. (See also Bemis, Franconeri, & Alvarez, 2008, for empirical evidence against sampling.) Barth et al. (2003) and Wood and Spelke (2005) may be right that people use global properties of large displays to determine approximate cardinality, but further research is necessary to determine whether such a procedure is both a reasonable guide to cardinality and consistent with the discrimination data.

5. Modifications to the Figure 2.3 model would also be needed to capture effects of chunking or grouping on enumeration. First, data from Halberda, Sires, and Feigenson (2006) suggest that adults can simultaneously group up to three subsets of dots based on color and can enumerate each subset separately using the magnitude system. Thus, the attentional mechanisms in the first part of Figure 2.3 must be able to partition items on the basis of color (and presumably other low-level visual properties) in addition to individuating items within the groups. This could be handled in Dehaene and Changeux's (1993) system by coding for (a limited number of) colors in addition to item location and size. Second, the upper tracks of the system can assign representations to groups or chunks, as well as to objects. Wynn, Bloom, and Chiang (2002) found that 5-month-olds are sensitive to the number of groups (2 vs. 4) of dots in a habituation task, where each group was a small set of dots moving in a swarm. Likewise, Feigenson and Halberda (2004) found that infants can succeed in an addition-subtraction task with four objects if these objects initially appeared in two spatially separated groups of two. This suggests that Figure 2.3 should frame the division between the upper and lower tracks in terms of number of chunks, rather than in terms of number of objects. Finally, Figure 2.3 is aimed at the way infants enumerate

visually presented objects that appear simultaneously. Further mechanisms would be necessary to explain infants' ability to deal with auditorily presented elements and other sequences.

6. A magnitude system of this sort would yield only a single output at a time, so one could think of magnitude addition as a three-place function of two addends and a time. This would preserve magnitude addition as a function. In such a system, however, the sum of two numbers would differ from one instant to the next (i.e., $+(5, 7, t) \neq +(5, 7, t + \Delta)$), whereas real number addition is constant over time. Any way you look at it, arithmetic with mental magnitudes lacks some of the familiar properties of arithmetic with reals. In particular, real-number addition does not have time as a parameter. (Similar considerations affect the suggestion that the output of magnitude addition is a unique distribution of values.)

7. Perhaps we could draw the same moral from the fact that, although natural-language semantics seems to depend heavily on Boolean operations, such as union and intersection (e.g., Chierchia & McConnell-Ginet, 1990), it seems to depend less heavily on specifically arithmetic operations, such as addition and multiplication (except, of course, for sentences that are explicitly about numbers).

8. Current neuropsychological evidence is also potentially relevant to the relation between language and number, but these results are partially conflicting and difficult to interpret. On the one hand, a close connection between calculation and language goes along with fMRI and ERP data showing activation of the left inferior frontal region (implicated in verbal association tasks) during exact calculation. Tasks involving numerical approximation recruit instead the bilateral intraparietal lobes (Dehaene, Spelke, Pinel, Stanescu, & Tsivkin, 1999). On the other hand, there appear to be empirical dissociations between linguistic and calculation abilities. For example, Rossor, Warrington, and Cipolotti (1995) and Varley, Klessinger, Romanowski, and Siegal (2005) describe global aphasic patients who are nevertheless able to perform correctly on written addition, subtraction, and multiplication problems, including those that depend on structural grouping (e.g., $50 - [(4 + 7) \times 4] =?$). There are also clinical cases of relatively normal language development with little numerical ability (Grinstead, MacSwan, Curtiss, & Gelman, 2005). It may be too early to draw any strong conclusions from the results of such studies.

9. One complaint about this argument (Margolis & Laurence, 2008) is that it incorrectly assumes that children treat the small number terms (e.g., "one") in (3) as ambiguous or as not truly denoting the corresponding number. This is because children would have to revise the denotations later when they find that "one" can also denote eleven, twenty-one, and so on, in case they find themselves learning the mod_{10} system. However, we can easily formulate the

argument without such an assumption: Imagine that what the child is learning is not the natural numbers, but a system in which the numerals loop back *after* the numerals that the child has already learned. For example, suppose the child is able to recite the count sequence to "nine." Suppose, too, the child is learning a system in which "one" denotes one, "two" two, ..., and "nine" nine, but "ten" denotes ten, twenty, thirty, etc., "eleven" denotes eleven, twenty-one, thirty-one, etc., and "nineteen" denotes nineteen, twenty-nine, etc. Of course, you could also hold that children are unable to learn a cyclical system of this sort, but this claim flies in the face of their success in learning the days of the week, the months of the year, the notes of a musical scale, and other such circular lists (see Rips et al., 2008). Finally, you could assert that, prior to making the inference in (4), children not only know that the first three numerals have fixed designations, but they also know that no looping in the numeral sequence is possible (the sequence continues without end) and that nothing other than the "$s(n)$" sequence can be a numeral. But such knowledge implies that the child's numerals already satisfy the axioms for the natural numbers (see Section 2.5.3). The inference in (4) maps these numerals onto cardinalities, but the child already has a representation of the natural numbers before performing the inference. This latter idea, however, is something that most psychologists deny, as I've mentioned in Section 2.2.1.

10. There is current debate in linguistic semantics and pragmatics as to whether noun phrases like "two dogs" denote exactly two dogs, at least two dogs, or an indeterminate meaning that is decided by context. The lower-bounded (at least two) sense can be obtained from (5) by omitting the last conjunct. I take no stand on the correct interpretation here, though such issues may become important if the child's understanding of number depends on knowledge of the natural-language count terms. See Carston (1998) and Musolino (2004) for accounts of this debate.

11. The distinction between numerical concepts and concepts of number partially resembles others that have appeared in the literature on number development. R. Gelman (1972; R. Gelman & Gallistel, 1978, chap. 10), for example, separates children's ability to determine the number of elements in a collection from their ability to reason about the resulting cardinality. For instance, deciding that there are three books in one pile and five in another requires enumerating the books, but deciding that the two piles have different numbers of books is a matter of numerical reasoning in Gelman's terminology. The distinction I'm driving at here, however, differs in that even numerical reasoning (in Gelman's sense) does not necessarily involve concepts of number. We can determine that two piles have different numbers of books by employing concrete representations of books rather than representations of number. Compare this judgment with the idea that five is greater than three, which *does*

seem to require concepts of numbers. Closer to the present distinction is Gelman and Gallistel's account of numerical versus algebraic reasoning: "Numerical reasoning deals with representations of specific numerosities. Algebraic reasoning deals with relations between unspecified numerosities" (R. Gelman & Gallistel, 1978, p. 230). However, even algebraic reasoning is about the cardinalities of physical objects rather than about numbers themselves. R. Gelman and Gallistel (1978, p. 236) do note, however, "the conceivable existence of another stage of development . . . . In this stage arithmetic is no longer limited to dealing with representations of numerosity. It now deals with that ethereal abstraction called number."

12. For recent debate about what the "How many?" task reveals about children's numerical competence, see Cordes and Gelman (2005) and Le Corre et al. (2006); however, the present point is independent of these more empirical issues. See also Carey and Sarnecka (2006) for cautions about inferring a type of number concept from experimental evidence.

13. The results on commutativity also seem to hold of other mathematical principles, though the data are much more incomplete. A second example is an understanding of the additive inverse principle (in the form: $a + b - b = a$), first studied by Starkey and Gelman (1982). Until they are about 4 years old, children are not able to appreciate the inverse relation between addition and subtraction in an addition-subtraction task (Vilette, 2002, Experiment 1). Although practice observing the counteracting effects of adding and subtracting the same number of concrete objects helps 3-year-olds perform more accurately, the benefit is no greater than that of observing the separate effects of addition and of subtraction (Vilette, 2002, Experiment 2). This suggests that successful children initially deal with the inverse relation $a + b - b$ by literally adding and then subtracting b objects. By contrast, 4- to 5-year-olds recognize the answers to such problems more easily than comparable ones of the form $a + b - c$ that don't allow them to use the inverse relation as a short cut (Bryant, Christie, & Rendu, 1999; Rasmussen, Ho, & Bisanz, 2003). In the latter studies, the terms of the problems are given in numeric form (with or without objects present), and children provide numeric answers (e.g., "How many invisible men do we have if we start with 14, add 7 more, and then take away 7?"). The gap between the performance of younger and older children makes it reasonable to conjecture that awareness of the inverse principle depends on some prior (but not necessarily school-taught) arithmetic.

14. I thank Susan Carey for pointing out the relevance of the How to Count principles in this context.

15. We defined *closure* in the following way: "If # is an operation defined on [a set of numbers] S, x # y is also in S for any x and y in S."

16. Another consequence of this position concerns the relation between logical reasoning and mathematics. I've argued that math concepts may depend on an underlying cognitive framework that includes recursion. Typical production systems for handling problem spaces (e.g., J. R. Anderson, 1983; Newell, 1990) also include limited logical abilities for dealing with conditionals and conjunctions and for instantiating or binding variables. The usual form of a production rule is: "If Condition$_1$ and Condition$_2$ and . . . and Condition$_k$ then take action A," in which mental action A occurs (e.g., a symbol is stored in working memory) if Conditions 1–k are met by the current contents of memory. Although there are competing cognitive architectures (e.g., connectionist ones), production systems and other classical systems have an advantage of providing basic resources like these that mathematical reasoning can build on. Much the same can be said about the resources that people need for explicit deductive reasoning in tasks that depend on logical connectives and quantifiers. I've suggested (Rips, 1994, 1995a) that certain aspects of explicit deductive reasoning (e.g., rules like modus ponens) are especially natural because they're inherited directly from this background architecture. Work in the foundations of mathematics appears to show that attempts to reduce mathematics to logic are problematic at best (see Giaquinto, 2002, for a review), and there is no reason to suppose that mathematical reasoning can be reduced to logical reasoning in any simpler way. But the current perspective suggests, nonetheless, that there may be important indirect connections between them, due to their very tight dependence on a common pool of cognitive resources. I know few systematic attempts in psychology to trace the relations between logical and mathematical thought (see Houdé & Tzourio-Mazoyer, 2003, for a start), but there is every reason to try to do so. See Chapter 6 in this book for further discussion of logical reasoning.

3

Causes

It's just one damn thing after another. After forgetting to open the garage door this morning, I backed my car into the door, splintering it. The actions I perform cause other events—my backing up caused the splintering. But events of other kinds—nonactions—have their effects too. With no help from me, last night's storm caused a branch to fall from a tree, putting a hole in my roof.

Much as we might like to forget them, we often keep track of events like these and the causes that unite them. Although we might not have predicted these events, we can remember and reconstruct the causal sequences after they occur. If the Causal Continuer theory of Chapter 1 is correct, we use these causal sequences to follow from moment to moment the identity of objects, including our own history and those of others. We also remember fictional stories in terms of the causal changes that compose their main plot line, remembering less about events falling on dead-end side plots (Trabasso & Sperry, 1985). We sometimes attribute causal powers to concrete objects as well as to events, but we can understand this sort of talk as an abbreviation for event causation. If Fred caused the glass to break that's because one of Fred's actions—maybe his dropping it—caused the breaking. I'll take event causation as basic in this chapter on the strength of such paraphrases.

We remember causes and effects for event types as well as for event tokens. Slamming heavy objects into more fragile ones typically causes the fragile items damage; repeating phone numbers four or five times typically causes us to remember them temporarily. Negotiating routine events (e.g., Schank & Abelson, 1977), constructing explanations (e.g., Lewis, 1986), and making predictions all require memory for causal relations among event categories. Causal generalities underlie our concepts of individual objects, as we observed in Chapter 1, but they also unite individuals into natural kinds, like daisies and diamonds, an idea we will pursue in Chapter 4 (e.g., Ahn & Kim, 2000; Barton & Komatsu, 1989; S. A. Gelman & Wellman, 1991; Keil, 1989; Rehder & Hastie, 2001;

Rips, 1989, 2001). Our knowledge of how beliefs and desires cause actions in other people props up our own social activities (e.g., A. M. Leslie, Friedman, & German, 2004; Wellman, 1990).

The importance of causality is no news. Neither are the psychological facts that we attribute causes to events, remember the causes later, and reason about them—although, as usual, controversy surrounds the details of these mental activities. Traditional psychological approaches to causality assume that we acquire causal information by extracting it from our experience of events. One possibility is that we can directly perceive causality (or can use a specialized perceptual module) to detect causal interactions. Another possibility is that we infer causality from correlational evidence—the co-occurrence of particular causes and effects. But for reasons we're about to review in Section 3.1, these purely bottom-up solutions are unlikely to succeed. Thus, the moral of the first part of this chapter will parallel that of Chapter 2: Don't count on getting from perceptual information to the more abstract concepts that embody numbers and causality.

One new approach to causal cognition that may alleviate these difficulties comes from research on Bayes nets in computer science (Pearl, 2000) and philosophy of science (Spirtes, Glymour, & Scheines, 2000). Many cognitive psychologists view the development of Bayes nets as an important breakthrough: For example, "until recently no one has been able to frame the problem [of causality]; the discussion of causality was largely based on a framework developed in the eighteenth century. But that's changed. Great new ideas about how to represent causal systems and how to learn and reason about them have been developed by philosophers, statisticians, and computer scientists" (Sloman, 2005, p. vii). And at a psychological level, "we argue that these kinds of representations [of children's knowledge of causal structure] and learning mechanisms can be perspicuously understood in terms of the normative mathematical formalism of directed graphical causal models, more commonly known as Bayes nets . . . . This formalism provides a natural way of representing causal structure, and it provides powerful tools for accurate prediction and effective intervention" (Gopnik et al., 2004, p. 4).

Bayes nets have several features that recommend them for cognitive purposes, so Section 3.2 examines their pluses and minuses. Here's the gloomy picture: The new methods are at heart data-analytic procedures for summarizing or approximating a bunch of correlations. In this respect, they're a bit like factor analysis and a lot like structural equation modeling. (If you think it surprising that psychologists would seize on a statistical procedure as a model for ordinary causal thinking, consider that another prominent theory in this area is Kelley's, 1967, ANOVA model; see Section 3.1.2, and Gigerenzer, 1991.) The idea that people use these methods to induce and represent causality flies in the face of evidence suggesting that people aren't much good at normatively correct statistical computations of this sort (e.g., A. Tversky & Kahneman, 1980). Offhand, it's much more likely that people have qualitative and error-prone representations of what causes what.

The rosier picture is the one about "great new ideas." Bayes nets provide a way of incorporating information about experimental manipulation or intervention, and so they go beyond slavish reliance on perception or correlation. As another plus, some versions of Bayes nets take a top-down approach that goes beyond mere statistical regularities. Bayes nets contain some of the structural characteristics that seem necessary in understanding people's concept of causality.

The jury is still out, and I won't be resolving this issue here. But sorting out the claims for the new causal representations highlights some important questions about the nature of causal thinking. It will also help fill in the causal view of object concepts from Chapter 1 and the similar view of natural-kind concepts that we will take up in the next chapter.

3.1 How Are Causal Relations Given to Us?

Here's a sketch of how a CD player works (according to Macaulay, 1988): A motor rotates a spindle that rotates the CD. As the CD turns, a laser sends a beam of light through a set of mirrors and lenses onto the CD's surface. The light beam lands on a track composed of reflecting and nonreflecting segments that have been burned onto the CD. The reflecting segments bounce the light beam back to a photodiode that registers a digital "on" signal; the nonreflecting segments don't bounce the light back and represent an "off" signal. The pattern of digital signals is then converted into a stereo electrical signal for playback.

You could remember this information in something like the form I just gave you—an unexciting little narrative about CD players. But the new psychological approach to causal knowledge favors directed graphs like Figure 3.1 as mental representations—"causal maps" of the environment (Gopnik et al., 2004). This graph contains nodes that stand for event types (e.g., one node represents the state of the CD player's motor as rotating or not rotating, another represents the CD turning or not turning). Directed links stand for direct causal connections between these events (the motor rotating causes the CD's turning; the laser producing a beam and the mirror-lens assembly focusing the beam jointly cause the beam to hit the CD's surface). Of course, no one disputes the fact that people can remember some of the information these diagrams embody. Although people can be overconfident about their knowledge of mechanical devices like this one (Rozenblit & Keil, 2002), they're

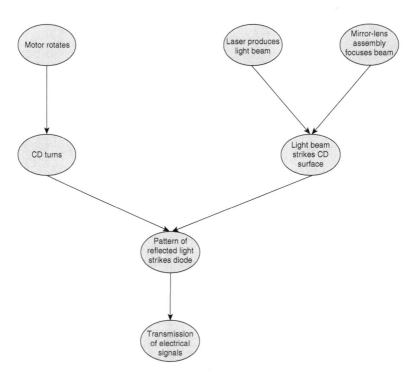

FIGURE 3.1 A directed graph representing the operation of a CD player, based on text by Macaulay (1988).

nevertheless capable of learning, say, that the CD player's motor causes the CD to turn. What's not so clear is how they acquire this cause-effect information, how they put the component facts together, and how they make inferences from such facts.

In this section, I'll consider the acquisition problem, deferring issues of representation and inference until the second part of this chapter. I concentrate on the possibility that people learn about causes and effects by observing and operating on their environment. Perhaps we can perceive interactions as causal, at least in the case of simple physical events, such as one object bumping into another. Perhaps we can infer cause-effect relations by remembering correlations between events and extracting probable causes from this pattern. Or perhaps we can discover causes by manipulating events or observing others' manipulations. As already hinted, I'll be suggesting that none of these strategies is likely to work if they operate in a purely bottom-up way. Identifying causes requires a healthy dose of theory to direct our search. We can't understand these abstract matters unless the appropriate schemas are already in place.

3.1.1 Causation in Perception

You're not likely to get much of the information in Figure 3.1 by passively observing a CD player, unless you already know about the nature of similar devices. But sometimes you do get an impression of cause from seeing objects move. Repeated sightings of an event of type E_1 followed by an event of type E_2 may provide evidence that E_1 causes E_2. Rather weak evidence, but evidence nonetheless. When we later see an example of the same sequence, we can infer the causal link. But psychologists sometimes claim there is a more intimate perception of cause in which an observer directly experiences one event causing another.

3.1.1.1 Perceptual Studies

In a famous series of demonstrations, Michotte (1963) rigged a display in which a square appeared to move toward a second square and to stop abruptly when they touched. If the second square then began to move within a fixed interval of the touching and at a speed similar to that of the first square, observers reported that the first square caused the second to move, *launching* it.[1]

Michotte's extensive experiments aimed to isolate the purely perceptual conditions that produce this immediate impression of causality, but there's a paradoxical quality to his efforts. The first square in the display doesn't actually cause the second to move. The display showed a 2-D projection of simple geometrical forms whose movements could be carefully controlled behind the scenes. (In those days before lab computers, Michotte engagingly created his displays using striped disks rotating behind slits or using pairs of moving slide projectors. Both then and now, however, it is obvious to observers in such experiments that they are not watching actual causal interactions.) Michotte's goal was therefore not to determine when people correctly detect causal relations in their environment but instead to uncover the cues that lead them to report causality.[2] Michotte himself discusses a number of situations in which people report one event causing another, even though the interaction is physically unlikely or impossible. In one such case, a square A moves at 30 cm/s and contacts another square B, which is already moving at 15 cm/s. If A comes to a halt and B moves off at a *slower* pace than before (7.5 cm/s), observers report a causal effect. "Such cases are particularly interesting in that they show that causal impressions arise as soon as the psychological conditions of structural organization are fulfilled, and indeed that they can arise even in situations where we know from past experience that a causal impression is a downright impossibility" (Michotte, 1963, p. 71). Michotte's project attempted to explain these causal impressions in noncausal terms: His descriptions of the crucial stimulus conditions don't presuppose one object causally influencing another. He believed that people's impression of causality arises as their perceptual systems try to resolve a conflict (e.g., in the launching event) between the initial view of the first square moving and the second square stationary and the final view of the first square stationary and the second moving. The resolution is to see the movement of the first object extending to the second, which Michotte called "ampliation of the movement" (which, I hope, sounds better in French).

Michotte (1963, pp. 351–352) believed that this resolution "enables us to understand why, when such a structure is established, participants can communicate adequately what they perceive only by saying that they *see* the [initially moving] object make the second go forward." How so? An obvious answer would be that this perceptual situation is similar to one real objects produce when they undergo causal interactions. The resolution that takes place in the experimental displays reminds the observers, perhaps unconsciously, of what happens when they view causal comings and goings in the ordinary environment, and they therefore interpret it the same way. But this answer is one Michotte rejects, since he consistently denies that the launching effect is due to acquired knowledge. This is why physically impossible cases, like the one described in the preceding paragraph, are important to him: They seem to rule out the possibility that observers are making an inference to causality based on experience.

The easiest way to understand Michotte's theory (though not in terms he used) is as the claim that people have a built-in causality detector, which is triggered by the conditions he attempted to describe. (For similar interpretations of Michotte in terms of Fodor's, 1983, perceptual input modules, see Leslie, 1986; Saxe & Carey, 2006; and Scholl & Tremoulet, 2000.) Since the detector is presumably innate, its operations don't depend on learning from previous experience. Moreover, the detector responds reliably but not perfectly. Toads dart at insects in their visual fields but can be tricked into darting at moving black-on-white or white-on-black spots, according to the old ethology chestnut (e.g., Ewert, 1974). In the same way, whenever the movement of an object "extends" to a second, people receive the impression of causality, whether or not the first object actually causes the second to move.

But this approach, like some moving spots, is hard to swallow. Although Michotte stressed that observers spontaneously report the events in causal language—for example, "the first square pushed the second"—the impression of causality doesn't seem as immediate or automatic as typical perceptual illusions. We can't help but see the apparent difference in line length in the Muller-Lyer illusion or the apparently bent lines in the Poggendorff and Hering figures (see, e.g., Gregory, 1978, for illustrations of these). And toads, as far as we know, can't help but unleash their tongues at moving specks. But Michotte's demonstrations allow more interpretative leeway.

Suppose Michotte was right that people possess an innate detector that's tuned broadly enough to be triggered by the displays his participants report as causal. The detector, of course, produces false positive responses to some displays that are actually noncausal (e.g., Michotte's displays), and it produces false negative or nonresponses to some causal ones (e.g., reflections of electro-magnetic rays in an invisible part of the spectrum). So what the detector detects is not (all or only) causal interactions but perhaps something more like abrupt transitions or discontinuities in the speed of two visible objects at the point at which they meet. This would include both the normal launching cases and the causally unlikely or impossible ones, such as slowing on impact. (Michotte might not have agreed with my specific characterization, but this general type of description should have been okay with him. Remember: his goal was to isolate the stimulus conditions that produce an impression of causation.) Nor do we ultimately take the output of the detector as indicating the presence of a causal interaction. In the case of Michotte's demos, for example, we conclude that no real causal interaction takes place between the squares, at least when we become aware of what's going on behind the smoke and mirrors. The issue of whether we *see* causality in the displays, then, is whether there's an intermediate stage between the detector and our ultimate judgment, a stage that is both relevantly perceptual and also carries a causal verdict. Because these two requirements pull in opposite directions, the claim that we can see causality is unstable.

Here's an analogy that may help highlight the issue. People viewing a cartoon car, like the ones in the Disney film *Cars*, immediately "see" the cartoon as a car (and report it as a car), despite the fact that it is physically impossible for cars to talk, to possess eyes and mouths, and to move in the flexible way that cartoon cars do. Although I don't recommend it, you could probably spend your career pinning down the parameter space (e.g., length-to-width ratios) within which this impression of carness occurs. But there isn't enough evolutionary time since the invention of cars in the nineteenth century for us to have evolved innate car detectors. The fact that we immediately recognize cartoons as cars even when they possess physically impossible properties can't be evidence for innate car perception. Michotte's evidence seems no stronger as support for innate cause detection. Although the issue is an empirical one, I'm willing to bet that the impression of carness generated by the cartoon cars is at least as robust as the impression of causality generated by launching displays.

A similar example comes from work by Heider and Simmel (1944), which overviews of event perception often group with Michotte's (e.g., D. R. Proffitt & Kaiser, 1995; Shiffrar, 2001). These investigators sought the stimulus conditions that give rise to impressions of people's actions and motives. (The emphasis on stimulus conditions rather than accuracy follows Michotte.) To do this, they presented participants with animations of geometric shapes (a big triangle, a little triangle, and a circle) moving in and about a larger rectangle, one of whose sides could open or close (see the source mentioned in Note 1 for an online demonstration). Most participants viewing this film interpreted it as if the shapes were people and their movements were actions (e.g., two individuals fighting or one individual chasing the other two). Participants also attributed to the shapes a range of emotions and motives, such as anger, fear, and frustration. As far as one can tell from reading Heider and Simmel's report, these impressions were as immediate as were the impressions of launching in Michotte's experiments. But do we want to say that the impressions of, for example, chasing and frustration are due to innate detectors? Heider and Simmel make no such claims. As they point out, the stimulus conditions that give rise to a chasing interpretation are ambiguous: If shapes A and B are moving one behind the other with A in front, then A could be leading B or B could be chasing A. The interpretation depends on whether A or B is the agent of the action. But observers can't determine which item is the agent from the immediate perceptual input; instead, it depends on what Heider and Simmel describe as "surrounding data"—that is, on contextual information.

Causality is an inherently abstract relation—one that holds not only between moving physical objects but also between subatomic particles, galaxies, and lots in the middle—and this abstractness makes it difficult to come up with a plausible theory that would have us perceiving it directly, as opposed to inferring it from more concrete perceived information.[3] There's no clear way to defeat the idea that "when we consider these objects with the utmost attention, we find only that the one body approaches the other; and the motion of it precedes that of the other without any sensible interval" (Hume, 1739/1967, p. 77).[4]

3.1.1.2 Dissociation Between Perceived and Inferred Causality

Recent evidence suggests that people's perceptual judgments about causality are independent of some of the inferences they make about cause.[5] Investigators have taken these dissociations to suggest that Michotte (1963) was right that perceived causality is an innate module. One such study (Roser, Fugelsang, Dunbar, Corballis, & Gazzaniga, 2005) employed two split-brain patients, presenting causal tasks to the patients' right or left hemispheres. In one task, the patients saw Michotte-type launching events that varied: (a) the spatial gap between the two objects at the moment the second object began to move, and (b) the time-delay between the point at which the first object stopped and the second object began moving. Both spatial gaps and time delays tend to weaken the impression of perceived causality in normal participants. And so they did in the split-brain patients, but with an important qualification. The patients' task was to choose whether the first object appeared to cause the second to move or whether the second object moved on its own, and their positive "cause" judgments were more frequent when there was no delay and no gap. This difference appeared, however, only when the patients' right hemisphere processed the display. Left-hemisphere processing showed no difference between conditions. A second task asked the same split-brain patients to solve a problem in which they had to use the statistical co-occurrence between visually presented events to decide which of two switches caused a light to come on. Patients were more often correct in this task when the displays presented the information to their left hemispheres than when they presented it to their right hemispheres.

Split-brain patients may process causal information in atypical ways, but investigators have found similar dissociations with normal participants. Schlottmann and Shanks (1992, Experiment 2) varied the temporal gap within launching events (as in Roser et al., 2005) and also the contingency that existed across trials between whether the first object moved and whether the second object moved. On some series of trials, the first object's moving was necessary and sufficient for the second object to move; on others, the second object could move independently of the first. Participants made two types of judgments on separate trials within these series: how convincing a particular collision appeared and whether the collisions were necessary for the second object to move. Schlottmann and Shanks found an effect of delay but no effect of contingency on judgments of the display's perceptual convincingness. Judgments of necessity, however, showed a big effect of contingency and a much smaller effect of delay.

These dissociations suggest—what should become clear in the course of this chapter—that causal thinking is not of one piece. Some causal judgments depend vitally on detailed perceptual processing, while others depend more heavily on schemas, rules, probabilities, and other higher-order factors. What's not so clear is whether the dissociations also clinch the case for a perceptual causality detector. The right hemisphere of one of Roser et al.'s (2005) split-brain patients could assess the perceptual quality of launching events even though it was unable to evaluate the impact of statistical dependencies. But this leaves room for the influence of other inferences on judgments about launching. Suppose, for example, that the launching judgments depend on whether observers are reminded of similar real-world interactions of objects. Unless the right hemisphere is unable to process these reminders, inference of this sort could still influence decisions about launchings. Similarly, Schlottmann and Shanks's (1992) finding shows that observers can ignore long-run probabilities in assessing the convincingness of a particular collision, but not that they ignore prior knowledge of analogous physical interactions (see Schlottman, 2000, for a careful assessment).

3.1.1.3 Studies of Infants

Developmental studies might also yield evidence relevant to Michotte's claim. If the ability to recognize causation is innate, we should find infants able to discriminate causal from noncausal situations. In fact, by about six or seven months, infants are surprised by events that violate certain causal regularities (Kotovsky & Baillargeon, 2000; A. M. Leslie, 1984; A. M. Leslie & Keeble, 1987; Oakes, 1994). In one such study, for example, Kotovsky and Baillargeon first showed 7-month-olds static displays containing a cylinder and a toy bug, either with a barrier separating them (no-contact condition) or with a partial barrier that did not separate them (contact condition). Figure 3.2 displays these two conditions at the left and right, respectively. A screen then hid the position that contained the barrier or

Familiarization, no contact
condition

Familiarization, contact
condition

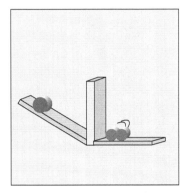
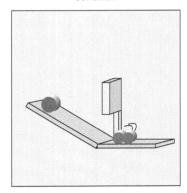

Test trial

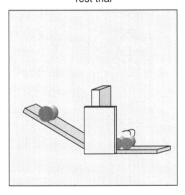

FIGURE 3.2 Familiarization and test conditions from Kotovsky and Baillargeon (2000).

partial barrier. In the experiment's test phase, the infants saw the cylinder roll down a ramp and go behind the screen, as shown at the bottom of Figure 3.2. The screen hid what would be the point of impact, but if the bug moved as if the cylinder had struck it, the infants looked longer in the no-contact than in the contact condition. If the bug failed to move, infants showed the opposite pattern of looking.

At seven months, then, infants appear to discriminate some cases in which simple launching events will and won't occur, but should we take this as evidence for innate perception of causality? Unfortunately, no evidence exists that would allow us to compare directly the class of interactions that Michotte's participants report as causal with the class infants react to. We don't know, for example, whether the "impossible" displays that Michotte's observers judge to be causal are also ones to which infants give special attention. What we do know, however, is that infants take longer than seven months to recognize causal interactions even slightly more complex than simple launching. For example, at seven months they fail to understand situations in which one object causes another to move in a path other than dead ahead, situations that adults see as causal (Oakes, 1994).

If the classes of interactions that adults and infants perceive as causal are not the same, this weakens the evidence for innate causality detectors. You could maintain that the perceptual impression of causality changes with experience, beginning from an innate starting point of very simple causal percepts, such as dead-on launchings. But this opens the door to objections to the very idea of perceiving cause. If learning can influence what we see as a causal interaction, then top-down factors—beliefs and expectations—can affect these impressions. Perhaps the learning in question is extremely local and low-level. But if not—if observers' impressions of cause change because of general learning mechanisms—then the impressions are a matter of inference rather than due to innate causality detectors. Much the same can be said about evidence that seven-month-olds' reaction to launching events depends on whether the objects are animate or inanimate (e.g., Kotovsky & Baillargeon, 2000). The animacy distinction goes beyond the spatiotemporal parameters Michotte isolated (see Saxe & Carey, 2006, for a review).

Uncertainty about causality detectors needn't affect the claim that the *concept* of causality is innate. This latter claim seems quite plausible, for reasons we will get to in Section 3.2.1.1. Children may have such a concept but be initially unsure to what perceptual data it applies. Moreover, nonperceptual, as well as perceptual, data may trigger such a concept. In fact, most theories of causality in psychology have avoided tying cause to specifically perceptual information. These theories take seriously the other aspect of Hume's (1739/1967) view, tying judgments of causality to the co-occurrence of events. Does recent research shed any light on this possibility?

3.1.2 Causation from Correlation

Even if we can literally perceive causality in some situations, we have
to resort to indirect methods in most. A careful look at a CD player's
innards can't disclose the causal link between the reflected pattern of
light and the transmission of sound signals at the bottom of Figure 3.1.
We may see the reflected light and hear the resulting sound, but we don't
have perceptual access to the connection between them. Similarly, we
can't see atmospheric pressure influencing the boiling point of a liquid
or a virus producing a flu symptom or other people's beliefs motivating
their actions. Experiments in science would be unnecessary if all we had
to do to isolate a causal mechanism is look.

Scientists, of course, aren't the only ones in need of hidden causal
facts. We need to predict how others will behave if we want to enlist
them in moving a sofa. We need to know what buttons to press if we
want to make a cell phone call or record an opera broadcast or adjust the
drying cycle to keep from scorching our socks. We need to know which
foods are likely to trigger our allergy, which windows are best for which
plants, which greetings will produce another greeting versus a stunned
silence or a slap in the face. We can sometimes rely on experts to tell us
about the hidden causes. Allergists are often good on allergies, botanists
on plants, and Miss Manners on manners. But sometimes we have to
proceed on our own, and the question is how ordinary people cope with
the task of recognizing causal relationships when they can't look them
up. The answer that psychologists have traditionally given to this question
is that people operate from bottom up, observing the temporal co-
occurrence of events and making an inductive inference to a causal
connection. They might passively register the presence or absence of a
potential cause and its effects or they may actively intervene, pressing
some buttons to see what happens. In either case, they decide whether a
cause-effect link is present on the basis of these results. This section
considers the more passive route to discovering causes, and the next
section looks at the more active one.

3.1.2.1 Cause, Contrast, Correlation

If we suspect event type C causes event type E, we should expect
to find E present when C is present and E absent when C is absent.

This correlation might not be inevitable even if C really is a cause of E. Perhaps E has an alternative cause C′; so E could appear without C. Or perhaps C is only a contributing cause, requiring C″ in order to produce E; then C could appear without E. But if we can sidestep these possibilities or are willing to define *cause* in a way that eliminates them, then a correlation between C and E may provide evidence of a causal relation.

Codifying this idea, Mill (1874) proposed a series of well-known rules or canons for isolating the cause (or effect) of a phenomenon. The best known of these canons are the method of agreement and the method of difference. Suppose you're looking for the cause of event type E. To proceed by the method of agreement, you should find a set of situations in which E occurs. If cause C also occurs in all these situations but no other potential cause does, then C causes E. To use the method of difference, which Mill regarded as more definitive, you should find two situations that hold constant all but one potential cause, C, of E. If E is present when C is present, and E is absent when C is absent, then C causes E.

Psychologists have mostly followed Mill's canons in their textbooks and courses on scientific methods.[6] If you're a victim of one of those courses, you won't find it surprising that psychological theories of how nonscientists go about determining cause-effect relations reflect the same notions:

> The inference as to where to locate the dispositional properties responsible for the effect is made by interpreting the raw data . . . in the context of subsidiary information from experiment-like variations of conditions. A näive version of J. S. Mills' method of difference provides the basic analytic tool. The effect is attributed to that condition which is present when the effect is present and which is absent when the effect is absent (Kelley, 1967, p. 194).

As an example (similar to one from Cheng & Novick, 1990), suppose you know that Calvin danced the tango last Thursday. To find out the cause of this dancing event, you need to examine potential causes that the outcome suggests: Maybe it was a disposition of Calvin's, maybe it was the tango's allure, or maybe it was something about the occasion that caused this specific instance of dancing. To figure out which of these potential causes was at work, you mentally design a study in which the three causes are factors (independent variables). The design will look something like what's in Table 3.1. You then populate the cells of this table with data you retrieve from memory or from further experience. Table 3.1 contains some hypothetical data, with the 1's standing for somebody dancing on a particular occasion, and the 0's standing for no dancing. If the pattern of data looks like what's in Table 3.1a, then Calvin dances on all occasions, whether it's the tango or some other type of dance, but other people never do. We have an effect for the person (Calvin vs. others) but no effects for either the occasion or the type of dance; so we might conclude that the reason Calvin danced the tango on this occasion is that he just likes dancing. On the other hand, if the data come out in the form of Table 3.1b, where Calvin and others don't do other kinds of dancing, but everyone dances the tango, we might conclude that the tango caused Calvin's dancing.

Kelley's (1967) ANOVA (analysis of variance) theory aimed to explain how individuals determine whether their reaction to an external object is due to the object itself (e.g., the tango) or to their own subjective response, and the theory focused on people, objects, times, and "modalities" (different ways of interacting with the entity) as potential factors. Cheng and Novick (1990, 1992) advocated a somewhat more flexible approach

TABLE 3.1   Two Contrasts for Assessing the Presence of a Causal Relation.

a.

	This Occasion		Other Occasions	
	Calvin	Other people	Calvin	Other people
tango	1	0	1	0
other dances	1	0	1	0

b.

	This Occasion		Other Occasions	
	Calvin	Other people	Calvin	Other people
tango	1	1	1	1
other dances	0	0	0	0

1's indicate that a person dances on a given occasion; 0's indicate not dancing in which people choose to consider a set of potential factors on pragmatic grounds:"Contrasts are assumed to be computed for attended dimensions that are present in the event to be explained" (1990, p. 551). According to this theory, people also determine causation relative to a particular sample of situations, a "focal set," rather than to a universal set. Within these situations, people calculate causal effectiveness in terms of the difference between the probability of the effect when the potential cause is present and the probability of the effect when the same potential cause is absent:

(1) $\Delta P = \mathrm{Pr}(\textit{effect}\,|\,\textit{factor}) - \mathrm{Pr}(\textit{effect}\,|\,\sim\textit{factor})$,

where $\mathrm{Pr}(\textit{effect} \mid \textit{factor})$ is the conditional probability of the effect given the presence of the potential causal factor and $\mathrm{Pr}(\textit{effect} \mid \sim\textit{factor})$ is the conditional probability of the effect given the absence of the same factor. When this difference, ΔP, is positive, the factor is a contributory cause of the effect; when it's negative, the factor is an inhibitory cause; and when it's zero, the factor is not a cause. Cheng and Novick also distinguish causes (contributory or inhibitory) from "enabling conditions"—factors whose ΔP is undefined within the focal set of situations (because they are constantly present or constantly absent) but that have nonzero ΔP in some other set.

We can illustrate some of these distinctions in the Table 3.1 example. In Table 3.1a, $\Delta P = 1$ for Calvin versus other people, but 0 for the object and occasions factors. So something about Calvin is a contributory cause of his dancing the tango at that time, and the tango and the occasion are noncauses. In Table 3.1b, the object (type of dance) factor has a ΔP of 1, whereas the person and occasion factors have ΔP's of 0; so the tango causes the event. Reversing the 0's and 1's in Table 3.1b, so that Calvin and others never dance the tango but always dance other dances, will produce a ΔP of -1. In this case, the tango is an inhibitory cause. A factor—perhaps, music—that is present in all the situations in the focal set would be an enabling condition if it turned out to have a positive ΔP in a larger sample of situations in which it was present in some and absent in others. The results in Table 3.1 are all-or-none, but the ΔP measure generalizes to situations in which the effect can occur within each cell sometimes but not always.

Related notions about cause derive from work on associative learning. Creatures learning that, say, a shock often follows a tone are remembering contingency information about the tone and shock or the pain or fear that the shock creates (note to animal lovers: these aren't my experiments). A number of researchers have proposed that this primitive form of association might provide the basis for humans' causal judgments (e.g., Shanks & Dickinson, 1987; Wasserman, Kao, Van Hamme, Katagiri, & Young, 1996). Data and models for such learning suggest that this process may be more complex than a simple calculation of ΔP over all trials. In particular, the associative strength between a specific cue (e.g., tone) and an unconditioned stimulus (shock) depends on the associative strength of other cues (lights, shapes, colors, etc.) that happen to be in play. The associative strength for a particular cue is smaller, for example, if the environment already contains stronger cues for the same effect. If these associative theories are correct models for judgments about a specific potential cause, then such judgments should depend on interactions with other potential causes, not just on "main effect" differences like those of the ANOVA model or ΔP. Evidence for these interactions in causal judgments appears in a number of studies (e.g., G. B. Chapman & Robbins, 1990; Shanks & Dickinson, 1987).[7] However, ΔP-based theories can handle some of these results if participants compute ΔP while holding other confounded factors constant (a conditional ΔP, see Cheng, 1997; Spellman, 1996). Also, under certain conditions (e.g., only one potential cause present), associative theories sometime reduce to ΔP (G. B. Chapman & Robbins, 1990; Cheng, 1997).[8] Because both associative and statistical models make use of the same bottom-up frequency information, we consider them together here (see the Section 3.1.2.4 on Power, below, for more on interactions).

3.1.2.2 Lots of Correlations

The same textbooks on methodology that extol Mill's canons of causal inference also insist that a correlation between two variables can't prove that one causes the other. (Little wonder that students universally despise methodology courses.) Because Mill's methods, the ANOVA theory, ΔP, associative theories, and their variants all work along correlational lines, how can they provide convincing evidence for causation?[9]

If these methods yield a positive result, the possibility always exists that some unknown factor confounds the relation between the identified cause its effect. Maybe Calvin's love of dancing didn't cause his dancing the tango Thursday, but instead the cause was his girlfriend's insistence that he dance every dance on every occasion (in the Table 3.1a example). If these methods yield a negative result for some putative cause, there's always the possibility that some unknown factor is suppressing the first. The tango's special allure might surface if Calvin and his girlfriend hadn't crowded other couples off the dance floor. If we can't identify a cause (due to possible confounding) and we can't eliminate a potential cause (because of possible suppression), how can we make any progress with these correlational methods? Of course, the ANOVA theory and the ΔP theory (unlike Mill's methods) are intended as models of everyday causal reckoning, and everyday reckoning may not consider confoundings or suppressors. Superstitious behavior may attest to people's unconcern about spurious causes and noncauses, as might the need for the textbook warnings about these weak inferences. Even children, however, can reject confoundings under favorable conditions (Gopnik et al., 2004; Koslowski, 1996, chap. 6). So we need an explanation of how people go beyond correlation in their search for causes.

Although a single contrast or correlation between factors may not be convincing evidence, multiple correlations may reveal more about the causal system, allowing us to do some reverse engineering. To see why this is so, let's go back to the diagram of the CD player in Figure 3.1. Both the rotating motor and the laser beam influence the final transmission of electrical signals. So we would expect both the rotation of the motor and the presence of the laser beam to be correlated with the transmission. The correlation between the motor and the light beam, however, should be zero, provided no further factors outside the diagram influence both of them. (If a power switch, for example, controls both the motor and the laser, then, of course, it will produce such a correlation. So imagine they have separate controls for present purposes.) Similarly, the diagram predicts that if we can hold constant the state of some of the variables in Figure 3.1, the correlation among other variables should go to zero. For instance, although a correlation exists between whether the CD is rotating and transmission of signals, we should be able to break the correlation by observing only those situations in which the intermediate variable, the light striking the diode, is constant. When light is not striking the diode, no correlation will appear between the rotating and the transmission. The causal relations among the different parts of the diagram put restrictions on what is correlated with what. Working backward from the pattern of correlations, then, we may be able to discern which causal relations are consistent with them. For example, the presence of a correlation between the rotation and the light beam would be a reason to think that the causal arrows in Figure 3.1 are incorrect. Statistical techniques like path analysis and structural equation modeling exploit systems of correlations in this way to test theories about causal connections (e.g., Asher, 1983; Klem, 1995; Loehlin, 1992).

We need to consider limitations of these methods, however, that are similar to those we noted for single correlations (Cliff, 1983). In the first place, confounding causes may exist that are not among the factors considered in the analysis. In the set up of Figure 3.1, we should observe a correlation between the light striking the diode and the transmission of signals, but we have no guarantee, based on correlations alone, that this is due to the direct effect of the diode on the signals (as the figure suggests). Rather the correlation could be due to the effect of some third, confounding variable on both the diode and the signal. The same is true for the rest of the direct connections that appear in the graph. Each direct connection is subject to exactly the same uncertainty about confoundings that we faced with single correlations.

Second, the pattern of correlations can drastically underdetermine the causal structure. Consider, for example, a completely arbitrary set of correlations among four variables A, B, C, and D. The causal connections in Figure 3.3a (i.e., A has a direct causal effect on B, C, and D; B has a direct effect on C and D; and C has a direct effect on D) will be perfectly consistent with those correlations, whatever they happen to be. For example, a path analysis based on these connections will *exactly* predict the arbitrary correlations. Moreover, so will any of the other 23 models in which the position of the variables in this structure is permuted—for instance, the one in Figure 3.3b in which D directly causes C, B, and A; C directly causes B and A; and B directly causes A. These are *fully recursive* models in path-analysis lingo, and they always fit the data perfectly. This underdetermination shouldn't be surprising: We're attempting to predict six correlations (e.g., the correlations between A and B, A and C, etc.).

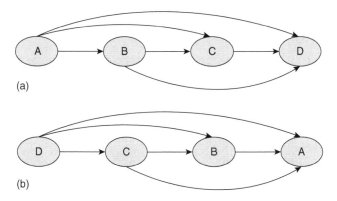

FIGURE 3.3 A hypothetical causal model for four variables in original form (a) and permuted form (b).

But to do so, we can make use of six parameters, corresponding to the weights on the six arrows in Figure 3.3a or 3.3b. If fewer arrows exist in the network, then perfect fits will not usually be possible. In general, though, two or more networks can provide equally good fits to a set of correlations, and noncorrelational information will then be necessary to decide between them (Klem, 1995; see also Pearl, 2000, for a discussion of Markov equivalent causal structures).

3.1.2.3 Causal Mechanisms and Schemas

To compound these difficulties for the bottom-up, correlation-to-causation, approach, the causal environment typically contains an enormous number of factors that could produce a given effect. Calvin, the tango, or the occasion may produce events that cause his dancing the tango on Thursday, but these factors are cover terms that contain many different potential causes: They serve as causal superordinate categories. Not all of Calvin's dispositions would plausibly cause him to dance, but we still have a seemingly unlimited number from which to choose. Is the cause his showmanship, his athleticism, his musical talents, his religious fervor, his distaste of being a wallflower, his fear of letting down his girlfriend, . . . ? Moreover, we needn't stop at people, objects, and occasions, as we've already noted. Maybe the cause is his girlfriend's demands, maybe it's bribery by the DJ, maybe it's cosmic rays, maybe it's his therapist's hypnotic suggestion, maybe it's a disease (like St. Vitus dance), and so on. Since we have no end to the possibilities, we have no way to determine for each of them whether it is the cause, making a purely bottom-up approach completely hopeless. This is the issue I raised in the introduction to this book: Because we can't possibly examine all correlations for a given effect, we need some further method to direct our search.

We should again distinguish the plight of the scientist from the task of describing laypeople's causal search. Laypeople may take into account only a handful of potential causes and test each for a correlation with the effect. Such a procedure may not be normatively correct, but it may be the recipe people follow. Yet if people use correlations over a restricted set of factors, an explanation of their causal reasoning would have to include an account of how they arrive at the restricted set. The factors they test are the factors they attend to, of course, but what determines what they attend to? People's causal thinking often aims at explaining some phenomenon, where what needs explaining may be a function of what seems unusual or abnormal within a specific context (Einhorn & Hogarth, 1986; Hilton, 1988; Kahneman & Miller, 1986). The explanation process itself depends on pragmatic factors, such as the explainers' interest or point of view, the contrast class of explanations they have in mind, the intended audience for the explanation, and the availability of evidence, among others (e.g., Brem & Rips, 2000; Hilton, 1990; Lewis, 1986; van Fraassen, 1980). The same goes for determining "the cause" of a phenomenon, which is a disguised way of asking for the main cause or most important cause.

Evidence supports the notion that people's search for causes relies on information other than correlation. Ahn, Kalish, Medin, and Gelman (1995) asked participants what kinds of evidence they needed to determine the cause of an event like the one about Calvin. (Ahn et al. used some of the stimulus materials from Cheng & Novick, 1990.) For example, participants had to write down questions that they would like to have answered in order to figure out the cause of (in this case) Calvin's *not* dancing the tango on this occasion. Ahn et al. predicted that if the participants were following the ANOVA or Cheng-Novick ΔP theory, they should seek information that fills out the rest of the design matrix in Table 3.1—the kind of information they could use to compute experimental contrasts or ΔP. Did other people dance the tango? Did

Calvin dance other kinds of dances? Did Calvin dance the tango on other occasions? And so forth. What Ahn et al. found, though, is that participants asked these sorts of questions only about 10% of the time. Instead, they asked what Ahn et al. call "hypothesis-testing" questions, which were about specific explanatory factors not explicitly mentioned in the description of the event. Participants asked whether Calvin had a sore foot or whether he ever learned the tango, and about similar sorts of common-sense causal factors. These hypothesis-testing questions showed up on approximately 65% of trials. Ahn et al. concluded that when people try to explain an event, they look for some sort of mechanism or process that could plausibly cause it. They have a set of these potential mechanisms available in memory, and they trot them out when they're trying to discover a cause.

People may also infer correlational information from their causal beliefs rather than the other way round. Psychologists have known since L. J. Chapman and Chapman's (1967; L. J. Chapman 1967) initial work on illusory correlations that causal expectancies can affect estimates of correlations (for reviews, see Alloy & Tabachnik, 1984; Busemeyer, 1991; Nisbett & Ross, 1980). Both clinicians and laypeople overestimate the correlation between diagnostic categories and certain test results, for example, between paranoia and unusual eye shapes in patients' drawings. This is probably because the judges' causal theories dictate a relation between the category and the result—paranoia causes patients to be especially aware of the way people look at them or of their own glances at others—since the true correlation is negligible.

Similarly, A. Tversky and Kahneman's (1980) experiments on causal schemas show that causal theories can dictate estimates of conditional probabilities. Participants in one experiment were asked to choose which of the following events is more probable:

(a) That a girl has blue eyes if her mother has blue eyes.
(b) That a mother has blue eyes if her daughter has blue eyes.
(c) The two events are equally probable.

The converse conditional probabilities in (a) and (b) are necessarily equal, according to Bayes' theorem, if the (marginal or unconditional) probability of being a blue-eyed mother is the same as being a blue-eyed daughter. (A follow up experiment verified that most participants think this equality holds.)[10] The results showed that 45% of participants correctly chose option (c). The remaining participants, however, chose (a) much more often than (b): 42% versus 13%. According to Tversky and Kahneman, these judgments are biased by knowledge that mothers are causally responsible for their daughter's eye color, whereas the daughter's eye color does not affect the mother's. This causal asymmetry produces an incorrect impression of asymmetry in the conditional probabilities.

Finally, Waldmann and his colleagues have shown that people's judgment about a cause can depend on causal background beliefs, even when correlational information is constant (Waldmann, 1996). Consider, for example, the fictitious data in Table 3.2, which exhibits the relation between whether a certain set of fruit has been irradiated and the fruit's quality in two samples, A and B. Summed over the samples, the quality of fruit is positively related to irradiation: ΔP is positive when irradiation is the factor and quality the effect (see the equation in (1)). Within each sample, however, the effect reverses. Both ΔP's are negative when calculated within sample, as shown in the bottom row of the table. This situation is an example of *Simpson's paradox*: When the number of cases in the cells are unequal, the size and even the direction of contingency statistics can depend on how the population is partitioned.[11] In Table 3.2, people should judge irradiation to be positively related to quality if they base their decision on the entire sample, but should make the opposite judgment if they attend to samples A and B separately. Waldmann and Hagmayer (2001, Experiment 1) manipulated participants' assumptions about the causal import of the samples by informing them in one

TABLE 3.2   Contingency Information from Waldmann and Hagmayer (2001).

	Sample A	Sample B	Total
Irradiated	16/36	0/4	16/40
Not irradiated	3/4	5/36	8/40
ΔP	−.31	−.14	+.20

The first two rows indicate what fraction of a group of fruit was good as a function of whether the fruit was irradiated or not and of whether it was from Sample A or Sample B. The top number in each fraction is the number of good fruit and the bottom number is the total number of fruit tested in that condition. Bottom row shows ΔP (i.e., Pr(good | irradiation) − Pr(good | no irradiation)) for the entire population and for each sample separately.

condition that sample A consisted of one type of tropical fruit and sample B consisted of a different type. In a second condition, participants learned that A and B were samples randomly assigned to two different investigators. Participants in both conditions, however, saw the same list of 80 cases (distributed as in Table 3.2) that identified the sample (A or B) and, for each piece of fruit, its treatment (irradiated or not) and its outcome (good quality or bad). All participants then rated how strongly the irradiation affected the fruits' quality. Although correlational information was constant for the two conditions, participants believed irradiation affected quality negatively when the samples were causally relevant (types of fruit) but affected quality positively when the samples were irrelevant (different investigators).

These findings imply that people probably don't form their judgments of cause from bottom up, except under the most antiseptic conditions. Contingencies, associations, and correlations are relevant to people's assessment of cause, but the role they play must be part of a much larger picture.

3.1.2.4 Power

As a step toward a more theory-based view of cause, we might analyze observed contingencies as due to two components: the mere presence or absence of the cause and the tendency or power of this cause to produce the effect (Cheng, 1997; Novick & Cheng, 2004). The cause can't bring about the effect, of course, unless it's present. But even when it is present, the cause may be co-opted by other causes or may be too weak to produce the effect in question. Ordinarily, we can observe whether or not the cause is present, at least in the types of experiments we have been discussing, but the cause's power is unobservable. In this vein, Novick and Cheng (2004, p. 455) claim that "Previous accounts, however, are *purely covariational* in that they do not consider the possible existence of unobservable causal structures to arrive at their output. In contrast, our theory explicitly incorporates into its inference procedure the possible existence of *distal* causal structures: Structures in the world that exist independently of one's observations" (emphasis in the original). On this theory, you can detect the nature of these distal structures only under special circumstances. When these special assumptions are met, the distal causal power isn't exactly an ANOVA contrast or ΔP, but it looks much like a normalized ΔP.

To derive the power of a cause C, suppose first that C is present in the environment. Then the effect, E, will occur in two cases: (a) C produces E (with probability p_c, the power of C), or (b) other alternative causes, collectively designated A, occur in the same environment and produce E (with probability $Pr(A \mid C) \cdot p_a$). Thus, the probability of E when C is present is:

(2) $Pr(E|C) = p_c + Pr(A|C) \cdot p_a - p_c \cdot Pr(A|C) \cdot p_a .$

The final term in (2) (after the minus sign) ensures that we count only once the case in which C and A both produce E.

When C is absent, only the alternative causes A can bring about E. So the probability of E given that C is not present is:

(3) $Pr(E|{\sim}C) = Pr(A|{\sim}C) \cdot p_a .$

Substituting these expressions in Equation (1), above, we get:

(4) $\Delta P = [p_c + Pr(A|C) \cdot p_a - p_c \cdot Pr(A|C) \cdot p_a] - [Pr(A|{\sim}C) \cdot p_a] .$

Solving (4) for p_c yields the following expression for the causal power of C:

(5) $p_c = \dfrac{\Delta P - [Pr(A \mid C) - Pr(A \mid {\sim}C)]p_a}{1 - Pr(A \mid C)p_a} .$

In the special case in which causes A and C occur independently (so that $Pr(A \mid C) = Pr(A \mid {\sim}C) = Pr(A)$), then Equation (5) reduces to:

(6) $p_c = \dfrac{\Delta P}{1 - Pr(A)\, p_a}$

$\quad\quad = \dfrac{\Delta P}{1 - Pr(E \mid {\sim}C)}$

The last expression follows because, by Equation (3), $Pr(E \mid {\sim}C)$ is equal to $Pr(A) \cdot p_a$ when A and C are independent. The interpretation of (6) may be clearer if you recall that ΔP is itself equal to $\Pr(E \mid C) - \Pr(E \mid {\sim}C)$, by the definition in Equation (1). In other words, p_c is the amount that C contributes to producing E relative to the maximal amount it could contribute. Thus, p_c, unlike ΔP, is immune to ceiling effects—situations in which E already occurs frequently in the absence of C—except in the extreme case in which $\Pr(E \mid {\sim}C) = 1$, where p_c is undefined. (To see this, suppose $\Pr(E \mid C) = .95$ and $\Pr(E \mid {\sim}C) = .90$. Then $\Delta P = .05$, a seemingly small effect for C because both $\Pr(E \mid C)$ and $\Pr(E \mid {\sim}C)$ are high. But $p_c = .50$, a much larger effect because of the correction in the denominator of (6).) The formulas in (5) and (6) define contributory causal power, but analogous ones are available for inhibitory causal power (see Cheng, 1997).

Does the power statistic, p_c, correspond to a concept of the potency of a distal cause, as Novick and Cheng (2004) claim? Why shouldn't we consider it another subjective measure that a particular cause will produce an effect—ΔP corrected for ceiling effects? As I mentioned earlier, the Cheng-Novick theory portrays causation as a two-step affair. If we want to predict whether C causes E, we need to know both the likelihood that C is present and also the likelihood that C will produce E. But granting this framework, we have some options in interpreting the latter likelihood. One issue is whether people think that "distal power" is a probabilistic matter at all, a question that Luhmann and Ahn (2005) raise. Setting aside subatomic physics, which is outside the ken of ordinary thinking about ordinary causal interactions, people may believe that causal power is all-or-none: Something either is a cause or isn't; it's not a cause with power .3 or .6. Of course, a potential cause doesn't always run to completion; intermediate steps of a process may fail. For example, a drunk driver might have caused an accident if his car hadn't been equipped with antilock brakes. But do we want to say that the causal power of the drunk driving was some number between 0 and 1?[12]

Novick and Cheng are likely right that people believe in external causes that have the power to produce certain effects. What's in question is whether you can model these powers as probabilities in a way that doesn't sacrifice basic intuitions about causality, which for ordinary events might be necessarily all-or-none (Luhmann & Ahn, 2005) and inherently mechanistic ("intrinsically generative," in White's, 2005, terms).

Power proponents could take the position that causal power describes an idealized, normatively correct measure that actual causal judgments merely approach. After all, our conclusion in Section 3.1.1 was that distal causal powers are the sorts of things we infer rather than directly apprehend. However, the causal power formulas in (5) and (6) don't necessarily yield normatively correct estimates. Like other measures of causal effectiveness—main effect contrasts, ΔP, path analysis coefficients, and similar measures estimated directly from co-occurrence data—the power formulas don't always yield the right result. Glymour observes (2001, p. 87) that there "is an obvious reason why [the power method] will not be reliable: unobserved common causes. We have seen that the estimation methods [for generative and preventive powers] are generally insufficient when there are unobserved common causes at work, and often we have no idea before we begin inquiry whether such factors are operating." If we already know the structure of the causal environment, we can safely use power-like calculations to estimate the strength of particular pathways, and in this context, power may be a normative ideal. But this presupposes some way other than power to arrive at the correct structure.

3.1.3   Causation from Intervention

We're finally in a position to return to the claims at the beginning of this chapter about "great new ideas" for representing causation. One of these ideas is the use of multiple correlations or contingencies, as in the path-analysis theories we glimpsed in Section 3.1.2.2. Perhaps people represent a causal system as a graph connecting causes to effects, along the lines of Figures 3.1 and 3.3. These graphs embody statistical relations—the pattern of conditional probabilities among the depicted events—that put constraints on what can be a cause of an effect. At a psychological level, we might encode this pattern of contingencies and then find the best graph—or at least a good graph—that fits them. The resulting structure is our subjective theory or causal model of the reigning causal forces. You could complain that this isn't exactly a new idea, deriving as it does from data-analytic work by Wright in the 1920s (see Wright, 1960, for a recap; see also Simon, 1953). But perhaps it's an innovation to take such diagrams seriously as mental representations—mental causal maps.

Further elaborations may constitute genuine advances. Let's see what these could be.

We noticed that graphical representations of multiple-correlation systems are open to problems of confounding and underdetermination. The very same pattern of correlations and partial correlations can be equally consistent with very different causal graphs, as the example in Figure 3.3 illustrates. Faced with this indeterminacy, though, scientists don't always throw up their hands. They can sometimes bring experiments to bear in selecting among the alternative causal possibilities. In the case of Figure 3.3, for example, imagine an experiment in which a scientist explicitly manipulates factor A to change its value. You'd expect this experiment also to change the value of B in the system of Figure 3.3a but not in that of Figure 3.3b. Intuitively, this is because manipulating a factor can have only a forward influence on its effects, not a backward influence on its causes. So intervention can discriminate the two causal frameworks. Of course, we can sometimes make the same discovery without getting our hands dirty if we know the time at which the factors change their values, since causes don't occur after their effects. In the world of Figure 3.3a, observing a change in A should be followed by observing a change in B, but this will not be true in Figure 3.3b.

Manipulating factors, however, has an advantage that goes beyond merely clarifying temporal relationships. By changing the value of a factor, we can often remove the influence of other factors that typically covary with it, isolating the former from confoundings. If we're interested, for example, in whether listening to Mozart improves students' math scores, we could randomly assign one set of students to listen to 15 minutes of Mozart and another to 15 minutes of silence before a math test. In randomizing, we're removing the influence of intelligence, social class, and other background factors that could affect both a tendency to listen to Mozart and to do well in math. In the graph of Figure 3.3a, suppose factor A is the social class of students' families, B is intelligence, C is listening to Mozart, and D is test performance. Then the manipulation just described deletes the links from social class and intelligence to Mozart listening. In the experiment we're contemplating, students with more intelligence are no more likely to listen to Mozart than are those with less intelligence. If we still find an effect of Mozart on test scores, this can assure us that Mozart listening affects the scores apart from the influence of the two background variables. This advantage for manipulating is due in part to the fact that intervention places additional constraints on the statistical relations among the variables (Pearl, 2000). If we manipulate Mozart listening as just described, we're essentially creating a new graphical structure—Figure 3.3a minus the arrows from social class and intelligence to Mozart listening—and we're demanding that the correlations change in a way that conforms to this remodeling.

Recent evidence suggests that adults, children, and even rats are sometimes aware of the benefits of explicitly manipulating variables in learning a causal structure (rats: Blaisdell, Sawa, Leising, & Waldmann, 2006; children: Gopnik et al., 2004; adults: Lagnado & Sloman, 2005; Steyvers, Tenenbaum, Wagenmakers, & Blum, 2003). For example, Gopnik et al. (2004) report an experiment in which 4-year-olds observed a stage containing two "puppets" (simple rods with differently colored balls attached). The experimenter could move the puppets in two ways: either out of the view of the children (by reaching under the stage) or in their view (by pulling them up and down). The experimenter told the children that one of the puppets was special in that this puppet could make the other move. The children's task was to decide which was special—say, the yellow or the green puppet. Children first saw the yellow and green puppets moving together as the result of the experimenter's concealed action. They then observed the experimenter overtly pulling up the yellow puppet while the green puppet remained stationary. Under these conditions, 78% of the children could identify the green puppet as the special one. Because the children saw the experimenter manipulate the yellow puppet without any effect on the green one, they could reason that the yellow puppet couldn't have been responsible for their initial joint movement and, thus, that the green puppet must be the cause. Purely association-based or correlation-based theories have trouble accounting for results like these, since such models don't distinguish event changes that result from interventions.

In more complex situations (and with college-age participants), however, the advantage for interventions is not as clear-cut (Lagnado & Sloman, 2005; Steyvers et al., 2003). According to Lagnado and Sloman, any benefit for intervention in their experiments was due to the simple temporal consequences mentioned earlier (that interventions must precede their effects) rather than to the statistical independencies that interventions create. Steyvers et al. (2003, Experiment 2) presented 10 observational trials about a three-variable system. They then allowed participants a single intervention, followed by an additional 10 trials based on that intervention. (No explicit temporal information was available during the observation or intervention trials.) Participants' ability to identify the correct causal structure increased from 18% before intervention to 34% after (chance was 5.6%); however, ideal use of the intervention in this experiment should have led to 100% accuracy. These results suggest that when the environment is simple (as in Gopnik et al., 2004) and only a small number of causal set ups are possible (e.g., X causes Y vs. Y causes X), people can use facts about interventions to test which alternative is correct. When the number of alternatives is larger, hypothesis testing isn't as easy, and people are less able to use the difference between observations and interventions to determine the causal arrangement. Investigators have also looked at participants' ability to use a previously learned causal structure to make predictions based on observations or interventions, and we will consider the results of these experiments in the section on reasoning later in this chapter. The present point is that the intervention/observation difference is not very robust when people must go from data to causal structure.

Perhaps one reason why people don't always pick up on interventions is that—as every experimentalist knows—interventions don't guarantee freedom from confounding. The literature on causal nets sometimes suggests that intervening entails only removing causal connections— links from the immediate causes of the variable that's being manipulated (i.e., the independent variable). But manipulations typically insert a new cause that substitutes for the old ones, and sometimes the new cause comes along with extraneous connections of its own. Take the Mozart effect. Randomizing participants to conditions removes the influence of intelligence and other participant-centered factors. But placing participants in a control group that has to experience 15 minutes of silence may have an aversive effect that could lower test scores to a greater extent than would merely not listening to Mozart (see Schellenberg, 2005). Figuring out the right manipulation isn't always an easy matter. Ambiguity about the possible effects of an intervention may lead participants to back off from such cues during causal learning. Of course, you can define "intervention" as a manipulation that does not affect any variable other than the targeted one (Gopnik et al, 2004; Hausman & Woodward, 1999), but this tactic is not much help to the working scientist or layperson, who often doesn't have advance knowledge of possible side effects of the manipulation.[13]

3.2 Reasoning from Causal Theories

We've just looked at the possibility that people discover causal relations by noticing the patterning of events in their surroundings. That method is problematic for both theoretical and empirical reasons. Theoretically, we're faced with an unlimited number of potential causal relationships of unlimited complexity, and correlation is often unable to decide among these rival causal arrangements. Empirically, we have found no compelling evidence that people have hard-wired cause detectors, so people probably don't automatically derive causal facts from event perception. Moreover, our ability to infer cause from event co-occurrence seems to depend heavily on higher-level beliefs about what sorts of events can cause others, on beliefs about how events interact mechanistically, and on pragmatic pressures concerning what needs to be explained.

The classic alternative strategy for deriving causal knowledge is a form of inference to the best explanation (Harman, 1965). We can start with theories about the potential causes of some phenomenon and then choose the best theory that explains the data. The best theory gives the right causal picture. In discussing path analysis (Section 3.1.2.2), I mentioned that several different models can fit a set of correlations equally well. The present proposal supplements the correlations with theoretical constraints (e.g., higher-level causal principles or factors such as simplicity, unity, or depth) that can help decide among the models. Of course, this form of inference doesn't give us certainty about our causal conclusions, since it depends on the range of alternatives we've considered, on the validity of the tests we've performed, and on the goodness of the data we've collected. But *no* method yields certainty about such matters. What could give us a better idea about correct causal relations than the best explanation that exploits them? This approach reserves a place for observational data, but the place is at the receiving end of a causal theory rather than at its source.

This top-down strategy, however, yields a host of further psychological problems. We still need to know how our theories or hypotheses develop if they don't arise purely from observation. We also need to consider how people use causal theories to make the sorts of predictions on which our inferences depend. In this last respect, the causal schemas or Bayes nets that we looked at earlier can be helpful. We noted that people don't always accurately construct such schemes from data, even when they can manipulate relevant variables. Nevertheless, once people settle on such a representation, it may guide them to correct conclusions.

3.2.1 Representing Causal Information: Causal Principles and Causal Theories

If we don't get causal information from innate perceptual cause detectors or from pure associative/correlational information, what's left?

3.2.1.1 Causal Primitives

According to one top-down theory of causality, we have, perhaps innately, certain primitive causal concepts or principles that we bring to bear on the events we observe and talk about, primitives that lend the events a causal interpretation. One possibility is that we possess a single primitive causal relation, *cause(x, y)*, that we combine with other concepts to produce more complex and specific causal descriptions (e.g., Dowty, 1979; McCawley, 1968; T. Parsons, 1990). Thus, we might mentally represent the sentence in (7a) as (7b):

(7) a. John paints a picture.
     b. cause(John paints, become(a picture exists))

Or perhaps there are several primitive causal relations or subtypes that vary in ways that distinguish among causing, enabling, and preventing, among others (e.g., Jackendoff, 1990; Schank & Riesbeck, 1981; Talmy, 1988; Wolff, Klettke, Ventura, & Song, 2005; see also Tufte, 2006, for related conclusions about causal graphs).

I suggested earlier that no strong evidence exists for innate cause detectors in perception, but also that lack of such detectors is consistent with innate causal concepts. The difficulty for the perceptual view is that scenes that are supposed to trigger causal impressions automatically we can usually interpret noncausally. But this Humean way of thinking about the perception of causation is exactly what we should expect if our interpretation of the scenes depends on how we apply our causal concepts. Having an innate concept of cause doesn't imply that external stimuli can force us to apply it. But having an innate (perceptual) cause detector—an input module in Fodor's (1983) sense—presumably does.

Of course, the existence of these causal concepts doesn't mean that perceptual or contingency information plays no role in our judgments about causality, and it doesn't mean that babies appear on the scene already knowing everything about causation that adults do. Percepts and contingencies can provide evidence about what we should investigate in order to uncover possible causal connections; however, they don't ordinarily provide a direct route to such connections. Similarly, having a causal concept may be necessary in understanding causal setups, but understanding exactly what causes what in a particular physical setting often requires further learning. Knowing that events can be connected causally doesn't automatically tell us, for example, how chemical reactions take place or how astronomical objects interact; it simply gives us one of the ingredients or building blocks. Infants may have some domain-specific theories in areas like psychology (Carey, 1985), biology (Atran, 1998), or physics (Spelke, Breinlinger, Macomber, & Jacobson, 1992) that provide particular information about causal relations in these areas, but even initial theories obviously undergo elaboration with experience and schooling, perhaps quite radically.

The existence of conceptually primitive causal concepts goes along with the idea that babies come equipped with the notions that events have causes, that the causes precede their effects, and that the causes bring about the effects in a mechanistic way. Bullock, Gelman, and Baillargeon (1982) propose principles along these lines—their Determinism, Priority, and Mechanism principles—and they suggest that children's and adults' later understanding of cause builds on these principles by adding information both about specific types of causal relations and about which environmental cues are most important when events interact. Preschoolers do not understand that scattering light causes rainbows, but they know that rainbows have some preceding mechanistic cause or other.

3.2.1.2 Causal Schemas

Many cognitive theories suggest that people maintain unified representations of causal systems. If the system is the CD player in Figure 3.1, then
memory for this information would include the individual causal relations
(corresponding to the arrows in the figure) together with some larger
structure that specifies how they fit together. Some theories represent
the structure in terms of propositions, as in (7b), with further embedding
for more complex situations (e.g., Gentner, 1983); other theories employ
more diagrammatic representations, similar to Figure 3.1 itself. The
unified representations in either case may speed search for the included
facts, make the included information less susceptible to interference,
and highlight certain inferences. Of course, a commitment to a unified
representation still leaves room for some flexibility in the representation's
abstractness and completeness. Causal schemas may be relatively sparse,
even for familiar causal systems (Rozenblit & Keil, 2002), and they may
sometimes amount to little more than top-level heuristics, such as "more
effort yields more results" (diSessa, 2000).

As cognitive representations, causal schemas don't necessarily carry
explicit information about the statistical relations among the included
events. People could possess a schema similar to that of Figure 3.1 and
still fail to notice the implications it has for statistical dependencies, such
as the ones we considered earlier (see Section 3.1.2). What sets Bayes nets
apart from other causal schemas in psychology is their tight connection
to statistical matters. Bayes nets depend essentially on a property called
the (Parental) Markov condition (Pearl, 2000; Spirtes et al., 2000). This is
the principle that conditioning on the states of the immediate causes—
holding constant the "parents" of a variable (or node) in the network—
renders that variable statistically independent of all other variables in the
net, except for those it causes (its "descendants"). Because the Markov
principle determines the causal links, the plausibility of Bayes nets as
psychological representations depends heavily on this principle. According
to Figure 3.1, if we hold constant whether the light strikes the diode, we
will make the transmission of electrical signals independent of the rest of
the variables in the figure. In Section 3.2.2, we examine the empirical
status of this assumption: Do people obey the Markov principle in their
inferences? In the meantime, we consider some theoretical issues that
surround Bayes nets as cognitive schemas.

3.2.1.3 Causal Bayesian Networks and Functional Causal Models as Causal Schemas

Although psychologists commonly cite Pearl (2000) as a source for the theory of Bayes nets, they gloss over the fact that Pearl presents three different versions of the theory, which provide successively more complex accounts of causality. What Pearl refers to as "Bayesian networks" are directed graphs of variables and links that observe the Markov principle we just reviewed. What Bayesian networks depict are the pattern of statistical dependencies and independencies among a set of variables. If a set of variables X is statistically independent of another set Y given Z, then the graph displays these independencies (the graph is a *D-map* in Pearl's, 1988, terminology). Conversely, if the graph displays X as independent of Y given Z, then the probability distribution contains this independency (the graph is an *I-map*). However, several different networks can be equally consistent with the pattern of statistical dependencies in a data set, for reasons mentioned in connection with Figure 3.3.

To overcome this indeterminacy problem, Pearl moves to a reformulated representation called "causal Bayesian networks." These networks have the same form as ordinary Bayes nets. They are still graphs, such as those in Figures 3.1 and 3.3. But causal Bayesian networks also embody constraints about interventions. These networks are answerable not just to the statistical dependencies inherent in the full graph of variables and links, but also to the statistical dependencies in the subgraphs you get when you manipulate or intervene on the variables. Within this theory, intervening on a variable means severing the connections from its parent variables and setting its value to a constant. For example, we could intervene on the "CD turns" variable in Figure 3.1 by disconnecting the CD holder from the motor and manually rotating it. Causal Bayes networks help eliminate the indeterminacy problem by requiring the representation to reflect all the new statistical relations these interventions imply.

In the last part of Chapter 1 and in Chapter 7 of his book, Pearl (2000) moves to a third kind of representation: "functional causal models." At first glance, not much difference appears between causal Bayesian networks and functional causal models, and this might make Pearl's claims about the latter models surprising. Functional causal models are given by a set of equations that have the form in (8):

(8) $x_i = f_i(pa_i, u_i), i = 1, 2, ..., n,$

where n is the number of variables in the network. Each of these equations specifies the value of one of the variables x_i based on the immediate (parent) causes of that variable, pa_i, and an additional set of variables, u_i, representing other unknown factors. In the case of Figure 3.1, for example, we can think of the node labeled "CD turns" as having the value 0 if the CD is not turning and 1 if it is turning (i.e., $x_{CD} = 0$ means the CD is not turning and $x_{CD} = 1$ means that it is). This value is determined by a function like that in (8), f_{CD}, that will depend on the value of the parent variable (whether the motor is turning) and of a variable u_{CD} (not shown in Figure 3.1) representing other unobserved factors that might interfere with the CD's operation. Pearl considers a special case of this representation, called "Markovian causal models," in which the graph is acyclic (i.e., contains no circular path from one node back to itself in the direction of the arrows) and the u terms are independent of each other. He proves that Markovian causal models are consistent with exactly the same probability distributions as the corresponding causal Bayes nets. "In all probabilistic applications of Bayesian networks . . . we can use an equivalent functional model as specified in [(8)], and we can regard functional models as just another way of encoding joint distribution functions" (Pearl, 2000, p. 31).

So what's the advantage of functional causal models that we didn't already have with causal Bayesian nets? (From now on, let's call the latter "causal nets" for short.) We noticed in discussing causal nets that their definition was given, not in terms of causal mechanisms, but in terms of probabilities. A causal net is just a Bayesian network that captures additional probability distributions, namely the ones we get by intervening on variables. With functional causal models, we are starting in the opposite direction, beginning with functions in (8) that completely determine the states of the variables rather than beginning with probabilities. This seems consistent with the lessons of the first half of this chapter. As Pearl (2000, p. 31) puts it, "agents who choose to organize their knowledge using

Markovian causal models can make reliable assertions about conditional independence relations without assessing numerical probabilities—a common ability among humanoids and a useful feature for inference." Everything operates in a deterministic way in functional causal models, with any uncertainty confined to our lack of knowledge about the values of the u_i's. Moreover, the system's equations in (8) are not just arbitrary functions that happen to give the correct x_i values. They reflect the actual causal determinants of the system, with pa_i and u_i being the true causes of x_i.

Pearl is explicit that an important benefit of functional causal models over causal networks is that the former deal correctly with counterfactual conditionals—statements of the form "If X had happened, then Y would have happened," such as *If Fred had taken the trouble to fix his brakes, he wouldn't have had an accident.* The truth of many counterfactual conditionals seems to depend on causal laws that dictate the behavior of events. The sentence about Fred is true or false because of the causal laws governing mechanical devices like brakes. If causal schemas record our understanding of causal laws, then they should enable us to make judgments about counterfactual conditionals. Pearl is clearly right that if functional causal models entail counterfactuals, then this gives them a leg up on ordinary causal nets. But in order to do this, the functions in (8) have to mirror these causal laws and must be constant over all causally possible situations. Pearl outlines a specific procedure that is supposed to answer counterfactual questions ("Would Y have happened if X had happened?") using functional causal models, and we'll look at the psychological plausibility of this hypothesis in more detail in discussing causal reasoning. In general, though, knowledge of causal laws (from the f_i's) and knowledge of the input states of the system (from the u_i's) should give us what we need to simulate how the system will work in all the eventualities it represents, including counterfactual ones.

The direction of explanation in Pearl's analysis is from causality (as given by the causal functions in (8)) to counterfactuals. But the opposite strategy also seems possible. Some philosophical analyses of causation—prominently, David Lewis's (1973a)—interpret causation in terms of counterfactuals. If event e would not have happened had c not happened, then e causally depends on c, according to this analysis. Psychologists have occasionally followed this lead, deciding whether one event in a story causes a second according to whether people are willing to say that the second would not have occurred if the first hadn't occurred (Trabasso & Sperry, 1985; Trabasso & van den Broek, 1985).

But even Lewis's theory uses causal laws to help determine a counterfactual conditional's truth. This truth depends on similarity among possible worlds, where similarity, in turn, depends on causal laws. The counterfactual "If c had not happened then e would not have happened" is true just in case there is a world in which neither c nor e happens that is closer to the actual world than any world where c doesn't happen but e does. And closeness to the actual world depends, at least in part, on whether the actual world's causal laws govern the alternative world. According to Lewis (1979, p. 472), the similarity relation must be governed by the principle that "it is of the first importance to avoid big, widespread, diverse violations of law." Lewis didn't intend his analysis to eliminate causal laws but to provide a new way of exploiting them in dealing with relations between individual events. So even if we adopt Lewis's theory, we still need the causal principles that the f_i's embody.[14]

Another possible complaint about functional causal models as psychological representations is that they don't come with enough structure to explain how people are able to learn them (Tenenbaum, Griffiths, & Niyogi, 2007). In figuring out how a device like a CD player works, we don't start out considering all potential networks that connect the key events or variables in the system. Instead, we take seriously only those networks that conform to our prior knowledge of what general classes of events can be causes for others. Because lasers are unlikely to turn motors, we don't waste time testing (or at least we give low weight to) functional causal models that incorporate such a link. According to Tenenbaum et al., people use higher-level theories to determine which network structures are possible, and this restricts the space of hypotheses they take into account. This objection seems right, since we do sometimes possess high-level knowledge (e.g., that diseases cause symptoms or that beliefs and desires cause actions) that shapes lower-level theories. But even in Tenenbaum et al.'s hierarchy, causal models are at center stage, mediating higher-level theory and data. This leaves us with an empirical issue: Assuming that functional causal models are possible psychological representations, how well do they explain people's ability to reason from their causal beliefs?

3.2.2 *Causal Reasoning*

The phrase "causal reasoning" could potentially apply to nearly any type of causal thinking, including the causal attribution that we considered in the first part of this chapter. The issue there was how we reason *to* causal beliefs from data or from other noncausal sources. Our considerations suggested that little reliable reasoning of this sort is possible without a healthy dose of top-down causal information already in place. But how well are we able to exploit this top-down information? Once we know a batch of causal facts, how do we use them in drawing further conclusions? Quite a lot of research in cognitive psychology has looked at indirect effects of causal relations on reasoning with conditional (*if . . . then*) sentences, and I review these results in the Appendix to this chapter. The following sections, however, examine reasoning with sentences that directly express causal information. (For general views of reasoning, see Chapter 6 in this book).

3.2.2.1 Reasoning from Causal Models: The Causal Markov Principle

We've seen that functional causal models (Pearl, 2000) provide an explicit representation of cause-effect relations, and they include normative constraints that should govern causal reasoning. In particular, Markovian causal models obey the causal Markov principle. We can therefore get a closer look at causal reasoning by teaching people causal connections that compose such a model and checking whether they follow the Markov principle in drawing inferences from it.

In a pioneering study of this kind, Rehder and Burnett (2005) taught participants explicit causal relations about fictitious categories, such as Lake Victoria shrimp or Neptune computers. For example, participants might be told that Victoria shrimp tend to have a high quantity of ACh neurotransmitter, a long-lasting flight response, an accelerated sleep cycle, and a high body weight. The participants learned that 75% of category members have these features. They also learned the causal relations among these features, both verbally and in an explicit diagram. For example, these participants might learn the "common cause" pattern in Figure 3.4a, in which high levels of ACh neurotransmitter in Lake

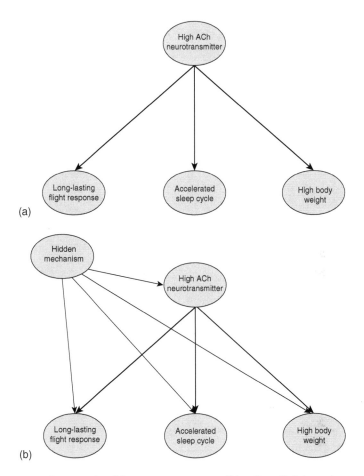

FIGURE 3.4 An example of the common cause condition from Rehder and
Burnett (2005, Experiment 1). (a) The network participants learned, and
(b) a possible alternative network to explain the empirical findings.

Victoria shrimp cause a long-lasting flight response, an accelerated sleep
cycle, and a high body weight. Rehder and Burnett then tested the
participants by giving them descriptions of a category member with an
unknown feature and asking them to rate how likely the category
member was to have that feature. How likely is it, for instance, that a
Victoria shrimp with high ACh, a long flight response, but no accelerated
sleep cycle, also has high body weight?

The interesting predictions concern the causal Markov principle:
Conditioning on the states of the parent variables renders a child variable

statistically independent of all other variables, except its descendants. In Figure 3.4a, if we know whether a Lake Victoria shrimp has high (or low) ACh, then the values of the lower-level features—flight response and body weight, for example—will be statistically independent of each other. If we're trying to predict whether a shrimp has high body weight, its high or low ACh level should influence our prediction. But as long as we know its ACh level, we needn't worry about whether it has any of the sister features (a long flight response or an accelerated sleep cycle), since these are not descendants of body weight. We can ignore these sister features because their only effects on body weight funnel through ACh.

What Rehder and Burnett (2005) found, however, is that participants systematically violated the Markov principle. Participants' estimates of the probability that a Lake Victoria shrimp has high body weight correctly depended on whether they were told it had high levels of ACh. But these estimates also increased if the shrimp had a long flight response and an accelerated sleep cycle, even when participants knew the ACh level. (See Rehder, 2006a; Waldmann & Hagmayer, 2005, Experiment 3; and Walsh & Sloman, 2007, for evidence of similar violations of the Markov principle in other types of causal systems.) Rehder and Burnett's participants had learned the common-cause structure in Figure 3.4a, which depicts the causal model, and the Markov principle is the central ingredient in defining the model. So why do participants flagrantly disregard the principle?

Rehder and Burnett propose that participants were indeed using causal nets, but nets with a configuration that differed from the one they had learned. According to this theory, the participants were assuming the presence of an additional hidden node, representing the category members' underlying mechanisms. The network in Figure 3.4b illustrates this structure, containing the new hidden mechanism node with direct connections to all the observed nodes. According to Rehder and Burnett (2005, p. 37), "to the extent that an exemplar has most or all of the category's characteristic features, it will also be considered a *well functioning* category member. That is, the many characteristic features are taken as a sign that the exemplar's underlying causal mechanisms functioned (and/ or are continuing to function) properly or normally for members of that kind. And if the exemplar's underlying mechanisms are operating normally, then they are likely to have produced a characteristic value on the unobserved dimension." Because participants don't know the state of the hidden mechanism, the sister nodes at the bottom of the figure are no longer statistically independent. Thus, participants' tendency to rely on these sister nodes no longer violates the Markov principle.

Rehder and Burnett show in further experiments that this hidden-mechanism theory also predicts the results from experiments using different network structures—for example, a net consisting of a single chain of variables and a "common effect" net with multiple causes for a single effect. For the latter networks, the underlying mechanism idea seems quite plausible, and the theory is consistent with models of causal centrality and psychological essentialism, as we'll see in the next chapter. Participants may suspect that a natural kind or complex artifact is likely to have some central cause or causes that hold the object together, an assumption that's in line with essentialist theories of categories (e.g., S. A. Gelman, 2003; Medin & Ortony, 1989). As Hausman and Woodward (1999) note, applications of the causal Markov principle have to ensure that all relevant variables are included in the model, that the causal system is analyzed at the right level, and that the included variables are not logically or definitionally related.

For common cause structures like Figure 3.4a, however, why would participants go to the trouble of positing an extra hidden mechanism when they already have an explicit common cause? Rehder and Burnett (2005, Experiment 2) also found the same pattern of results—violations of the Markov constraint—when participants learned a common cause structure like Figure 3.4a for a nonsense category, daxes, whose features were arbitrarily labeled A, B, C, and D. Even if hidden mechanisms are reasonable for shrimp and computers, where you might suppose underlying causes lurk, why would you assume them for an obviously fictitious category? Why believe in hidden mechanisms governing well-functioning daxes? You would at least expect some decrease in the nonindependence effect when the category gives participants less reason to suppose that an underlying mechanism is at work. But the extent of the Markov violations for daxes is about the same as that for natural kinds and artifacts. Although participants may have been positing hidden mechanisms, a simpler alternative might be that they were reasoning in a more primitive way. Perhaps they were assuming that the dominant values of a category's features tend to cluster together, without worrying much about the exact causal set up. Participants may have been short-circuiting the Bayes net, relying instead on the belief that the greater the number of typical shrimp features an item has, the more likely it is to have other typical features. Ditto for daxes. Participants weren't completely ignoring the causal structure, since they recognized the role of direct causes. But they may have given little thought to implications for the indirectly connected variables.

3.2.2.2 Reasoning from Causal Models: Observation versus Intervention

We found limited support (in Section 3.1.3) for the idea that people exploit interventions in order to discover the workings of a causal system. Although people use interventions within very simple systems, their ability to do so seems to fall off rapidly with even moderately complex networks. This difficulty may reflect general information-processing limits, since the number of possible causal nets (acyclic directed graphs) increases exponentially with the number of variables (see Rips & Conrad, 1989). A more sensitive test of people's understanding of the intervention/observation difference is to give people the relevant causal relations and to see whether they can predict the difference between intervening on a variable and passively observing its values.

Two series of experiments provide support for sensitivity to interventions. Sloman and Lagnado (2005, Experiment 6, p. 26) gave one group of participants the problem in (9):

> (9)   All rocket ships have two components, A and B. Movement of Component A causes Component B to move. In other words, if A, then B. Both are moving. Suppose Component B were prevented from moving, would Component A still be moving?

A second group received the same problem, except that the final question was changed to *Suppose Component B were observed not to be moving, would Component A still be moving?* If an external process manipulates a variable—in this case, prevents Component B from moving—the internal causal connections to that variable are no longer in force, and we can't reliably use them to predict the state of the cause (Component A).

By contrast, if normal internal causes are intact—if B is merely observed not to be moving—then the state of the effect provides diagnostic information about the cause. In line with this difference, 85% of participants responded "yes" to the intervention question, but only 22% did so for the observation question. Waldmann and Hagmayer (2005, Experiment 1) also found an observation/intervention difference, using more complex five-variable systems that they presented to participants in both verbal and graphical formats.

It may seem odd, at first glance, that causal nets (or models) make correct empirical predictions in the case of the intervention/observation difference but largely incorrect predictions in the case of the causal Markov principle. This divergence might be due to differences between studies, but in fact, both results have appeared within the same experiment (Waldmann & Hagmayer, 2005, Experiment 3). On second thought, though, why should these principles necessarily hang together? We associate both the observation/intervention distinction and the Markov principle with causal nets because causal modelers have given clear formal treatments for both. And the Markov principle, in particular, does seem tightly connected to causal nets because of the role it plays in their construction. But causal nets aren't the only way to formulate knowledge about interventions. The basic idea that you can't use the state of a manipulated variable to make inferences about its normal causes may simply be a piece of commonsense knowledge that's independent of the specific representation it gets in causal nets and functional causal models.[15] Evidence for correct understanding of interventions is support for correct causal reasoning but not necessarily support for causal nets.

3.2.2.3 Reasoning from Causal Models: Counterfactuals and Cause

There's one more piece of the causal net puzzle we need to consider. Pearl (2000) motivated functional causal models on the grounds that these models give a better way to deal with counterfactual questions. Functional causal models, but not causal nets, can tell us whether a different effect would have occurred if a cause had taken a value other than its actual one. Do functional causal models correctly predict people's reasoning with counterfactuals?

To handle counterfactual statements within the causal-model framework, we need a set of structural equations, like those in (8), that specify the state of each variable in terms of the state of its parents and of unobserved factors. In the simplest possible case, consider a two-variable system, such as that in (9). Assume for the sake of the example that the variables are dichotomous, either on or off, which we will code as 1 or 0. We can then specify the f functions as in (10):

(10)   a. $A = u_A$
       b. $B = A \cdot u_B$,

where A is the variable for Component A, and B for Component B. In other words, Component A will operate ($A = 1$) provided some external process turns it on (the error variable, u_A, has the value 1); Component B will operate ($B = 1$) provided both that its error variable, u_B, is 1 and that Component A is operating.

To determine the answer to a counterfactual question in this case—for example, *Suppose Component B were not operating, would Component A still operate?*—we follow a series of three steps, according to Pearl (2000, Theorem 7.1.7): We first update the probability of the u variables to reflect current evidence about the actual state of affairs. If we assume that the two components are operating in the actual state, as in (9), then $u_A = u_B = 1$. Second, we modify the causal model for an intervention on the event mentioned in the antecedent (*if* clause) of the counterfactual. For the sample question just mentioned, we modify Component B in the usual way by orphaning B from its parent A and setting its value to a constant (0, in this case), while also keeping the u variables fixed. This entails changing the equation in (10b) to $B = 0$, since the antecedent states that Component B is not operating. Finally, to determine whether Component A would still operate, we compute its value (i.e., the value of A in (10a)) in the modified model, using the updated background variables. Since we have $u_A = 1$, the equation in (10a) gives us a positive answer.

According to functional causal models, the answer to our sample counterfactual question should be the same as what we would get if the question had directly mentioned manipulating Component B.

For example, we should get the same answer ("yes") to the question in (11a) as to the question in (11b):

(11) a. Suppose Component B were not operating, would Component A still operate?
b. Suppose Component B were prevented from operating, would Component A still operate?

Question (11b) is also counterfactual and differs from (11a) only in making the intervention explicit. Sloman and Lagnado's (2005) Experiment 5 directly compared answers to straight counterfactuals, such as (11a), and prevention counterfactuals, such as (11b), but found a significant difference between them (68% of participants answered "yes" to the straight counterfactual and 89% "yes" to the prevention counterfactual). A similar difference appeared for scenarios describing a slightly more complicated three-variable system (Sloman & Lagnado, 2005, Experiment 2).[16]

Because counterfactuals were the main motive for introducing functional causal models, we should ask why these predictions fail. Participants may have been making mistakes in the experiments just cited, but we should also consider the possibility that the theory itself gives an incorrect account of how people should interpret counterfactuals. As a second example, consider the simple device in Figure 3.5, which contains just three parts, A, B, and C. The device works in the following way: Component A's operating always causes component B to operate; component A's operating always causes component C to operate; and component B's operating always causes component C to operate.

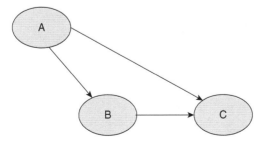

FIGURE 3.5 A hypothetical device in which component A's operating always causes both components B and C to operate, and component B's operating always causes component C to operate (see Rips, 2010b).

Suppose, too, that A, B, and C are all currently operating, and ask yourself the question in (12):

(12) If component B were not operating, would component C be operating?

A reasonable line of thought in this setting is to take the failure of B as evidence that A is not operating. Because A always causes B to operate, then B not operating is diagnostic of A not operating. And if neither A nor B were operating, then neither would C, since A and B are C's only causes. The answer to (12) would therefore be "no," and most participants (60.4%) go along with this decision (Rips, 2010b).

However, a "no" answer contradicts Pearl's theory of counterfactuals. If we work through Pearl's (2000) procedure—intervening on component B by removing the arrow from A and setting B to 0—then A should still be operating ($A = 1$). And because A is operating, C will be operating as well (see Rips, 2010b, for a derivation that parallels the one for (10)). Thus, Pearl predicts a "yes" answer to (12), contrary to the modal answer.

You could again dismiss the majority response as erroneous, but many participants were able to justify their "no" answer in ways that seem quite sensible. For example, one participant wrote, "If B is not operating, it is not causing C to operate. This also means that A is not operating because it always causes B to operate. Therefore, none are operating." A second participant came up with a similar justification: "For component C to operate, either A, B, or both must be operating. It is given that B is not, and this means that A must also not be operating. Therefore, C could not operate." Because these responses are defensible, we might wonder why Pearl's algorithm can't handle them. Pearl's motive for cutting some causal ties to the past is clear. In a deterministic system, such as those conforming to (8), no change to the actual event can occur without some alteration to its causes. To envision component B not operating, we need to imagine a change causally upstream from B, else B would continue to operate just as it does in the actual world. We must also make this change leaving as much as possible of the causal structure intact, since arbitrary changes to preceding causes give us no way to determine whether a counterfactual sentence is true or false. But although some break with the past is necessary, we needn't make this break by causally isolating the event mentioned in the antecedent of the counterfactual. As the example in (12) shows, we may have to trace further back to some of the causes of the antecedent event in order to see which of them is most likely to have produced the alteration. Determining which of the preceding causes must be changed may depend on which is most mutable (Kahneman & Miller, 1986), as well as which is powerful enough to bring about the new effect (see Dehghani, Iliev, & Kaufmann, 2007).

These reflections may help explain the differences between straight counterfactuals and prevention counterfactuals in Sloman and Lagnado's (2005) experiments. Prevention counterfactuals, such as (11b), require explicit manipulation of the event that the antecedent of the conditionals describes. The scenario in (9) suggests that if someone had prevented Component B from operating, the intervention occurred directly at B. But the straight counterfactual (11a) allows more room for interpretation. We're free to imagine different ways for B to have stopped operating, some of which might plausibly involve the failure of A. This ambiguity relates to one we have met before in our study of causal models (in Section 3.1.3). We noted that intervening on an event means more than removing an old cause. It also entails substituting a new cause, and the way in which the intervener does this can have important consequences. The present point is that if all we know is that some event has changed from the actual situation to a counterfactual one, we have a choice of mechanisms for understanding that change.

This difficulty with Pearl's (2000) account of counterfactuals doesn't mean we have to give up causal models. Other theories of counterfactuals based on causal schemas may provide better approaches to cases like (12). (For one promising account, see Hiddleston, 2005.)[17] Nevertheless, people's representations of causal models are necessarily incomplete depictions of event interactions, since any event has a causal history stretching back over enormous temporal distances. We can indicate our ignorance about these prehistories by including explicit representations of uncertainty, such as Pearl's *u* variables. But part of our causal reasoning consists in filling in some of these missing pieces, for example, in considering what sort of disturbance could have brought about a hypothetical event. These considerations may come from knowledge not captured in the causal systems.

3.3 Concluding Comments

Causal theorizing is essential, both in everyday thinking and in scientific endeavors. The implication of the first part of this chapter is that we probably don't do such thinking by strictly bottom-up observation. We can interpret simple displays of colliding geometric shapes as instances of pushings, pullings, and other causal events. Similarly, we can interpret other swarming movements of geometrical shapes as instances of actions—for example, chasings, catchings, and fightings. But we can also take a more analytical attitude to these displays, interpreting the movements as no more than approachings, touchings, and departings with no implication that one shape caused the other to move. No convincing evidence suggests that the causal interpretations are hardwired or impenetrable in the way standard perceptual illusions often are. The evidence is consistent with the idea that we see these demos as causal, but probably only in the way that we see certain visual arrays as cows or toasters. This suggestion is reinforced by the fact that, although seven-month-old infants may register some of these animations as special, other demos that adults report as causal are not distinctively so for these infants. Doubts about innate perceptual causality detectors do not extend to innate causal concepts, but causal concepts, innate or learned, must have sources that aren't purely perceptual (see Rips, 2010a).

Are the sources of causality co-occurrence frequencies? Here we run into both empirical and conceptual difficulties. On the empirical side, people are obviously limited in which potential causes they can test using frequency-based methods. Moreover, even when an experimenter tells participants about the relevant candidates and provides the relevant frequencies, the participants appear guided by prior hypotheses in their evaluation of the data. Theoretically, the frequency-based or correlation-based methods—main effect contrasts, ΔP, conditional ΔP, Rescorla-Wagner strength, power, and path coefficients—all give incorrect answers in certain causal environments, especially when there are hidden confounding factors. Explicit manipulation or intervention can remove some of the ambiguities by eliminating the confoundings, just as in scientific experiments, but current research suggests that people are often unable to make use of such information, except in very simple settings. The empirical results agree with the conclusions of Waldmann (1996) and others that people pursue knowledge of cause in a largely top-down fashion. The theoretical results suggest this might be the right thing to do.

A top-down approach implies that people begin with hypotheses when they assess or reason about cause. But this leaves much room for variation. Causal hypotheses could be anything from fragmented bits of information about a system to highly integrated and consistent theories. Bayes nets provide one way to represent causal information in schematic form, and these nets have many advantages in understanding causal situations, especially in the context of data-mining and analysis. They provide a way to factor a situation into statistically independent parts, and they therefore clarify the kinds of conclusions we can draw from specific observations and experiments. Should we also take Bayes nets to be the mental representations that people ordinarily use to store causal facts in memory?

Bayes nets go beyond a vague commitment to causal schemas: They embody strong assumptions about the relation between the causal links in the model and statistical regularities, and they generate predictions about how people reason about interventions and counterfactuals. They may well be consistent with the way people learn about new causal situations, though they may require additional constraints or heuristics to achieve this. In simple cases with small numbers of variables, they produce correct predictions for both children's and adults' reasoning. There seems little doubt, for example, that people recognize the distinction between observation and intervention that Bayes nets embody.

On the other side of the balance, we've found little evidence that people observe the causal Markov condition, the key ingredient in Bayes net's construction. Bayes nets tie the presence or absence of causal links to the presence or absence of statistical dependencies in the data. But participants' reasoning with causal information doesn't always agree with predictions based on these dependencies. And without the Markov principle, we're back to a position not much different from ideas about cognitive schemas, models, scripts, frames, or theories that preceded Bayes nets (see Section 2.5.1 of this book for references to these theories).

Bayes nets are also oddly inarticulate as cognitive representations. Proponents of Bayes nets have generally been uninterested in the way people express causal regularities, presumably because people's talk about cause is filtered through pragmatic channels, obscuring their underlying beliefs. But although this can be true, people's causal reasoning can depend on whether a cause or set of causes is necessary or sufficient. Likewise, their reasoning can depend on the differences between independent ("alternative") and interactive ("additional") causes (see Appendix). While we can derive information of this sort from the underlying conditional probabilities that go along with Bayes nets, we can't get them from the graphs alone. Two arrows running into an effect could equally represent two independent, individually sufficient causes of that effect or two causes that are only jointly sufficient. The same is true for contributory versus inhibitory causes. In addition, people make a wealth of adverbial distinctions in the way causation takes place. They distinguish, for example, between pushings, shovings, and thrustings in ways that don't seem recoverable from the bare networks or even from their underlying conditional probabilities or functional equations. These limits on expressibility may not be fundamental ones, but they do lessen the appeal of Bayes nets as cognitive maps of our causal environment.

To accord with the facts about human causal thinking, we need a representation that's less nerdy (less tied to statistical dependencies) and more discursive. We shouldn't jettison Bayes nets' insights, especially insights into the differences between intervention and observation. But we should be looking for a representation that better highlights people's talents in describing and reasoning about causation and that downplays purely quantitative phenomena.

Appendix

Reasoning with Conditional and Causal Sentences

Cognitive psychology has tiptoed up to the issue of how people reason from causal beliefs. Instead of looking at inferences from explicitly causal statements, psychologists have more often investigated causal reasoning in the context of ordinary conditional (*if . . . then*) sentences. A number of experiments have attempted to demonstrate that inferences from conditionals depend on whether the conditionals' content suggests a causal relation (e.g., Cummins, Lubart, Alksnis, & Rist, 1991; Staudenmayer, 1975; Thompson, 1994). The conditionals in these experiments are indicatives, such as *If the car is out of gas, then it stalls*, rather than the counterfactual (or subjunctive) conditionals discussed in Section 3.2.2.3 (*If the car had been out of gas, it would have stalled*). Because indicatives are less closely tied to causal relationships than counterfactuals, people may reason with such conditionals in a way that does not depend on causal content.

The results of these studies show, however, that causal content affects the conclusions people are willing to draw. For example, Thompson (1994) compared arguments like the ones in (A1) to see how likely her participants were to say that the conclusion logically followed:

(A1) a. If butter is heated, then it melts.
       The butter has melted.
       Was the butter heated?

b. If the car is out of gas, then it stalls.
The car has stalled.
Is the car out of gas?

Arguments (A1a) and (A1b) share the same form in that both have the structure: *If p then q; q; p?* So if participants attend only to this form in deciding about the arguments, they should respond in the same way to each. However, people's beliefs about cars include the fact that running out of gas is just one thing that could cause a car to stall, whereas their beliefs about butter include the fact that heating butter is virtually the only way to get it to melt. If people rely on these beliefs in determining whether the conclusions logically follow, they should be more likely to endorse the argument in (A1a) than the one in (A1b), and indeed, they do. The difference in acceptance rates is about 40 percentage points.

Thompson (1994) and others view these results as due to people's knowledge of necessary and sufficient conditions (see also Ahn & Graham, 1999). Heating butter is both necessary and sufficient for its melting, whereas running out of gas is sufficient but not necessary for a car stalling. Thus, given that the butter was melted, it was probably heated; but given the car has stalled, it may not be out of gas. The same point is sometimes made in terms of "alternative" causes or "additional" causes (e.g., Byrne, 1989; Byrne, Espino, & Santamaria, 1999; Cummins et al., 1991; De Neys, Schaeken, & d'Ydewalle, 2003; Markovits, 1984). An alternative cause is one that, independently of the stated cause (e.g., running out of gas), is able to bring about the effect, and an additional cause is one that must be conjoined with the stated cause in order for the effect to occur. The explanation of the difference between (A1a) and (A1b) is then that participants know of no alternative causes for the conditional in (A1a) that would block the inference, but they do know of alternatives for the conditional in (A1b)—perhaps an overheated engine or a broken fuel pump. Giving participants further premises or reminders that explicitly mention alternative or additional causes also affects the conclusions they're willing to draw (Byrne, 1989; Byrne et al., 1999; De Neys et al., 2003; Hilton, Jaspars, & Clarke, 1990).

The general framing in terms of necessary and sufficient conditions, though, raises the issue of whether the experiments are tapping reasoning with specifically causal relations or with more abstract knowledge. Some of the experiments cited above (Ahn & Graham, 1999; Thompson, 1994) demonstrate similar effects with conditionals that are about noncausal relations (e.g., conditional permissions such as *If the licensing board grants it a license, then a restaurant is allowed to sell liquor*). Perhaps people reason about necessity and sufficiency, with causal information merely setting up these beliefs. Likewise, you can interpret the results as due to participants' use of conditional probabilities (Evans & Over, 2004; Oaksford & Chater, 2003, 2007). According to Oaksford and Chater, for example, people's response to the question in (A1a) depends on the conditional probability that butter is heated given that it is melted, and the response to (A1b) reflects the conditional probability that the car is out of gas given that it has stalled. Since the first of these is likely to be greater than the second, participants should answer "yes" more often for (A1a) than (A1b). According to both the necessity/ sufficiency and the probabilistic theories, people's beliefs about causation informs the way they represent these problems, but their reasoning is carried out over representations that don't distinguish causes from other relations.

We may be able to get a more direct view of how people reason about causes by looking at experiments that give participants statements containing the word *cause* or its derivatives. A number of studies have found that people make different inferences from statements of the form *p causes q* (or *q causally depends on p*) than from ones of the form *If p then q* (Rips, 1983; Sloman & Lagnado, 2005; Staudenmayer, 1975). For example, Staudenmayer (1975) observed that participants were more likely to interpret explicit causal statements as implying a two-way, if-and-only-if, connection. For example, *Turning the switch on causes the light to go on* was more likely than *If the switch is turned on then the light goes on* to entail that the light goes on if and only if the switch is turned on. Many causal arrangements, however, don't lend themselves to such a two-way interpretation. *My turning on the switch causes the light to go on* is a case in point, since the light's going on could be caused by someone else turning the switch. Staudenmayer included examples like these, in which the cause is not necessary for the effect. But if causal statements don't force an if-and-only-if interpretation, why the difference between causals and conditionals in the results? Perhaps *cause* allows more freedom of interpretation than *if.* Although a two-way interpretation is possible for both *if* and *cause* in some situations (for pragmatic or other reasons), people may be more cautious about adopting it in the case of *if.*

In another respect, however, *cause* is more selective than *if.* Consider the arguments in (A2):

(A2)   a. If the gear turns then the light flashes.
           The bell rings.
           Therefore, if the gear turns then both the light flashes and
           the bell rings.
       b. The light flashing causally depends on the gear turning.
           The bell rings.
           Therefore, both the light flashing and the bell ringing
           causally depend on the gear turning.

The conclusion of (A2a) seems to follow, since we understand the conditionals as statements about an existing state of affairs. The gear's turning means that the light will flash, and since the turning presumably won't affect the bell's ringing, then if the turning occurs, so will the flashing and the ringing. However, the conclusion of (A2b) does not follow. Intuitively, the conclusion asserts a causal connection between the gear's turning and the bell's ringing that goes beyond anything asserted in (A2b)'s premises. In line with this impression, I found that, although 60.2% of participants agreed that the conclusion of arguments like (A2a) had to be true whenever the premises were true, only 31.0% agreed to the conclusion of items like (A2b) (Rips, 1983).

These differences between *cause* and *if* reflect fundamental differences in their meaning. Formal semantics for conditional sentences is a controversial matter (see Bennett, 2003). But people may evaluate them by temporarily supposing that the *if*-part (antecedent) of the sentence is true and then assessing the *then*-part (consequent) in that supposed situation (Stalnaker, 1968).[18] In these terms, *if* relates the current situation to a similar one (or similar ones) in which the antecedent holds. Conditionals can thus depend on circumstances that may not be a direct effect of the antecedent but simply carry over from the actual situation to the supposed one. This explains why we tend to judge that the conclusion of (A2a) follows. *Cause,* however, is not a sentence connective, but a predicate that connects terms for events. In order to create parallel structures between conditionals and causals in these experiments, investigators have to rephrase the antecedent and consequent as nominals (e.g., *the gear turns* in (A2a) becomes *the gear turning* in (A2b)), but the nominals still refer to events. Whether a causal sentence is true depends on exactly how these events are connected and not on other circumstances that may happen to hold in a situation in which the cause takes place. In this respect, causal sentences depend on the specifics of the expressed relation, just as ordinary predicates like *kiss* or *kick* do. Whether *John kisses Mary and Kate* is true depends on whether the appropriate relation holds between John and Mary and between John and Kate, and whether the gear's turning causes both the light's flashing and the bell's ringing likewise depends on whether the right causal connection holds between these events. The conclusion of (A2b) fails to follow from the premises, since the premises entail no such connection.

This point about the difference between conditionals and causals may be an obvious one, but analyses of *cause* can sometimes obscure it. For example, some formal treatments of action, like McCarthy and Hayes's (1969) situation calculus, represent these actions (a type of cause) as a function from a situation that obtains before the action to one that obtains after it. But although we may be able to think of both *if* and *cause* as types of functions between situations, the truth of a causal depends more intimately on the way in which the resulting state of affairs is brought about. We judge that "if c occurs then e occurs" on the basis of whether e holds in the situations that we get by supposing c is true, but this is not enough to support the assertion that "c causes e." Similarly, causal modal logics (e.g., Burks, 1977) represent the causal necessity or possibility of conditionals. Such logics, for example, can symbolize sentences of the type "It is causally necessary that if c occurs then e occurs," with the interpretation that "If c occurs then e occurs" in all possible worlds that retain the actual world's causal laws. However, causally necessary conditionals aren't equivalent to causals. It is causally necessary that if $5 + 7 = 12$ then $5 + 8 = 13$, since $5 + 7 = 12$ and $5 + 8 = 13$ are true in all possible worlds, including the causally necessary ones. But $5 + 7 = 12$ doesn't cause $5 + 8 = 13$ (or anything else, for that matter), since arithmetic facts don't have causal properties.

NOTES

Thanks to Jonathan Adler, Russell Burnett, Douglas Medin, and Brian Scholl for helpful comments on an earlier version (Rips, 2008) of this chapter.

1. For a computer animation of the Michotte effect, see: http://cogweb. ucla.edu/Discourse/Narrative/Heider_45.html. The same site also contains a replica of Heider and Simmel's (1944) demonstration, discussed later in this chapter.

2. Michotte (1963) is inconsistent on how to understand these reports. On the one hand, he emphasizes the phenomenal character of the observers' experiences: "Now the responses in these conditions given by the subjects always relate, of course, to the physical 'world' . . . . But the physical 'world' in question here is no longer the world of physical *science*, as revealed by measuring instruments; it is *the world of things, as it appears to the subject* on simple inspection, his 'phenomenal world', disclosed in this case by the indications which he gives as a human 'recording instrument'. Thus, when he says that A 'pulls B' or 'pushes B', he is referring to an event occurring in a world which appears as external to him, an event of which he thinks himself simply a witness and which he is merely describing" (p. 306). But one page later, on the other hand, Michotte retreats to a position in which statements about what an observer sees are no more than abbreviations for what the observer reports: "Throughout this book there often occur expressions such as 'what the subject sees', or 'the impression received by the subject', and so on. These expressions are clearly only abbreviations, and are used to make the text less cumbersome. They in fact refer to the subjects' verbal responses and they therefore mean 'what the subject says or asserts that he sees' or 'that of which the subject says or asserts that he has an impression', and so on" (p. 307, Note 5, emphasis in the original in both these passages).

3. Fodor (2003, chap. 3) argues that even if observers directly perceive an event in the display, it's likely to be a lower-level one like square x pushing another y (which is indeed what observers report, according to Michotte) rather than square x causing y to move. There's no reason to think, according to Fodor, that perceiving an event like a pushing entails perceiving the causing. Although *x pushes y* may imply *x causes y to move*, we may get the causing from the pushing by inference rather than by direct perception. This distinction may seem unimportant to investigators, who may be satisfied that at least one type of causal interaction (pushing or launching) is directly perceived, but it is a reminder that the conclusions about direct perception have limited scope.

4. For a more detailed critique of Michotte, see Rips (2010a).

5. I'm grateful to Brian Scholl for pointing out the relevance of these experiments.

6. For example, according to a methodology textbook by Pelham and Blanton (2003), "Most researchers who wish to understand causality rely heavily

on the framework proposed by the nineteenth-century philosopher John Stuart Mill," (p. 63). Similarly, Cook and Campbell (1979) note, "A careful reading of chapters 3 through 7 will reveal how often a modified form of Mill's canons is used to rule out identified threats to valid inference" (p. 19). Or, in more detail, "The conditions necessary for arriving at explanations were set forth in the nineteenth century by the philosopher John Stuart Mill. . . . Mill argued that causation can be inferred if some result, X, follows an event, A, if X and A vary together and if it can be shown that event A produces result X. For these conditions to be met, what Mill called the joint method of agreement and difference must be used. In the joint method, if A occurs then so will X, and if A does not occur, then neither will X" (Elmes, Kantowitz, & Roediger, 1999, p. 103, emphasis in the original). The joint method is the third of Mill's canons, which he regarded as superior to the method of agreement but inferior to the method of difference.

7. A normative problem also affects ΔP (as Cheng, 1997, argues). Since ΔP does not take into account the presence of other causes, it can yield a misleading index of the strength of any particular cause. For example, if other causes usually bring about the effect, then ΔP for the target cause will be systematically too small. In general, measures of causal strength run into normative difficulties by ignoring the structure of the causal system (e.g., the possible presence of confounding factors). Glymour (2001) shows that this problem affects not only ΔP but also conditional ΔP, Rescorla-Wagner strength, power, multiple regression coefficients, and others.

8. G. B. Chapman and Robbins (1990) and Cheng (1997) prove that under simplifying assumptions Rescorla and Wagner's (1972) theory of associative conditioning reduces to ΔP. (In general, however, the equivalence does *not* hold; see Glymour, 2001, citing earlier work by Danks.) A prominent member of my own faculty once declared that no graduate student from our cognitive program should get a Ph.D. without having studied the Rescorla-Wagner model. So here's the idea: Suppose that a creature is learning a relation between a set of conditioned stimuli $C_1, C_2, \ldots, C_n$ (e.g., lights, tones, etc.) and an unconditioned stimulus U_j (e.g., shock). Then the change to the associative strength, ΔV_i, of a particular stimulus C_i on any trial is a function of the difference between the asymptotic level of strength that's possible for the unconditioned stimulus and the sum of associative strengths for all the conditioned stimuli:

$$\Delta V_i = \alpha_i \beta_j (\lambda_j - \Sigma V_k),$$

where α_i is the salience of cue C_i, β_j is the learning rate for U_j ($0 \le \alpha, \beta \le 1$), λ_j is the asymptotic level of strength possible for U_j, and the sum is over all cues in $C_1, C_2, \ldots, C_n$ present on the trial. The asymptote λ will have a high value (> 0) when the unconditioned stimulus is present and a low value (perhaps 0) when it is absent on a trial. No change occurs to the strength of C_i if it is not present on a trial ($\Delta V_i = 0$). The important thing to notice is that the change in strength for an individual cue depends on the strength of all others present. See Shanks and Dickinson (1987) for a discussion of the Rescorla-Wagner theory and other learning models as applied to causal judgments.

9. Psychologists tend to see ANOVA methods as superior to correlational ones in isolating the cause of some phenomenon. But as far as the statistics goes, there's no important difference between them, since ANOVA is a special case of multiple correlation/regression. The perceived difference between them is due to the fact that psychologists use ANOVA to analyze designed experiments but use correlations to analyze observational ones. Manipulation does have advantages over passive observation for reasons discussed in the following section.

10. Bayes' Theorem is a mathematical relation between the conditional probability $\Pr(A|B)$ and the converse conditional probability $\Pr(B|A)$. We can express the theorem in one of its forms as follows:

$$\Pr(A|B) = \frac{\Pr(B|A)\Pr(A)}{\Pr(B)}.$$

In the present case, let A = *a mother has blue eyes* and B = *a daughter has blue eyes*. Then, if $\Pr(A) = \Pr(B)$, the two conditional probabilities will also be equal.

11. "Simpson's paradox" is not a true paradox but an algebraic consequence of the fact that the difference between each of two proportions a/b − c/d and e/f − g/h can be positive (negative) while the aggregate difference (a + e)/(b + f) − (c + g)/(d + h) can be negative (positive), as the numbers in Table 3.2 illustrate. Simpson (1951, p. 240) pointed out that this leaves "considerable scope for paradox and error" in how we interpret the two-way interaction between the remaining factors (i.e., the two that don't define the partition between a-d and e-h). For example, should we say that irradiation is positively or negatively related to the quality of fruit in Table 3.2?

12. These cases may also violate assumptions necessary in deriving p_c and, if so, lie outside the domain of the power theory (see Luhmann & Ahn, 2005).

13. A variation on an example of Sloman's (2005, pp. 57–59) illustrates the same ambiguity. Suppose peptic ulcers result either from bacterial infections of a certain sort or from taking too many aspirin and similar drugs. Peptic ulcers, in turn, cause burning pains in the gut. In this situation, we may be able to intervene on someone's ulcer by administering a drug—Grandma's special formula, in Sloman's example—that cures the ulcer and thereby relieves the pain. But what should we conclude about whether the bacteria or the aspirin continue to be present after the intervention? The natural thing to say is that this depends on how Grandma's formula works. If it acts as a kind of barrier that

protects the stomach lining, then perhaps the presence of the bacteria or the aspirin is unchanged. But if it works by destroying the bacteria and neutralizing the aspirin, then, of course, neither will exist after the intervention. Sloman is careful to stipulate that Grandma's special formula "goes directly to the ulcer, by-passing all normal causal pathways, and heals it every time." But how often do we know in the case of actual interventions that they route around all normal causal channels? Isn't the more usual case one where the intervention disrupts some causal paths but not others and where it may be unclear how far upstream in the causal chain the intervention takes place?

14. The old way of exploiting casual laws involved deducing causal relations between individual events from general "covering" laws plus particular statements of fact (see Hempel, 1965). See the papers in J. Collins, Hall, and Paul (2004), for recent work on the counterfactual analysis of cause. For a theory that attempts to derive knowledge of necessity and possibility more generally from counterfactual conditionals, see Williamson (2007, Ch. 5).

15. This isn't to deny a relation between the causal Markov condition and the idea of intervention. Hausman and Woodward (1999, p. 553) argue that "the independent disruptability of each mechanism turns out to be the flip side of the probabilistic independence of each variable conditional on its direct causes from everything other than its effects." But their argument requires a number of strong assumptions (each variable in the Bayes net must have unobserved causes and these unobserved causes can affect only one variable) that may not always be true of the representations people have of causal systems. See Cartwright (2001) for a general critique of the causal Markov condition, and Cartwright (2002) for a specific critique of Hausman and Woodward's "flip side" claim.

16. Section 3.2.2.2 discussed a similar experiment from Sloman and Lagnado (2005, Experiment 6). That experiment compared counterfactuals describing explicit prevention with those describing explicit observation (*Suppose Component B were observed not to be moving . . .*). The present study (Sloman & Lagnado, 2005, Experiment 5) compares a case of explicit prevention with a vanilla counterfactual that mentions neither prevention nor observation [see (11a) vs. (11b)].

17. Hiddleston (2005) proposes a causal network theory of counterfactuals along the following lines: Given a causal network with variables A and C, we can evaluate the truth of the counterfactual *If A = a then C = c* by considering all minimally different assignments of values to variables in the network such that A = a. If C = c is true in all these minimal assignments, then so is *If A = a then C = c*. An assignment is minimally different, roughly speaking, if (a) it has as few variables as possible whose value is different from that in the actual situation but all of whose parents have the same values, and (b) among the variables that are not effects of A, it has as many variables as possible whose values are the same as

in the actual situation and all of whose parents are also the same. This theory is consistent with participants' majority answers to counterfactual questions such as (12). (See Rips, 2010b.)

18. Of course, a suppositional theory needs to be worked out more carefully than can be done here. In particular, the supposition can't be such as to block all modus tollens arguments that entail the falsity of the conditional's antecedent.

4

Kinds

This is more of a mixed-pickles story than most.

A. J. Liebling, *The Wayward Pressman*

Our knowledge of natural kinds, such as frogs or daisies or silver, extends beyond actual circumstances and holds as well in merely possible circumstances that we've not experienced. We're willing to affirm that if Frederick were a frog, he would have webbed feet and long hind legs, even though we have no previous knowledge of Frederick or have knowledge that he is a (human) prince instead. We assume that if a frog has a biological property, such as having glyco-lymphide as a neurotransmitter, then other frogs have glyco-lymphide, even though we have no previous knowledge of this property. Although we may ultimately base these conjectures on knowledge about natural kinds' actual properties, we don't limit our hypotheses to those about the actual world. Natural concepts such as FROG have a status that allows them to play a role in counterfactual conditionals and hypothetical inductive inferences, as in the examples we just glimpsed (see, e.g., Brandom, 1988, 1994).

Similarly, our knowledge of natural kinds includes information that is resistant to exceptions. Linguists and philosophers, for example, have described *generic sentences*, such as *Lions have manes*, as ones that are true, despite the existence of obvious and sometimes numerous exceptions (such as female lions and immature male lions; see Krifka et al., 1995; S.-J. Leslie, 2008). Likewise, research on nonmonotonic logic in AI has sought systems that can reason with such sentences without making mistakes or becoming inconsistent when exceptions arise (e.g., Ginsberg, 1987).

Cognitive psychology, however, has mostly treated beliefs about categories in terms of what's normal or usual rather than in terms of what's law-like or exception-resistant. Early theories of perceptual categorizing (e.g., Posner & Keele, 1968, 1970; Reed, 1972) emphasized the role of prototypes, consisting of average values of category members along their physical dimensions. According to these theories, if people have to classify, for example, schematic faces into two previously identified sets, they mentally compute a prototype for each set, where the prototype specifies the average values of the members of that set on dimensions like width of mouth, length of nose, and distance between eyes. To decide which set a novel face belongs to, people then determine the similarity between the new face and each of the category prototypes. Finally, people assign the new face to the set whose prototype is closest to this new item.

The importance of normal or average values of category members persists in many cognitive theories of everyday categories. In Eleanor Rosch's well-known theory (e.g., Rosch, 1978; Rosch & Mervis, 1975), membership in these categories depends on the typicality of an instance with respect to the category. Typicality of the instance depends, in turn, on how many of its stimulus values the instance shares with members of the target category and how few values it shares with members of rival categories. The best examples of lions—the most typical ones—are those that have properties that are most widespread among lions (and least widespread among cougars, cheetahs, and tigers). On this view, then, both typicality and category membership come down to possessing properties (values of attributes, such as having a tawny color) that are common in a census of the target category (see A. Tversky, 1977, for a similar view of typicality). Although Rosch (1978) held that there might be no single prototype for everyday categories, she nevertheless believed that these categories depend on the prevalence of properties among their instances.

Recent theories have sometimes taken over this view of everyday categories as based on average values, although the mental representations that contain them tend to be more complex. Hampton (1995a, p. 104), for example, retains the notion of a prototype as a "generalization or abstraction of some central tendency, average or typical value of a class of instances falling in the same category," and E. E. Smith, Osherson, Rips, and Keane's (1988) prototypes are composed of attribute-value combinations, with each value weighted (in part) by the subjective frequency of the value among category instances. To be sure, some psychological theories don't rely on prototypes, but many of these alternatives also appeal to the properties of (samples of) existing category members. For instance, in exemplar theories of categories (e.g., Hintzman, 1986; Medin & Schaffer, 1978; Nosofsky, 1986), decisions about membership depend on the similarity of new items to previously encountered and remembered instances. Exemplar models do not compile average values or distributions of properties for a category in the way prototype theories do, but they remain tethered to a sample of actual category members. (For more on the exemplar theory, see Chapter 5 in this book.)

I examine other psychological theories of categories later in this chapter and in the following one, but for now the issue is this: If our concepts of natural kinds are based on our mental surveys of members of these categories, as they seem to be in prototype or exemplar theories, then what allows these concepts to resist exceptions, generalize to novel instances, and support counterfactual conditionals? To see the difficulty here, compare lions to a nonnatural category, such as things in offices weighing between 40 and 50 pounds. An inventory might convince you that such things are typically beige and rectangular. But you would probably be more hesitant to attribute beige and rectangular to a new member of this category than to attribute tawny color and lionlike shape to new members of the lion category. Similarly, you would never suppose that if Calvin were to weigh 45 pounds and were to step into an office, he would be beige and rectangular; but you might well think that if Calvin were a lion he'd be tawny and lion-shaped. On-the-spot perceptual recognition of objects as members of natural kinds may depend on average or typical stimulus values. As the questions just raised make clear, though, once we begin considering the role natural kinds play in other forms of thought, we're forced to consider these kinds' modal properties—properties that the members of the kind *might* have or *must* have across (possibly counterfactual) circumstances.

We met a similar problem in Chapter 1 in trying to determine how we're able to think about individual objects' behavior in situations that have not actually occurred. That chapter suggested that knowledge of the causal forces that sustain an object during its existence provides the information we need to envision these nonactual situations. The present chapter considers a similar solution to the problem about categories. Causal laws governing the kinds in question give us generalizations about these kinds that are more robust than simple statistical generalizations. In fact, for natural kinds like lions or daisies, some of the same causal laws that govern an individual may also be responsible for the existence of the category. The lion species may be supported, in part, by the causes that maintain individual lions. Of course, to play this role, our beliefs about causal forces have to go beyond statistical generalizations. But this accords with the conclusions of Chapter 3: Although people may use correlations to aid them in detecting causes, they nevertheless believe that causes are more than just co-occurrence patterns.

In the first part of this chapter, I look at some psychological evidence that pins down the modal qualities of natural kinds (e.g., daisies, lions, copper); in the second part, I examine some approaches that may have a chance of explaining these qualities. The second part compares two general ideas about modal properties, which I'll call the "intrinsic" and the "interactional" views. The intrinsic view allies itself with psychological essentialism (e.g., S. A. Gelman, 2003; Medin & Ortony, 1989) in holding that people believe the modal properties of natural kinds are the results of a single necessary property residing within each instance of the kind. The interactional view maintains instead that these kinds depend on a set of co-operating causes, some internal and some external to a member of the kind. Although each view can claim some advantages, I'll be arguing that the interactional view comes closest to beliefs about these matters, at least for adults. The view of kinds therefore meshes with the view of individuals that I presented in Chapter 1.

The aim of this chapter is to grapple with the question of how seemingly objective categories like lions could have properties that extend beyond the set of their actual members. In thinking about this issue, we should keep in mind that natural kinds are not just arbitrary sets of objects that *occur* in nature, but they are groupings of objects that *share* an underlying nature. Frogs are natural kinds but the set consisting of frogs and daisies are not, despite the fact that both frogs and daisies are found in nature. Cats are a natural kind but pets are not, since there is no underlying nature common to pets. Dogs are natural kinds but seeing-eye dogs are probably not. Seeing-eye dogs have an underlying nature by virtue of being dogs, but no further nature that makes them seeing-eye dogs. Exactly what constitutes a natural kind is one of the issues that this chapter addresses: We need to understand what constitutes an underlying nature for the categories in question. For the time being, however, we can get along by thinking of typical examples of natural kinds, such as biological species and chemical elements.

4.1 Modal Characteristics of Natural Categories: Psychological Evidence

In recent cognitive studies of natural kinds, there seem to be three main ways in which beliefs about these categories could be said to be modal: First, natural kinds govern people's ideas about the distribution of their relevant properties, even in the face of contradictory perceptual evidence. Second, these categories dictate conditions under which individuals belong to the category, again despite possible perceptual evidence to the contrary. And third, people believe in determinate ways of resolving questions about category membership, although they may have no personal knowledge of what these tests might be. Let's look at these experiments to explore the nature of these beliefs' modal character. Although I briefly examine children's ideas about these matters, the main goal is to determine the final or steady state of these beliefs among adults.

4.1.1 Natural Kinds and Induction

We think that certain biological properties of lions, such as having lungs, having four legs, or having a specific genetic makeup, are potentially true of all members of the lion category. Thus, if we learn that a new biological property is true of a particular lion, we're likely to think that other lions have the property as well. If you learn that Leigh has Type K blood serum, for example, you're likely to think that other lions also have it. Type K blood is presumably a type of blood, even though it's not a type you've heard of. Since types of blood are the sorts of properties that run along biological lines, you're willing to generalize them to other lions. You could be wrong. Maybe lions, like people, have more than one blood type. But your willingness to generalize is an important aspect of your knowledge of categories. Of course, not all properties generalize across natural kinds: Leigh's particular pattern of cuts and bruises is not the sort of property that is likely to be true of other lions. The power of natural kinds to guide generalization therefore depends on the type of relation that holds between property and kind.

4.1.1.1 Category-Based Inductive Inferences in Children

Even toddlers go along with generalizing by kind. As early as 14 months, children generalize an animal's activity more often from one (toy) animal to another than from the animal to an artifact (Mandler & McDonough, 1998). For example, after they have seen an experimenter demonstrate a dog drinking, they tend to imitate the drinking more often with a lamb than with a train engine. When the activity is not specific to animals, however, they generalize about equally to an artifact as to another animal. They generalize getting-cleaned-with-a-sponge from the dog to the train engine about as often as to the lamb.

Mandler and McDonough (1998) found little sensitivity to distinctions within the category of land animals. But by 2 or 3 years, children more often generalize familiar properties to novel instances of the same lower-level category than to novel instances of other categories (S. A. Gelman & Coley, 1990; Waxman, Lynch, Casey, & Baer, 1997). For example, Waxman et al. told children that a (pictured) animal had a specific (but unpictured) property and then asked them whether the same property was true of other animals. The children learned, for instance, that a particular collie had the property of "helping us take care of sheep." The children then had to decide whether other collies, other dogs (e.g., setters), and other animals (e.g., caribou) had this property. The results indicated that children generalized the property to other dogs more often than to nondog animals. Training on contrasting properties of subcategories (e.g., setters "help us find birds," whereas Samoyeds "help us pull sleds") further restricted the range of the children's generalization.

Somewhat older children (4-year-olds) are usually willing to generalize unfamiliar biological properties (e.g., *having cold blood*) by category, even when perceptual appearance is placed in direct opposition to category membership. Gelman and Markman (1986) told children that one dinosaur (a pictured apatosaurus) had cold blood and a pictured rhinoceros had warm blood, as in Figure 4.1. The children were then asked whether a second dinosaur (a triceratops) had warm or cold blood. These children preferred generalizing cold blood from the dinosaur over generalizing warm blood from the rhino, even though the picture of the triceratops looked more similar to the rhino than to the apatosaurus.[1]

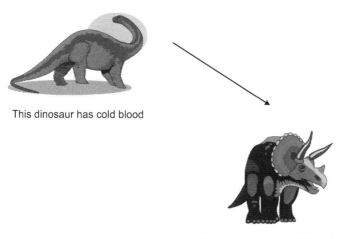

This dinosaur has cold blood

Does this dinosaur have cold blood or warm blood?

This rhinoceros has warm blood

FIGURE 4.1   One trial from Gelman and Markman's (1986) study of category-based induction in children. Children chose to generalize a property from a perceptually dissimilar but same-category member (the dinosaur) rather than from a perceptually similar but different-category member (the rhino). (The pictures in this figure are not those used in the original study.)

Of course, children don't always generalize properties in an adult-like way. Carey (1985, chap. 4) found that 4-year-olds are much more apt to generalize unfamiliar properties (e.g., *having a spleen inside*) from people to other familiar animals, such as dogs, than from dogs to people. Carey takes this result to indicate that younger children organize their knowledge of the animal domain in terms of their beliefs about specifically human properties rather than in terms of biological characteristics (however, see Medin & Waxman, 2007, for other interpretations). Carey (1985) and S. A. Gelman and O'Reilly (1988) also found that 4-year-olds are less willing than early grade-school children to generalize unfamiliar properties from one member of a natural kind to a member of a second kind within the same superordinate category. (See Chapter 1, Note 8, of this book for the distinction between basic, superordinate, and subordinate categories.) For example, the younger children are more hesitant to generalize the property *has leukocytes all through it* from a dog to a horse than were the older children. Evidence is somewhat inconsistent on whether preschool children recognize that natural kinds are more likely than artifacts to promote generalization (S. A. Gelman, 1988; S. A. Gelman & O'Reilly, 1988), presumably because these children are just mastering the relevant knowledge.

In sum, these results suggest that 4-year-olds understand that animal and plant species support inductive generalization, and they have a rough idea of which properties generalize and which don't. Still, children 4 or younger apparently don't have a clear sense of the mechanisms that support generalization over species or of the differences between these mechanisms and those at work in artifacts. Finally, even 8-year-olds have difficulty recognizing the importance of sample size and sample variability in induction based on natural kinds (Gutheil & Gelman, 1997).

4.1.1.2 Category-Based Inductive Inferences in Adults

Early theories of category-based inductive inference in adults (Osherson, Smith, Wilkie, Lopez, & Shafir, 1990; Rips, 1975) consisted of a two-part process: a direct and an indirect transmission of the target property. According to these theories, when people are told, for example, that cows have a novel disease and are asked to estimate the likelihood that bats also have the disease, they consider both the similarity between cows and bats (direct transmission) and also the similarity or typicality of cows with respect to mammals in general (indirect transmission). These two routes to an inductive conclusion appear in Figure 4.2. The first route accounts for the finding that people judge it more likely that the disease will generalize from cows to horses than from cows to bats. The second route accounts for the fact that people judge it more likely that the disease will generalize from cows (a typical mammal) to bats (an atypical mammal) than from bats to cows.

The Similarity-Coverage model.   Osherson et al. (1990) have elaborated this theory in their Similarity-Coverage model to describe simultaneous generalization from several different categories. This model is able to

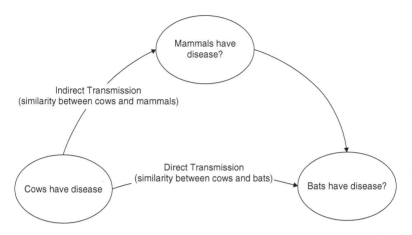

FIGURE 4.2 An example of the Similarity-Coverage model (Osherson et al., 1990)
as applied to the problem:

Cows have disease X.

Bats have disease X.

The model computes the strength of the conclusion as a weighted average of the
direct similarity between cows and bats (direct transmission route) and the similarity
between cows and all mammal species (indirect transmission route).

predict, for example, how likely people think it is that bats have Vitamin
Z, given the information that cows, lions, and mice have Vitamin Z. We
can write this argument in the standard format in (1), where the sentences above the horizontal line are called the *premises* and the sentence
below the line the *conclusion* of the argument:

(1)   Cows have Vitamin Z.
       Lions have Vitamin Z.
       Mice have Vitamin Z.

       Bats have Vitamin Z.

Applied to an argument of this sort, the Similarity-Coverage model
computes direct transmission as the similarity of the conclusion item
(bats) to the most similar of the premise categories. In argument (1), bats
are more similar to mice than to either cows or lions; so the similarity
between mice and bats determines the degree of generalization due to the
direct route. The model computes indirect transmission in a related way,
by first determining the smallest superordinate category containing all the

categories in the premises and conclusion—presumably, mammal in the case of argument (1). The model then finds the average similarity between the premise categories and each species of mammal known to the participant. Thus, indirect transmission of Vitamin Z would be due to the average similarity of cows, lions, and mice, on one hand, to horses, pigs, bears, and the rest of the mammal species on the other. (The model again calculates the joint similarity of cows, lions, and mice to another species as the similarity of that species to the most similar of those three premise categories.) The overall strength of the argument will be a weighted average of the similarity from the direct and the indirect routes.

Osherson et al. (1990) show that the Similarity-Coverage model can explain many phenomena associated with arguments such as (1) that contain biological-seeming, but unfamiliar, properties.[2] In addition to the similarity and typicality results just discussed, the model's indirect transmission route can also explain why participants judge arguments like (1) stronger than matched arguments such as (2):

(2)   Rabbits have Vitamin Z.
       Squirrels have Vitamin Z.
       Mice have Vitamin Z.

       Bats have Vitamin Z.

According to the model, this result, which Osherson et al. call *premise diversity*, occurs because cows, lions, and mice, as a group, are more similar to other mammal species than are rabbits, squirrels, and mice. The first group is more diverse in that it better spans the range of mammals than the second does. Thus, mammals in general will be more likely to have Vitamin Z, given the premises of (1) than the premises of (2). The model also applies to arguments in which the conclusion category is at a higher level than the premise categories—for example, arguments in which *mammals* substitutes for *bats* in (1) and (2). For these *general* arguments, the direct and the indirect routes collapse; both become just the average similarity of the premise categories to all mammal species. Thus, the model also predicts that argument (1) will be stronger than (2) when *mammals* appears in place of *bats* in the conclusions.

Perceived similarity—direct and indirect—is the engine of the Similarity-Coverage model. Sloman (1993) has shown that many of the phenomena that the Similarity-Coverage model explains can also be handled by a single-route similarity theory. This theory represents each of the categories as a set of predicates or features (e.g., *living, has a mane,* and *roars* in the case of lions), and it predicts the strength of arguments such as (1) and (2) to be the proportion of the conclusion category's features that are included among those of the premise categories. For example, this *Feature-Based* theory explains premise diversity (e.g., the greater strength of argument (1) than (2)) on the assumption that more diverse premise categories will usually contain more of the conclusion category's features than less diverse premise categories. This one-route similarity model has some strengths and weaknesses relative to Osherson et al.'s (1990) two-route model, but since similarity is the driving force in both models, we can consider them together here.

Questions about the Similarity-Coverage model. Although the Similarity-Coverage model is successful in unifying a large set of findings, it runs into a number of difficulties (as does the earlier theory in Rips, 1975). The most obvious of these is that the model is completely insensitive to the type of property that's being projected from the premises to the conclusion. As Osherson, Smith, and Shafir (1986) noted in earlier work, the similarity idea "oversimplifies the psychology of argument strength."

Some results of Heit and Rubinstein (1994) illustrate the problem (see Osherson et al., 1986, for an earlier example). These investigators employed triples of animal categories, such as bears, tunas, and whales, in which the first and third categories shared certain anatomical properties (e.g., mammalian ones) and the second and third shared behavioral properties (e.g., swimming). Heit and Rubinstein used these category triples to construct arguments, such as the examples in (3) and (4), varying both the anatomical or behavioral consistency of the categories and the anatomical or behavioral nature of the predicates:

(3)   a. Bears have a liver with two chambers that act as one.
       _____
       Whales have a liver with two chambers that act as one.

       b. Tunas have a liver with two chambers that act as one.
       _____
       Whales have a liver with two chambers that act as one.

(4)   a. Bears usually travel in a back-and-forth or zig-zag trajectory.

Whales usually travel in a back-and-forth or zig-zag trajectory.

b. Tunas usually travel in a back-and-forth or zig-zag trajectory.

Whales usually travel in a back-and-forth or zig-zag trajectory.

A theory based entirely on the similarity between the named categories must predict that participants should select the (a)-items as stronger in both (3) and (4) or should select the (b)-items as stronger in both. For example, if the combination of direct and indirect routes in Figure 4.2 yields the result that (3a) is a stronger inference than (3b), then participants should also choose (4a) over (4b), since these arguments involve exactly the same categories. This is not, however, the result that Heit and Rubinstein obtained. Instead, participants found (3a) stronger than (3b), but (4b) stronger than (4a). The categories in the (a)-items are the ones that share their anatomical natures, whereas the categories in the (b)-items share behavioral natures. The premise category in (3a), bears, is therefore a better predictor of the anatomical property *having a liver with two chambers* than is the premise category in (3b). By contrast, the premise category in (4b), tunas, is a better predictor of the behavioral property *traveling in a back-and-forth trajectory* than the premise category in (4a). (For similar findings, see Ross & Murphy, 1999).

The Similarity-Coverage model attempted to sidestep such problems using fictitious biological properties, such as having Vitamin Z, but related difficulties affect the model even for this unfamiliar material. These difficulties become apparent when we try to apply the Similarity-Coverage theory to some of the results on children's inferences. As we noticed earlier, S. A. Gelman and Markman (1986) found that 4-year-olds prefer generalizing an unfamiliar biological property by category than by perceptual similarity. For example, when the children learned that "this dinosaur" (an apatosaurus) has cold blood and that "this rhinoceros" has warm blood, they ventured that "this [new] dinosaur" (a triceratops) has cold rather than warm blood (Figure 4.1). Osherson et al. (1990) reconstruct Gelman and Markman's task as involving a choice between two contrary arguments. One argument is: Apatosauruses have cold blood; therefore, triceratops have cold blood. The other argument is: Rhinos have warm blood; therefore, triceratops have warm blood. The stronger of these two arguments should determine the child's response. Which argument is stronger depends on the relative weight given to the direct and indirect routes in Figure 4.2. On the one hand, the argument from the apatosaurus to the triceratops, according to the model, is mainly warranted by the indirect transmission of cold blood through dinosaur. On the other hand, the argument from the rhino to the triceratops will mainly depend on direct similarity. Thus, the Similarity-Coverage model is consistent with the result, provided that the children place more weight on indirect than direct transmission.

But although the Similarity Coverage model is consistent with the Gelman-Markman finding, it doesn't *explain* the result, since the model provides no reason why indirect transmission should dominate direct transmission in this setting. On an intuitive account, the children are generalizing correctly because the property is biologically relevant, and apatosauruses and triceratops are in the same relevant biological category (i.e., dinosaurs), whereas rhinos and triceratops are not. This is essentially Gelman and Markman's view (see also Markman, 1989, chap. 5; and S. A. Gelman, 2003). If the property-to-be-projected is an accidental one, such as *can eat a cupful of food* or *has feet that get cold at night*, then children do not generalize by kind any more often than by perceptual similarity (S. A. Gelman & Markman, 1986, Experiment 3). Similarly, children as young as 4 years generalize inborn characteristics but not acquired ones (Springer & Keil, 1989, Experiment 3). But this is just the sort of dependence on properties that pure similarity theories, including the Similarity-Coverage model, can't handle.[3]

Finally, in carrying out an inductive inference with an unfamiliar property, people sometimes consider connections between premise and conclusion categories that don't hinge on similarity at all, and this leads to mispredictions for the Similarity-Coverage approach. For example, Lopez, Atran, Coley, Medin, and Smith (1997) report that the Itzaj (Mayan natives of Guatemala) do not exhibit the premise diversity effect—the contrast between arguments (1) and (2) above. For example, Itzaj informants were told that coconut palms and royal palms have one disease and that coconut palms and basket whists have another (where coconuts, royal palms, and basket whists are all palm trees known to the informants). When asked whether all other palms were more likely to have the first disease or the second, the Itzaj informants split their vote, despite the fact that coconuts and basket whists are more diverse than coconuts and royal palms in Itzaj folk taxonomies. As justification for preferring the less diverse argument, Itzaj explained that both coconuts and royal palms are tall trees and are therefore more likely to spread a disease by contact with others in the rain forest. According to the Similarity-Coverage approach, the diversity effect depends on participants using the indirect transmission route in Figure 4.2, as mentioned earlier. Since coconuts and basket whists are jointly more similar to other palms than are coconuts and royal palms, indirect transmission predicts more generalization from the former pair. At least some Itzaj, however, prefer to reason with more direct causal connections between category members, short-circuiting the similarity-based method (for related evidence, see also Coley, Medin, Proffitt, Lynch, & Atran, 1999; Medin, Lynch, Coley, & Atran, 1997; J. B. Proffitt, Coley, & Medin, 2000; and Shafto & Coley, 2003).

The Gap model.   Osherson et al. (1986) were well aware of the limitations of theories based purely on similarity. In proposing their Similarity-Coverage model, Osherson et al. (1990) hoped to avoid some of these problems by using unfamiliar biological properties, about which people have few prior beliefs. Since these predicates are unfamiliar, "they are unlikely to evoke beliefs that cause one argument to have more strength than another" (p. 186), and they can thereby isolate the effects of categories on inductive inference. The results by S. A. Gelman and Markman (1986) and by Heit and Rubinstein (1994), however, suggest that their biological flavor leads people to assume that the predicates generalize according to specifically biological mechanisms rather than according to overall similarity. In some cases, people may assume these mechanisms run along taxonomic lines. If horses have Vitamin Z, for example, then perhaps the mechanisms responsible for Vitamin Z production in horses is also at work in biologically related species such as donkeys, or even in all mammals. Hence, donkeys (or mammals) have Vitamin Z. In other cases, people may reason that the relevant causal mechanism is external to the organism. Perhaps horses have Vitamin Z by virtue of eating certain kinds of feed; so other animals that eat the same feed should also have Vitamin Z. The Similarity-Coverage model may provide better fits to the data in the former case, since biological (taxonomic) relationships play a role in determining indirect transmission between species. But in neither case is global similarity likely to be the guiding principle.

In their later work, Osherson, Smith, Shafir, and their colleagues (Osherson, Smith, Myers, Shafir, & Stob, 1994; Osherson, Smith, Shafir, Gualtierotti, & Biolsi, 1995; E. E. Smith, Shafir, & Osherson, 1993) have attempted to account for arguments with more familiar properties by proposing a related theory, called the *Gap model*.[4] The model applies to arguments similar to those in (1)–(4) in which the subject nouns of the premises and conclusion name a category. However, the predicates can differ in the premises and conclusion, and they describe more familiar properties. Osherson et al.'s (1995) examples and experiments typically involve complex predicates, such as *have skins that are more resistant to penetration than most synthetic fibers* or *have a visual system that fully adapts to darkness in less than five minutes*.[5] The Gap model's mechanisms are somewhat complicated, and I present the details in the Appendix to this chapter. But I can illustrate the basic ideas of the model in terms of the simple argument in (5):

(5)   Lions are at least 5 feet tall.

       House cats are at least 5 feet tall.

To determine the inductive strength of (5), we need to assume that the premise is true and assess the conclusion on this basis. According to the Gap model, we do this by recalibrating facts about the premise category (adjusting the height of lions) and then applying the recalibration to the conclusion category. In the case of (5), the model computes the difference between the usual height of lions (say, 4 feet) and the value specified by the predicate (5 feet). The difference (1 foot) represents the amount that lions would have to increase in height in order for the premise to be true. The model then increases the height of house cats by the same amount, but weighted by the similarity between lions and house cats. For example, if lions and house cats are quite similar—for example, .8 on a 0 to 1 scale—then the new height of house cats will be boosted by .8 (5 − 4) = .8. If the subjective height of house cats is ordinarily 1 foot, their recalibrated height will be 1.8 feet, and the model determines the likelihood that house cats with a subjective average size of 1.8 feet could be 5 feet tall. This probability measures the strength of the argument, according to the Gap model. (See Note 20 if you're worried about the meaning of the probability statement.)

Questions about the Gap model.   The role that similarity plays in the Gap model leads to some questions about the theory. By contrast with the Similarity Coverage model, in which overall similarity between categories matters, the Gap model considers similarity with respect to properties "potentiated by the predicate" (E. E. Smith et al., 1993, footnote 5). This decision seems on the right track, since, for example, no matter how similar a toy stuffed lion is to a flesh-and-blood lion, learning that a lion is 5 feet tall may have minimal effects on your estimate that the toy is 5 feet tall (Carey, 1985). However, how do we determine which properties the predicate potentiates? The model would run into problems if it restricted the similarity computation to the property the predicate *denotes.* In (5) the predicate denotes a value on the height dimension. Potentiating only height would mean determining similarity according to the difference in height between lions and house cats in (5). But suppose that instead of house cats, the conclusion category was cougars and that the subjective height of cougars is 2 feet (see the Appendix). Do we want to adjust the height of cougars more than the height of house cats because the difference in height between cougars and lions is smaller than that between house cats and lions?

Examples like these led E. E. Smith et al. (1993, p. 93) to conclude that when the critical dimension is obvious, as in (5), people no longer use similarity in calculating the strength of the argument. Still, you might well believe that some relevant relationship between the premise and the conclusion categories (apart from height) affects the strength of arguments like these. Argument (5) becomes less plausible when we substitute for "house cat" an inanimate object of approximately the same size. For example, argument (5) seems noticeably weaker when the conclusion category is Coke bottles, even assuming that Coke bottles have exactly the same height as house cats.

We can put this point in a more general way: In evaluating arguments for inductive strength, we are invited to assume the premises are true, and we must then determine the believability of the conclusion. In assessing the conclusion, we could take into account the similarity between premise and conclusion categories (as in the Similarity-Coverage model) and the relative degree to which conclusion and premise categories fall short of the predicate's value (as in the Gap model). But we also need to understand why or how the premise is supposed to be true—a

theme that has already appeared in the discussion of causality and counterfactual conditionals in Chapter 3. This is because the factors that make
the premise true may determine how the premise information generalizes (see Heit, 2000, for a similar conclusion). We noticed in discussing
the Vitamin Z examples that how the property generalizes depends on
whether the premises are true because the animals produce the vitamin
internally or because they obtain it externally from food. Similarly, the
results from Lopez et al. (1997) and Shafto and Coley (2003) suggest that
the believability of the conclusion depends on people's notions of how
a disease is transmitted. And, likewise, the strength of arguments like
(5) may be a function of how we imagine the premise could become
true: If it's a matter of feline growth hormone or some other biological
factors, we would probably find (5) much stronger than the comparable
argument with Coke bottles as the conclusion category. If it's a matter of
general stretching or other purely physical-mechanical factors, however,
we might find the two arguments equivalently strong (or, more likely,
equivalently weak). These considerations of how the premises become
true go beyond a simple comparison between the categories or between
the predicate's properties and those of the categories. They also depend
on the causal dependencies that are in place (see Burstein, Collins, &
Baker, 1991; Collins & Michalski, 1989; Hadjichristidis, Sloman, Stevenson,
& Over, 2004; Kemp & Tenenbaum, 2009; Rehder, 2006; and Shafto,
Kemp, Bonawitz, Coley, & Tenenbaum, 2008, for theories of induction
partly based on such dependencies).

A pair of studies by Sloman (1994, 1997) demonstrates the importance of these external causal factors. In these experiments, participants
received arguments, such as (6) and (7), and they estimated the conditional probability of the conclusion given the premise. In (6), for example, they estimated the probability that zoologists are required by law to
receive rabies vaccines regularly, given that ranchers are. The participants
also estimated the probability of the conclusion alone (without the
premise information)—for example, the probability that zoologists are
required by law to receive rabies vaccines. The arguments had premises
that suggested an explanation that either carried over to the conclusion
(as in (6)) or did not carry over (as in (7)). For example, ranchers might
be required to get rabies vaccines because of their exposure to animals, a
risk also common to zoologists. Ranchers try to control animal breeding,

however, in order to improve their livestock, a goal that may not be relevant to zoologists.

(6)   Ranchers are required by law to receive rabies vaccines regularly.

Zoologists are required by law to receive rabies vaccines regularly.

(7)   Ranchers try to control the breeding of animals.

Zoologists try to control the breeding of animals.

Sloman found that estimates of the conditional probability of same-explanation items, such as (6), were higher than estimates of the probability of the conclusion alone. (E.g., the estimated probability that zoologists are required by law to receive rabies vaccines *given that* ranchers are so required was higher than the estimated probability that zoologists are required by law to receive rabies vaccines.) Thus, the premise boosted the likelihood of the conclusion for these arguments. By contrast, the premise of the different-explanation items, such as (7), either reduced the conditional probability of the conclusion or produced the same estimate as the isolated conclusion. (E.g., the estimated probability that zoologists try to control the breeding of animals *given that* ranchers are so required was less than or equal to the estimated probability that zoologists try to control the breeding of animals.) Sloman concludes that people arrive at their conditional probability estimates by considering reasons why the premise and the conclusion might hold. If the reasons for the premise are consistent with the reasons for the conclusion (as in (6)), then the premise enhances the likelihood of the conclusion. If the reasons for the premise are not consistent with those for the conclusion (as in (7)), then no such enhancement takes place.

To explain these data, a proponent of the Gap model would have to contend that: (a) the predicate of an argument evokes a corresponding set of properties in the representation of the categories (animal handling frequency? frequency of controlling breeding?); (b) the conclusion category's values on these dimensions are recalibrated; and (c) the probability of zoologists having the properties is assessed relative to the recalibrated values. But granting these assumptions, why should the conclusion probability of (7) remain unchanged or decrease? A simpler hypothesis is that the causes for requiring rabies vaccinations apply to both ranchers and zoologists, whereas the causes for wanting to control breeding of animals applies to ranchers but is irrelevant to zoologists.

Hypothesis-testing theories of category-based induction. The idea that general causal knowledge affects inductive strength suggests that we could treat the conclusion of arguments, such as (1)–(7), as analogous to a scientific hypothesis and the premises of the arguments as evidence for this hypothesis. We could then use theories of hypothesis testing or confirmation to explain judgments of inductive strength as a special case. This idea goes back at least to Carnap (1950). Recently, a number of investigators (Heit, 1998, 2000; Kemp & Tenenbaum, 2009; McDonald, Samuels, & Rispoli, 1996) have proposed psychological models of category-based induction along these lines. For Heit, the probability of the conclusion given the premises is just the probability of a hypothesis (that the conclusion is true) given the evidence (provided by the premises). So we can apply Bayes' theorem to obtain this probability, assuming some prior distribution of probability over potential hypotheses. In the case of argument (8), if we have the prior probability that a hypothesis will be true of cows, horses, mice, and all other mammals, and the prior probability that it will be true of cows, horses, mice, but not all other mammals, then Bayes' theorem allows us to calculate the probability that the hypothesis is true of all mammals, *given* that it is true of cows, horses, and mice:

(8)   Cows have Vitamin Z.
Horses have Vitamin Z.
Mice have Vitamin Z.

Mammals have Vitamin Z.

This approach is similar to some of the reasoning theories that we will examine in Chapter 6, though the present theories target only category-based inductive arguments. (For a statement of Bayes' Theorem, see Chapter 3, Note 10, of this book.)

McDonald et al. (1996) propose that factors that affect hypothesis testing in empirical studies—in particular, the amount of evidence, the scope or range of the given hypothesis/conclusion, and the number of alternative hypotheses—can also predict judged argument strength. In arguments like (8), the amount of evidence comes down to the number of (mammal) subcategories that the premises specify as having the property in question (cows, horses, and mice, in this example),[6] the scope of the hypothesis is the size of the conclusion category (the total number of mammals or number of types of mammals), and the alternative hypotheses are possible alternative explanations that the premises bring to mind (e.g., that having Vitamin Z is restricted to land-based mammals). Heit (1998, 2000) and McDonald et al. (1996) both show that hypothesis-testing theories can account for many of the same phenomena that the Similarity-Coverage model does. Kemp and Tenenbaum (2009) and McDonald et al. (1996) also produce impressive correlations to actual judgments of argument strength.

These hypothesis-testing theories, unlike the Similarity-Coverage approach, also generalize immediately to arguments about familiar properties. For example, if we have the prior probabilities that a specific property (e.g., having good eyesight) is true of the different combinations of the premise and conclusion categories, we can again plug into Bayes' theorem to compute the conditional probability that the property holds of the conclusion category given that it holds of the premises' categories. Whether people use Bayes' theorem to test hypotheses is a controversial matter (see, e.g., A. Tversky & Kahneman, 1974). For that reason, Heit (1998) and Kemp and Tenenbaum (2009) propose their theories as accounts of the goals of inductive inference (what needs to be computed) rather than as processing models (see the discussion of Oaksford and Chater's theory in Chapter 6 of this book).

The ability of these models to describe or explain phenomena from experiments on induction depends on the prior distributions, and as Heit (1998) notes, Bayes Theorem provides no account of where these distributions come from. Heit plausibly suggests that people might estimate the distributions from known properties of the categories or from higher-order beliefs about the distributions of properties across categories (Goodman, 1955; Shipley, 1993). Kemp and Tenenbaum (2009) show that the prior probabilities can sometimes be derived from assumptions about the structure of the category and assumptions about how the property is distributed over the structure. For example, given a taxonomic structure for the mammals and a statistical process defined over it, the structure and the statistical process can yield prior probabilities that each combination of mammals will have a property. Different types of property will call for different structures and different processes. If the induction problem concerns mammals having a specific neurotransmitter, then we can reasonably assume that a taxonomic structure underlies the property and that the property spreads across the taxonomic tree. If the problem concerns mammals having a specific food-based disease, however, then people may assume that the relevant structure is a predator-prey network and that the disease spreads probabilistically from prey to predator (Shafto et al., 2008). The difficulty, then, is similar to one we met in assessing the Gap model: To make the Gap theory work properly, we need to know the underlying properties responsible for the "gap." To make the Bayesian model work properly, we need to know the underlying structures and processes that determine property distributions.

The role that prior probabilities play in Heit's (1998) and in Kemp and Tenenbaum's (2009) approach corresponds in part to the number of alternative hypotheses in McDonald et al.'s. In their experiments, McDonald et al. (1996) measure the alternatives empirically by providing participants with a list of premises from arguments like (8) and asking them to construct hypotheses about sets of objects in the domain that might reasonably have the property. This measure significantly predicted judged argument strength from a separate group of participants who inspected the full arguments (same premises plus conclusions). The success of this prediction, though, raises the issue of how the participants arrived at their alternative hypotheses. What about the premises tempted participants to suppose that the property in question might generalize in one way rather than another? Similarly, in the Kemp and Tenenbaum framework, how do people decide in the case of argument (8) that the proper underlying structure is taxonomic, predator-prey, or one of what would appear to be an unlimited set of alternatives? Maybe Vitamin Z is administered by veterinarians. Maybe it depends on sources of drinking water. Maybe it depends on interactions between exposure to sunlight and internal chemistry. Moreover, category-based induction can also require reasoners to revise their beliefs about the underlying structure for purposes of entertaining a counterfactual premise, as we noted in discussing the Gap model. Since resolving these issues itself depends on inductive inference, these versions of the hypothesis-testing theory also presuppose some important reasoning processes that occur offstage.

Hypothesis-testing theories provide a general and useful framework for thinking about argument strength but leave unexplored some cognitive prerequisites that are essential for the theories' success.

4.1.1.3 Summary

What does category-based inductive inference tell us about the nature of categories? Natural categories and their properties are not uniformly scattered in a vast property soup, but they cluster in ways that support further inferences even about unfamiliar properties. To take advantage of this nonuniformity and to project properties across categories, people may reason that similar categories support similar properties, either directly (Sloman, 1993), taxonomically, or both (Osherson et al., 1990; Rips, 1975). Or they may reason more abstractly that the distribution of new properties should follow the distribution of old ones (Heit, 1998) or follow the contours of linguistic practices in naming (Coley, Medin, & Atran, 1998). What hooks natural kinds to their properties are often causal laws, and people may be able, at least on some occasions, to marshal these laws to support their inferences. Lassaline (1996) provides evidence that when people have explicit causal information connecting known properties to the properties they are trying to generalize, this information increases judged argument strength, without increasing judged similarity between the premise and conclusion categories. Rehder and Hastie (2001) also found that people generalize more from instances that embody known causal relations than from instances that violate one or more causal relations. Similarly, Rehder (2006b) reports that a known cause for the to-be-projected property decreases the effect of similarity (as well as related effects, such as typicality and diversity).

The Gap model (E. E. Smith et al., 1993; Osherson, Smith, Myers, et al., 1994; Osherson, Smith, Shafir, et al., 1995) captures an essential insight: People conceive ways in which the inductive premises could become true, adjust the conclusion category in light of these alterations, and evaluate the strength of the argument as the likelihood of the conclusion in this changed context. In outline, this idea resembles proposed methods for evaluating the truth value of counterfactual conditionals, such as *If lions were 5 feet tall, then house cats would be 2 feet* (see, e.g., Levi, 1996; Stalnaker, 1968; and the causal theories of counterfactuals that I reviewed in Chapter 3 in this book). According to this method, you judge the counterfactual by revising your beliefs to accommodate the antecedent (lions are 5 feet tall). If the consequent information (house cats are 2 feet tall) is true in the revised set of beliefs, then the counterfactual as a whole is true as well. This correspondence between assessing the inductive strength of arguments and assessing the truth of counterfactuals is not surprising, since the same causal principles may sometimes support both (Goodman, 1955).

Current psychological models of category-based induction, however, scant the details about how people carry out the belief adjustment that is central to this endeavor. I have tried to argue that the process isn't necessarily as simple as revising values on prespecified dimensions. Instead, we use our knowledge of which aspects of categories are changeable, what the causes of these changes are likely to be, and how the consequences of these changes affect other categories. This isn't, of course, a substantive theory of category-based induction, but it may point to ingredients missing in current theories. Perhaps the best way of viewing current research in this area is as illustrating default strategies that people adopt when explicit knowledge is unavailable.

4.1.2 Natural Categories and Their Transformations

The research we have just examined derives information about categories from the role they play in inductive reasoning. Positing new information about a category in the premise of an argument can force us to modify our beliefs about the category for purposes of the inference. Which modifications we make—which aspects of the category are easily modifiable and which are not—can provide evidence about (our beliefs about) the category's structure. (Nisbett, Krantz, Jepson, & Kunda, 1983, make a similar point about the homogeneity of a property within a category.) Subjecting a category to this sort of inferential pressure gives us a test of the category's make up. Since the properties that the premises ascribe to the category can be counterfactual, the induction paradigm identifies beliefs about what *might* be true or what *must* be true of the category in unrealized situations. These are beliefs about a category's modal properties, not merely beliefs about what's normal or average in our own experiences.

We might consider another way to examine these modal properties. Instead of attributing a property to a category and studying how the property generalizes, you can change a property of a category member and check whether the individual retains its category membership. Consider, for example, beliefs about Leigh, an individual lion. Changes in Leigh's external appearance are perfectly consistent with her remaining a lion, whereas other changes—particularly in her internal make-up—cause both children (S. A. Gelman & Wellman, 1991; Keil, 1989) and adults (Barton & Komatsu, 1989; Rips, 1989) to think that Leigh no longer counts as a lion. We've seen some examples of such transformations in Chapter 1. Judgments about these transformations, of course, rely on inductive inference, just as judgments about explicit arguments do in the research described in the previous section. The corresponding argument here might be similar to (9):

(9)   Leigh is a lion at time *t*.
      Leigh undergoes cosmetic surgery so that her external appearance becomes identical to that of a tiger at *t* + 1.

      Leigh is a lion at *t* + 1.

However, because such arguments differ in content from those of experiments on category-based induction, we will consider transformations separately here.

4.1.2.1 Evidence from Transformations of Category Members

Keil's (1989) studies of natural kinds created conflicts between the appearance of an individual organism and the more fundamental properties of its inner constitution, parentage, or progeny. Some of his experiments told children about discoveries in which scientists find that an organism that appeared to be a member of one category (e.g., horses) has the inner parts, parents, and offspring of another (e.g., cows). Other experiments provided stories of normal organisms of one category whose external appearance changes permanently to resemble that of another category (e.g., a horse that a doctor alters to have stripes and to eat wild grasses like a zebra). Both sets of studies provided evidence that between kindergarten and second grade, children come to appreciate the more theoretically important properties and to discount the more superficial ones. Further growth in this knowledge continues through at least fourth grade. Keil (1989) argues, however, against the view that younger children are prisoners of external appearance (see also Keil, Smith, Simons, & Levin, 1998). Temporary changes (e.g., a horse in zebra costume or a horse with stripes that wash off in the rain) do not lead kindergartners to suppose that an organism has switched categories. Nor do changes that make an animal resemble an inanimate object (e.g., a porcupine made to look like a cactus) convince them that the animal has transmuted.

In simple settings, even preschool children are sensitive to the importance of internal properties (S. A. Gelman & Wellman, 1991). Four- and five-year-olds usually deny that an animal whose insides have been removed is still an animal. For example, they answer "no" to grizzly questions like: "What if you take out the stuff inside of the dog, you know, the blood and bones and things like that and got rid of it and all you have left are the outsides? Is it still a dog?" At the same time, they usually affirm that an animal whose outsides are removed is still an animal. They answer "yes" to: "What if you take off the stuff outside of the dog, you know, the fur and got rid of it and all you have left are the insides? Is it still a dog?" They also know that natural kinds are likely to have natural-kind insides, whereas artifacts have artifact insides, despite lack of detailed knowledge about the insides' structure (Simons & Keil, 1995). Moreover, older four-year-olds appreciate that an animal or plant of one species raised among those of another species will retain its category membership—for example, that a watermelon seed planted in a cornfield will produce watermelons rather than corn (S. A. Gelman & Wellman, 1991). The evidence is less clear, however, that preschool children can predict which of an organism's properties—for example, its physical traits versus its beliefs and preferences—are the likely products of its birth parents and which are the products of its adoptive parents (Solomon, Johnson, Zaitchik, & Carey, 1996; Springer, 1996).[7]

Controversy about these results (and the developmental results we glimpsed earlier) centers on the question of whether they reflect increasing sophistication of a preexisting base of biological knowledge or, instead, the emergence of biological knowledge from a nonbiological—social or psychological—precursor (e.g., Atran, 1998; Carey, 1985, 1995b; Inagaki & Hatano, 1993; S. C. Johnson & Carey, 1998; Keil, 1995;

Medin & Waxman, 2007). For our purposes, however, the outcome of this controversy isn't as important as the clues the experiments yield about people's eventual beliefs about natural kinds. Since children have never witnessed horses cross-dressing as zebras or horses that have undergone cosmetic surgery to look like zebras, their answers don't reflect mere experience of these events. Analogies from transformations that children *have* witnessed might be a source of information; but if this is so, the analogies must take into account the fact that transformations preserve category membership in some domains but not others. Older children realize that changing the external appearance of a horse can't change it into a zebra, but changing the external appearance of a coffee pot may well change it into a bird feeder (Keil, 1989). They also know that internally caused changes in size and changes in parts are permissible for animals but not for artifacts, such as light bulbs or telephones (Hall, 1998; Rosengren, Gelman, Kalish, & McCormick, 1991).

By the time they are adults, people's analogizing, if any, is probably not based on pure similarity, since experiments produce dissociations between judgments of similarity and judgments of category membership for these transformations. In one experiment (Rips, 1989), participants read stories about a member of one natural kind (e.g., a reptile) who undergoes a transformation to resemble a member of another kind (e.g., a fish) but is still able to have normal offspring of the first kind. These participants rated the transformed animal more likely to be a member of the first kind, but more similar to the second. In a separate study, participants read stories about animals whose immature form resembles one category but whose mature form resembles another. Participants rated the immature form as more likely to be a member of the second kind, but as more similar to the first.

Older children and adults, then, possess relatively abstract knowledge that certain sorts of properties are important to category membership, that other properties are not as important, and that which properties are which depends on the domain of the object in question (Barton & Komatsu, 1989; Keil, 1995; Prasada & Dillingham, 2006). For example, most adults judge that molecular structure (and not external appearance) determines which individuals are members of animal and plant categories. Molecular structure, however, is clearly less important for artifact categories than for natural kinds (Barton & Komatsu, 1989).

4.1.2.2 Essentialist Interpretations of the Transformation Studies

Do the results just discussed show more than that some properties are more important than others for category membership? Do they imply that people hold some properties of objects to be *essential* for category membership? Psychological essentialism is an important strand in research on concepts, and it is closely tied to theme of this book, since it asserts that people believe that organisms *must have* specific properties to be true members of their kind.

In examining this issue, we can begin with a formulation by S. A. Gelman and Hirschfeld (1999), since they have taken pains to clarify the scope of essentialist ideas (see also S. A. Gelman, 2003). First, Gelman and Hirschfeld distinguish their position from earlier philosophical views: Essentialism in this context is a *psychological* claim about people's beliefs— beliefs about the make up of natural kinds and certain other categories— not a claim about the actual (metaphysical) composition of these kinds (see also Medin, 1989; Medin & Ortony, 1989). Second, Gelman and Hirschfeld distinguish the *causal* essentialism they promote from a *sortal* essentialism that deals with word meaning. Causal essentialism is belief in a "substance, power, quality, process, relationship, or entity that *causes* other category-typical properties to emerge and be sustained and confers identity," whereas sortal essentialism is knowledge of a "set of defining characteristics that all and only members of a category have" (S. A. Gelman & Hirschfeld, 1999, pp. 405–406). Gelman and Hirschfeld reject sortal essences on the grounds that "given the past thirty years of research on categorization, it is extremely unlikely that people represent features that can identify all and only members of a category . . . , regardless of how confident they are that such features exist" (p. 407; see Section 4.1.3, below, for further discussion of this claim).[8]

Table 4.1 attempts to flesh out the claims of causal essentialism in a way that is consistent with psychological views of this topic. Causal essentialism is a theory about people's (especially, children's) everyday beliefs about natural kinds, and the characteristics in the table have the status of beliefs. Thus, causal essentialism holds at a minimum that people believe essential forces are responsible for particular objects being members of natural kinds and for the typical properties these objects

TABLE 4.1   Possible Characteristics of Cognitive Essentialism About Natural Kinds

Characteristic	Description
Potency	Essential properties are responsible for an object's being a member of a natural kind.
Productivity	Essential properties are responsible for (a possibly unlimited number) of a member's other properties.
Objectivity	Essential properties exist in nature (do not depend on human convention).
Intrinsicness	Essential properties exist within individual category members (do not depend on other objects).
Uniqueness	Natural kinds have one essential property (or, at most, a small subset of essential properties) common to all members.
Distinctiveness	Different natural kinds have different essential properties.
Identity-of-members	Essential properties are responsible for tracing a member of the kind across possible situations.
Identity-of-individuals?	Essential properties are responsible for tracing an individual across possible situations.
Discreteness?	An object has the essential properties of a natural kind either completely or not at all.
Prepotency?	No additional factors can override essential properties.

Note: As part of a psychological theory, the descriptions should be prefaced by "People believe that . . . "

have as members. Table 4.1 displays these two characteristics under the headings *potency* and *productivity*. In addition, people believe these essential forces are *objective*, existing in nature apart from people's interests and beliefs. However, if causal essentialism were just a belief that something or other (some natural "substance, power, quality, . . . ") causes the properties of category members, it would be unobjectionable but toothless. People obviously believe that something causes lions to have the properties they possess. A more interesting version of the theory is that people not only believe in such causes but can actually describe them. Part of the doctrine of psychological essentialism, however, is that people often aren't able to describe such causes in any detail, sometimes representing them simply as a wild card or "placeholder" (Medin & Ortony, 1989).

A second possible strengthening of causal essentialism that is closer to Gelman and Hirschfeld's theory is that people believe not just that the properties of category members are caused but also that the same cause is responsible for all the typical properties of all members of a category.

This cause is *intrinsic*, subsisting in the individual members and independent of other objects. The essential cause is also a *unique* cause that is responsible for all Leigh's liony properties, and for other lions' liony properties as well. Thus, the essential properties provide a unitary explanation for what are otherwise merely correlated external traits. Presumably, also, *distinct* causes produce the typical properties of other categories, so that essential causes differentiate the categories. Essence of lion must differ from essence of tiger.

This claim about belief in unique and distinctive causes is an interesting one, since it is possible that many of the categories that our animal and plant terms denote are not in fact associated with such causes (see, e.g., Dupré, 1993; Sober, 1980; and the discussion in Section 4.2 of this chapter). However, it is not easy to be precise about how uniqueness and distinctiveness play out in causal essentialism. In the case of uniqueness, for example, the spirit of the proposal seems consistent with a small number of causal factors being jointly responsible for Leigh's lionhood. However, the possibility of a large number of alternative causes seems incompatible with essentialist intuitions. Perhaps uniqueness and distinctiveness should be spelled out in terms of belief in individually necessary and jointly sufficient causal factors, but this reformulation may also be unclear for reasons discussed later (see Section 4.1.3). People's beliefs may themselves be imprecise about these matters, going little beyond the notion that lions have one root cause and tigers another.

In their definition of causal essentialism, quoted above, Gelman and Hirschfeld also assert that causal essences confer "identity" on category members. This could mean that the causes are responsible for an individual's being a category member—for example, for Leigh's identity as a lion-in-good-standing. This is the characteristic that we have already labeled *potency* in Table 4.1, and the studies just cited bear on this claim. However, "identity" in this context can also mean the object's continued existence as the numerically same member (or even as the numerically same individual) across situations. (See Chapter 1 for the difference between numerical and qualitative identity.) As another Michigan essentialist puts it, "People in diverse cultures consider . . . essence responsible for the organism's identity as a complex, self-preserving entity governed by dynamic internal processes that are lawful even when hidden. This hidden essence maintains the organism's integrity even as it causes the organism to grow, change form, and reproduce" (Atran, 1998, p. 548). Identity over time (maintenance of "the organism's integrity" over change) goes beyond mere membership in a superordinate category. In this sense, essential causes are responsible not only for Leigh's being a lion, but also for her being the very same lion (or same individual) in different settings and at different times. An essence is able to perform this function because the essence dictates conditions of identity and individuation for category members, as in the sortal theory of identity that I described in Chapter 1 (see Hirsch, 1982, and Wiggins, 1980).

For now, we can take the causal essentialist doctrine to mean that a unique essence is causally responsible for each individual lion's membership in the lion category, for its lionlike properties, and for its identity as the same lion or the same object in different possible situations; a distinct essence is responsible for each individual tiger's tigerlike properties, for its membership in the tiger category; and so on. Table 4.1 summarizes these characteristics of psychological essentialism, along with some other potential characteristics we will consider later. Because ambiguity exists about whether the essential properties supply criteria of identity for members of natural kinds as such or identity for individual objects in themselves, we distinguish these characteristics in the table, labeling the first *identity of members* and the second *identity of individuals*. Psychological essentialists seem committed to at least the first of these traits (e.g., identity as the same lion). Commitment to the second (e.g., identity as Leigh) is not so clear, and we register it in the table as an optional characteristic of essentialist doctrine. (See Chapter 1 and Section 4.2.2.1, below, for further discussion.)

The characteristics of Table 4.1 are important here because essential properties are one obvious source of natural kinds' modal qualities. The identity characteristic, in particular, gives us a way of thinking about which object is the same lion in different possible situations and so a notion of the range of properties that could possibly be true of her. We therefore need to examine essentialist theories closely. An immediate question, then, is whether the evidence supports causal essentialism. Do people think natural kinds possess unique and distinctive causal essences or do they merely hold a *minimal* view that some causes or other are responsible for natural kinds' properties, membership, and persistence (Strevens, 2000)?

4.1.2.3 Questions About the Transformation Studies

The studies I've reviewed provide evidence about which properties of objects sustain membership in a natural category across transformations. Internal mechanisms and descent, for example, are important in this respect, whereas external appearance and location are not. The studies may also support the idea that people take the former factors as essential for category membership, in some sense of "essential" that we have begun to fill out. Most of the criticism of the transformation experiments has focused on the essentialism claim, and we examine these issues here as they come up in recent empirical work. (I'll postpone discussion of essentialism's theoretical pros and cons until Section 4.2.)

A more general objection to the transformation studies, however, is that they tap people's higher-level thinking about natural kinds, but shed no light on how people recognize category members in everyday encounters (E. E. Smith & Sloman, 1994). In deciding whether an animal you are observing is a horse or a zebra, you don't typically examine the animal's pedigree or genetic markers but rely instead on superficial perceptual properties in making the decision. This is the equivalent of Muggsy's approach in the excerpt from *The Lady Eve* that I quoted in Chapter 1. You may use deeper—unobservable or theoretical—aspects of the organism mainly in special situations when correct classification or inference is very important (for scientific purposes, say), or when no superficial properties happen to be available. This point is well taken, since it limits the scope of conclusions from the transformation studies. Our purpose here, however, is to examine people's beliefs about natural kinds' modal properties, and for this reason we need to look beyond immediate perceptual recognition and categorizing.

Objections to specifically essentialist claims have focused on two issues—one having to do with the relation between essence and membership, and the other with transformations of members versus entire species. The thinking behind the first of these problems is that if essences are unique and distinctive in the way we supposed earlier, then something is a horse if and only if it has horse essence. We should come across no intermediate cases of animals that are only partly horses. However, Kalish (1995, Experiment 1) found that participants rated atypical organisms as members of natural kinds to some degree. For example, they rated a zebra as "sort of a horse" and a wolf "sort of a dog." As Kalish notes, these intermediate ratings might reflect the uncertainty of participants' beliefs about category membership (e.g., McCloskey & Glucksberg, 1978) rather than their belief that category membership is uncertain: They may be unsure whether zebras are horses rather than being sure that zebras are partial horses. In addition, essentialists might assume (as do S. A. Gelman & Hirschfeld, 1999) that an organism can possess essential properties to a greater or lesser extent. If so, then essentialism is compatible with categories that are graded rather than all-or-none, in accord with Kalish's data.[9]

Essentialists can't evade this fuzzy-membership objection quite so easily, though. Even if objects possess an essential property to a variable degree (so that, for example, a zebra can have a partial helping of horse essence), we would at least expect degree of membership to track degree of essence. The more essence of a natural kind something has, the better a member of the kind it should be. For instance, assuming that H_2O is the essence of water, then the more H_2O a substance has, the better it should be as a type of water. Malt (1994) has shown, however, that whether people call a substance "water" is not even monotonically related to their belief about the percentage of H_2O in the substance. For example, participants judged ocean water to contain 79% H_2O but saliva (a nonwater) to contain 89%.

The second type of experimental objection to psychological essentialism comes from judgments about discoveries and transformations. Braisby, Franks, and Hampton (1996) provide evidence that discoveries about the intrinsic properties of natural kinds do not always affect participants' judgments about the existence of these categories. In one key condition in this experiment, participants read stories, such as (10a), in which an individual category member is discovered to lack a key property of the category. In a second condition, they read stories, such as (10b), in which all members of the category are discovered to lack the property (Braisby et al., 1996, p. 256):

(10)   a. You have a female pet cat named Tibby who has
          been rather unwell of late. Although cats are known
          to be mammals, the vet, on examining Tibby
          carefully, finds that she is, in fact, a robot controlled
          from Mars.

b. You have a female pet cat named Tibby. For many years
   people assumed cats to be mammals. However, scientists
   have recently discovered that they are *all*, in fact, robots
   controlled from Mars. Upon close examination, you discover
   that Tibby too is a robot, just as the scientists suggest.

Participants then answered questions about the existence of cats and
about whether Tibby is a cat, given each discovery.

The predictions these authors make on behalf of essentialism come
from philosophical theories of reference developed by Kripke (1972) and
Putnam (1975). These theories hold, roughly speaking, that the referent
of natural-kind expressions, such as "water" or "cat," is fixed at the time
of their introduction by local samples of the kind in question. Thus,
whether an arbitrary specimen falls under these terms depends on
whether it is in the same kind as that of the local sample. If present-day
scientific theories are correct, then whether a substance is correctly
termed "water" depends on whether its molecular structure is identical
to that of the local samples, and whether an object is correctly termed a
"cat" depends on whether its genetic structure (or other underlying
properties or relations) is the same as that of the original cat examples.[10]
In the case of stories like Braisby et al.'s (10a), if participants (a) share the
Putnam-Kripke intuitions and (b) interpret the story to mean that Tibby
is discovered not to possess the property that determines the same-kind
relation to original cat samples, then they should judge that the kind cat
exists but that Tibby is not a member of the kind. For (10b), if participants assume that the same-kind relation for cats now depends on being
a Martian-controlled robot, then they should again assert that cats exist
but, this time, that Tibby remains a cat (see Braisby et al., 1996, Table 4.1).
Braisby et al. found 47–89% agreement with essentialist predictions for
the (10a)-type stories and 73–87% agreement with these predictions for
the (10b)-type stories (where the range depended on how the questions
were framed; see Braisby et al., 1996, Table 7). But despite the fact that
agreement with essentialist predictions was often high, these investigators
concluded, based on the remaining discrepancies, that "our evidence
indicates that people do not, in fact, believe that things have essences, if
essences are interpreted according to the model provided by Kripke and
Putnam (even though people may sometimes behave as if they did)"
(Braisby et al., 1996, p. 270).

One reaction to both Malt's (1994) and Braisby et al.'s findings is that they are irrelevant to the claims about causal essentialism that we considered in the preceding section (S. A. Gelman & Hirschfeld, 1999). Gelman and Hirschfeld (1999) complain on this score, "Critically, H_2O represents a sortal not causal essence, and accordingly [Malt's] study provides evidence only against the classical view of category meaning" (p. 408). Similarly, they claim against Braisby et al. that "on a *causal* essentialist view, the essence need not provide necessary and sufficient clues for determining reference . . . , and accordingly the experiments are relevant to a sortal (not causal) essentialist view" (ibid.).

Psychological essentialists and their opponents agree that people do not possess a set of necessary and sufficient criteria that determine the meanings of the terms they use. Essentialists' rejection of "sortal essentialism" secures this agreement. The issue that divides these groups is therefore whether experiments like Malt's and Braisby et al.'s cast doubt on *beliefs* in essence. Do people believe natural kinds have an essence even though they can't describe it? S. A. Gelman and Hirschfeld's (1999) position may be that these experiments do no more than provide further evidence that people don't know what the essential (necessary-and-sufficient) features are, but opponents might well contend this is too narrow an interpretation. The intent of Braisby et al. (1996) was not merely to show that people lack *mammal* as a necessary feature for *cat* but also to prove they lack the high-order belief that essence determines the denotation of natural kind terms (see the quotation from Braisby et al. in the paragraph before last). The issue for both sides of the debate is a metacognitive one: Do beliefs about essence play an important role in thinking about kinds?

One way to reconcile proponents and opponents of essentialism would be to suppose that proponents are right about people's theories of kinds' physical makeup, whereas opponents are right about people's theories of meaning. Perhaps people think that essences cause animals, plants, and other natural kinds to have the properties they do, but they don't believe that essences play a role in determining the referents of expressions for these kinds. This would be to invoke the distinction between causal and sortal essentialism at a higher level: People's ideas about reference and meaning could be partly independent from their ideas about biology, chemistry, physics, and other domains of natural kinds.

There are limits, however, to the distance that can separate beliefs about the nature of kinds from beliefs about the meaning of kind terms—between ideas of what a kind is and of what the term for the kind applies to. Suppose you are a causal essentialist and believe that causal factors exist distinguishing lions from other species. The news that these causal factors were absent in Leigh would presumably affect your belief about whether the term "lion" correctly refers to her. Thus, causal essentialists have little room to maneuver between: (a) object O has the causally essential properties of a category C, and (b) the name of category C correctly refers to O. If a property is causally crucial in determining whether something is a lion, then it is also crucial in determining whether "lion" is true of it in causally possible circumstances. To put this slightly differently: What reason could you have for affirming that people believe natural kinds have essences while denying that they believe that terms for natural kinds are associated with necessary and sufficient properties? People may indeed be uncertain about what sorts of properties can function as necessary and sufficient for purposes of meaning, as I discuss later, but it is hard to see why such qualms wouldn't apply equally to essences.[11]

Recall, too, that the empirical evidence in favor of causal essentialism that we reviewed earlier depends on altering causal factors for a member of a kind and quizzing participants about whether it remains a category member—for example, whether a lion whose insides are scooped out is "still a lion" (S. A. Gelman & Wellman, 1991) or whether a goat with altered chromosomes is "still a goat" (Barton & Komatsu, 1989). This type of question is, in fact, not very different from that posed in (10a); so denying the relevance of Malt's and Braisby et al.'s studies may be self-defeating for causal essentialists.

The results of Braisby et al. (1996) and Malt (1994) bear on causal essentialism as a psychological theory, but they don't necessarily defeat it. A majority of participants supported essentialist predictions in Braisby et al.'s experiments; so the difficulties these data pose for essentialism depend on how seriously you view departures from complete agreement. As we just noted, a causal essentialist could dissent from some of the Kripke-Putnam intuitions about (10a) and (10b) without sacrificing the idea that essential underlying causes determine kind status. Such an individual might believe, for example, that what fixes cathood once and for all is having a brain of a certain sort and not other causes that scientists happen to discover. Such a person would judge that no cats exist in worlds in which all catlike objects are (brainless) robots, such as that in (10b). This would cause the person to depart from Braisby et al.'s essentialist predictions, although the person could still be said to be a causal (and even a sortal) essentialist.[12] In the case of Malt's (1994) experiment, essentialists might invoke the sorts of pragmatic considerations mentioned in Note 11 (see Abbott, 1997, for an argument of this sort). Or they could deny that water, as laypeople conceive it, is a natural kind. What laypeople (but not chemists) count as water may depend on its source (lakes but not tissues of organisms) and the purpose it serves (irrigating plants but not developing photographs).

Some difficult issues remain, though. I've already raised the question of whether possession of essences must be all or none. A second question is whether essentialists can consistently think that factors in addition to underlying causal ones can affect what's water—factors like the use to which the substance is put or the location in which it is found (Malt, 1994; see also Hampton, 1995b). Similarly, could an essentialist believe, for example, that H_2O helps determine what's water, but that certain impurities (e.g., tea extract) disqualify a mixture as water whereas others (e.g., soil) do not? To what extent can causal essentialism admit exceptions in causally possible circumstances? These issues depend on further details of the essentialist position, and I postpone discussion until we have had a look at some additional evidence. To record uncertainty about these matters for now, I list in Table 4.1 the characteristics of *discreteness* (essences are all-or-none) and *prepotency* (nothing can override essences) with question marks to indicate that these items are ones on which essentialists might differ.

4.1.2.4 Direct Assessments of Causal Structure

The transformation experiments suggest that 4- to 7-year-olds come to think underlying causal properties are important in deciding membership in natural kinds, more important than properties of the members' external appearance. We would therefore expect that the stronger or more central a causal factor—for example, the more effects it has—the more important for membership it might be. In line with this prediction,

Ahn (1998, Experiment 1) reports a negative correlation between (adult) participants' ratings of the likelihood that a specific factor causes other properties for a kind and their ratings that members of the kind could lack that factor. For example, participants judged that having goat genetic code was very likely to cause a goat to give milk and to have four legs, and they also judged that it was very unlikely that "a goat would still be a goat if it were in all ways like a goat except that it did not have a goat's genetic code."

Investigators have also explored the role of causal factors by constructing artificial "natural" kinds in which these factors explicitly vary (Ahn, 1998; Lombrozo, 2009; Rehder, 2006b; Rehder & Hastie, 2001; Sloman, Love, & Ahn, 1998). Participants might learn, for example, about a fictitious type of flower that has certain attributes, with causal (or other) relations that run between these attributes. The participants then judge whether novel instances that possess some of these attributes and lack others belong to the category. By varying the attributes and their relations, the investigators have used this technique to determine whether the causal status of an attribute (central vs. peripheral cause), the causal structure of the kind (one cause with many effects vs. many causes of a single effect), the qualitative nature of the characteristic (molecular vs. functional), and the type of category (natural vs. artifact) affect category decisions. The results from these studies suggest that participants' knowledge about the relations between attributes is critical for category membership. Knowledge that an interattribute relation is missing can cause participants to decide that an instance is unlikely to be a category member (Ahn, 1998; Rehder & Hastie, 2001; Sloman et al., 1998).

This paradigm has produced some null or conflicting findings, however. There is no evidence that internal attributes (e.g., having Eucalyptol in their petals) matter more for membership in natural kinds than do functional attributes (attracting insects) when causal status is constant, and there is no evidence that internal attributes are more important for natural kinds than for artifacts under the same circumstances (Ahn, 1998). Nor is there consistent evidence that explicitly describing the relation as causal has a greater impact on categorization than describing it as temporal or merely labeling it as a "dependency" (Sloman et al., 1998; but see Lassaline, 1996, for evidence that causal relations promote inductive generalization more powerfully than temporal ones). Finally, some studies have found that a missing cause has more impact than a missing effect (Ahn, 1998; Sloman et al., 1998), but others have not (Rehder & Hastie, 2001). In Rehder and Hastie's study, what mattered was the number of causal relations that an attribute enters into rather than the attribute's initial position in a causal network (but see Marsh & Ahn, 2006). Similarly, an experiment by Lombrozo (2009) suggests that the advantage for an initial cause depends on whether participants concentrate on mechanical causal explanations—what physically brings about a particular effect. The advantage disappears if the participants focus instead on the effect's functional role—the purpose that the effect serves in the category's operation. Although causal relations affect categorization in all these studies—participants are less likely to classify an instance as a category member if it is missing an attribute within a causal structure—the special status of initial or internal causes is uncertain.

We should treat these findings with caution, especially since the techniques are new ones. Different studies use somewhat different methods. If we take the null results seriously, however, they may provide a challenge to essentialism. Essentialists might try to explain away these results on the grounds that "artificial" natural kinds aren't representative of "natural" natural kinds. Natural kinds don't have causal structure in which, for example, functional properties cause molecular ones; so the way participants treat these items may not be relevant to the way they think about real kinds. But essentialists' hands are tied here by their commitment to psychological essentialism as a representation or pattern of beliefs. They can't appeal to the way natural kinds *really* are to dismiss these experiments, particularly since some of the same theorists express doubts about scientific versions of essentialism (S.A. Gelman & Hirschfeld, 1999). If people believe that natural kinds have central causes that are important in producing the kinds' properties and in differentiating one kind from another, then why doesn't this show up as differences in performance in tasks that disrupt these relations?

A better strategy for proponents of causal essentialism might be to maintain that the cover stories in these experiments are simply not convincing enough to engage assumptions about natural kinds. (Or, perhaps, they are so convincing that they override people's everyday assumptions; B. Rehder, personal communication, August 3, 2001.) In addition, factors other than causal status can affect categorization, and some of these may overwhelm benefits due to initial or internal causes (Ahn & Kim, 2000). Of course, essentialists could accept the idea that what matters to natural-kinds concepts is simply the presence of causal forces and not whether these forces are internal to category members. But for reasons I take up later (see Section 4.2.2), this may concede too much to anti-essentialism.

4.1.2.5 Summary

The transformation studies quiz participants about whether a hypothetical change or discovery about an object prevents that object from being a member of a natural kind. Grade-school children and adults can perform these contrary-to-fact decisions, and they judge that certain changes to biological kinds (e.g., evisceration) do alter membership whereas other changes (e.g., external disguises) do not. Similarly, anyone who has had the usual dose of high school chemistry is likely to know, for example, that a hydrogen atom that has captured an extra proton is no longer hydrogen but something else (helium). They believe that atomic number differentiates the elements and is responsible for some of the elements' properties, but that the size, shape, texture, or color of a sample of the element does not. Those who think otherwise get very low grades.

Critics of the transformational studies point to limits on people's willingness to base their category decisions solely on central causal properties. Category membership may also depend on practical aspects of the natural kind—in the case of water, for example, where the substance is found and what people use it for. This may indicate some slippage between the scientific use of natural-kind terms and our everyday use. For complex natural kinds (e.g., biological ones) that depend on many causal relations, people may believe that membership in the kind is graded rather than all-or-none. They may also think that the attributes most important for membership are ones that take part in many causal relationships (or causal relations of particular types) rather than ones that are the central cause (source of most effects) or ones that are internal to the exemplars. These latter issues are not yet settled and warrant further research.

Do these limitations leave intact anything we could plausibly call "causal essentialism" or "psychological essentialism"? We'll return to this issue in Section 4.2. Nevertheless, the transformation studies make explicit what appears implicit in the induction experiments: People believe the causal goings-on in natural kinds sustain inferences about what's possible for these kinds. In the case of the induction studies, causal relations help determine the range of properties that members of a kind can possess (given information about the properties of some of these members). In the transformation studies, causal relations help determine membership itself—the range of properties a member can possess and "still be" a member of that kind.

4.1.3 Natural Categories and Their Definitions

A truism among cognitive psychologists is that people are unable to produce properties for natural kinds that are both individually necessary and jointly sufficient for category membership. As we've seen, this is the reason proponents of causal essentialism reject "sortal essentialism," while maintaining that causal properties differentiate natural kinds. Fodor (1981, p. 283) has elevated the same idea to a general principle:

> Indeed, it seems to me to be among the most important findings of philosophical and psychological research over the last several hundred years (say, since Locke first made the reductionist program explicit) that attempts at conceptual analysis practically always fail.

The issue about necessary and sufficient properties involves questions about the types of properties that can legitimately play those roles. Any set of properties that are logically equivalent to *is a lion* is necessary and sufficient in one sense. For example, *being either a walnut or a lion* and *being a nonwalnut* are logically necessary and jointly sufficient for *being a lion*, but such properties are surely not the sort that are relevant to psychological claims.[13] Traditionally, necessary and sufficient properties are supposed to be more primitive than the things they define, but this notion of primitiveness is not easy to explicate.

The published evidence on this issue is not completely one-sided, however. Support for the truism comes from two studies in which participants explicitly listed properties for given categories, such as fish (Hampton, 1979), or listed properties for each of a set of subcategories (e.g., salmon, trout, and sardine) within larger categories (Rosch &

Mervis, 1975). Judges then decided which of these properties applied to all and only members of that category—for example, whether any of the properties listed for fish are true of all and only fish. The finding from these studies is that few of the listed properties were common to all members, and those that were common also tended to apply to non-members. Thus, few if any properties are both necessary and sufficient. Hampton found, for example, that properties such as *is alive*, *lives in water*, and *is cold-blooded*, which his judges deemed true of all fish, are also true of nonfish, such as shrimp and tadpoles.

The results change, however, when the participants, rather than the judges, label the properties as necessary and sufficient. McNamara and Sternberg (1983) asked participants to decide which of a set of properties were necessary for membership in specific natural kind and artifact categories (which properties "exemplars of the word must have to be exemplars"). They asked separately which properties or sets of properties were sufficient (which properties "guaranteed that some object or person was an exemplar of the given word"). On average, participants identified properties as both necessary and sufficient for 4.4 of 8 natural-kind terms and 4.0 of 8 artifact terms. For example, participants identified the property *hardest substance known* as both necessary and sufficient for diamonds. Thus, McNamara and Sternberg (1983, p. 470) concluded, "Our investigations have led us to believe that the evidence against the definitional theories is less compelling than some have argued." These results are the more surprising because McNamara and Sternberg's criteria for being necessary or sufficient are more stringent than Hampton's or Rosch and Mervis's. To qualify as necessary in Hampton's study, a property need only be true of all listed category members; but in McNamara and Sternberg's, the property must be one that any member *must* have in order to be a member.

The results of these studies may differ because of differences in the stimulus categories or because of different standards adopted by judges versus participants (see C. Johnson & Keil, 2000; Murphy & Medin, 1985; and B. Tversky & Hemenway, 1984, for criticisms of property-listing methods). Medin (1989) and Murphy and Medin (1985) have also questioned whether participants in McNamara and Sternberg's experiment were truly judging the necessity and sufficiency of the properties; perhaps, instead, they were reporting on the importance of these properties in their beliefs about the category (see Section 4.2.2.4).

Similar ambiguities surround evidence about the role of definitions in language understanding. In the 1970s and early 1980s, investigators used a number of techniques to determine whether understanding and producing sentences depend on the "definitional complexity" of individual words. If, for example, *bachelor* can be defined as *unmarried man*, then sentences containing *bachelor* should be more complex than those containing *man*. Hence, if people have to translate the more complex, defined words into their simpler, undefined components in order to process such sentences, then sentences with *bachelor* should be more difficult to understand and to produce than ones with *man*. Experiments using sentence completion, sentence construction, word-relatedness judgments, and phoneme monitoring techniques turned up negative results on this score (e.g., Fodor, Garrett, Walker, & Parkes, 1980; Kintsch, 1974, chap. 11). You could take these results to suggest that there are no definitions—no singly necessary and jointly sufficient properties—for most natural language terms. However, a more cautious reading of the evidence is that effects of definitional complexity are rare in immediate language understanding and production. Positive effects are more common in tasks that require active inferences—for example, tasks where participants must determine the truth of a sentence from a picture (Clark, 1974; Just & Carpenter, 1971).

We may need to recognize, then, that if necessary and sufficient predicates for a term exist, people need not consult them whenever they encounter the term. But perhaps people look up the mental definition when it becomes helpful in deeper interpretation. (See McNamara & Miller, 1989, for possibilities along these lines, and Chapter 5 in this book for one way of drawing the distinction between representations *of* and *about* a category.)

People may have not only direct beliefs about properties of category members but also beliefs about the properties of such properties. They may think, for example, not only that fish are cold-blooded, but also that cold-bloodedness is a necessary property of fish. They may also entertain these higher-order beliefs in the absence of lower ones, believing that necessary and sufficient properties exist for natural kinds, even though they are unsure of which properties fill this role (S. A. Gelman, 2003; Malt, 1990; Medin & Ortony, 1989; Shipley, 1993). Such second-order beliefs about the origin and nature of natural kinds are frameworks for people's conceptions and are part of psychological essentialism, as we noted earlier. One source of evidence about these beliefs comes from a study by Malt (1990), who asked participants to consider objects that were in between two well-known categories—for example, a fish that "seems to you to be sort of halfway between" a sardine and an anchovy. Participants were to explain the category membership of the item by selecting one of the three choices in (11):

(11)   a. It's probably one or the other, but I don't know which.
        b. You can think of it as either one.
        c. It can't really be either one, then.

For natural kinds, such as sardines/anchovies, participants tended to select option (11a), whereas for artifact categories (e.g., a vehicle that was between a car and a truck), participants chose option (11b).

Not everyone subscribes to the existence of underlying objective criteria for natural kinds. Kalish (1995) found that participants are less likely to think that facts settle membership in animal categories than in well-defined categories, such as odd numbers. Nevertheless, on approximately 70% of trials participants said that disputes about membership in animal species could be settled by facts. People apparently believe, then, that criteria can decide membership in some natural kinds, even when they themselves are unable to make the judgment. Likewise, kindergartners apparently believe that a chimeric animal, midway between a chicken and a turkey must be one or the other and not a hybrid (Keil, 1989, chap. 11).

4.1.4 Summary of Experimental Findings

Transformation studies make it clear that people think some properties of an object can change its membership in a natural kind. If you splice into Leigh-the-lion the genetic structure of a tiger, then she's no longer a lion but a tiger with a lion's appearance (e.g., Rips et al., 2006). But not all properties are relevant to membership in natural kinds. Painting stripes on Leigh does not change her status as a bona fide lion; she remains a lion with a tiger's appearance.

How does this square with the difficulty in finding definitions for kind terms? If people know which properties are critical for lionhood and which aren't, why can't they use such properties to define *lion*? Methodological differences among the studies may be partly responsible. Transformation studies sometimes ask participants whether certain named properties determine category membership, whereas experiments on "necessary and sufficient properties" have asked participants to produce their own property lists. People may have more difficulty generating necessary and sufficient properties than recognizing such properties when they see them. Second, transformation studies often allow participants to be vague about the crucial properties in a way that is difficult or impossible in studies in which the participants must name the properties. It's one thing to know that something about a lion's insides makes it a lion and another to know exactly which something is responsible. Similarly, knowing that cosmetic alterations don't change membership in natural kinds doesn't entail knowing exactly which properties maintain membership. People's vagueness about these properties is one of the motivations for the view that people have only a placeholder for essential properties. Third, participants may think there is something wrong with listing a predicate like *having lion DNA* as a property of lions: *Having lion DNA* is circular in the sense of presupposing an understanding of lions. *Having lion DNA* does denote a necessary property of lions. Nevertheless, listing *lion DNA* may seem unhelpful in the same way listing *being a lion* is; these predicates don't provide an independent way of identifying the category in question. If participants see their task as providing properties that could aid someone in picking out lions, then "lion DNA" is useless if all one knows about it is that it's inside lions.

You could try interpreting the differences between the transformation and the definition studies by appealing to the distinction between causal and sortal essentialism—between beliefs about kinds and beliefs about meaning. But the methodological variations we've just examined—in recognition versus production, in level of precision, and in epistemic or pragmatic demands—provide a more plausible account. The property-listing experiments that serve as evidence about lack of necessary and sufficient properties (e.g., Hampton, 1979; Rosch & Mervis, 1975) did not ask participants for definitions per se. They asked instead for properties true of all and only category members. What's at stake in these experiments is participants' knowledge about lions, not their knowledge of lion definitions. This conclusion jibes with our earlier one (see Section 4.1.2.3) that we should be careful about excluding evidence that appears on the surface to be about the meaning of kind terms rather than about the nature of natural kinds.

Of course, the evidence from definition and transformation experiments is not completely discordant. Malt's (1990) experiment shows that people sometimes believe there are facts of the matter about membership in natural kinds. Investigating an object in the proper way can disclose, in principle, properties that resolve its kind status. Thus, natural kinds possess a type of objectivity—natural kinds are kinds *in nature*—that serves as their hallmark and that differentiates them from conventional kinds. McNamara and Sternberg's (1983) study suggests that people sometimes do identify properties of natural kinds that they think guarantee membership and that are necessary for continued existence in the kind. This result tallies with evidence by Barton and Komatsu (1989) and others that I discussed in the context of the transformation studies.

The explicitly modal character of these judgments is important, since it implies that people are basing their responses not merely on what's true of existing members of the category but on what's possible for them. To say that having a property is necessary for continued existence in a natural kind is not just a statement about the properties that all members of the kind happen to possess; it's a statement of the range of possibilities that are open to members. This is the same moral we drew from the induction experiments: People's knowledge of natural kinds yields inferences about what's possible for these kinds. The central question we are left with, then, is what psychological mechanisms could support such judgments?

4.2 What Explains Natural Categories' Modal Status?

The evidence shows that people are able to make judgments about natural kinds that extend beyond a tally of their members' properties. People can judge what would be true of members of these kinds under conditions that the kinds never undergo. In the second part of this chapter, I evaluate some suggestions about what makes such judgments possible. The first section reviews cognitive theories of ideals as ways of explaining beliefs about natural kinds' potential. The final section then turns to two metaphysical views of the source of natural kinds' modal properties and asks whether a psychological version of one or the other could also serve as the basis of beliefs about kinds.

4.2.1 Do Ideals Underlie Beliefs About Kinds?

Ideals are potential characteristics of objects that would best enable them to serve their category's goals. Foods with zero calories best fulfill the goal of the category diet foods; so having zero calories is an ideal for this category. Barsalou (1985) found that for explicitly goal-derived categories, such as diet foods, items that fell closer to the ideal (as determined by participant ratings) were also judged better examples of the category. It's sad, but true, that green tea (no sugar with that) is a better example of a diet food than are french fries. For other sorts of categories, including natural kinds and artifacts, closeness-to-ideals seemed to play some role in determining goodness of the example, but the effect was smaller than that of how close the item was to the category's central tendency. For instance, good examples of the category fruit are items like peaches and apples that are highly similar to other fruit; however, good examples of fruit also include items like strawberries and bananas that fall near the ideal of what people like to eat (but are not especially similar to other fruit). Lynch, Coley, and Medin (2000) likewise found that among tree experts the best examples of trees are those that are least "weedy" (i.e., least messy). Central tendency played a lesser role in determining which trees are good examples.

Natural kinds sometimes serve human goals, and evidence from Barsalou (1985), Lynch et al. (2000), and Malt (1994) shows that how well an object fulfills these goals can affect how typical it seems. Perhaps we can also regard as ideals, not only properties that fulfill goals, but also any extreme value on a dimension. Neither of these senses of ideal, however, is of much help in understanding the type of normativity we need in order to explain the induction and transformation studies. Unfamiliar properties of apples or peaches are more likely to generalize to other fruits than are unfamiliar properties of bananas, despite the fact that they all satisfy human goals. Our knowledge of how properties of natural kinds are transmitted (and of how some properties depend on others) dictates these inductive patterns; they don't rely on how well category members serve goals (unless, of course, the property is itself goal-oriented). And serving such goals is not likely to affect continued existence in the category. Several species of citruses are inedible, but they're fruits for all that. Exceptions may occur in cases where humans have a role in creating the natural kinds, as in species of pets and crops. We may reason that breeders would have promoted certain properties or subspecies at the expense of others, given the breeders' goals. But such categories are more like artifacts than natural kinds, and they would produce different patterns of judgment in relevant induction and transformation studies.

If we include among ideals those values that are extreme on some dimension (in addition to those that are optimal), we do no better in explaining the induction and transformation experiments. Members of natural kinds that are near extremes are no more likely to share their properties, and moderating their extreme values would not threaten their status as members. In isolated cases, extreme items may have greater inductive potential, as in the Itzaj example mentioned in Section 4.1.1.2. Some Itzaj believe that tall trees are more likely to transmit a novel disease than short ones. But this is because the causal path of transmission incidentally runs through the extreme instances—big trees come into physical contact with a larger number of other trees than do short ones—and not because of anything about extremity itself. In other Itzaj examples, culturally important species (e.g., jaguars) carry greater inductive potential than less prominent ones (Atran, 1998). However, plenty of other extreme values don't promote induction—for example, extremes of tree color or bark texture. Ideals are of great interest in the study of categories, especially categories of artifacts and goal-derived ensembles, and they probably affect performance in other cognitive spheres (Medin, Goldstone, & Markman, 1995). However, the normative qualities of ideals aren't the qualities that are likely to explain the data we reviewed earlier, at least for members of Western culture.

4.2.2 Two Frameworks for Natural Kinds

Beliefs about causal laws (and perhaps certain other dependencies) underwrite notions about what is possible for members of natural kinds. As Putnam (1990, p. 74) puts it, "To say that something is impossible is to say that nothing has the capacity to bring it about." This view, however, leaves many details to fill in. How exactly do causal beliefs shape our thinking about natural kinds?

Two main suggestions about natural kinds are consistent with their modal standing and may help in seeing what's at stake. According to one view, natural kinds depend for their existence on certain internal properties of instances that dictate their category membership and many of their other (internal and external) properties. Let's call this the *intrinsic view*. The other tradition is perhaps of more recent origin and focuses less on internal properties than on the causal role kinds play in relation to other things. We can call this the *interaction view*. It is possible to trace the sources of these views, but the present goal is to sketch their main features, not to produce a historical account. These aren't, of course, the only frameworks for thinking about natural kinds, but they're the ones most relevant for cognitive approaches.

In presenting these views, I start by describing them directly as theories about the structure of kinds, bypassing their potential as descriptions of people's beliefs. We can then see how well they fare in the role of psychological theories.

4.2.2.1 The Intrinsic Theory

Imagine that a small number of properties intrinsic to an object establish which natural kind the object belongs to. "Intrinsic" is difficult to define precisely, but somehow the object's possessing the property does not depend on the existence of other objects. In particular, an object's intrinsic properties do not depend on us. Human interests and goals may be important in determining the way we classify artifacts, social kinds, and other categories, but except for the cases of human tampering mentioned earlier (see Section 4.2.1), they don't affect natural kinds' intrinsic properties. We discover such properties, we don't invent or construct them, and they therefore have an objective status. Moreover, these properties are productive. Intrinsic properties of natural kinds are responsible for an unlimited number of other properties; so we never come to an end of information about them. These characteristics of intrinsic kinds coincide, then, with the first three properties in Table 4.1. In general, we can think of causal essentialism (the psychological theory) as the hypothesis that people *believe* natural kinds are intrinsic kinds.

With this understanding, the Table 4.1 characteristics can do double duty as properties of intrinsic kinds and as properties of essentialist beliefs.

Essential properties are exactly those intrinsic properties that are crucial for natural-kind membership. Other intrinsic and extrinsic properties are accidental to membership. An essential property in this sense is not merely one that all and only members of a category happen to possess, but a property that an object *must* have to be a category member and, possibly, to exist at all. The set of essential properties are usually said to be "necessary and sufficient," but the relevant sense of these terms is stronger than "every actual member has each essential property and every essential property is possessed by each actual member." Essential properties are properties that a member of the kind has across causally possible worlds or states or circumstances.[14] Unless this is so, essential properties would be worthless for purposes of explaining natural kinds' modal properties—for example, explaining why these kinds can determine the truth of counterfactual conditionals, such as our earlier example *If Calvin (a particular human) were a lion, he'd be tawny colored*. These sentences are true, according to the intrinsic view, because the essential property of the kind carries over to nonactual situations (e.g., ones in which Calvin is a lion instead of a human), producing the kind's typical characteristics. If a natural kind's essential property changed from one situation to another— if lions in other possible worlds had what is human essence in this one— then all bets would be off about whether such sentences are true.

Recall that the purpose of the present chapter is to examine theories of natural kinds' modal characteristics. Essential properties seem to be a logical source of such features. But if essential properties are simply ones that people feel are important in our actual situation and not ones that continue to be true in counterfactual contexts, then essentialism is unhelpful for our purposes. Essentialists need essential properties to hold across possible situations in order to explain, for example, why if sheep were raised by cows, they'd still grow up to be sheep, or why if melon seeds were planted in a cornfield, they would still produce melons rather than corn.

Essential properties make for distinctness between different kinds. If two objects belong to different natural kinds, then they must differ on at least one essential property. We therefore also have intrinsicness, uniqueness, distinctiveness, and identity from Table 4.1 as part of the intrinsic package.

The intrinsic view does not demand that arbitrary combinations of natural kinds are themselves natural kinds. There is no natural kind consisting of just daisies and aardvarks. However, some natural kinds may stand in subordinate-superordinate relations. In particular, according to the usual intrinsic view, if one object is a member of two different natural kinds, then one kind must be superordinate to the other. How many levels exist in the hierarchy of natural kinds is a question that exercised philosophers and scientists from ancient to modern times (e.g., Atran, 1995, 1998; Lovejoy, 1936). The answer presumably depends on how many levels meet the criteria in Table 4.1. One possibility is that there is only a single level of intrinsic kinds, with higher and lower levels being arbitrary sets. If so, this special level contributes the essential properties to its members. In Leigh's case, for example, the lion kind might be the one responsible for her essential properties; higher categories such as mammals and lower ones such as South Asian lions are then nonintrinsic kinds, perhaps imposed by people for classificatory convenience.

If only one privileged level exists, then this kind can decide the conditions of the object's existence. Take away the properties associated with being a lion and Leigh not only resigns from the lion category, but ceases to exist entirely. On this strong version of the intrinsic story, "to be for a thing is to be a thing of a certain kind, to have a certain essence" (Loux, 1991, p. 7; see, also, Grene, 1963, p. 211, for a similar interpretation). This would provide a link between the sortal theory of Chapter 1 and essentialism about categories. On other weaker versions of the intrinsic story, no special level exists, and several categories to which an object belongs provide criteria for sameness and persistence of the object, but only *as a member of that kind*. In this case, Leigh's membership in the lion category yields principles for determining whether something is the same lion as Leigh across circumstances (*identity-of-members* in Table 4.1), but not necessarily whether something is the same entity (i.e., *identity-of-individuals*).

On any version of the intrinsic view, though, the essence of a natural kind is responsible for the modal characteristics of kind members. Essence determines what's possible for the member. Thus, if we think of essence as being some sort of internal causal force, as seems consistent with this view, then this causal essence determines the limits on what a category member can do and be.

4.2.2.2 The Interaction Theory

The interaction view agrees with the intrinsic view in taking natural kinds to be objective and productive. The starting point for this view, however, is not the role of internal properties in the kinds, but the role of the kinds in causal relations. Roughly speaking, natural kinds are the sorts of entities that causal laws relate. Chemical kinds, for example, are the things that participate in law-governed reactions with each other, and biological kinds the things that participate in law-governed biological relations involving reproduction, descent, and other matters (Fodor, 1974; Quine, 1969). The objectivity of natural kinds, on this view, then, is on a par with the objectivity of the causal interactions these laws describe. Similarly, to the extent that we can continue to discover new laws interrelating natural kinds, we can continue to discover new facts about the kinds themselves. The productivity of a natural kind's properties is on a par with the productivity of the causal relations in which the kinds participate.

An object's membership in a natural kind depends on whether the object instantiates the laws for that kind, and preserving this relationship entails a harmony or equilibrium between laws and kinds. If certain objects or subcategories prove to be exceptions to a law involving the whole kind, then this may be a reason to suspect that the exceptions belong to some other kind. Alternatively, we may suspect that "laws" that violate the integrity of a natural kind are erroneous. This does not mean that kind membership is arbitrary, but it does mean that membership is more complex than the presence or absence of fixed internal properties. Table 4.2 summarizes this idea under the heading of *instantial membership*, which replaces the notion of the potency of essential properties (the method of establishing membership for intrinsic kinds in Table 4.1). For similar reasons, the existence of the entire category will depend on *relational* rather than purely intrinsic matters. Moreover, the interlocking of kinds and laws implies that natural kinds are *projectible*. Because causal laws and kinds are tailored to each other, natural kinds will support induction and counterfactual conditionals (Goodman, 1955). For example, if we learn that all known members of a natural kind have some property P, then we can predict that a new member will also have P, provided that

TABLE 4.2   Possible Characteristics of Interactional Kinds

Characteristic	Description
Instantial membership	Members of a natural kind are objects that instantiate the causal laws in which the kind participates.
Productivity	A kind's causal interactions are responsible for (a possibly unlimited number of) a member's properties.
Objectivity	Causal forces governing kinds exist in nature (do not depend on human convention).
Relationality	Existence of kinds depends on causal interactions with other objects.
Nonuniqueness	Natural kinds participate in many types of relevant causal relations. Individual members need not be part of each such relation.
Partial distinctiveness	Members of different natural kinds participate in different but possibly overlapping types of causal relationships.
Identity-of-members	Clusters of causal properties are responsible for tracing a member of the kind across possible situations.
Identity-of-individuals?	Clusters of causal properties responsible for tracing an individual across possible situations.
Projectibility	Natural kinds allow their properties to apply to new members and support counterfactual conditionals

Note: As part of a psychological theory, the descriptions should be prefaced by "People believe that . . . "

P is itself projectible.[15] Under the same proviso, we can also suppose (counterfactually) that if something were a member of the same natural kind, then it too would have P.

Further differences between interactional and intrinsic kinds depend on assumptions about the (lack of) uniqueness and distinctiveness of a kind's causal relations. Nothing about interactional kinds demands that only one type of causal interaction is crucial to the kind. In fact, we've just noted that the possibility of discovering new laws is needed to explain natural kinds' productivity. Hence, the types of causal relations associated with an interactional kind are not unique in the way that essences are unique to intrinsic kinds. Moreover, although causal laws group objects in kinds, the causal interactions need not be common to all or only members of the kind, except as a limiting case (Wilson, 1999). A second sort of equilibrium prevails among a kind's causal properties: Subsets of the properties will causally support other subsets in overlapping and mutually reinforcing ways (Boyd, 1999; see also Keil, 1989, 1995, and

Kornblith, 1993). However, single members of the kind need not have all relevant causal properties. The causal properties are not discrete in the sense of Table 4.1—either all present or all absent in individual category members—and no single property will be prepotent in dominating the influence of all others. Also, nothing prevents members of different kinds from having some of the same relevant causal properties. In this sense, then, causal properties only *partially distinguish* kinds (see Table 4.2). Of course, certain properties may turn out to be more central or less mutable than others are, but this will depend on the particular configuration of causal forces that surround the kind.

Because of the interdependence of cause and kind, limits on the kind are limits on what the associated causes support. Questions about whether a kind can undergo certain changes and questions about the concomitants of such changes are questions about the causal interactions governing these transformations. If there are no essential properties, these issues aren't decidable simply by inspecting whether intrinsic properties are preserved. Instead, we have to defer to the same kind-cause harmony that determines membership in the first place.

4.2.2.3 The Intrinsic View as Beliefs About Natural Kinds

Let's suppose that people believe natural kinds are intrinsic kinds. How does this stack up against the evidence we've reviewed? At first glance, belief in intrinsic kinds comports well with results from the transformation experiments, which helped make the notion of psychological essentialism popular. Essential properties are those that can't be transformed away while still leaving an object's membership intact. So if children have a grip on which sorts of properties are essential for kinds, then they'll appreciate that some transformations (i.e., those involving nonessential properties) preserve kind membership, whereas other transformations (i.e., those involving essential properties) don't. This follows from the potency and identity properties in Table 4.1. One potential qualification is that relatively little direct evidence exists that people can identify essential properties, but the intrinsic view is consistent with this inability: Vague knowledge of these properties is sufficient for dealing with some transformations but not for describing the properties precisely (as discussed in Section 4.1.4). Children and even adults may know the sorts of properties that are essential (e.g., that they're inside an animal), but not precisely which properties these are. Thus, they can say that a dog whose insides have been removed is no longer a dog, yet they may not know exactly which of the inside parts are critical. Perhaps a more serious qualification is the lack of evidence that intrinsic attributes count more toward membership than relational (functional) attributes (see Section 4.1.2.4). Absence of more direct evidence for essential properties is a weakness of the intrinsic view.

The intrinsic view explains some types of category-based induction. One of the theory's selling points is that because all members of a kind are alike with respect to essential properties, then any property that is itself essential (or depends heavily on the essential ones) will be similarly uniform across members. Once you know that such a property is true of one member, it must also hold of all others by a sort of "super-inductive" inference (as Harper, 1989, calls it). There's no need to locate a convincingly large sample of members that possess the property before agreeing with the conclusion. A single instance may suffice (Nisbett et al., 1983; Thagard & Nisbett, 1982). So far, so good for the intrinsic view.

This advantage, however, should be balanced against the fact that other mechanisms must supplement essential properties in order to explain typicality effects in inductive inference. How could essential properties account for why people prefer generalizing from dogs to mammals over generalizing from opossums to mammals? Dogs and opossums equally share essential mammal properties. We might try to explain such findings by invoking similarity based on nonessential properties, as in earlier models of category-based induction. But our review of such findings suggests that people make use of deeper knowledge of causal relationships in making such judgments, not just surface similarity. Adding nonessential causal relations to the intrinsic view in order to handle these results is a concession to the rival interaction theory.

For counterfactual inductive inferences, the intrinsic view encounters similar difficulties. Consider argument (12), which seems reasonably strong:

(12)   Pekinese can leap over cars.

Dobermans can leap over cars.

To explain the inductive strength of (12) via essential properties, we need to assume that whatever essential properties Pekinese have are responsible for their leaping prowess. Suppose you think the premise is true. Then you probably also think that Dobermans have a similar set of essential properties that will allow them to leap cars. But what if you think the premise is false (as you probably do)? In that case, in order to suppose the premise true for the sake of the argument, you either have to assume that Pekinese have acquired new essential properties or that something else—some other, nonessential causal mechanism—is responsible for their remarkable leaping skill in this counterfactual setting. However, the first alternative is out for intrinsic kinds: Essential properties are exactly those properties that *can't* change across possible circumstances. Altering Pekinese's essential properties makes them ex-Pekinese, not Pekinese high-jumpers. Changing essential properties of dogs, mammals, or animals has exactly the same consequence, since these properties are among the essential properties of Pekinese. So essential properties are useless in explaining category-based induction with counterfactual premises. The same point can be put directly in terms of judgments about counterfactual conditionals. The statement *If Pekinese were able to leap over cars, then so could Dobermans* is presumably true, but not because Pekinese would have new essential properties in situations consistent with the antecedent.

The same problem holds for intrinsic kinds even if people have only "placeholders" for essential properties. If people believe that some unknown property P is essential for Pekinese, then P must be true of Pekinese in at least all causally possible situations in which Pekinese exist—counterfactual as well as factual situations. For this reason, you can't assume for the sake of argument (12) that Pekinese have adopted some new essential property P', which replaces P and enables them to jump higher. The very nature of essential properties implies that Pekinese do not exist without P.

This inability to explain category-based inferences via essential properties doesn't mean that the intrinsic view can't deal with such inferences at all. We could still invoke other (nonessential) intrinsic properties or, for that matter, relational properties to explain the inductive strength of these arguments.[16] But that means the intrinsic view ends up explaining modal phenomena in two different ways. On the one hand, natural kinds' essential properties determine, for example, limits on the possible transformations that members can undergo and still count as members. On the other, some separate modal device is needed to explain possible effects that members have when counterfactual changes occur, as in argument (12). Essential properties can't be the sole source of natural kinds' modal characteristics, and this seems to undercut the motivation for positing essential properties in the first place. If we take this deficiency together with the general lack of evidence that intrinsic properties are privileged in those studies that have manipulated causal relations explicitly (see Section 4.1.2.4), we have some grounds for skepticism about the intrinsic view as people's everyday theory about natural kinds.

4.2.2.4 The Interaction View as Beliefs About Natural Kinds

How does the interaction view stack up? This view is more general than the intrinsic view, in a sense, since interactional kinds could have some of their key causal properties essentially. So to make the comparison between the views sharper and more interesting, let's suppose that the interaction theory rules out essential properties. In this guise, the interaction view bears similarities to Rosch's (1978) theory: The view assumes that our beliefs about natural kinds depend on clusterings of properties. Things with fins tend to have gills; things with feathers tend to have wings; and so on. According to the interactional view, however, causal relations replace mere statistical co-occurrences in order to explain these relations. Transformation experiments might seem at first to be weak spots for this view, since a few of these studies (e.g., Barton & Komatsu, 1989; S. A. Gelman & Wellman, 1991) suggest that people think a change to certain properties entails a change in kind membership. Aren't the changed properties therefore essential ones?

No. Properties that change an object's kind are not necessarily essential properties. If the interaction view is correct, membership in a natural kind may depend on many interacting properties. If enough of these properties are disrupted, for example, by eviscerating an organism, then the organism is no longer a category member. But no single property (or small subset of properties) need be essential in this situation. The fact that interactional kinds have no essential properties, then, doesn't mean that members of these kinds can't cease to be members. Objects are members of interactional kinds in virtue of instantiating causal laws (see Table 4.2). So if a member begins violating enough of these laws (whereas other members continue to instantiate them), then we should consider the object no longer a member of the kind in question.

The interaction view can also handle category-based induction. Individual members of interactional kinds have overlapping causal properties; hence, new properties that are bound up with the old ones will tend to carry over to other members of the same kind. Overlap in these properties won't guarantee that a new biological property that Leigh has—say, having Enzyme E—will hold for all lions. But, in fact, we usually *aren't* certain about such matters. Whether other lions have the enzyme depends on how it is hooked up to other liony properties and on the connections among these mediating properties, as discussed earlier (see the sections on category-based induction). Property distribution is an empirical matter, not one about which we can have absolute confidence. On this, the interaction view coincides with intuition.

The interaction view accounts for inferences based on counterfactual information in a uniform way. To accommodate the counterfactual, we have to suppose that the properties of a kind (or of a member of the kind) differ from what they are in the current state of affairs, making adjustments in causally dependent properties. The strength of the inference will then depend on what these adjustments lead us to think will be true in the adjusted state. One advantage of interactional kinds, then, is parsimony: Why posit two modal mechanisms when only one appears necessary?

The interaction view also explains the general lack of evidence for definitions, since no essential properties exist to supply the definitions. In those few studies reporting that people do provide definitions for natural kinds, the interaction view can interpret these definitional attributes as important, perhaps even universal properties, but not essential ones (as Medin, 1989, and Murphy & Medin, 1985, suggest). This seems consistent with the actual examples these studies cite. For example, being the hardest substance known is true of diamonds, but it's not essential since it leaves open the possibility of discovering harder substances. (If a harder substance *x* were discovered, we wouldn't refer to *x* as diamonds.) A potential difficulty for interactional kinds, however, is Malt's (1990) finding that people think that an object in between two natural kinds is "probably one or the other." A crisp division between kinds supports the intrinsic view's distinctiveness over the interaction view's partial distinctiveness (see Tables 4.1 and 4.2). The strength of this objection depends on the reliability of the effect (Kalish, 1995) and on issues of wording—for example, on how participants interpreted "probably" in "probably one or the other." The interaction view is consistent with causal forces producing a fairly clear separation between kinds, making in-between cases "improbable."

A second potential disadvantage of interactional kinds is that the tight connection between kinds and laws may put natural kinds out of reach of children and adults who don't know the relevant science. Young children don't know what chemical laws govern kinds like water, and neither did adults before modern times. We might be tempted to say, for this reason, that these people can't have interactional kinds, even though they appreciate water as a category distinct from other liquids. Maybe early kinds are intrinsic kinds, whose status changes to interactional kinds if a person happens to acquire the key scientific principles. Children might start out with a simplified causal schema that specifies a unique, distinctive organizing cause per kind and later graduate to a more differentiated set of laws that provide the basis for an interactional, theory-based kind. A number of authors (e.g., Keil, 1989; Kornblith, 1993) have pointed out that an innate psychological bias toward expecting intrinsic kinds may help children acquire later knowledge of interactive ones.

Should proponents of interactional kinds concede that early kinds are intrinsic? Clearly, beliefs about kinds change as we add knowledge about laws that govern the kinds. But is the start state belief in a single internal cause or belief in multiple—possibly fragmentary, possibly false—interactive ones? It seems at least as plausible to suppose that children begin by assuming that what makes Leigh a lion is a set of causes (e.g., having lion cubs, having a lion mom, dominating other animals) as to suppose they start with a single intrinsic cause. Skepticism about interactional kinds seems to arise from doubts about children's knowledge of causal principles, but the lawlike character of natural kinds is also part of the intrinsic story. The intrinsic view softens its position by positing that people have beliefs in such causes, without knowing the causes' descriptive content; but the same move is open to proponents of interactional kinds. Similarly, if an innate bias toward intrinsic kinds fosters later knowledge of science, a bias toward interactional kinds should do better.

The most serious complaint about interactional kinds is that they are too unconstrained, especially if they amount to no more than the bland notion that natural kinds have some causes or other.[17] Intrinsic kinds come with a stronger organizing principle: a unique central cause produces an organism's surface characteristics. Thus, intrinsic kinds explain the impression that their members distribute statistically around a common type, and they motivate a search for the type's source. By contrast, interactional kinds seem less disciplined, since multiple forces shape the kinds. Still, the interactional view can hold that natural kinds result, not just from any combination of forces, but from special conditions that yield instantial membership, productivity, identity, partial distinctiveness, and the other characteristics in Table 4.2. You might also question whether positing a single root cause is the best or most intuitive explanation for distributional characteristics. Intrinsic kinds must posit interfering forces to explain why category members aren't cookie-cutter versions of each other. Interactional causes seem an equally reasonable source of variability. Likewise, although belief in a central cause can drive inquiry in everyday life and in science, so could belief in cooperating causes. If we discovered that there were no essential causes for plant and animal species, would that squelch our curiosity about their origins and properties?[18]

4.3 Summary and Concluding Comments

People have knowledge of what is possible for members of natural kinds, not just knowledge of what is presently true of them. People may not be able to volunteer properties that objects must have in order to be members of these kinds. But they make consistent judgments both about the membership of hypothetical objects that have gained or lost properties and about what these hypothetical changes imply for other kinds of objects. How is this knowledge of the possible possible?

The second part of this chapter examined whether causal information could provide the basis for natural kinds' modal properties. Knowledge about causal principles may be helpful because such principles apply not just to natural kinds as they currently are but also to kinds in other potential situations. To be more specific about the kind-cause relation, however, we need to know how people think causal forces shape natural kinds. One possibility is that kinds depend on a single intrinsic cause that is responsible for an object's membership, typical properties, identity, and distinctness from other kinds. This is the intrinsic view that Table 4.1 summarizes, and it captures current ideas about causal (psychological) essentialism. An alternative possibility, outlined in Table 4.2, sees natural kinds as constellations of causal forces. Both conceptions take natural kinds to be objective groupings "in nature" with a potentially unlimited number of properties to be discovered, but interactional kinds depend on a set of meshing causes rather than a unique internal essence.

Maybe we can find room for both kinds of kinds. For example, adults might believe that chemical kinds are intrinsic, but biological kinds interactional.[19] Intrinsic kinds seem better equipped to handle judgments that membership in natural kinds is all-or-none. Interactional kinds have the advantage of explaining the inductive and transformation data in a unified way. Intrinsic kinds force us to distinguish between essential properties responsible for change in membership, and nonessential, but modal, properties responsible for other counterfactual changes; interactional kinds can do both jobs with the same causal forces.

Appendix

The Gap Model

To understand the Gap model's assumptions, let's consider arguments (A1) and (A2) [argument (A1) is identical to (5) above]:

(A1)   Lions are at least 5 feet tall.

House cats are at least 5 feet tall.

(A2)   Lions are at least 5 feet tall.

Cougars are at least 5 feet tall.

There is a discrepancy (a "gap") between the property expressed by the predicate (*are at least 5 feet tall*) and the corresponding property of the members of the premise category (lions). Lions can be 4 feet tall, but probably not 5 feet. Evaluating the strength of such arguments requires assuming that the premise is true and then determining to what extent the conclusion is true under that assumption. Assuming the premise is true, in turn, means reducing or eliminating the gap. According to the Gap model, we do this by recalibrating the conclusion category (house cats in argument (A1) and cougars in (A2)) by adding to it (some function of) the difference between the value of the property expressed by the predicate (*is 5 feet tall*) and that possessed by the premise category (lions).

As an illustration of this recalibration process, let's assume that the actual height of lions is 4 feet, cougars 2 feet, and house cats 1 foot. Then the recalibrated size of house cats in the context of argument (A1) will be the actual height of house cats plus the difference between 5 feet and the height of lions: $1 + (5 - 4) = 2$ feet. The Gap model assumes, however, that the extent of the adjustment also depends on the similarity between the premise and conclusion categories (and on the similarity between the premise and conclusion predicates, when these differ). For these purposes, similarity is measured on a scale from 0 (not at all similar) to 1 (maximally similar). This fractional value of similarity multiplies the difference between the value of the predicate and the premise category before adjustment. For example, if the similarity between lions and house cats is 0.8, then the recalibrated height of house cats will be not 2 feet, but $1 + 0.8(5 - 4) = 1.8$ feet. For the moment, let's assume that the similarity between cougars and lions is the same as that between house cats and lions; if so, cougars' recalibrated height will be $2 + 0.8(5 - 4) = 2.8$ feet.

To calculate the probability of the argument's conclusion given its premise, the Gap model determines how likely it is that the recalibrated conclusion category will have the value of the predicate. The probability of the conclusion of (A1), given the premise, is then the probability that 1.8 foot house cats are 5 feet tall, and the probability of the conclusion of (A2), given the premise, is the probability that 2.8 foot cougars are 5 feet tall.[20] The Gap model computes these probabilities as:

$$\Pr(conclusion \mid premise) =$$
$$\frac{min(recalibrated\ value\ of\ conclusion\ category,\ value\ of\ conclusion\ predicate)}{value\ of\ conclusion\ predicate}$$

For example, if the recalibrated height of a house cat is 1.8 feet, as above, the probability of the conclusion of (A1), given its premise, is $min(1.8, 5)/5 = .36$. Similarly, if the recalibrated height of a cougar is 2.8 feet, then the probability of the conclusion of (A2), given its premise, is $min(2.8, 5)/5 = .56$. This agrees with the intuition that (A2) is a stronger argument than (A1).

NOTES

This chapter is a revision of Rips (2001a). Thanks to Serge Blok, Douglas Medin, and Daniel Osherson for comments on an earlier version of this chapter and to Beth Proffitt for conversations about the material in Section 4.1.

1. See S. A. Gelman, 2003, for further studies along these lines. Gelman and Markman pretested properties like *having cold blood* to make sure the children didn't already know, for example, that the triceratops had cold blood; so the properties were unfamiliar to these children. We can be confident, then, that the children were making a novel inference. As an anonymous reviewer has pointed out, we don't have this assurance for familiar properties, such as drinking from a cup, that appear in some other studies.

2. Osherson et al. (1990) call these properties "blank predicates." People probably interpret them, however, as fictitious or unfamiliar biological properties rather than as purely unknown or nonsense predicates. As Osherson et al. (1990, p. 186) note, "blank predicates are recognizably scientific in character." I'll therefore drop "blank predicate" in favor of "unfamiliar biological predicate" in what follows (as do McDonald, Samuels, & Rispoli, 1996).

3. Proponents of the Similarity-Coverage model could argue that S. A. Gelman and Markman (1986) labeled their items in a way that emphasized category membership (see Figure 4.1); hence, the fact that children favored the indirect route in their inferencing was due to features of the experimental setup. For example, Gelman and Markman told children that "this dinosaur" (the apatosaurus) has cold blood, that "this rhinoceros" has warm blood, and asked whether "this dinosaur" (the triceratops) had cold or warm blood. Repetition of "dinosaur" might have emphasized the indirect transmission route through the corresponding category. (See also Sloutsky & Fisher, 2004, who argue that the labels provide young children, but not adults, with an additional source of direct similarity.) This argument gains support from Medin, Lynch, Coley, and Atran's (1997) finding that even experts prefer to generalize across natural kinds when their common genus is linguistically marked (e.g., Norway maple and sugar maple) than when it is not (Ohio buckeye and horsechestnut). In Gelman and Markman's experiment, however, the preference for generalization-by-category cannot be explained by mere repetition of the common noun ("dinosaur"). S. A. Gelman and Markman (1986, Experiment 2) found similar results when they used synonyms instead of exact repetitions. Could mention of the category itself (by whatever noun) have driven participants to the indirect route for generalization? Although this is possible, it still won't explain the difference in results for biological and accidental properties.

4. The formulation of the Gap model changes somewhat from the earlier to the later papers in this series; the description here and in the Appendix follows Osherson et al. (1995), since this article introduces improvements and generalizes the earlier versions.

5. The complicated nature of these predicates may have led some researchers to dismiss the Gap model. However, the choice of predicates is probably the result of the authors' desire to find properties that are both realistic and whose distribution people don't already know. Use of truly familiar properties runs the risk of participants determining their answer based on their prior belief in the

conclusion rather than by reasoning from the premises. Clearly, the intent of the Gap model isn't to account for only complex predicates like *have skins that are more resistant to penetration than most synthetic fibers*.

6. Sheer number of subcategories might not be the best measure of amount of evidence, as McDonald et al. (1996) acknowledge. For example, replacing cows with bisons, horses with zebras, and mice with voles seems to make argument (8) weaker, presumably because the new categories are less frequent or less important members of the mammal category. McDonald et al.'s discussion does not make it clear how best to analyze amount of evidence.

7. A potential ambiguity about these results is that they may reflect children's pragmatic uncertainties about labeling rather than their beliefs about category membership. They may believe, for example, that a dog whose fur has been shaved is no longer a dog but still have no better word for it than "dog." The yes/no format of the questions may reduce this worry, since children don't have to produce their own label for the furless creature, but it is still possible that when children are asked "Is it still a dog?" they hesitate to say "no" for lack of a better descriptor. This alternative view must explain, however, why children do say "no" when they are told that the dog's insides are removed. This view would be forced to the position that both transformations cause children to believe that the creature is a nondog, but only the more radical transformation is enough to overcome the tendency to agree to the "dog" label.

8. Unfortunately, the terminology is confusing here, because sortal essentialism is related to, but not the same as, the sortalism we ran into in Chapter 1. "Sortal essentialism," as S. A. Gelman (2003; S. A. Gelman & Hirschfeld, 1999) uses the term, is the claim that category terms have definitions specifying necessary and sufficient conditions for category membership (sometimes called "criteria of application"). Sortalism about identity is the claim that category terms have definitions specifying necessary and sufficient conditions for identity and individuation—that is, for determining whether one category member is identical to another ("criteria of identity"). You could be a sortal essentialist without being a sortalist about identity if you think category terms have definitions but these definitions don't determine the identity of individual category members over time. You could be a sortalist about identity but not a sortal essentialist if you believe that the meaning of category terms determine identity over time but not category membership. The traditional view in philosophy is that many terms supply criteria of application, but only special terms ("sortals," roughly, basic level count nouns) supply criteria of identity. As we'll see in a moment, psychological essentialists are probably committed to sortalism about identity, but they deny commitment to "sortal essentialism." See also Section 4.2.2.1 for further discussion of the relation between essentialism and sortalism.

9. Some versions of essentialism, however, do require all-or-none categories; see Ellis, 1996, for one such version. In further research Diesendruck and Gelman (1999) found a greater number of all-or-none judgments for animal

categories than for artifact categories (i.e., participants were more likely to say that something was either definitely a fish or definitely not a fish than that something was either definitely a tool or definitely not a tool). Even for animal categories, however, there were some intermediate membership judgments. See also Malt (1990).

10. According to these theories of reference, which properties are essential depends ultimately on which properties actually do determine sameness of kind to local samples, not on what current scientific theories happen to say. So whether H_2O is an essential property of water depends on whether present-day chemistry is true.

In more recent work, Putnam (1990) allows for greater distance between everyday use of natural kind terms and their use in science:

> I would now distinguish ordinary questions of substance-identity from scientific questions. I still believe that ordinary language and scientific language are interdependent; but layman's "water" is not the chemically pure water of the scientist, and just what "impurities" make something no longer water but something else (say, "coffee") is not determined by scientific theory. (p. 69)

Malt's evidence on everyday uses of "water" seems to confirm this lay sense of the term. See also Boyd's (1999) distinction between everyday natural kinds and scientific natural kinds.

11. This is not to say that properties that are central to membership in a natural kind are exactly the same as those that people use to pick out members of the kind or those they believe are most important in applying the kind term (Sloman & Ahn, 1999). Whether an animal has stripes may be important in whether "zebra" appropriately applies to it, but having stripes is not causally crucial for determining whether it is a zebra. This is because a term's appropriateness is partly a pragmatic matter; it depends on not misleading others. Nevertheless, the point remains that if essence determines kind membership, then essence also determines whether it's correct to apply the name of the kind to an instance.

12. Other departures from essentialist predictions in Braisby et al. (1996) may depend on details of the wording of the stories and the probe questions. In the case of stories like (10b), in which a discovery is made about all cats, Braisby et al.'s results show that on 87% of trials participants endorsed statement (a) and rejected (b), in accord with the essentialist predictions (see their Table 7):

(a) Cats exist.
(b) Cats do not exist.
(c) Cats do exist and people's beliefs concerning cats have changed.
(d) There are no such things as cats, only robots controlled from Mars.
(e) Tibby is a cat, though we were wrong about her being a mammal.
(f) Tibby is not a cat, though she is a robot controlled from Mars.

Most participants also endorsed the statement (c) and rejected (d)—again in agreement with essentialism—but the percentage decreased to 73%. Similarly, 76% of participants agreed with (e) and disagreed with (f). The decrease may have been due to the complexity of the statements in (c)-(f). The fact that participants had read in (10b) that all cats, including Tibby, are robots controlled from Mars may have encouraged some of them to go along with (d) and (f), since the second clause in each statement coincides with that information.

In the case of (10a), where a discovery is made about Tibby, 89% of participants accepted (a) and rejected (b), supporting essentialist predictions. However, only 46% rejected both (c) and (d), and only 47% rejected (e) and accepted (f), which are the options Braisby et al. (1996) believe essentialists should take (see their Table 1). It is not obvious, however, that an essentialist would have to reject (c). (Doesn't it count as a changed "belief about cats" that robots are present that look just like cats?) The story in (10a) also begins with the statement that "you have a female pet cat named Tibby," which may have prompted the discrepant responses to (e) and (f). (The percentages cited here are from Braisby et al., 1996, Experiment 2, which introduced procedural improvements over their Experiment 1.)

13. Daniel Osherson has emphasized this point (personal communication, February, 2001).

14. Proponents of intrinsic kinds hold that all essential properties are necessary and sufficient in this strong sense; but for reasons similar to those discussed earlier (see Section 4.1.3), they may not hold the converse. Logically necessary and sufficient properties (e.g., *being a walnut or a lion* and *being a nonwalnut*) may not be essential, since they don't comport with other characteristics, such as potency and productivity (see Table 4.1). We can leave it as an open question for these proponents, however, how to separate true essential properties from others that are "merely" necessary and sufficient.

15. We can perform induction over some properties of natural kinds but not others, as we've noted earlier in this chapter. For example, we're willing to project having a particular neurotransmitter from one lion to another but not having a particular pattern of cut and bruises. If we know the causal laws that govern the kind in at least a general way, we can let these laws dictate which properties we can project successfully. If we don't know any relevant laws, we may have to resort to weaker inductive methods, governed by the usual statistical and methodological principles for sampling. (See Godfrey-Smith, 2003, for a discussion of projectibility that acknowledges different methods of induction.)

16. Essentialists need not appeal to essential properties to explain all forms of inductive reasoning. We can perform induction with nonessentialized categories, and induction sometimes depends on purely statistical considerations of the sort familiar in survey sampling, as discussed in the previous note. If inspection

reveals that most randomly sampled mammal species have property P, then you might reasonably conclude on statistical grounds that a new mammal species will have P, in the absence of further information about P's nature. But statistical reasoning and other weak methods don't seem up to explaining the strength of arguments like (12). The results we've reviewed in Section 4.1.1.2 suggest that people's inductive reasoning about such arguments often depends on causal explanations about the categories in question. If essences don't supply these causes, we have to seek some other source (nonstatistical and nonessential) to do so. The issue is what resources an intrinsic theory would need to explain these causes.

17. This point is due to Douglas Medin (personal communication, October 11, 2000).

18. Notice that both intrinsic and interactional kinds pose similar problems of circularity. A potential explanatory circle runs between a natural kind and its essence (Q: What's a lion? A: Whatever is caused by lion essence. Q: What's lion essence? A: Whatever causes lions.), and the same circle runs between a natural kind and the causal laws in which it participates. People might be content with such circular beliefs for a while, but very tight circles are likely to seem feeble eventually.

19. See Sober (1980) for a metaphysical view along these lines.

20. Of course, taken literally, the probability is 0 that something 1.8 feet tall is 5 feet tall. So we should consider the values to represent approximations or central tendencies rather than exact points. According to this interpretation, the question is how likely it is that something estimated to be 1.8 feet tall could really be 5 feet tall. This difficulty is probably the motivation for Osherson et al.'s use of more complex predicates whose exact values participants are unlikely to know.

5

Thoughts

It's easy to spot the fault lines in psychologists' current theories of meaning. On the one hand, the goal for many investigators is to have a theory that explains which instances are members of specific categories. Given a perceptually presented daisy (or a description of a daisy), how do people recognize this object as a member of the category of daisies (or flowers or gifts)? How do they decide that it's not a member of the category of daffodils (or fruits or pajamas)? We've already met theories of this sort in discussing kinds in Chapter 4. On the other hand, the goal for a second group of investigators is to have a theory of concepts that explains sentence understanding. For the sentence about daisies you read several lines back, how did you understand its meaning based on the meaning of its component words, for example, *daisy*? These two goals— explaining classification and explaining sentence understanding—are sufficiently different that investigators have usually pursued them in isolation. The result has been that theories of concepts designed for one goal may have little in common with theories designed for the other, as we will see.

This division between theories of classifying and theories of understanding is unsatisfying, because intuition suggests these two abilities are related. Classifying something as (say) an upside-down daisy would seem to depend on our ability to make sense of what an upside-down daisy might be, and the same goes for our ability to understand a sentence like *That's an upside-down daisy*. In both cases, we seem to combine information associated with *upside-down* with information associated with *daisy* to arrive at the thought of an upside-down daisy. It would be surprising if the mental process that gives the phrase *upside-down daisy* its significance were unrelated to the process that tells us what's an upside-down daisy. (We drew a similar conclusion in Chapter 4 in examining the difference between "sortal" and "causal" essentialism.) This relationship doesn't imply that classifying and understanding are *identical*, and in particular, it doesn't imply that understanding *upside-down daisy* is nothing but knowing how to determine whether something is an upside-down daisy. Far from it. But at least in the case of novel, multiword phrases, classifying something as a member of the category named by the phrase seems to depend on combining the meanings of the phrase's words into a complex thought.

Psychologists have run into difficulty, though, constructing a theory that explains how people classify things in categories named by phrases. In the first place, some of the most promising theories of classification appear to be cognitively inert—the mental representations that underlie these theories simply don't combine readily with others. These theories offer no obvious way to bond the representation of *upside-down* to the representation of *daisy*. Second, even where combination rules are possible, these rules are sometimes at odds with facts about sentence comprehension. So we have an impasse: We need a way to explain people's ability to understand multiword phrases and to classify instances as members of the categories such phrases denote, but the available options seem unacceptable for theoretical or empirical reasons. Similarly, we worked hard in Chapter 4 to understand the properties of kind concepts, such as DAISY, that allow these concepts to support reliable inferences. For example, we considered ways in which DAISY could support novel inferences from *Daisies have Enzyme E441* to *Daffodils have Enzyme E441*. However, any progress we've made on this front depends on relating information about the concept to information about the entire statement (e.g., from DAISY to *Daisies have Enzyme E441*). We carry out inferences at the level of the statements (or associated propositions), not at the level of lexical concepts. Obstacles to transferring this information from concepts to propositions create problems for explaining people's confidence in these inferences.

I won't be offering in this chapter a theory that overcomes these obstacles, but instead will be settling for a more modest, diagnostic goal. In the first section of this chapter, I argue that one reason for the current impasse is that no monolithic theory can cope with all the demands on a cognitive system for combining lexical information. Thus, there is a reason for the rift, mentioned earlier, between theories of classifying and theories of understanding. One type of "sentence understanding" or "comprehension" is independent of classifying (and related cognitive operations); so any adequate theory must have parts that divide the labor of combining lexical knowledge. This suggestion goes along with earlier theories that have taken a two-factor approach to concepts (e.g., G. A. Miller & Johnson-Laird, 1976; Osherson & Smith, 1981). Earlier dual theories, however, assigned classification to one mental component and concept combination to another component, endorsing the split we found unsatisfying. In Section 5.2, I claim instead that both components must combine lexical information, but lexical information of different sorts. In other words, a second type of "sentence understanding" accompanies classifying for categories named by phrases. This second type of understanding extends the approach of Chapter 4. The third section of the present chapter attempts to show that this distinction between two types of lexical combination can help deal with an important family of objections that appears to demonstrate that psychological concepts can't combine.[1] Some suggestions about the shape of an adequate theory appear in Section 5.4.

5.1 Psychological Theories of Concepts and Concept Combination

Let's take a quick tour of some recent theories of classifying in order to see why such theories have difficulty explaining novel items such as *upside-down daisy* or *green firetruck*. I'll concentrate here on what seem to be the most viable current models in cognitive psychology: Exemplar theories, which represent categories as remembered instances, and Theory theories (aka "Knowledge-based theories"), which, roughly speaking, represent them as internal encyclopedia entries (see Murphy, 2002, for an extensive review). Other psychological models, such as Schema theory or Prototype theory, can be seen as variations or hybrids of the Exemplar and Theory ideas, and they introduce no new considerations for combining concepts. Schema-based theories seem to be virtually identical to Theory theories, according to standard accounts (e.g., Rumelhart & Norman, 1988), as I mentioned in Chapter 2. I stick to the "theory" terminology here simply because it is more common in this context (see Note 3 below). "Prototype" has been applied to many different representations—according to some, they are theory-like entities (e.g., E. E. Smith, Osherson, Rips, & Keane, 1988); according to others, they are average instances or best examples (e.g., Posner & Keele,

1968)—but in neither case do they possess representational powers that differ from Exemplars or Theories when it comes to combining lexical information or forming new thoughts.

5.1.1 The Exemplar Theory

According to a generic version of the Exemplar theory, deciding to classify an instance *i* as a member of some category *C* is a matter of determining the similarity between *i* and members of *C* that you have previously encountered and remembered. If *i* is similar enough to these *C* exemplars (and dissimilar enough to the exemplars of other potential categories), then you will also classify *i* as a *C*. This type of model has enjoyed a good deal of empirical success, especially in experiments in which participants learn artificial categories (e.g., two disjoint sets of geometrical forms or dot patterns) and then attempt to classify a new item as a member of one of them (Hintzman, 1986; Medin & Schaffer, 1978; Nosofsky, 1986).

However, Exemplar models run into some difficulties as accounts of how we understand multiword phrases and even as accounts of how we classify instances as members of categories named by such phrases. For suppose you've never before heard or read the noun phrase *upside-down daisy* and have never before encountered an example of one. Nevertheless, you would probably have no trouble understanding this phrase and would be able to decide whether or not something was an upside-down daisy (provided, of course, you can recognize daisies). Since you can't recall any upside-down daisies, Exemplar models can't explain these cognitive feats of yours without further assumptions. Even proponents of Exemplar models have come to acknowledge these limitations (Medin & Shoben, 1988). This is a familiar point: Multiword phrases and sentences make it possible to express an extremely large, probably infinite, number of novel concepts for which no instances have been encountered or stored. A theory like the Exemplar model, in which concepts (or concept representations) consist solely of traces of instances, can't get started explaining these novel items.

This deficiency is connected with lots of other troubles the Exemplar model has with natural language categories. For instance, the Exemplar model fails to explain how you can have the concepts WITCH,

UNICORN, and TELEPATHY, and presumably, ELECTRON and BLACK HOLE. The Exemplar model also predicts incorrectly that your concept of Nebraskans is the same as your concept of flight-insurance salesmen in case it happens by chance that all and only the Nebraskans you've met are flight-insurance salesmen. The point about multiword phrases is that it amplifies these deficiencies because of the large number of potential concepts they introduce that have few or no exemplars. Of course, if the Exemplar model had a way to produce exemplars of upside-down daisies, telepathy, and so on, from exemplars of simpler categories, then these problems wouldn't be so severe. But this would sacrifice the idea that exemplars are always *remembered* instances, and the process of manufacturing novel instances goes far beyond the capacity of any proposed Exemplar theory.

5.1.2 The Theory Theory

Although the Exemplar model won't give us any help in dealing with concept combination, other current theories may do better. One that seems promising has emerged from studies of changes in children's thinking about natural kinds (Carey, 1985; S. A. Gelman & Markman, 1986; Keil, 1989; Markman, 1989), from studies of the coherence of categories (Murphy & Medin, 1985), and from studies of differences between judgments of similarity and judgments of category membership (Ahn & Dennis, 2001; Rips, 1989, 1991; Rips & Collins, 1993). According to a generic version of this theory, people represent categories as mini-theories that describe facts about those categories. Thus, deciding that instance *i* is a *C* comes down to determining whether *C*'s mini-theory can best explain the properties manifested by *i*. There have also been a number of attempts, which we'll look at shortly, to extend this Theory theory to concept combination.[2]

The Theory theory's approach to classifying builds on an analogy to scientific classification. The analogy goes something like this:

A scientist uses his or her theories of different species to decide which one a given specimen belongs to.

An ordinary individual uses his or her mini-theories of different categories to decide which one a given object belongs to.

Let's not quibble as to whether people's beliefs about categories deserve the name "theory" or even "mini-theory" (see Murphy, 2002, p. 61, who demurs on this point). The beliefs in question may be sketchy, naive, stereotyped, or incorrect. People may use "placeholders" instead of descriptions for properties they believe exist but don't know how to flesh out (see Chapter 4 of this book). But most investigators who have defended the Theory theory assume that the beliefs include, whenever possible:

(1)   a. People's ideas about what makes an instance a member of the category,
       b. Some specification of the normal or default properties that such an instance possesses, and
       c. Some account of the relation between (a) and (b)

These are exactly the points we discussed in connection with natural kinds in Chapter 4. Some of the items in (1a–c) may be missing in particular cases; but if they're available, they'll be part of the mini-theory. In the case of daisies, for example, the mini-theory might state that daisies are flowers distinguished by a particular genetic structure and ecology (not further specified for us laypeople), that they usually grow in temperate habitats, have yellow centers and white petals, and that the genetic structure and the ecology cause these latter characteristics. For a math category like that of odd numbers, the mini-theory might tell us that odd numbers are positive integers that are not evenly divisible by 2, that their final digit is 1, 3, 5, 7, or 9, and that number theory defines them that way.[3]

Mini-theories are less susceptible than Exemplar models to troubles with the meanings of words. They have no difficulty with witches, since you can easily build a mini-theory that happens to have no instantiations. And they have no problem with Nebraskan insurance salesmen, since your theory of Nebraskans can differ from your theory of flight-insurance salesmen, even if their instantiations are the same in your experience.

Still, at least three problems haunt the Theory theory. First, and most important in the present context, theories don't easily combine. Given a mini-theory of daisies and a mini-theory of upside-down things, how can we construct a mini-theory of upside-down daisies? We'll review (in Section 5.3 of this chapter) several different versions of the combination problem, but for the moment, we can simply note that theories aren't the sort of things that combine in an obvious way.

Second, if we must possess a theory in order to understand a term or a sentence in which the term appears, then it would seem to be impossible to understand our own requests for information about the term. As Komatsu (1992) points out, if I have no theory of what sassafras is, then *sassafras* has no meaning for me, and neither does the sentence *What's sassafras?* The Theory theory implies that I understand *What's sassafras?* as *What's . . . ?* (i.e., *sassafras* has *no* meaning in this query). If I also have no theory about erbium, for example, then *What's erbium?* also translates as *What's . . . ?* So *What's sassafras?* and *What's erbium?* should mean the same thing to me, contrary to fact. Although the Theory theory has no problems with categories like witches that happen to be empty, it does have difficulties with categories for which a person has no theory.

Third, as Fodor (1994) has argued, the Theory theory leads to a holistic view of comprehension that is difficult to sustain. A psychological version of this criticism goes like this: Suppose that part of my theory of *daisy* is that daisies cause hayfever. As an expert on allergies, you then present evidence that eventually convinces me that daisies don't in fact cause hayfever. My new belief would then seem to contradict my old one in the way that *Daisies do and don't cause hayfever* is contradictory. According to the Theory theory, however, my old and new beliefs don't conflict, since the meaning that I attach to *daisies* has changed in the interim. My old belief was about flowers-that-cause-hayfever, whereas my new one is about flowers-that-don't-cause-hayfever, since causing or not causing hayfever was part of my theory of daisies and, hence, part of what *daisy* means. Because the two beliefs differ in this respect, they are no more contradictory than *Roses cause hayfever* and *Daffodils don't cause hayfever*. But this result is intuitively unacceptable: I've clearly changed my mind about daisies and have not just changed the subject.

The holism issue that Fodor raises goes beyond the problem of how people recognize inconsistent beliefs and, according to Fodor, beyond what a psychological account can provide. However, the daisy example indicates that the Theory theory already runs into trouble explaining purely psychological phenomena. Some psychologists in the concepts-and-categories area tend to dismiss problems like these, viewing them as issues in linguistic semantics that have little to do with concepts, thoughts, or conceptual combination. This dismissal illustrates the schism in the field that I mentioned at the very beginning of this chapter. But I don't think these issues can be compartmentalized away quite so conveniently. If a psychological theory stipulates that the mental representation of daisies is X and if representing daisies as X makes it impossible for people to disagree with their own remembered beliefs and with the beliefs of others, then the theory is in serious trouble for psychological reasons.

Theory theorists sometimes overlook these difficulties, perhaps because they read into the examples features of the surface structure of the accompanying sentences. The surface form seems to make it clear, for example, that *Daisies cause hayfever* and *Daisies don't cause hayfever* are contradictory; so this doesn't seem to be a problem for the Theory theory. But notice that the Theory theory doesn't include the surface appearance of a term as part of its theory or its meaning. Viewed from the perspective of the Theory theory, the two sentences about hayfever are equivalent to something like these two:

> Old me: Flowers that have white petals and . . . and that cause hayfever cause hayfever.
> New me: Flowers that have white petals and . . . and that don't cause hayfever don't cause hayfever.

and these sentences are both true and, hence, consistent with each other, as claimed.

Surface form sneaks into these discussions because surface form or some other stable component can supply part of what's missing in the Theory theory, as we'll see in Section 5.2. On its own, however, the Theory theory doesn't have the resources to indicate when one mental theory is supposed to be directed to the same thing as another and hence no way to rule out the possibility that every change in theory is a change in subject matter. Yoking both the hayfever-causing theory and the non-hayfever-causing theory of daisies to the term *daisy* at least begins to indicate that these two theories are supposed to be about the same thing. The surface spelling of a term in natural language won't quite fix this problem, though. Homonyms like *mold* show that sameness of surface spelling isn't a good guide to the intended subject matter. Nevertheless, surface form suggests a more promising approach than those we've looked at so far, and several investigators have tried to avoid difficulties

with theories by marrying them to some other type of mental representation that stays fixed as theories change. I think that a dual approach is
in fact the best route to a satisfactory treatment of concept combination.
This path, however, is also mined with difficulties we need to sort out,
and these difficulties will occupy us in the rest of this chapter.

5.2 Dual Versus Unitary Models of Concept Combination

A number of researchers have noted that mental theories and related
approaches are too variable, both interpersonally and intrapersonally, to
fulfill all the functions that a representation of categories must serve, and
they have proposed representations with multiple parts that divide these
functions among them (e.g., G.A. Miller & Johnson-Laird, 1976; Osherson
& Smith, 1981; E. E. Smith, Shoben, & Rips, 1974). Of course, people's
ideas about categories do sometimes waver over time, and individual
differences exist among people about specific categories (Barsalou, 1987;
McCloskey & Glucksberg, 1978). Nevertheless, these changes must be
constrained in some way in order to avoid the consequences we've just
discussed.

My goal is to see whether a dual approach that combines theories
with other forms of representation can salvage the Theory theory, and
we'll find it helpful in this endeavor to look at earlier dual models to see
how they fare. Dual models' usual approach is to posit one sort of representation for the variable aspects of belief about categories and a second
sort for fixed aspects, with the task of combining concepts assigned to
the latter. However, several reasons suggest that this way of parceling
concept combination can't be right: Both fixed and variable representations must combine.

5.2.1 Osherson and Smith's Proposal

The best-known argument for a dual theory is due to Osherson and
Smith (1981), and it was a direct reaction to problems of concept
combination. Osherson and Smith were addressing earlier proposals that
the mental representation of a category is a prototype—a representation of
the category's best examples (e.g., Posner & Keele, 1968; Rosch, 1978).

The main thrust of their paper is that the only known proposal for computing the prototype of a complex concept from the prototypes of its elementary constituents is fuzzy set theory, a method for generalizing ordinary set theory to allow for degrees of set membership (Zadeh, 1965). Osherson and Smith demonstrate, however, that fuzzy set theory yields incorrect predictions about the typicality of instances with respect to categories named by phrases like *striped apple*, incorrect predictions about the judged truth of universally quantified sentences such as *All grizzly bears are inhabitants of North America*, and others (see, also, Roth & Mervis, 1983). Because of these difficulties, Osherson and Smith tentatively propose a dual theory: a *core* representation that combines concepts, determines truth values, and handles other aspects of meaning, coupled with a group of *identification procedures*, including similarity to prototypes. Osherson and Smith's arguments have provoked many challenges. Most of these claim that modifications to fuzzy set theory (e.g., Oden, 1984; Zadeh, 1982) or other combination rules (supervaluations, according to Kamp & Partee, 1995; stack theory, according to Jones, 1982; idealized cognitive models, according to Lakoff, 1987) can get around the mispredictions and salvage prototypes. I won't pursue this controversy, since I'm not concerned with prototypes or fuzzy sets per se (but see Osherson & Smith, 1982, 1997, for replies to some of their critics).

Of interest in the present context is Osherson and Smith's suggestion that combining concepts is a job for the core and not for prototypes. This idea, though, seems to conflict with some of the intuitions they appeal to. For instance, Osherson and Smith (1981) claim that an apple covered with regular stripes will be more typical of the category of striped apples than of the category apples, contrary to a prediction they derive from fuzzy set theory. (E. E. Smith & Osherson's, 1984, and E. E. Smith et al.'s, 1988, experiments confirm this hypothesis for a variety of adjective-noun combinations.) But this claim presupposes that intuitions about typicality exist even for novel composites like striped apples. Unless you're a devotee of the concept-combination literature, you've probably not encountered the phrase *striped apples* before and don't have a previously stored representation for them. Yet you can judge certain instances typical (and others atypical) striped apples. This intuition seems to imply that the information responsible for these typicality judgments comes from representations about stripes and about apples. So Osherson and

Smith appear to be committed to the idea that prototypes can combine after all. Of course, none of this forces the conclusion that typicality ratings for composites like *striped apple* are a function of typicality *ratings* for the components, *striped* and *apple*. Osherson and Smith's arguments make any such function unlikely. However, the typicality ratings of novel composites must derive from *some* information people have about the components, and in later work E. E. Smith et al. (1988) provide an explicit model (their Selective Modification model) of how this can be done.

The particular model that Smith et al. propose for combining prototypes has again been the target of criticism (e.g., Medin & Shoben, 1988; Murphy, 1988). What's important here, however, is that no one is currently claiming that the failure of fuzzy-set theory threatens the possibility of combining prototypes, mini-theories, or similar representations. If such representations are necessary for classifying and judging typicality, then people must presumably combine them in order to classify instances or judge the typicality of members of novel, complex categories (e.g., upside-down daisies or striped apples).

5.2.2 A Challenge to Dual Theories

You might think that dual models, with their extra degrees of freedom, ought to accommodate all the evidence that researchers have found in support of unitary theories. You should be surprised to find investigators offering experimental results favoring unitary over dual approaches. Hampton (1988), however, makes just this sort of case.

Here's Hampton's position: Dual theories explain typicality in terms of identification (i.e., classification) procedures, but explain category membership in terms of the core. How typical a particular weapon is, for example, depends on the properties of the instance that help you recognize it as a weapon. Whether it's actually a weapon, however, depends on definitional information in the core. Moreover, dual theories also assign the composition process to the core, especially when logical or set-theoretic relations are involved, such as conjunction (intersection), disjunction (union), or negation (complementation). Thus, people's judgments about whether an instance is a member of a conjunction should obey standard set-theoretic rules. For instance, if participants think that something is not a weapon, they should also think that it's not a weapon-which-is-a-tool. If $i \notin C$, then according to elementary set theory, $i \notin (C \cap D)$. However, people's decisions don't always follow this pattern. Participants in Hampton's study tend to deny, for example, that a screwdriver is a weapon, but are likely to affirm that it's a weapon-which-is-a-tool (or tool-which-is-a-weapon). Hampton calls these cases "overextensions." Dual theories are consistent with the possibility that participants rate screwdrivers more *typical* of weapons-which-are-tools than of weapons; logic doesn't constrain the identification procedures responsible for typicality ratings. (These are analogous to the Osherson-Smith results that we just looked at.) But according to Hampton, dual theories are not consistent with the finding that participants rate screwdrivers more likely *to be* weapons-which-are-tools than weapons. So dual theories must be incorrect.

This argument addressed Osherson and Smith's earlier theory in which the core had exclusive right to compositionality. Later dual models (e.g., E. E. Smith et al.'s, 1988, theory) allow composition of prototypes or mini-theories, as we've just seen. However, dual theories—even current ones—would still be in trouble if the core is solely responsible for category membership. According to the recent Smith-Osherson approach, the core does indeed operate according to logical principles. Thus, if something is not a weapon, it's also not a weapon-which-is-a-tool. Even if composition can also occur with mini-theories, illogical membership decisions are out, as long as the core handles membership.

One troublesome aspect of this argument, however, arises from some additional data in these intriguing studies. Although 94% of participants in Hampton's (1988) first experiment agreed that *CD is a type of D* (e.g., garden furniture is a type of furniture), only 34% of them agreed that *All CD is D* in preference to *Some CD is not D*. For example, some participants believe that garden furniture is a type of furniture, while allowing that some garden furniture is not furniture. (See Carlson, 1982, for related linguistic evidence.) It seems quite reasonable to suppose that the same holds for the constructions Hampton used in his other experiments. That is, participants may have thought that some weapons-which-are-tools are not weapons. Participants might believe, for example, that *weapons-which-are-tools* means tools that have been pressed into service as weapons but don't fully qualify as weapons. Thus, a screwdriver might be a weapon-which-is-a-tool if someone uses it maliciously to inflict an injury; yet it might not count as a weapon (perhaps because the screwdriver's designer didn't intend it as one; see Bloom, 1996; Keil, 1989; and Rips, 1989). But if this is true, then the argument against dual theories stalls. If you believe that not all weapons-which-are-tools are weapons, then no logical inconsistency arises in supposing that a screwdriver is a weapon-which-is-a-tool but not a weapon. In that case, the overextensions would seem to be in complete accord with a core that combines concepts in a strictly logical way and decides membership based on this composite.

The assumption of the argument seems to be that a logical core can't help but interpret weapons-which-are-tools as the set intersection of weapons and tools. But what could justify such an assumption in the face of participants' claims to the contrary? No theory (certainly not Osherson & Smith's) claims that *all* adjective-noun phrases have the interpretation adjective-and-noun. Big fleas aren't both big and fleas, artificial flowers aren't both artificial and flowers, and good dancers aren't (always) both good and dancers. The semantics of these expressions (and, hence, their logical cores) have to reflect the correct interpretation of the phrases, which is not always conjunctive (intersective). The X-which-is-Y constructions may seem on first glance to have a better claim to a uniform X-and-Y meaning than adjective-noun phrases. But look again: X-which-is-Y phrases are often nonconjunctive. Fleas which are big aren't both big and fleas, flowers which are artificial aren't both flowers and artificial, and dancers who are good aren't both good and dancers, at least on one natural reading of these relative clauses. Osherson and Smith's theory predicts that core representations combine according to the correct semantic analyses of these phrases, not that they blindly combine according to a conjunctive rule. If the correct analysis of phrases like weapons-which-are-tools is not conjunctive, then we can't blame the Osherson-Smith theory for predicting that it is.

This being so, then even if the core operates in an all-or-none manner according to logic and set theory, we have no grounds for thinking that dual theories are in a worse position than unitary models in explaining overextensions.

5.2.3 Some Amendments to Dual Theories

Although unitary models don't provide an advantage over dual models, we haven't established that dual models can overcome the problems that plagued the Theory theory. If we combine both mental theories and some fixed, core-like representation, can we get around the difficulties raised in Section 5.1.2 or do we merely inherit those difficulties? This question is especially pressing for the problem of combining concepts: We've just seen that both the fixed and variable representations in dual models must combine in order to explain categorization and typicality, but how do we combine variable theories? Section 5.3 is devoted to a discussion of this issue and attempts to establish that current arguments aren't fatal to theory combination. Before exploring this problem, though, let's look at mental theories' other headaches. Even if theories can combine appropriately within dual models, don't we still have difficulties with null theories and holism?

Dual approaches seem of genuine benefit in cases where a person has no theory for a particular category, but to see this we need to alter the usual conception of dual theories, along the lines I hinted earlier. Previous dual models usually conceived of the fixed or core representation as a definition or a set of the more important theoretical properties that qualify an instance as a category member. The problem, however, is that true definitions are tough to find for natural language categories, as is often pointed out (e.g., by Fodor, 2008; see Chapter 4 in this book for a discussion of this problem). Moreover, substituting important theoretical properties for definitional ones turns the core representation into a theory; so a core of this sort has exactly the same liabilities as the unitary Theory theory that we started with. Another possibility—one we encountered in Chapter 4—is to assume that the core includes people's belief in an essence for the category, even if these same people can't describe this essence (Medin & Ortony, 1989). Although this might work for natural kinds, however, both psychological essentialists and nonessentialists tend to doubt whether people think that artifacts like umbrellas and chairs have essences (S. A. Gelman, 2003; Sloman & Malt, 2003, though see Bloom, 1996, for a dissenting opinion). If there are no essences to occupy artifacts' core, then we are back to the null theory problem for these concepts.

Instead of coupling mental theories with a definitional core, we might instead pair them with a different sort of representation. Let's distinguish the mental representation *about* a category—the general information we have about the category—from the representation *of* that category. In the case of elementary categories like daisies or sassafras, for example, the representation *of* the category can consist of just an unchanging atomic symbol, a word-like entity in the language of thought. The representation *about* daisies or sassafras, however, might be the associated mini-theory, in the sense of (1a–c). So on this view, a concept is a pair of psychological representations. Moreover, these parallel representations can be maintained at the level of more complex concepts of the type that natural language expresses in phrases or sentences. As an example, consider *upside-down daisy* again. The term *daisy* is associated with a fixed representation of daisies—the mentalese word for daisies—and a representation about daisies that spells out the more important beliefs about them. (The representation about daisies is itself written in mentalese, of course, just as an encyclopedia uses the same natural language to express both the explained term and the body of the entry.) The representation of upside-down daisies might be something like the logical form of that phrase—a set of symbols structured by logical-syntactic relations—whereas the representation about upside-down daisies will be some mini-theory that tells us what they are like.[4]

I am not claiming that the representation-of and the representation-about a category exhaust all that is interesting and important about the meaning of an expression. Arguments by philosophers from Frege (1892/1970) to Putnam (1988) strongly suggest that no purely psychological account can do justice to all our intuitions about meaning. Part of the semantic story will probably have to include external causal connections that run between the referents and their representations. The representation-of a category might provide a "hook" for these connections. (For proposals about how to combine the psychological and nonpsychological aspects of meaning, see Block, 1985, and Field, 1977.) But the point I'm emphasizing here is that the difficulties of the preceding section also create trouble within cognitive psychology. Thus, in addition to external semantic relations, I believe there are also two parts to mental representations, parts that serve different cognitive functions.

How does this double representation help? Well, for one thing, representations-of categories give us a possible way out of the null theory problem. Since the representations-of sassafras and erbium can be different (even if I have no further information about either of them), so will the representations-of the questions *What's sassafras?* and *What's erbium?* Hence, we're no longer committed to the idea that these sentences have the same cognitive significance. Similarly, representations-of categories can explain how a person recognizes when a disagreement exist with his or her own previous beliefs. Even under rather different theories about daisies (i.e., different representations-about daisies), the representation-of daisies can be the same, and this will indicate the intended contrast.[5]

Notice that we're not assuming that each term in natural language must correspond to just one representation-of; you can have two or more such representations for homonyms like *mold* or *bow*.[6] You can also have distinct representations-of witches and unicorns, despite the fact that neither has any instances. This means that we can't guarantee that representations-of categories will stand in a one-one relation to the sets they denote. As we would expect from the reasons given by Putnam (1988) and others, same categories will sometimes map onto different representations-of. The null set, for example, will map onto both the representation-of witches and the representation-of unicorns on this view. What we can assume is that enough such representations exist to make the distinctions we need in understanding utterances.

The distinction between representation-of and -about categories is different enough from the core/identification distinction to warrant the new terminology. The representation-of a category jettisons definitions or essences in favor of a simple atomic symbol (in the case of word level concepts) or a structured set of these symbols (in the case of more complex expressions). If any definitions are available, they are relegated to the representation-about the category, along with other information. (We could reconstruct the traditional distinction between core and identification procedures within the latter representation if this proved necessary.) Although the distinction hasn't appeared (as far as I know) in the literature on concepts and categories, it isn't unprecedented, since it's close to multiple-layer approaches to text comprehension (e.g., Just & Carpenter, 1987, chap. 9; Kintsch, 1988; see also the distinctions among labels, cores, and identification procedures in Miller & Johnson-Laird, 1976).

We're not done examining difficulties for the Theory theory; but I think the only hope of getting off the ground with it lies in accepting some sort of distinction between representations-of and representations-about categories. Let's grant that this distinction can be worked out in adequate psychological detail for elementary concepts so we can see how far it will get us in dealing with complex concepts.

5.3 Concept Combination and Mental Theories

According to the Theory theory, classifying an instance is often a matter of determining which mini-theory best explains what we know of it. If this is true of categories named by novel phrases, such as *upside-down daisy* or *green firetruck*, then there must be some way of constructing theories of these categories too. This theory-construction process would be a combinatorial procedure—a computable function—that produces an account of what it means to be a member of such a complex category, along the lines of (1a–c).

The dual approach of the last section is also committed to such a procedure. We've modified the usual Theory theory to accommodate facts about constancies in comprehension, adding a representation-of categories that stays the same across changes in a person's beliefs about a category. The representation of *upside-down daisy* would simply indicate that *upside-down* modifies *daisies*. But we're also retaining the idea that categorizing and other mental processes make use of theories or representations about both simple and complex categories. The representation about *upside-down daisy* would be a mini-theory of upside-down daisies. Since people presumably don't have a representation about a novel category like this prior to encountering the corresponding phrase, they must have some way to construct it. In general, if classifying is a matter of applying mini-theories, then some theory-composition is necessary, since people clearly don't come equipped with a stock of memorized mini-theories for all such categories.

As I noted in connection with Osherson and Smith, the combinatorial process need not be direct in the sense of taking a typicality rating (or degree of membership) as input and producing a typicality rating (degree of membership) as output. Although the procedure must predict typicality and membership for complex categories, input to the procedure could include the full mini-theories of the component categories. What we require is that the procedure be computable within human information-processing constraints.

Alas, a family of arguments in the literature suggests that no such theory-combining process could exist. Most of these arguments were in fact directed, not at the Theory theory, but at earlier Prototype theories of concepts (e.g., Rosch, 1978); however, the criticisms apply quite broadly to cognitive models of concepts based on prototypes, family resemblances, exemplars, semantic networks, inferential roles, mini-theories (including schema theories), meaning-as-use, and many other notions. The general form of the criticism is that:

(2)   a. In any adequate account, concepts must be compositional (i.e., complex concepts must be a function of their elementary constituents), and

b. Concepts based on mini-theories, prototypes, and so on, aren't compositional.

According to this line, if concepts are mini-theories, for example, then your mini-theory of upside-down daisies must be a function of your mini-theories of upside-down things and daisies; but no available function meets these specifications; hence, concepts aren't mini-theories. We'll be concerned here with the anti-Theory implications; but bear in mind that if the general criticism is right, it cuts down nearly all models of concepts in psychology, as well as many in linguistics and philosophy.

Premise (2b) is the focus of the debate about concept combination, but (2a) also merits some clarification. This premise is an empirical claim about human understanding of natural language. The notion is that people are able to interpret a potentially infinite range of novel sentences, as we noted earlier, and that by far the most plausible explanation of this ability is that they compute sentence meanings by combining the meanings of individual words or lexemes according to syntactic and semantic rules. Although you've never heard the sentence *Robert contemplated a tub of newt soup*, you can easily understand it by semantically combining the meanings of its component expressions, *Robert*, *contemplated*, and so on. This standard linguistic claim about compositionality, however, is compatible with the fact that many (but finitely many) complex expressions in English and other languages are not compositional. For example, we don't understand the meaning of *ivy league* by combining the meanings of *ivy* and *league*, this being an obvious idiom. Noncompositional expressions like this will become important later in this chapter, but they must be the exceptions rather than the rule. If all multiword phrases were only interpretable as single chunks or idioms, we couldn't possibly explain the enormous range of sentences people can potentially understand. Humans' finite memory capacity rules out this hypothesis. Because no clear alternative to premise (2a) presents itself, let's assume it in what follows.

The criticism in (2) plays out in different ways according to how the author supports premise (2b), and practically every variation has been tried. For uniformity, let's call a complex concept (e.g., your representation-about upside-down daisies) a *composite*, and its elementary constituents (e.g., your representations-about daisies and upside-down things) its *components*. In these terms, you can deny compositionality because no composites of the requisite sort exist (e.g., no prototypes for complex concepts; see Fodor, 1981, 1994). Or you can argue that the best current hypotheses about the compositional function (e.g., fuzzy-set functions applied to prototypes) are flawed and that a better hypothesis is unlikely to come along (Osherson & Smith, 1981, 1982). Or you can argue that no such function is possible, since it's indeterminate which aspects of the components are inherited by the composite (S. L. Armstrong, Gleitman, & Gleitman, 1983). Or you can argue that any such function must presuppose some further properties that are unacceptable on independent grounds (e.g., the analytic/synthetic distinction; see Fodor, 1994; Fodor & Lepore, 1991, 1992, chap. 6). Taken together, these variations present a formidable challenge to cognitive models relying on mini-theories, prototypes, schemas, and so forth, a challenge that's formed a basis of debate about concepts since the early 1980s.

Argument (2), however, hasn't stopped researchers from exploring the possibility that mini-theories, schemas, and so on, might be compositional after all. This research has produced several models that are supposed to compute the form of a composite (e.g., about upside-down daisies) from that of the components (representations about upside-down things and daisies), where the representations in question are of the sort that argument (2) is supposed to demolish. Evidence for these models comes from experiments in which participants decide whether instances are members of complex categories, rate instances for typicality within such categories, and list properties that describe the categories (e.g., Franks, 1995; Gagné & Shoben, 1997; Hampton, 1987, 1988; Huttenlocher & Hedges, 1994; Murphy, 1988; E. E. Smith et al., 1988; Wisniewski, 1997). Table 5.1 (from Medin & Rips, 2005) provides a brief summary of some of these models. But how is this possible? Argument (2), in some of its variations, doesn't seem susceptible to empirical disconfirmation. On the one hand, if a principled reason exists why no function can take components into composite concepts, then something must be wrong with the empirical research. On the other, if the research confirms the investigators' models, then something is wrong with argument (2).

Let's take a closer look at the dilemma that argument (2) poses for the Theory theory. Clearly, the argument applies most forcefully to unitary models in which mini-theories are the sole representation for categories. As we'll see, dual theories can avoid some of these problems. But the argument also creates difficulties for dual theories, since both parts of the model are compositional, at least according to the view I outlined earlier. In order to find out if we can avoid the consequences of argument (2), we need to examine specific versions of this objection. The goal will be to see whether we can find a way around (2) and preserve our intuition that people combine theories when they classify items in complex categories like *upside-down daisies*.

5.3.1 Indeterminacy Arguments

One version of argument (2) that seems to tell against dual theories comes from S. L. Armstrong et al.'s (1983) critique of prototypes. Among other criticisms, Armstrong et al. note that prototypes make "understanding compositional (phrase and sentence) meaning look altogether hopeless. One reason is that if you combine, say 'foolish' and 'bird' into the phrase 'foolish bird' it is no longer a fixed matter—rather it is indeterminate— which *foolish* elements and which *bird* elements are intended to be combined" (p. 272). If we rephrase this point in terms of mini-theories, the problem is that some of the information in our mini-theory of birds will

TABLE 5.1   Some Theories of Concept Combination (from Medin & Rips, 2005).

Model	Domain	Representation of Head Noun	Modification Process
Hampton (1987)	Noun-Noun and Noun-Relative-Clause NPs (conjunctive NPs, e.g., *sports that are also games*)	Schemas (attribute-value lists with attributes varying in importance)	Modifier and head contribute values to combination on the basis of importance and centrality
Smith, Osherson, Rips, and Keane (1988)	Simple Adjective-Noun NPs (e.g., *red apple*)	Schemas (attribute-value lists with distributions of values and weighted attributes)	Adjective shifts value on relevant attribute in head and increases weight on relevant dimension.
Murphy (1988)	Adj-Noun and Noun-Noun NPs (esp. nonpredicating NPs, e.g., *corporate lawyer*)	Schemas (lists of slots and fillers)	Modifier fills relevant slot; then representation is "cleaned up" based on world knowledge.
Franks (1995)	Adj-Noun and Noun-Noun NPs (esp. privatives, e.g., *fake gun*)	Schemas (attribute-value structures with default values for some attributes)	Attribute-values of modifier and head are summed, with modifier potentially overriding or negating head values.
Gagné and Shoben (1997)	Noun-Noun NPs	Lexical representations containing distributions of relations in which nouns figure	Nouns are bound as arguments to relations (e.g., *flu virus* = virus causing flu).
Wisniewski (1997)	Noun-Noun NPs	Schemas (lists of slots and fillers, including roles in relevant events)	1. Modifier noun is bound to role in head noun (e.g., *truck soap* = soap for cleaning trucks). 2. Modifier value is reconstructed in head noun (e.g., *zebra clam* = clam with stripes). 3. Hybridization (e.g., *robin canary* = cross between robin and canary)

be true of many, but not all birds; many but not all birds fly, for example. So when we combine our mini-theory of birds with that of foolish things to produce a mini-theory for foolish birds, should we include the information that they fly? For all we know on first encountering this phrase, foolish birds may include only ostriches. Because we have no principled way of making such decisions, no compositional function could take the mini-theories of components to the mini-theory of their composites.

Armstrong et al. mentioned this idea only rather briefly (pp. 272 and 297), however, so perhaps it could benefit from examination. What does it mean to say that it's indeterminate which properties of the component theories we should posit of the composite? One possible meaning is that no function could combine mini-theories in a way that ensures that properties of the composites are typically *true* of the categories. Thus, whether to include the predicate *flying* in our mini-theory of foolish birds is indeterminate since we have no way of knowing on the basis of the theories of the components whether most foolish birds fly. Of course, we can't insist that the projected predicate be true of all foolish birds. As just noted, a basic feature of mini-theories is that they contain information that isn't invariably true of the corresponding category; that's how *flying* can be a part of the bird mini-theory in the first place. So the problem is *not* that the composite for foolish birds contains *flying* and a few foolish birds happen to be flightless. But if we project flying in this way, shouldn't at least *most* foolish birds fly? And if this is a requirement, compositionality of mini-theories appears doomed; for how could such an account guarantee that a projected predicate apply correctly in most cases? Even if we knew that, say, 90% of birds fly and that 90% of foolish things fly, we could still find that 0% of foolish birds fly.

However, this sense of "(in)determinate" imposes too strict a requirement on compositionality of mini-theories. Mini-theories, remember, are part of a *psychological* explanation of how laypeople classify objects, judge their typicality, explain their properties, and so on. They are not scientific theories of the relevant domains. Thus, a mini-theory doesn't have to be true of all, or even most, instances in order to fulfill its role. It only has to mirror people's beliefs about the domain, and research on naive physics (e.g., Clement, 1983; McCloskey, 1983a, 1983b) is enough to remind us that people's beliefs about even well-behaved domains can be radically false. But if we don't use truthfulness as a criterion for mini-theories of components, why should we apply this as a standard for mini-theories of composites? People might well come to include *flying* in their mini-theory of foolish birds based on their belief that most birds fly. The fact that this projection may turn out wrong—even the possibility that *no* foolish birds fly—isn't by itself troublesome for this approach. Errors are often what we expect from newly created theories (they've certainly turned up often enough in mine).[7]

A better case can be made for indeterminacy when the properties of the components conflict. To take a well-known example from Reiter and Criscuolo (1981), suppose your mini-theory of Quakers says they are pacifists and your mini-theory of Republicans says they are nonpacifists. If you now have to create a mini-theory for Republican Quakers, which property should you assign to it? Are Republican Quakers pacifists or not? Which property to attribute in this situation seems genuinely indeterminate, assuming you have nothing else to go on. One possible decision is to do nothing: to withhold attributing either pacifist or nonpacifist because neither is fully warranted (Horty, Thomason, & Touretzky, 1987; Touretzky, 1984). Another possibility is to use the discrepancy itself to rationalize one or the other choice (Reiter, 1980). Hastie, Schroeder, and Weber (1990) report that participants who were asked to decide about the properties of members of groups such as female mechanics or Republican social-workers sometimes justified their decision in terms of entry conditions for such roles ("a woman would have to be especially strong to be a mechanic") or effects of these roles on their occupants ("after awhile she'd come to be just as loud and street-smart as the others"). Either of these decisions is appropriate, or at least appropriate in some cases: At certain times, a more cautious wait-and-see attitude seems best in these property clashes, especially if we have a lot riding on which of the rival properties holds. At others, a bolder approach is called for, especially when we're pressed to make a decision. Then we need to use whatever scraps of causal information are available to reach a conclusion.

The upshot is that we may have no single way to put together a composite mini-theory from its components, no single function from components to composites. At first glance, then, we seem to be in the clutches of argument (2): Mini-theories must be compositional, given the sort of dual-model that I'm advocating, but indeterminacy shows they're not.

At second glance, though, all that the conflicting-properties problem really shows is that we don't have a *unique* way to compose mini-theories. We may have several distinct compositional functions rather than just one. This would be problematic for unitary models, since it would entail the sort of instability we wrung our hands over earlier (see also Rey, 1983). Stability isn't so crucial, however, for the representation-about a category, since we have a representation-of the category for this purpose. What *is* crucial is that mini-theories compose in a way that explains categorization and typicality of instances in novel categories, and for these purposes, the situation posed by the Republican Quaker example isn't necessarily a problem. The fact that people have multiple mini-theories of Republican Quakers doesn't mean that they are left without a method of classifying instances in that category or deciding how typical they are. Individual differences may appear in these decisions—different typicality rankings, for example. But this is a consequence we can live with (see Barsalou, 1987). For even in a scientific context, different investigators are likely to have different theories when they first encounter new applications.

In short, we don't have to give up compositionality in order to account for evidence cited in favor of indeterminacy. Instead, we can give up the notion that only one compositional function exists for representations-about categories. We clearly need *some* restrictions on these functions, of course, and we're about to consider further difficulties they face. But no one has formulated the indeterminacy objection with sufficient precision to show that it's a real obstacle to combining mini-theories.

5.3.2 Arguments Based on Emergent Properties

The indeterminacy issue is a question about which predicates of components we should assign to the composite. However, a converse problem exists here as well. Suppose we have a predicate that's part of the composite mini-theory; if mini-theories are compositional, then that predicate must have come from (or be predictable from) the component mini-theories. But the trouble is we can easily find many exceptions to this principle. For example, the predicate *is pulled over your head* is typically true of casual shirts, but not of casual things in general nor of shirts in general (Murphy, 1988). Similarly, aquatic mammals have blowholes for breathing, even though this isn't generally true either of aquatic things or of mammals (Hampton, 1988). The presence of these "emergent" properties yields another variation on argument (2): If mini-theories have emergent properties, then mini-theories aren't compositional, and since concepts must be compositional, concepts can't be mini-theories. Fodor and Lepore (1991, 1992) raise this problem as a general argument against semantic theories based on the conceptual role that a word or phrase plays in mental processing (theories that include mini-theories, prototypes, schemas, etc.).

Evidence on emergent properties comes from studies by Hastie et al. (1990), Kunda, Miller, and Claire (1990), Medin and Shoben (1988), and Murphy (1988). Murphy (1988) showed that participants rate properties like *is pulled over your head* as more typical of casual shirts than of either casual (things?) or shirts. In a similar vein, Medin and Shoben found that participants rated round watches, for example, as more typical of conventional watches than of digital watches, but they rated rectangular watches as more typical of digital than of conventional ones. Since being rectangular is probably not typical of either digital things or watches, we can take *rectangular* as an emergent property of the composite.[8]

Assuming this evidence is decisive, we have one version of argument (2) that seems correct: Mini-theories aren't compositional since no function can account for the relative prominence or typicality of the composite predicates. But notice that the evidence for this conclusion comes from the mini-theories that we eventually settle on after acquiring experience with the referents of these expressions, and not necessarily from the mini-theories that we form on hearing a novel phrase. As all the investigators of emergent properties have noted, many of these properties depend crucially on our "real-world background knowledge" of the phrases' referents—on "extensional feedback" in Hampton's (1987) terms. You know, for example, that casual shirts are pulled over your head because of your experience with casual shirts. If you had neither seen nor heard about casual shirts, yet did know something of shirts and casual things, then you would not be able to predict that casual shirts are typically pulled over your head and not buttoned completely up the front.

(Styles change. Next summer all casual shirts might be Hawaiian shirts, Heaven forefend.) Likewise, before about 1970, you presumably wouldn't have been able to predict that digital watches would typically be rectangular, there being no extant digital watches.

Something is fishy, though, about emergent properties based on extensional feedback. The goal of combining mini-theories, in our sense, is not to compose mature mini-theories, the ones we ultimately believe, but to compose the mini-theories we construct on first encountering a concept. What we want to explain is how people classify or judge the typicality of instances with respect to *novel* composites, and for this reason what's relevant are initial mini-theories, rather than mature ones. Most of the emergent properties we find in the experimental literature, such as *rectangular* for digital watches and *is pulled over your head* for casual shirts, can't be part of these initial mini-theories, since these properties aren't predictable. Thus, when we confine ourselves to initial mini-theories, emergent properties may not pose such a problem for compositionality. Whether mini-theories (or other classes of entities) are compositional or not depends on what we take to be the domain and range of the compositional function.

5.3.3 Emergent Properties, Continued: The No Peeking Principle

People believe that casual shirts are typically pulled over the head and that digital watches are typically rectangular (or at least they did at the time of these experiments). But the reasons for their belief must lie outside the process that produces the initial composites from their components. In order to affirm their belief in these properties, people must already know something about the composite that can't be captured simply by combining the components. Similarly, in processing sentences, people sometimes retrieve the same unpredictable emergents. They may infer from *Martha glanced at her digital watch* that the watch was rectangular. What this shows, however, is that they are able to retrieve or infer *rectangular* from previously existing facts about digital watches, not that *rectangular* "emerges" from their representations of watches and digital things.

The difficulty here is similar to the one we encountered in discussing indeterminacy. Requiring cognitive models to account for unpredictable properties of composites seems to be imposing an overly restrictive standard. What the models are trying to explain is how people combine mini-theories of the components to get a mini-theory of the composite. Why insist that these models predict, not only the initial mini-theories, but also how these initial theories will change as the result of later experiences? The usefulness of such models doesn't require them to predict future trends in fashion (how casual shirts will fasten) or technology (the shape of new-fangled watches), especially since the people they are modeling aren't notably good at this. Critiques based on unpredictable emergents of this sort transgress what we can call the "No Peeking" principle: No compositional theory of concepts can be required to peek at (have foreknowledge of) the referents of the composites.[9]

The No Peeking principle doesn't necessarily mean, however, that the critics are wrong about the weakness of earlier models. Some emergent properties may be predictable (can be inferred from the mini-theories of the components) and therefore don't violate the No Peeking principle. If so, then these properties could provide genuine counterexamples to the selective modification model (E. E. Smith et al., 1988) and other similar ones. Some potential examples come from an experiment that Wen-chi Yeh and I conducted (Yeh & Rips, 1992) in which we asked separate groups of undergraduate participants to list properties for familiar adjective-noun combinations (e.g., *smoky chimney*), unfamiliar combinations (e.g., *smoky apple*), and for the adjectives and nouns individually (*smoky*, *apple*, and *chimney*). The unfamiliar combinations are of interest here, since these items were probably new to our participants, and the properties participants listed for them were less likely to come from foreknowledge of the combinations' referents.

In fact, participants listed a number of "emergent" properties for these unfamiliar items, where we determined their emergent status by comparing the properties to those listed for the separate adjectives and nouns. Emergent properties in this study were those that two or more participants (of 10) listed for the combination, but no participant listed for either the adjective or the noun. For instance, three participants mentioned *dried* as a property of smoky apples and two participants mentioned *bad tasting*, but neither of these were mentioned as predicates of apples or of smoky. Our participants were quite likely inferring such properties from their knowledge of apples and smoky things, perhaps using some kind of plausible or causal reasoning (e.g., C. Johnson & Keil,

2000; Kunda et al., 1990).[10] If so, these examples create problems for an approach like Smith et al.'s, since the model doesn't have the resources to project the attributes correctly.[11]

But although predictable emergent properties like these are trouble-some for some psychological theories, they don't suffice to show that mini-theories can't be compositional. Emergent predicates, as defined in these experiments, are ones that participants acknowledge for the composite but not for the components: They are not *inherited* from the components, in the sense of being copied from them. But what matters for compositionality (and for argument (2)) is not inheritance but *computability*. As long as a computable function projects the predicates of the composite from the components, we have no reason to insist that every composite predicate be literally identical to a component predicate. The function could include a variety of intermediate steps to decide what should belong to the final product, could draw on background knowledge of certain sorts, and the product could contain predicates that depend on interactions among components and the background. (The last section of this chapter contains a brief sketch of how this might work for the *smoky apple* example.) As Murphy (1988) and others have noted, mini-theories have an advantage here, since they incorporate causal and relational information that can help make this kind of prediction possible.

This might be the right time for a recap of the No Peeking idea. I'm claiming: (a) that mini-theories have to combine in order to account for data from experiments on categorization and typicality of instances with respect to phrasal concepts. (b) Emergent properties suggest that mini-theories can't combine, since the emergents don't come from the components. (c) We can get around part of this apparent contradiction by requiring only that the composites be computable (we don't also demand that properties of the composites be literal copies of properties of the components); this allows us to deal with the predictable emergents. But (d) this still leaves the problem of emergents that aren't computable or predictable from the components. The No Peeking principle attempts to resolve this remaining problem (and so make the world safe for models of mini-theory combination) by relieving these models of the need to account for unpredictable emergents during initial comprehension of the relevant phrases. Thus, No Peeking is not a constraint on theories of concept combination (you needn't be forbidden to do what's impossible); it's a constraint on criticisms of these theories—criticisms based on the emergent-property version of argument (2).

No Peeking does not deny the obvious fact that a mature representation-about a composite can contain unpredictable emergents, as in the *digital watch* and *casual shirt* examples. These models *should* represent the mature version of the *digital watch* concept as containing the property *rectangular*, since people add *rectangular* to their digital-watch mini-theory as they gain experience with digital watches. Nor does No Peeking limit the kind of information that can go into composite representations, with one important exception: Initial representations of a composite can't draw on extensional information that becomes available only after we've formed these representations.

5.3.4 Emergent Properties, Concluded: The No Compounds and No Lexicalizations Corollaries

Whether or not a property violates the No Peeking rule may not be an easy call. I'm supposing that no reasonable model of concepts could contain the sort of information that would allow you to project that casual shirts are pulled over your head from knowledge of casual things and shirts. I'm also supposing that any reasonable model of concepts (certainly any reasonable mini-theory theory) should be able to represent the facts about smoky things and apples that would allow you to infer that smoky apples might taste bad. But exactly what information a component contains is not a clear-cut matter, and hence we may not always know when we're peeking beyond it.[12] It may be possible, though, to point to some linguistic indicators of when No Peeking is in jeopardy.

For instance, Kamp and Partee (1995) distinguish compounds from modifier-head constructions, noting that the latter, but not the former, are compositional. Heavier stress on the first word of a noun-noun expression tends to indicate a compound rather than a modifier-head construction. For example, "*brick* factory" is factory that makes bricks, but "brick *factory*" is a factory made of bricks. Kamp and Partee claim that native speakers ordinarily can't interpret novel compounds based on their components' meaning, although they can interpret novel modifier-head constructions in this way (see also Gleitman & Gleitman, 1970).

If this is correct, then theories of concept combination can't be saddled with the job of projecting a mini-theory for compounds. People can coin compounds, so they are productive in a certain sense (Clark, 1983; Downing, 1977). In the right setting—for example, when we've just decided which car we should take to run our grant proposal to the Federal Express office—we can use the phrase *the grant-proposal car* to refer to that vehicle. But we can't completely interpret compounds like these just from our mini-theories of cars and grant-proposals. For in other circumstances, *the grant-proposal car* could equally well mean the car that you (or your university's president) bought with your grant or the car that just ran over a grant proposal or the car that you wrote a grant proposal in or the car that you wrote a grant proposal about, and so forth. To interpret such compounds in the intended way, the right composite concept has to be available beforehand from some external source, rather than from mini-theory combination alone. Thus, the productivity of compounds doesn't contradict the notion that compounds are not compositional.[13]

Of course, people can make informed guesses about the meaning of compounds. Compound nouns—ones of the form $N_1 N_2$—hint at a relation between N_1 and N_2, and we can try to fill in the relation based on what we know about these components. In fact, Downing (1977) and Wisniewski (1997) have shown that participants find it possible to try to interpret unfamiliar noun compounds such as *pan car, moose ladder*, and *vase pencil*. They sometimes explain these combinations by imagining a relation between the nouns (*moose ladder* = ladder for moose to use in fording rivers) or by positing a property of the second noun that's suggested by the first (*moose ladder* = a sturdy ladder). These results provide clues about the ways people employ mini-theories in conjecturing about unfamiliar combinations. However, this process probably can't converge to yield the correct interpretation of established compounds, since there are simply too many plausible candidates to consider. Why isn't a bull ring a ring through a bull's nose rather than a ring in which bulls are fought? Why isn't a Swiss burger a banker from Zurich rather than a hamburger topped with Swiss cheese (Sadock, 1984)? As Downing (1977) puts it (with respect to the compound *lipstick*), "through consistent usage to denote members of a specific referent class, this compound has come to carry semantic material not directly derivable either from the constituents of which it is composed or from the underlying relationship on which it is based" (p. 820). Interpreting such phrases in the canonical way entails looking beyond the component concepts and consequently violates No Peeking: No Peeking gives us a "No Compounds" principle as a corollary.

Compounds, though, are only one type of construction that contains information not derivable from its components. These constructions range from obvious idioms (e.g., *in a trice, on the house*) to more transparent phrases (Fillmore, 1978; Sadock, 1984). For instance, the phrase *short pants* in American English (another item from Murphy, 1988) isn't completely idiomatic, since short pants tend to be shorter than pants that aren't shorts. But *short pants* isn't compositional in the way that *short tie* or *short tiger* is. *Short pants* (= *shorts*) doesn't mean pants that are shorter than most pants, since if it did we would have to count pants that had shrunk slightly in the wash as short pants. *Short pants* is a lexicalized phrase, that is, one whose meaning constitutes an independent entry in the mental lexicon, and we can't compute its meaning from its components. This is consistent with the fact that the property *exposes your knees*, which is typically true of short pants according to Murphy's participants, probably wouldn't be true if *short pants* were compositional in the way *short tiger* is. As in the case of the unpredictable emergents, we can't expect models of concept combination to project properties like *exposes your knees*, since such properties are not determined by combining *short* and *pants*. We can therefore add to the No Compounds principle a "No Lexicalizations" principle. Unfortunately, lexicalized phrases are so varied that no simple linguistic test identifies them in the way in which stress identifies compounds.

Those proposing specific models of concept combination will need some principled way to decide when a phrase is a lexicalized expression. Similarly, for unpredictable emergent properties. Such a model would beg the question if it identified lexicalized phrases solely as those phrases the model was unable to explain. But I'm not here proposing a model for concept combination or defending any existing models. The strategy is simply to do some spadework by exploring prior objections and, perhaps, to clear a conceptual space for later theories. For these purposes, it's enough to point to clear examples of lexicalized expressions (e.g., *lipstick*) and to note that whatever the correct test of such expressions, potential models of concept combination shouldn't be held accountable for them.

To sum up, I'm suggesting that many of the psychologists who've focused on concept combination have tried to have it both ways: They've tried to construct models of concept combination to explain how we understand multiword composites based on their component representations. And at the same time, they've tried to accommodate in these models emergent predicates that are true or typical of the composites but not of the components. They assume that these emergent predicates arise from "background knowledge" or "extensional feedback" about what these phrases denote. This isn't by any means a silly move on the part of these investigators, since some of what we know about the composites includes such emergents, and some of these properties do "emerge" in concept combination (predictable emergents, as in the *smoky apple* example). What's problematic about this strategy, though, is that many emergent properties—the ones that violate the No Peeking principle and its corollaries—presuppose the very concepts that these models are supposed to derive. Such properties don't emerge in combining concepts, but are retrieved from preexisting composites. The only hope of reconciling concept combination (where the concepts are mini-theories) with argument (2) is to recognize that the unpredictable emergents are not the product of combination at all.

5.4 Is Concept Combination Possible?

I began this chapter by mentioning that some of the tension in the literature on meaning in psychology is due to the opposing demands of categorizing and language understanding. Categorizing often draws on a great deal of knowledge about the relevant items, tempting theorists to include this knowledge in the representation. Language understanding can be knowledge-intensive, too; but it also depends on the stability of representations from person to person and from occasion to occasion. This tempts theorists to streamline the representations to include only what's essential, since vagaries in knowledge make communication and memory unreliable. In Section 5.2 of this chapter, I've tried to defuse some of this tension by distinguishing between representations-of and representations-about categories. Representations-of categories can be uniform in order to anchor memory and communication, whereas representations-about categories can vary to make room for differences in knowledge. Moreover, the same distinction goes some way to resolve disputes about how concepts combine, since some of the tasks of combination that are difficult for rich representations (e.g., mini-theories) can instead be handled by the representation-of categories.

We noticed, however, that representations-about categories couldn't completely duck concept combination. If these representations are responsible for categorizing and typicality judgments, then they have to combine in order to explain how we can make these judgments for novel categories we construct from familiar ones. This combination process is also likely responsible for our earlier intuition that some of the same operations occur when we decide that something is an upside-down daisy as when we comprehend the sentence *That's an upside-down daisy*. But if representations-about categories have to combine, they face some immediate problems about completeness. We can be uncertain which information from the components to include in the composite, and we sometimes find emergent information in the composite that has no counterpart in the components. The distinction between representations-of and -about categories is still helpful in this dilemma, however, since it focuses discussion on the bona fide difficulties. First, we can tolerate some uncertainty (and some individual differences) in what information to include in combining representations-about categories, since we have representations-of components to compensate. Second, there is no need to account for all emergent properties: Concept combination has to explain beliefs about novel combinations; but it doesn't have to explain accretions that turn up after these categories become familiar (properties that violate the No Peeking rule). Indeed, argument (2) suffices to show that compositionality fails for these accretions.

The difference between representations-of and -about categories doesn't solve all the problems of concept combination. We still need a positive proposal about what this process is like: One that allows for fairly complex knowledge integration in order to capture the properties of novel composites (including any genuine emergents). One that permits us to withhold judgment about these properties in cases of genuine indeterminacy. But one that doesn't simply invoke "background knowledge" or "real-world knowledge" in an undisciplined way to get the process out of trouble. I don't have a proposal of this sort to advance, but there are some hints in the research literature (e.g., C. Johnson & Keil, 2000) about its general shape.

Returning to the analogy that motivates the Theory theory, we might view combining theories as similar to scientists' application of a general theory to a specific domain. Given a general theory of chemistry, we might try to apply it to organic compounds to get a theory of organic chemistry. Of course, applications in science aren't always straightforward matters, and parallel difficulties will probably appear in producing new mini-theories. But, so far, nothing about this suggestion makes it seem impossible. At least in the case of simple noun phrases, which have been the usual target of investigation in this area, the suggestion comes down to using the mini-theories of the components, T_1 and T_2, to produce a new mini-theory T_3 that explains a category to which T_1 and T_2 are jointly relevant. Clearly, T_3 won't be merely the conjunction of T_1 and T_2, not even if we think of mini-theories as sets of sentences. That's in part because mini-theories contain properties that hold by default, and these defaults don't necessarily hold for the composite—the T_1 defaults may conflict with the T_2 defaults, as in the case of the pacifism or hawk-ishness of Republican Quakers (see also Thagard, 1988, 1997). Still, we can assume joint relevance of T_1 and T_2 on pragmatic grounds—why would a speaker or writer invoke them together if they weren't relevant (Sperber & Wilson, 1986)?—and this permits us to work backward in order to infer what T_3 might be like. In easy cases, this might be simply a matter of further specifying T_1 or T_2 to take into account the other mini-theory. But drastic reorganization might well be required in order to explain how joint relevance is possible and to elaborate probable causes and consequences. The think-aloud results from Hastie et al. (1990), cited earlier, seem consistent with this sort of analysis, since participants appear to be hypothesizing possible circumstances in which both mini-theories (e.g., those for Republicans and social workers) might apply.

The move from the mutual relevance of T_1 and T_2 to a new theory T_3 that explains this relevance recalls other cases of diagnostic causal reasoning that we've encountered in Chapters 3 and 4 in this book. In discussing counterfactual reasoning in Chapter 3, we noticed that assessing the truth of a counterfactual requires determining why the antecedent is true, followed by use of this explanation to evaluate the consequent. For example, in answering the question *If component C were not working, would component D be working?*, we may need to determine the most likely reason why C is not working and then figure out what this reason implies for the operation of D (Rips, 2010b). Similarly, we saw in Chapter 4 that category-based induction sometimes depends on determining how the premise could be true and then applying this explanation to the conclusion. This pattern of reasoning is also similar in some respects to what goes on in categorizing. As I've mentioned, categorizing often involves an inference of the form: Category C's mini-theory provides the best explanation of instance i's known properties (relative to the mini-theories of other potential categories); therefore, i is probably a C. From this perspective, theory combination looks like nearly the converse of categorizing, since we're searching for the mini-theory T_3 that would provide the best explanation for instances to which both T_1 and T_2 are relevant.

To see how this mode of reasoning works in concept combination, take the case of smoky apples. How could our mini-theories of smoky things and apples both be applicable to the same category? As a start, our mini-theory of smoky things might specify that they're the result of exposure to heat, usually for an extended period. Our mini-theory of apples is consistent with the possibility that they could be exposed to heat in this way. Furthermore, these mini-theories give us some predictions about the probable effects of this treatment, for instance, that an apple might become dried, hot, blackened, or bad tasting, all of which were properties mentioned by participants in Yeh and Rips's (1992) study. In this way, we can put together a rich composite view, a new mini-theory, of what smoky apples are like that incorporates predictable emergent properties.

How we flesh out this explanatory process in any particular case will depend on the nature of T_1 and T_2, and on how they are jointly relevant; so we should probably expect to find a variety of strategies in constructing the composite mini-theory (Hastie et al., 1990; Kunda et al., 1990; Wisniewski, 1997). Not surprisingly, this process resembles the type of theory combination that occurs in scientific contexts when two noncompeting theories apply to some of the same phenomena. The composite theory can specify a number of different kinds of relations between the two components: T_3 can portray T_1 as a theory of a whole to which T_2 is a theory of a part, T_1 as a theory of a structure for which T_2 is the theory of its function, or characterize the mutual causal relations between the phenomena described by T_1 and T_2 (Darden & Maull, 1977). This can entail adjustments between the two original theories and can yield predictions based on the new co-ordination between them.

This abstract way of putting the matter, of course, isn't a substitute for a detailed theory of how the process works. Plenty of uncertainties still exist about the nature of such a model of concept combination. What I hope to have shown, however, is that the project deserves cognitive scientists' attention. If we clear away the tasks that *no* such model could perform, we may be left with a chance of designing a helpful theory for the remaining ones.

NOTES

Thanks are due to Dedre Gentner, Evan Heit, Philip Johnson-Laird, Boaz Keysar, Ken Livingston, Arthur Markman, Edward Wisniewski, Wen-chi Yeh, and especially Larry Barsalou, Jerry Fodor, Edward Smith, and Roger Tourangeau for their comments on an earlier version of this chapter. (The earlier version appeared as Rips, 1995b.)

1. As mentioned in earlier chapters, psychologists tend to use the term "concept" to mean a mental representation of a category or individual, whereas philosophers use it to denote (roughly) a relation that mediates expressions and their referents. So if you find yourself saying things like "concepts ain't in the head" (Burge, 1979; Putnam, 1975), then philosophy is your native tongue.

2. Not all the investigators just cited would subscribe to the generic version of the Theory theory set out here, and many disagreements exist among proponents (see chapter 4 in this book for some variations). My purpose is not to taxonomize the different versions of the Theory theory but simply to provide a relatively neutral account for purposes of seeing how it fares with concept composition. (For similar studies of explanation-based categorization in artificial intelligence, see DeJong, 1988, and Schank, Collins, & Hunter, 1986.)

3. You can think of these mini-theories as something like small-scale, mental encyclopedia entries for categories, as mentioned earlier. Maybe a cognitive Wikipedia stub. But I won't be concerned with the "packaging" of this information here. If you like, mini-theories might be sets of sentences. Or they might be regimented as schemas (Rumelhart & Norman, 1988) or frames

(Brachman & Schmolze, 1985) or idealized cognitive models (Lakoff, 1987). The representational format is often crucial for deriving predictions; but for our purposes, what's important is the type of information these mini-theories specify, and in this respect, one of these representational formats is about as good as another (Hayes, 1979). I'll use "mini-theory" as a cover term for this set of proposals. There's also no reason to quibble about how much information, in addition to (1a–c), a mini-theory should contain. Perhaps mini-theories should include images or procedures or heuristics. For present purposes, it won't matter whether or not these are bundled with the mini-theories. If you're still squeamish about "theory" or "mini-theory" in this context, feel free to substitute "knowledge-based" or a similar term of your choice.

4. Representations-of categories (and corresponding representations-of for larger expressions) are close to what I take to be the traditional Language-of-thought (LOT) hypothesis (Fodor, 1975, 2008). Representations-of, like LOT expressions, consist of word-like symbols that can combine according to syntactic rules. Representations-about categories, however, play no role in the LOT story of meaning or concepts (for reasons given in Fodor, 1994). LOT theories presumably don't deny that people represent facts about novel categories such as *upside-down daisies*; for example, people can mentally represent the information that upside-down daisies probably can't grow. What LOT-ites deny is that this sort of information is a compositional function of information about daisies and about upside-down things. We will examine some of the reasons for this position in the following section.

However, if representations-of and representations-about are both written in mentalese, why say that they are two different *kinds* of representation? The answer is that they are differentiated not by their internal properties—both are strings of mental symbols—but functionally by the kind of information they convey about a category and by their role in psychological processing. For a related functional distinction, see Burge (1999). An anonymous reviewer pointed out a parallel between the representations-of and "lemmas" in psycholinguistics, where a lemma is "a representation of the meaning and the syntactic properties of a word. For instance, the lemma of the word *bird* specifies the conceptual conditions for the appropriate use of the word, and indicates, among other things that the word is a noun" (Roelofs, 1996, p. 308). (What lemmas *don't* contain is information about the word's pronunciation.) But the representation-of a category does not include "conceptual conditions for the appropriate use of the word," since conditions of use (or application) belong to the representation-about a category.

5. As mentioned earlier, the holism problem goes beyond the question of how we identify disagreements among statements and probably can't be settled within a purely cognitive account. The present suggestions are meant to explain the psychological aspects of the problem that the Theory theory can't account for. If the content of the representation-of daisies is determined externally, as it

is in many contemporary philosophical theories, then the meaning of *daisy* can change as a function of the external relations even if the representation-of is fixed. This seems to be the content of a critique of the present proposal by Laurence and Margolis (1999), but it seems to be no more than a restatement of the traditional externalist semantic position of Putnam (1975) and Burge (1979). No psychological theory is proof against externalist changes in meaning, however. The best we can do is to ensure that the internal representations don't introduce unwarranted shifts in meaning.

6. If there are two representations-of corresponding to a homonym like *bow*—one for part of a ship and another for a movement of the body—then the question arises of how people get from the word *bow* to the correct representation. One possible story is that people access both representations initially and may select one of them later, based on the discourse context (Swinney, 1979). It seems plausible that the selection process could call on the representation-about the utterance to decide which representation-of is correct; so interplay could occur between the representations during later stages of sentence comprehension. None of this seems damaging to the idea that representations-of and representations-about are distinct, since we've just seen that we can have the former without the latter.

7. Errors of this sort would be troublesome, however, if we demand that composition gives us, not just our initial mini-theory of foolish birds, but the mature mini-theory we arrive at after we've hung around foolish birds for awhile. I discuss this demand in the following section.

8. These results don't rule out the possibility that these typical emergent predicates of the composite are also atypical predicates in one of the components, and so we need to be careful about what "emergence" means in this context. You know that the predicate *is pulled over your head* is true of some shirts, and it may therefore be part of your mini-theory of shirts. However, this predicate doesn't characterize most shirts, and so is less typical of shirts than of the subcategory of casual shirts. What the results suggest is that there is no *systematic* way in which a compositional function could promote just those predicates that will be typical in the composite (e.g., *is pulled over your head*) and demote those that will be atypical (*buttons completely up the front*).

9. Violations of the No Peeking principle also relate to arguments about context-sensitivity in comprehension. For example, psychologists sometimes cite Halff, Ortony, and Anderson (1976) as showing that the meaning of *red* changes when it is used in phrases like *red fire engine, red wine, red brick,* and *red hair*. People know that the objects these phrases denote ordinarily differ in hue. (Halff et al. asked participants about the color of the objects, not the meaning of *red*.) They know, in other words, the hue of red fire engines and can relate this to the hue of red wine. But this information can't be derived from combining the concepts associated with the words in these phrases, since the hue can't be predicted from knowledge of red things and knowledge of fire engines (unless, of

course, you already know about the hue of red fire engines). Knowledge of the precise hue violates No Peeking. In our terms, if the representation about adjective-noun phrases is compositional, then there must be a way to combine the representation about *red* with that for nouns that doesn't depend on prior knowledge of the referents of the entire phrase. Although we could construe "comprehension" in such a way that comprehending a phrase like *red wine* includes inferences about the typical color of red wine (R. C. Anderson, 1990), nevertheless people with no prior concept of red wine can also correctly comprehend this phrase (see Johnson-Laird, 1987).

10. See, also, Tourangeau and Rips (1991) for emergents like these that arise in comprehending metaphors. I also owe to Tourangeau the following points about inheritance vs. projectibility.

11. The same evidence also rules out purely statistical models of concept combination (e.g., Huttenlocher & Hedges, 1994). Of course, at some preliminary stage in interpreting *smoky apple*, people's representations may be the ones the Smith et al. model posits and that the emergent properties arise only in a later elaboration or inference phase (E. E. Smith & Gray, 1995). Evidence from Potter and Faulconer (1979) and Springer and Murphy (1992), however, suggests that access to some emergent properties is as fast or faster than access to properties of the components (but see Swinney, Love, Walenski & Smith, 2007). The present point, though, is not to defeat or defend the Smith et al. model, but only to suggest that some predictable emergent properties pose a more authentic challenge to the model than those unpredictable emergents that infringe the No Peeking principle.

12. Differences in available information can sometimes blur the line between Peeking and No Peeking. Imagine that you've not yet formed the concept *casual shirt,* but in every casual event you've attended, you've noticed that people have always worn shirts that are pulled over the head rather than buttoned up the front. If you then encounter the phrase *casual shirt*, you might infer that casual shirts are pulled over the head. This seems a perfectly legitimate form of mini-theory combination. Does it violate No Peeking? I'm inclined to think not, since the facts about being pulled over the head are already part of your ideas about casual things. True, the property *being-pulled-over-one's-head* may not appear on anyone's list of properties of such things, since it's not very salient. However, it's in the *casual* mini-theory for all that, given the details of this case. This contrasts with a situation in which you have to interpret *casual shirts* without the benefit of the sort of experience just described. Then you presumably can't infer that casual shirts are pulled over one's head. This contrast shows that which properties violate No Peeking will depend on differences in people's mini-theories of the components. But this is what we should expect and does not cast doubt on the validity of No Peeking.

13. J. N. Levi (1978) argues that no well-defined class of compound nouns exists and that the properties of frontal stress and semantic specialization sometimes

don't coincide. The fact remains, however, that people can't interpret certain noun-noun phrases by combining their components, and frontal stress is one (perhaps imperfect) predictor of these items.

Levi goes on to argue that a wide class of noun-noun and adjective-noun constructions—ones she calls *complex nominals*—have semantic interpretations that can be spelled out in terms of nine specific relations that can connect the two components. Thus, a *grant-proposal car* is nine-ways ambiguous among: car that causes grant proposals, car that has grant proposals, car that makes grant proposals (I'm still in the market for one of these), car that is in a grant proposal, and so on. Other authors set the number of possible implied relations anywhere between four and infinity (see Bauer, 1983, p. 184). However this may be, noun-noun combinations exist that people can't interpret without either prior knowledge of their referents or heavy contextual support. For example, you can't predict from *egg* and *plant* that *eggplant* means aubergines rather than turnips. Hence, you can't fault theories of concept combination for failing to generate from *egg* and *plant* such predicates as *grows above ground* and *typically purple*. In general, noun-noun combinations seem to be about the worst place to look for evidence of concept combination, which make it odd that so many cognitive psychologists have focused on them.

6

Reasons

Time and again we are led by our thought beyond the scope of our imagination, without thereby forfeiting the support we need for our inferences.

Frege, *Foundations of Arithmetic,* §60

We started with single, word-like concepts in the early chapters of this book and moved to composite, phrase-like thoughts in the previous one. Our glimpse of how people arrange their concepts into thoughts shows that even simple arrangements strain existing theories of cognition. The effort to understand complex constructions is crucial, though, since these thoughts are the typical vehicles for mental activities such as problem solving, decision making, learning, and reasoning. Of these skills, reasoning occupies a special place for our purposes: The study of reasoning focuses on people's ability to detect and to deploy connection between thoughts, connections that make thoughts seem possibly or necessarily true. In fact, we've seen many examples of studies that test cognitive theories by asking people to reason about specific notions—for instance, inductive reasoning as tests of theories of natural kinds and counterfactual reasoning as tests of theories of causality. But these studies leave us with a more general question: How does one group of thoughts manage to transmit conviction to others?

As most psychologists look at it, reasoning is a mental process that produces new representations from old ones. But, of course, not every process of transforming representations qualifies as reasoning. For example, suppose that mental representations include mental sentences similar to the items in (1):

(1) a. Calvin scandalizes Catherine.
     b. Catherine scandalizes Calvin.

You can produce a new representation by reversing an old one, yielding (1b) from (1a) in this example, but no one thinks that merely reversing sentences amounts to reasoning. Additional restrictions on the mental process are necessary before we would agree that reasoning is going on.

Distinguishing clearly between reasoning and other mental processes, though, is not an easy task. This is partly because reasoning is an integral component of other abilities: Decision making, categorizing, language processing, and problem solving, as well as aspects of spatial cognition, all involve some type of reasoning. To make matters worse, what we identify as reasoning may depend on not just internal features of the process itself, but also external properties, such as the role that the process plays in mental life as a whole or the fit between the process and certain normative standards. The ground here is too swampy to start from.

The strategy in this chapter is to begin with some clear examples of reasoning and to try to discern some patterns among them. If we can understand the commonalities and distinctions among different types of reasoning, we may get a better grip on their fundamental features. As I mentioned in the Introduction, coming to a reasoned conclusion means understanding what *would* be the case under specified assumptions or suppositions. Often these suppositions are purely hypothetical, describing states of affairs that have never actually existed and that we have never experienced. By examining different types of reasoning, we may get closer to grasping the cognitive abilities that make this sort of thinking possible. Exploring reasoning types will also allow us to examine some of the main theories of reasoning, since these theories differ in how they divide the reasoning domain.

As a first example, then, suppose that sentence (2a) is true:

(2)   a. Nobody wanted seconds on seal-blubber sherbet.
       b. Miriam didn't want seconds on seal-blubber sherbet.

From (2a), (2b) easily follows. (2b) is an *entailment* of (2a), in that (2b) must be true if (2a) is true. In this respect (and despite its silly subject matter), the relation between these two statements is the same as that between the axioms and the resulting theorems in mathematics: The axioms entail the theorems. This relation between (2a) and (2b) contrasts with that between (1a) and (1b), since Catherine could utterly bore Calvin at the same time that he scandalizes her. (1a) could be true while (1b) is false.

What's important about entailment, for our purposes in this book, is its apparent necessity. From any sentence of the form *Nobody F's*, where *F* is any predicate, we can correctly conclude that *n doesn't F*, where *n* is any name that refers to an existing creature. Inferences corresponding to this relationship are probably so commonplace that they go unnoticed in ordinary thinking. But what is responsible for our ability to identify entailments?[1]

Of course, reasoning also makes use of relations between statements or mental representations that are not entailments. The truth of (3a), for example, doesn't guarantee the truth of (3c)—and so does not entail it—but (3a) makes (3c) more likely:

(3) a. Few people wanted seconds on seal-blubber sherbet.
     b. Seal-blubber sherbet revolted Miriam.
     c. Miriam didn't want seconds on seal-blubber sherbet.

The support that (3a) gives (3c), though not perfect, is more solid than the support that (1a) gives (1b). In this case, (3a) provides a statistical reason for (3c), and this type of relationship is also common in ordinary thought. Other sorts of nonstatistical (and nonentailment) relations exist, however, that provide reasons. For example, (3b) warrants (3c) on causal grounds.

A key question in the psychology of reasoning is whether people recognize entailments and discriminate them from other reason-supplying relations. We noticed that the relation between *Nobody F's* and *n doesn't F* is a necessary one, holding in all possible situations or states of affairs. This is obviously not the case for the relation between (3a) and (3c) or between (3b) and (3c), since situations exist in which the first statement in each pair is true and the second false. Our ability to recognize this distinction suggests that people do discriminate entailments from other forms of inferential support, but of course, the entailment relation in (2) and the statistical and causal support relations in (3) aren't themselves instances of reasoning. Reasoning or inference is a psychological matter—a mental process, as we've already noted—not a strictly logical or statistical one. On the one hand, a single mechanism may be responsible for apprehending the support that (2a) lends (2b) and that (3a) or (3b) lends (3c)—perhaps a process that measures the degree of support that one sentence gives another on a single psychological continuum. According to this story, people register that (2a) provides stronger warrant for (2b) than (3a) does for (3c) (and, similarly, (3a) is stronger support for (3c) than (1a) is for (1b)), but the difference is a quantitative rather than a qualitative matter. On the other hand, recognition of these types of support may rely on qualitatively different processes. Recognition of entailments might be psychologically privileged, and if so, the task is to specify the mental characteristics responsible for entailments' distinctiveness.

I try to make the case in this chapter for the second possibility: that a distinct cognitive process is responsible for our ability to recognize entailments as logically necessary relations. I try to show that current unitary theories of reasoning—those in which all forms of reasoning are due to a single psychological process—don't have the resources to explain what's special about our recognition of entailments. In doing so, I review some of the main theories of deduction that have been in play during the last few years (since, roughly, 1995), although I briefly describe earlier views when current ones depend on them. I also draw on some recent behavioral and neuropsychological evidence for dissociations between deductive and inductive reasoning. If the type of reasoning responsible for entailments is unique, however, then this places a special burden on theories of deduction. What sort of faculty could apprehend these necessary relations? I also consider here some alternative ways of dividing reasoning abilities, including those based on content, and argue that these accounts fail to provide a plausible theory of deduction.[2]

6.1 Reasoning's Natural Kinds

The tradition in logic is to define an *argument* as a pair, consisting of a first statement (or set of statements) called the *premise(s)* and a second statement called the *conclusion*. The same tradition writes these statements in a list-like form, with the premises above a horizontal line and the conclusion below, as we saw in Chapter 4. For example, (2) would appear as (2′) in this format, and the argument from (3a) to (3c) as (3′):

(2′)   Nobody wanted seconds on seal-blubber sherbet.   (premise)

Miriam didn't want seconds on seal-blubber sherbet. (conclusion)

(3′)   Few people wanted seconds on seal-blubber sherbet. (premise)

Miriam didn't want seconds on seal-blubber sherbet. (conclusion)

The horizontal line in these arguments symbolizes a "thus" or "therefore" relation, and according to some theories, the job of evaluating an argument is determining the strength of the thus. Arguments like (2′) that embody an entailment are *valid* or *deductively correct*. Arguments like (3′) are *inductively strong* if they are not valid yet have premises that lend support to the conclusion. The question here is whether such differences in logical assessment correspond to psychologically real processes. Do people have distinct procedures for dealing with the relation between the premise and conclusion of (2′) versus (3′)?

Several recent proposals suggest the answer to this question is "no." According to these *unitary* theories, the step in (2′) and the one in (3′) exemplify the same process. Perhaps all reasoning is a matter of probabilistic thinking (or, alternatively, manipulating mental models, increasing coherence among beliefs, or some other process). Of course, different reasoning problems will force some variation in processing, but these variations may be unimportant from a cognitive standpoint. We can put them down, perhaps, to changes in the problem's subject matter, response requirements, and other details. What matters for reasoning, according to unitary proposals, is a single type of thinking applied to varying content and contexts. These unitary approaches appear in the left half of Figure 6.1, which provides a rough taxonomy of reasoning theories (e.g., the rational-probabilistic theory and the mental-models theory are types of the unitary approach, as we will see later.)

Several proposals offer an opposite answer to our question about kinds of reasoning—that reasoning abilities come in several psychologically interesting flavors. The right half of Figure 6.1 indicates a number of these *partitioning* theories. Of special interest here is a psychological approach along the lines of the traditional division between deductive and inductive reasoning: Maybe deductive processes are responsible for dealing with entailments via abstract logical concepts (e.g., concepts such as *nobody* in (2a)), and separate inductive processes are responsible for adjusting degrees of belief. The latter type of process might handle the inference from (3a) to (3c), for example, potentiating the belief that Miriam will avoid seconds if few people wanted them. I argue here that

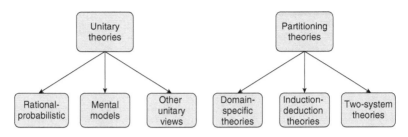

FIGURE 6.1 A taxonomic view of recent theories of reasoning.

this approach makes the most sense of our judgment that it is necessarily true that if (2a) then (2b).

The induction/deduction approach, however, does not exhaust partitioning approaches to reasoning. For example, developmental and evolutionary psychologists hold out the possibility that minds are partitioned according to domains of knowledge rather than according to deductive versus inductive reasoning. As the result of innate capacities or as the product of conceptual change, children acquire clusters of concepts and associated reasoning principles that are roughly similar to scientists' theories of domains like biology, chemistry, and physics. (These conceptual domains are similar to the mini-theories of Chapter 5, but on a grander scale, and include proprietary inferences.) Moreover, reasoning abilities that are local to these domains might have special properties, such as being easier to perform or more obvious to untutored people than general inference principles. As a theory of reasoning, the domain-specific view (in the version we will consider here) presupposes that inference procedures differ from domain to domain. This contrasts with a view in which domains differ only in the types of knowledge they contain and in which all domains use the same general inference procedures.

We also need to consider a final, quite popular, family of partitioning views in which reasoning abilities differentiate according to their mode of operation: one type largely conscious, sequential, symbolic, analytic, and explicit, and the other unconscious, parallel, connectionist, holistic, and implicit. Both processes could apply to the very same material and could yield contradictory conclusions about it (e.g., Evans, 2003; Sloman, 1996a, 1996b; and the contributions to Evans & Frankish, 2009). These theories share with the induction/deduction view the idea that types of reasoning are not always domain specific, but they propose independent distinctions among reasoning mechanisms. Deduction could be conscious or unconscious, explicit or implicit, sequential or parallel, perhaps even symbolic or connectionist, and the same is true of induction.

6.2 The Reasoner's Toolkit

Before examining unitary and partitioning approaches, we need to look briefly at two concepts that play an important role in both types of theories and that come up repeatedly in later parts of this chapter. One of these is the idea of a reasoning heuristic—a rule of thumb or method of approximation for particular types of reasoning problems—which we first encountered in Section 0.3.2 of this book. The other notion is that of conversational implicatures. These are (nondeductive) inferences that a given statement suggests because of the conversational context in which it occurs. All the theories we will review incorporate these two mechanisms to explain some discrepancies between reasoning data and the theories' predictions.

6.2.1 Heuristics

The idea that people use heuristics in reasoning is practically as old as the field itself. In the context of judgment and decision-making, heuristics gained prominence with the remarkable studies of Tversky and Kahneman (1974), but you could view people's ability to evaluate entailments in much the same way (see Pollard, 1982, for some possible connections between the two). When people have to decide whether one statement entails another, their judgments sometimes depart from the dictates of standard systems of logic. The pattern of these judgments over a set of problems can suggest that people are employing a heuristic rather than engaging in thorough analysis. The grande dame of these heuristics is the *atmosphere effect* of Sells (1936) and Woodworth and Sells (1935). This effect describes a tendency for people to go with the tone or atmosphere that the premises set when evaluating certain kinds of entailments. To understand the atmosphere effect, however, we need to look at an ancient form of argument called "Aristotelian" or "categorical" syllogisms.

Categorical syllogisms are a fixed set of arguments consisting of two premises and a conclusion. The importance of these arguments in logical theory evaporated at the end of the nineteenth century, at just about the time that psychologists took them up. Psychologists continue to study them, partly because of the large amount of accumulated data on syllogisms that can provide a basis for current theorizing. A categorical *statement* has one of the forms: *All A are B, Some A are B, No A are B*, and *Some A are not B*, where *A* is the subject term and *B* the predicate term of the statement. A categorical *syllogism* is an argument consisting of two categorical premises and a categorical conclusion. In traditional syllogisms, the subject term of the conclusion also occurs as one of the terms of the second premise, and the predicate term of the conclusion also occurs as one of the terms of the first premise. One final term, the middle term, occupies the two remaining positions in the premises. The argument in (4) follows this pattern:

> (4)   Some Volleyball League members are Bridge Club members.
>   Some Chess Team members are Volleyball League members.
>   --
>   Some Chess Team members are Bridge Club members.

In (4), *Volleyball League members* is the middle term; *Chess Team members* and *Bridge Club members* are the end terms (the subject and predicate of the conclusion).

What Woodworth and Sells (1935) found was that when people judge whether the conclusion of a syllogism logically follows from the premises, they tend to favor conclusions that have the same form as the premises. So if the premises are both of the form *All A are B*, participants will tend to choose a conclusion of the same form; if both premises are of the form *Some A are B*, as in (4), they'll go with a conclusion of that form; and so on. When the two premises have different forms, participants choose a conclusion that is particular (either *Some* or *Some . . . not*) if either premise is particular, and they choose a negative conclusion (either *No* or *Some . . . not*) if either premise is negative. In (4), for instance, the conclusion shown is the one that atmosphere selects, despite the fact that it is not an entailment of the premises. (Fred could be in the Volleyball

League and the Bridge Club; Susan in the Chess Team and the Volleyball League; but no one in both the Chess Team and the Bridge Club. Then the premises would both be true and the conclusion false.) As Woodworth and Sells noted, this response tendency connects with the fact that *for deductively correct syllogisms*, if either premise is particular the conclusion must also be particular and if either is negative the conclusion must also be negative. The atmosphere error is to take these necessary conditions to be sufficient ones, and for this reason, we can view the atmosphere effect as a heuristic rather than an arbitrary response bias.

Wetherick (1989; Wetherick & Gilhooly, 1990) has suggested a related heuristic called "matching." Matching "proposes simply that, where the logic of the situation is not immediately apparent to a subject, he or she may generate a response that has at least the appearance of rationality by selecting a logical form corresponding to that of the more conservative premise; that is, the premise making an assertion about the smaller proportion of members of the class designated by the subject term" (Wetherick & Gilhooly, 1990, p. 107). When the premises of a syllogism are of the same form, matching agrees with atmosphere in selecting that form as the conclusion. When the premises are of different forms, one of which is *All*, matching selects the form of the *other* premise (*Some, Some . . . not*, or *No*) for the conclusion. When one premise is *Some* and the other *No*, matching prefers a *No* conclusion. Matching apparently expresses no preference in arguments that have both a *Some* and a *Some . . . not* premise or ones that have both a *Some . . . not* and a *No* premise. Woodworth and Sells mentioned a similar kind of "caution" heuristic.

6.2.2 Implicatures

Woodworth and Sells (1935) also observed another tendency that may be responsible for some remaining errors on syllogisms. In everyday speech, *Some A are B* sometimes conveys the idea that *Some A are not B*, and conversely *Some A are not B* conveys *Some A are B*. So if atmosphere points to a *Some* conclusion, participants may substitute *Some . . . not*; if atmosphere yields *Some . . . not*, participants may substitute *Some*.

We can understand this tendency, as well as part of the caution or matching heuristic, as an effect of conversational pragmatics (Grice, 1989;

Sperber & Wilson, 1986). Although *All A are B* may be true, strictly speaking, when no A's exist, you would mislead your conversational partners in making such a statement in such circumstances. For example, to say that *All members of the Bridge Club are members of the Volleyball League* is conversationally inappropriate in a context in which the Bridge Club has no members. If the speaker knows there aren't any Bridge Club members, why didn't he or she say so? Likewise, the statement *No A are B* might be true but misleading in the absence of some A's (that are not B's).

We can understand the relationship between *Some* and *Some . . . not* in much the same way. Although *Some A are B* is compatible with *All A are B* (they can be true at the same time), a speaker would mislead listeners in saying *Some A are B* if she knew the stronger statement is true. (If the speaker knew that *All A are B*, why would she use the weaker *Some*?) *Some A are B* conveys conversationally that it is not true that *All A are B*, hence, *Some A are not B*. In the opposite direction, *Some A are not B* is true but inappropriate if *No A are B*; but if it is not true that *No A are B* then *Some A are B*. These inferences—from *All* to *Some*, from *No* to *Some . . . not*, from *Some* to *Some . . . not*, and from *Some . . . not* to *Some*—are species of *conversational implicatures* in H. P. Grice's phrase. If we write *X conversationally implies Y* as $X \Rightarrow Y$, then we can abbreviate these relations as in (5):

(5)   a. All A are B $\Rightarrow$ Some A are B
       b. No A are B $\Rightarrow$ Some A are not B
       c. Some A are B $\Rightarrow$ Some A are not B
       d. Some A are not B $\Rightarrow$ Some A are B

Oops! If conversational implicature ($\Rightarrow$) is a transitive relation, then the implicatures in (5) lead to contradictions. For example, *All members of the Bridge Club are members of the Volleyball League* implicates *Some members of the Bridge Club are members of the Volleyball League* by (5a), and this in turn implicates *Some members of the Bridge Club are not members of the Volleyball League* by (5c). But the first and last of these statements are contradictory. Similarly, we can get from *No A are B* to *Some A are B* via (5b) and (5d), but these two are again contradictory. These reflections show that we cannot treat all the implicatures in (5) on a par with entailments, which *are* transitive. (Medieval logic, for example, regarded (5a) and (5b) as entailments, but not (5c) or (5d).) Isolated in particular conversational settings, however, the implicatures help preserve the cooperativeness of speakers and listeners (Horn, 1989). Suppose a speaker says *Some A are B*. If we believe the speaker is cooperative and is in a position to know whether all A are B, then we can take the speaker as suggesting that *Some A are not B*. Drawing a further implicature from this implicature, however, is not appropriate without a change in conversational circumstances.[3]

Participants tend to go along with the implicatures in (5) when experimenters ask about them directly (Begg & Harris, 1982; Newstead & Griggs, 1983). The participants will agree, for example, that *Some members of the Bridge Club are members of the Volleyball League* follows from *All members of the Bridge Club are members of the Volleyball League*, in line with (5a). Whether such implicatures affect responses to syllogisms is more controversial (Newstead, 1995). Four traditional syllogisms have conclusions that follow only if (5a) or (5b) applies to the premises. (6) is one example:

(6)   All Volleyball League members are Bridge Club members.
      All Volleyball League members are Chess Team members.

      Some Chess Team members are Bridge Club members.

Implicature (5a), applied to either premise, ensures that there are some Volleyball League members, and this secures the conclusion of (6). When participants have to choose a conclusion in a multiple-choice format (*All, Some, No, Some . . . not*, or *No Valid Conclusion*), 24% select the conclusion that follows from (5a) and (5b) for the four key syllogisms (Dickstein, 1978, Table 3). When participants receive the entire syllogism, as in (6), and have to decide whether the conclusion follows, 51% go along with the same four items (Rips, 1994, Table 7.6). These figures are close to chance percentages, although the response distributions are far from uniform in the multiple-choice study.

A further ten syllogisms have conclusions that follow only if (5c) and (5d) apply to the premises. For example, if we assume that the second premise in (7) guarantees that some Chess Team members are *not* in the Volleyball League (by (5c)), then these Chess Team members can't be in the Bridge Club (by the first premise), yielding the conclusion shown:

(7)   All Bridge Club members are Volleyball League members.
      Some Chess Team members are Volleyball League members.

      Some Chess Team members are not Bridge Club members.

Newstead (1995) shows that the percentage of responses that can be attributed to (5c) and (5d) in such problems is not large: 21% when participants must select their response from a list of alternatives (*All, Some, Some . . . not, No,* and *None of these*), and 20% when participants must produce their own conclusion (Newstead, 1995, Table 4). The figure is still only 31% when participants see entire syllogisms (Rips, 1994, Table 7.6). Moreover, the tendency to make such responses correlated only weakly with the participants' tendency to endorse (5c) or (5d) when they appeared as independent arguments in Newstead's study.

People seem to accept the implicatures in (5) when they directly apply. Although they have also been incorporated in theories of syllogistic reasoning, as we are about to see, the evidence for this assumption is not as clear-cut. This may be due to the additional processing they require or to the fact that unrestricted use of these implicatures yields contradictory sentences.

6.3 Unitary Theories

With the concepts of heuristics and implicatures in mind, let's return to the question of how many inference processes people have. Unitary views maintain the positive thesis that a single principle (or small set of principles) governs all forms of reasoning. But, of course, you can always achieve unity on the cheap by ignoring potentially important differences. Equally crucial to unitary views is the negative thesis that no psychologically interesting distinctions exist that its single principle sweeps under the rug.

A case can be made, for example, that all thinking depends on a set of logic-like principles that perform basic cognitive tasks, such as search and comparison. Production-system theories (e.g., J. R. Anderson, 1993; Newell, 1990) come close to this ideal; even closer are explicitly deduction-based approaches (Rips, 1994). Theories like these are unified in the positive sense, since they claim to be able to explain in principle (not only reasoning but) all cognitive tasks based on their chosen set of primitives. Such theories, however, are not necessarily committed to the negative thesis that no substantive differences exist among types of reasoning. Although these systems could carry out both inductive and deductive reasoning with their primitive search and comparison operators, induction and deduction might each possess distinctive cognitive properties. A close analogy would be to the way a single computer language can execute vastly different types of programs. The programs themselves can have quite different characteristics even though the same underlying computer operations execute them. Whether a theory of reasoning belongs on the unitary or the partitioning side of Figure 6.1 is a matter of degree, depending as it does on the relative importance attached to unifying principles versus substantive differences. Nevertheless, the unitary theories discussed here are all committed to the idea that something is wrong with traditional splits among reasoning abilities, and committed, as well, to an account that is supposed to encompass them.

6.3.1 The Rational-Probabilistic Model

The relation between (2a) and (2b) is an entailment, whereas the relations between (3a) and (3c) and between (3b) and (3c) are not. Still, it is possible to view both as points on a continuum of what we can call *argument strength* (similar to the inductive strength of the arguments we considered in Chapter 4). Statement (2a) lends maximum strength to (2b)—the same degree of strength that (2b) lends itself—as indeed all entailments do. Statement (3a) gives some strength to (3c), though less than the maximum. This suggests that, for the type of reasoning in which people evaluate the inferential relation between one statement and another, all we need is a single cognitive process for strength assessment.

6.3.1.1 Conditional Probability as a Measure of Argument Strength

The best-known unitary strategy uses probability theory to adjust the strength of belief in the conclusion based on belief in the premises. Suppose we have a function Pr that measures your belief in statements. In particular, Pr is a function from statements to real numbers between 0 and 1, such that the greater your belief in statement s, the greater the value of $Pr(s)$. So, $Pr(Miriam\ didn't\ want\ seconds\ \ldots)$ is your degree of belief in the conclusion of (2′) or (3′), repeated here:

(2′)   Nobody wanted seconds on seal-blubber sherbet.

        Miriam didn't want seconds on seal-blubber sherbet.

(3′)   Few people wanted seconds on seal-blubber sherbet.

Miriam didn't want seconds on seal-blubber sherbet.

How should belief in the premise affect belief in the conclusion? Well, that would seem to depend on how the two statements are related—on the likelihood that the conclusion is true given that the premise is true. We can designate this likelihood Pr(Conclusion | Premises), and it will also be a number between 0 and 1. This is the degree of belief you would have in the conclusion if you were sure of the premise. Assuming your degrees of belief obey the axioms of probability theory, this number is the conditional probability of the conclusion given the premises, the same Pr function that we used in Chapter 3 (see Note 5 below for a statement of these axioms). The simpler expression Pr(Conclusion) is the (unconditional) probability of the conclusion. Proponents of the rational-probabilistic model subscribe to the idea that Pr(Conclusion | Premises) is the normatively correct way to adjust your degree of belief in the conclusion given that you've come to believe fully in the premises. In the case of (3′), Pr(*Miriam didn't want seconds . . .* | *Few people wanted seconds . . .)* is the degree of belief in Miriam didn't want seconds that you should come to have if you fully believed that few people wanted seconds.

We can extend this treatment to the argument in (2′). Here, a situation in which nobody wanted seconds is a case in which Miriam doesn't want seconds; so when we calculate Pr(*Miriam didn't want seconds* | *Nobody wanted seconds*), the result will be 1 (i.e., the maximum degree of belief). This fits the intuition that it must be true that Miriam does not want seconds, given that nobody does. Similarly, Pr(*Few people wanted seconds* | *Nobody wanted seconds*) is 1 as well, and this is in line with the thought that few people wanted seconds follows logically from nobody did. All this hints that Pr(Conclusion | Premises) might work as a general measure of argument strength, both in the case of entailments like (2′) and nonentailments like (3′). We will later find good reasons to question the idea that conditional probabilities of 1 always correspond to entailments, but let's see how far we can get with Pr(Conclusion | Premises) as a guide to argument strength.

Do we update our degrees of belief with conditional probabilities? This proposal runs into issues of computational feasibility, since one statement can have many (direct and indirect) probabilistic effects on others. Artificial intelligence offers systems that reduce this complexity, although they don't eliminate it (Pearl, 1988), a point we touched on in Chapter 3. Still, for purposes of evaluating single arguments, such as (3'), Pr(Conclusion | Premises) might be reasonable. One qualification about using Pr(Conclusion | Premises) as an index of argument strength, however, is that completely worthless arguments should ideally have equal and minimum argument strength, but this is not the case for Pr(Conclusion | Premises). For example, Pr(Conclusion | Premise) is greater for argument (8a) than (8b), despite the fact that their common premise provides no warrant for either conclusion:

(8)   a. Vincent Price owned a celery plantation.

One hippo will fit in Fred's van.

b. Vincent Price owned a celery plantation.

Fifty hippos will fit in Fred's van.

The reason for this difference in conditional probabilities is that the likelihood that the premise and conclusion of (8a) are both true is greater than the likelihood that the premise and conclusion of (8b) are both true. According to the usual definition of conditional probability, Pr(Conclusion | Premise) = Pr(Conclusion and Premise) / Pr(Premise).[4] Because the premises of (8a) and (8b) are the same, the conditional probability of (8a) will be greater than that of (8b). This suggests that we can get an improved measure of argument strength by normalizing by the probability of the conclusion, perhaps along the lines of (9):

$$(9) \quad \frac{Pr(Conclusion|Premises) - Pr(Conclusion)}{1 - Pr(Conclusion)}$$

We can use (9) as the measure of argument strength if Pr(Conclusion | Premise) > Pr(Conclusion), setting argument strength to 0 otherwise. This has advantages similar to those of the causal power statistic (Cheng, 1997), which we glimpsed in Chapter 3. However, a large number of probabilistic measures exist in the literature on confirmation that could also fill the role of argument strength (see Kyburg, 1983, and Fitelson, 1999, for theoretical comparisons, and Tentori, Crupi, Bonini, &

Osherson, 2007, for an empirical comparison of these). Even with these refinements, however, you could question whether probability alone suffices to define a reasonable measure of argument strength. Perhaps we should also consider the potential value of the information that the conclusion provides, the degree to which we are willing to stick out our necks in accepting the conclusion, and other parameters (see I. Levi, 1996, for an alternative measure of inductive support that incorporates such factors).

The main problem with Pr(Conclusion | Premises) from a psychological point of view is that people's judgments sometimes fail to track the restrictions that probability theory imposes on this function (Osherson, Smith, & Shafir, 1986; A. Tversky & Kahneman, 1980). Recall the example from A. Tversky and Kahneman (1980) that we examined in Chapter 3. People tend to find argument (10a) stronger than argument (10b), despite the fact that their conditional probabilities are approximately the same:

(10) a. A mother has blue eyes.

Her daughter has blue eyes.

b. A daughter has blue eyes.

Her mother has blue eyes.

In general, the straightforward use of Pr(Conclusion | Premises) is not likely to capture the way people draw inferences.[5] Further evidence of the difficulties people have with conditional probabilities appears in Bar-Hillel and Falk (1982), Falk (1992), Johnson-Laird, Legrenzi, Girotto, Legenzi, and Caverni (1999), and Shimojo and Ichikawa (1989). But perhaps we can patch up this account by drawing on the sorts of heuristics and implicatures we discussed earlier (see Section 6.2). This is the approach the Rational-Probabilistic model takes.

6.3.1.2 Probability + Heuristics in the Rational-Probabilistic Model

The idea that people rely on probability to change their beliefs collides with the fact that their judgments sometimes contradict essential properties of probability theory. But perhaps heuristics can help explain these deviations, while at the same time approximating the correct probabilistic relationships. This is a view that Oaksford and Chater (1998) adopt in their unitary view of reasoning. According to this rational-probabilistic framework, probability theory supplies a normatively appropriate account of what reasoning should be, but is also "descriptively adequate"—it provides a true description of the choices people make in confronting an inference problem. The way in which people mentally go about reasoning, however, need not involve actually calculating probabilities. Instead, people may use heuristics that operate within human processing limitations (e.g., limited memory capacity), that yield correct behavior, at least in the aggregate, and that also explain discrepancies from the probabilistic standards. "The theoretical accounts of reasoning we have discussed do not require that people possess quantitatively accurate probabilistic reasoning abilities. Thus, any apparent tension between the probabilistic approach to rational analysis of reasoning that we advocate and experimental data on probabilistic reasoning is illusory" (Oaksford & Chater, 1998, pp. 277–278).

A normative probabilistic approach to syllogisms.   Let's look at this two-part framework as it applies to syllogisms (Chater & Oaksford, 1999). On the probabilistic side, Chater and Oaksford associate each categorical statement type with a conditional probability: *All A are B* will be true only if $Pr(B \mid A) = 1$; *Some A are B* will be true only if $Pr(B \mid A) > 0$; *Some A are not B* will be true only if $Pr(B \mid A) < 1$; and *No A are B* will be true only if $Pr(B \mid A) = 0$. Chater and Oaksford extend their theory to arguments whose premises and conclusion contain statements with *Few* and *Most*, in addition to *All*, *Some*, and *No*; but we concentrate here on traditional syllogisms for purposes of comparison to other approaches. The conditional probabilities of the two premises of a syllogism will sometimes restrict the conditional probability of the conclusion. If the resulting conditional probability of the conclusion is 1, then an *All* conclusion is warranted; if it is greater than 0, a *Some* conclusion; and so on. For example, in argument (11), the first premise yields $Pr(\text{Bridge Club} \mid \text{Volleyball League}) = 1$, and the second yields $Pr(\text{Volleyball League} \mid \text{Chess Team}) > 0$. This guarantees that $Pr(\text{Bridge Club} \mid \text{Chess Team}) > 0$, which licenses (11)'s conclusion:

(11) All Volleyball League members are Bridge Club members.
Some Chess Team members are Volleyball League members.

Some Chess Team members are Bridge Club members.

Notice, however, that in justifying the conclusion of (11) in this way, we are not calculating Pr(Conclusion | Premises). Instead, warrant for the conclusion comes from a stronger premise-conclusion relationship, namely, deducibility under the axioms of probability theory (see Chater & Oaksford, 1999, Appendix B). Given the conditional probabilities of the premises (and certain simplifying assumptions), we can *prove* that the conclusion must have a conditional probability that is, in this case, greater than o. Chater and Oaksford show that this deducibility relation sanctions mostly the same syllogisms that standard logic also approves. The main exceptions concern arguments like (4), repeated here as (12), which are correct according to the Chater-Oaksford system (1999, Table 2), but not in logic:

(12) Some Volleyball League members are Bridge Club members.
Some Chess Team members are Volleyball League members.

Some Chess Team members are Bridge Club members.

Chater and Oaksford accept (12) as correct because of (statistical) independence assumptions they make, but is (12) a normatively appropriate argument? In our earlier example, Fred is on both the Volleyball League and the Bridge Club, Susan is on both the Volleyball League and the Chess Team, and nobody is on both the Chess Team and the Bridge Club. Then the premises are straightforwardly true, and the conclusion just as straightforwardly false. Some participants in syllogism experiments are willing to go along with the conclusion in (12), but the issue here is whether this response is normatively correct. My guess is that a simple counterexample, along the lines just mentioned, would be enough to convince these participants that their answer was in error.

Heuristic approximations. According to Chater and Oaksford's (1999) framework, however, people don't themselves perform derivations or probabilistic calculations in evaluating syllogisms. Instead, they employ a set of heuristics that I summarize in (13), omitting aspects that do not apply to traditional syllogisms:

(13) a. The preferred conclusion should have the same form as that of the premise with lowest rank in the following order of "informativeness": *All* > *Some* > *No* > *Some . . . not*.

   b. The next most preferred conclusion is the one that follows from that of (13a) by one of the implicatures in (5).

   c. If the most informative premise has a rank that is too low, according to the ordering *All* > *Some* > *Some . . . not* ≈ *No*, respond "no valid conclusion."

   d. If the conclusion produced by (13a) or (13b) is *Some . . . not*, avoid this conclusion as too uninformative.

To see how these heuristics work, we can compute the conclusions for some of the syllogism examples we've encountered so far. Syllogism (6), for example, has two *All* premises; so (13a) predicts an *All* conclusion, and (13b) a second-place *Some* conclusion by (5a). Since the premises are highly informative, reasoners should select these two conclusions (instead of "no conclusion follows"). Syllogisms (7) and (11) each have one *All* and one *Some* premise; so (13a) predicts a *Some* conclusion and (13b) a *Some . . . not* conclusion by (5c). Since at least one of the premises is highly informative, the *Some* conclusion should be selected by (13c); however, (13d) would tend to suppress the *Some . . . not* conclusion. Syllogism (12) has two *Some* premises. This means that (13a) and (13b) will again support *Some* and *Some . . . not* conclusions. (13d) will eliminate the *Some . . . not* conclusion, leaving *Some*. But because the premises are somewhat less informative than in (6), (7), or (11), people should be more apt to respond "no valid conclusion," in accord with (13c).

What is the psychological status of the heuristics in (13)? Perhaps we can think of (13a)–(13c) as the result of people's attempt to be conservative about the conclusions they reach—a generalization of Woodworth and Sell's (1935) caution principle. However, (13d) operates in the reverse direction, eliminating conclusions that are too conservative. (13a) is also quite similar to Wetherick's (1989) matching heuristic, which we discussed earlier. (13a) breaks a tie present in the matching strategy by preferring *Some . . . not* over *All*, *Some*, or *No*; however, this is again contravened by (13d).

Chater and Oaksford (1999), however, justify (13) not as a single interpretable strategy but as a reasoner's way of approximating the correct answers (as given by the probability principles that we discussed in the previous subsection). How good is this approximation? The exact degree depends on specifying the heuristics more exactly. We need to know in the case of (13c), in particular, just how low in the informativeness rank the premises must be before people will say that no valid conclusion exists. However, we might be able to see how good the approximation is by setting these parameters to their optimal values. Suppose that participants receive an entire syllogism (premises and conclusion) and must decide whether the conclusion follows. If the conclusion is not one that heuristics (13a) or (13b) propose, then we can assume the participants will respond that the conclusion does not follow. Similarly, if the conclusion is of the form *Some . . . not*, participants should again say that it doesn't follow by (13d). If the stated conclusion meets the criteria of (13a), (13b), and (13d), however, the participants can respond that the conclusion follows as long as the most informative premise is above threshold, according to (13c). Let's assume that the probability that they do so mirrors the true probability that syllogisms with such a premise are correct (following Chater & Oaksford's probabilistic standard and confining the calculation to syllogisms that meet (13a), (13b), and (13d)). For syllogisms whose most informative premise is *All*, this probability is .28; for *Some*, .20; and for *No* or *Some . . . not*, .06. Under these assumptions, participants should say that only 5% of syllogisms follow. Since nearly all traditional syllogisms are in fact invalid, these statistical participants will be correct on 92% of arguments overall (again, by the Chater–Oaksford standard; i.e., counting arguments like (12) as correct). However, such participants are not able to discriminate accurately between valid and invalid items: Although they are 96% correct on invalid syllogisms, they are only 24% correct on valid ones. The success of the model depends in part on a built-in bias toward "doesn't follow" responses.

As a way of approximating correct syllogistic reasoning, (13) has its problems, at least when it comes to differentiating valid from invalid items. Chater and Oaksford (1999) do show, however, that these heuristics produce reasonable fits to participants' actual responses (using different parameter settings) and can be extended to accommodate nontraditional arguments with *Most A are B* and *Few A are B*. The heuristics also have the advantage over the atmosphere and matching biases (see Section 6.2.1) of being able to predict responses that "no conclusion follows." The latter strategies always settle on one of the categorical conclusions (*All . . .* , *Some . . .* , *Some . . . not . . .* , or *No . . .*).

6.3.1.3 Evaluating the Rational-Probabilistic Model

One intuition that lies behind the rational-probabilistic model is that inference typically leads to conclusions that later considerations can overturn. The premise of (14a), for example, may make its conclusion seem likely, but adding a second premise, as in (14b), may cause us to reconsider our belief in the conclusion:

(14)   a. Martha owes $50,000 on her Zephyr card.

           Martha will cancel her vacation to St. Tropez.

        b. Martha owes $50,000 on her Zephyr card.
            Martha owns 1000 shares of Berkshire Breakaway.

            Martha will cancel her vacation to St. Tropez.

Artificial intelligence research has labeled reasoning *nonmonotonic* if the addition of new premises can weaken support for the conclusion. (See Ginsberg, 1987, for an introduction to such research; for psychological evidence of such weakening, see the suppression effects of Byrne, 1989, and Byrne, Espino, & Santamaria, 1999, mentioned in the Appendix to Chapter 3.) If what warrants an inference is the conditional probability of the conclusion given the premises—Pr(Conclusion | Premises) —then we should expect nonmonotonicity. Adding additional information to the "given" part (in this case, adding additional premises) can decrease the corresponding conditional probability. For example, Pr(Conclusion | Premise) in (14a) is higher than Pr(Conclusion | Premises) in (14b). By contrast, standard systems of deductive logic are monotonic:

Adding further premises to a valid argument can't change the argument into an invalid one. If all reasoning is subject to possible downward revision of this sort, then perhaps Pr(Conclusion | Premises) is the right foundation for a unitary psychology of reasoning. Such a theory might apply not only to probabilistic or uncertain arguments, as in (14), but also to arguments that can embody entailments, such as syllogisms, as Oaksford and Chater (1998) have argued.

This program has met with some success in predicting experimental results for syllogisms and for other staple tasks in the psychology of deduction (see Oaksford & Chater, 1994, for a second example). Applying the theory isn't always a straightforward matter, though. Although the probabilistic base of the theory is supposed to be both normatively and descriptively adequate, descriptive adequacy is sometimes hard to find. The rational-probabilistic approach should have a home court advantage in explaining judgments of probability, but we've seen that counterexamples, such as those of Tversky and Kahneman, are explained away, since the account "do[es] not require that people possess quantitatively accurate probabilistic reasoning abilities." In the case of syllogisms, descriptive adequacy is also little in evidence. The syllogisms that Chater and Oaksford's (1999) theory deems correct are roughly the same as those correct in logic (with the exception of arguments such as (12), which are problematic for their theory). People's judgments about syllogisms, however, are far from these normative standards. To take up the slack between its normative dictates and the empirical data, the theory posits heuristics that are supposed to approximate the normative at one end while producing the data patterns at the other. The main problem with the syllogism theory is that this is simply not possible, since the gap is too big between people's responses and normative dictates.

Second, a curious feature of this tactic is that the probabilism that motivates the theory does not play a big part in the final production. The normative aspect of the theory derives the conclusion of syllogisms from the premises via strict mathematical derivations, while people's thinking about these syllogisms depends on heuristics rather than on probabilistic calculations. Probability may be crucial to providing a unitary theory of reasoning; but if so, it operates behind the scene.

Finally, the probabilistic motivation may not be correct. For example, consider the conditional probability of the conclusion of (15) given its premise:

(15)   Calvin randomly chooses a real number between 3 and 4.

Calvin does not choose π.

Because there are an infinite number of reals between 3 and 4, the likelihood of choosing π is 0; hence, the likelihood of *not* choosing π is 1. However, the conclusion of (15) does not follow deductively from its premise.[6] If it did, the same would be true for each real number between 3 and 4. Although all deductively correct arguments in classical logic have conditional probabilities of 1, the converse is not true. If both deductively correct arguments (e.g., (2′)) and some that are not deductively correct (e.g., (15)) both have Pr(Conclusion | Premises) = 1, then we can no longer discriminate the deductively correct items from the deductively incorrect ones according to whether the conditional probability is 1 or lower than 1. We must either deny that people have this ability (lumping (2′) and (15) together), or we must acknowledge that people have other ways of evaluating goodness of arguments. I will present evidence in this chapter that the latter option is the correct one (see Section 6.4.2).

6.3.2 Diagrammatic Theories

In reasoning about logic or math problems, people often find it helpful to use diagrams to keep track of assumptions. Similarly, people may find it helpful on such problems to use internal, mental diagrams or imagery, as in Hadamard's example in the Introduction to this book. Traditional diagrams, such as Venn diagrams or Euler circles, are handy in determining entailments for sentences with quantifiers, for example in syllogisms (see Gardner, 1958, for an account of these). So a natural thought is that mental Euler circles, or something like them, might provide a unifying framework for reasoning. The central intuition is that we can use diagrams to represent specific states of affairs or circumstances—ways that the world (or part of it) might be. If these mental diagrams are logically exhaustive, then the premises of an argument entail its conclusion just in case the conclusion is true in every diagram in which the premises are true. And even if the premises don't entail the conclusion, they may still lend it strength if the conclusion is true in most of the diagrams in which the premises are true. Other things being equal, the greater the proportion of premise diagrams in which the conclusion is true, the greater the strength of the argument, with maximum strength accruing when the conclusion is true in all such diagrams.

Proposals along these lines for deductive reasoning go back at least to Erickson's (1974) theory of syllogisms and to DeSoto, London, and Handel's (1965) theory of simple transitive inferences (e.g., if Fred is taller than Mary and Fred is shorter than Bill, then who is tallest?). Erickson proposed, for example, that people approach syllogisms such as (6)–(7) and (11)–(12) by representing the premises as mental Euler circles, combining the premise circles, and checking whether a conclusion is true in all possible combinations. As an example, Figure 6.2 shows the Euler circle representations for the four categorical statements and the possible combined representations for the syllogism in (6). According to this theory, errors on these problems are due to people failing to consider all possible Euler representations of each premise or failing to consider all possible premise combinations. In this section, we will look at a closely related theory of syllogisms, but our main interest is in determining the extent to which diagrams can serve as a general theory of reasoning.

6.3.2.1 Mental Models for Argument Strength

Johnson-Laird et al. (1999) propose a theory of probabilistic reasoning based on mental diagrams. According to their account, the probability of a conclusion given a set of premises is our old friend Pr(Conclusion | Premises), but calculated from diagrams that represent possible ways in which the premises are true. To take a simple example, suppose you know that Martha is either in St. Tropez or in St. Moritz. What's the probability that she's in St. Tropez? In other words, what's the probability of the conclusion, given the premise of (16)? (This may seem like a trick question, but read on.)

(16)   Martha is in St. Tropez or Martha is in St. Moritz.

Martha is in St. Tropez.

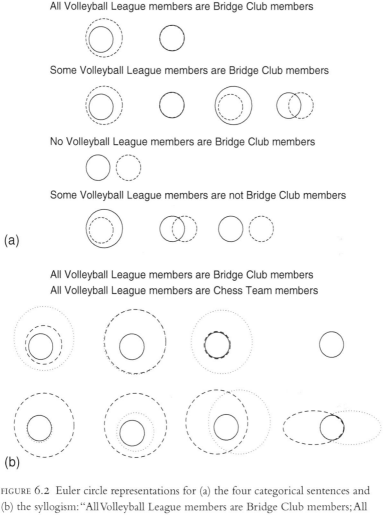

FIGURE 6.2 Euler circle representations for (a) the four categorical sentences and (b) the syllogism: "All Volleyball League members are Bridge Club members; All Volleyball League members are Chess Team members; Therefore, Some Chess Team members are Bridge Club members." Circles with solid outlines represent Volleyball League members, circles with dashed outlines represent Bridge Club members, and circles with dotted outlines represent Chess Team members.

To find out, according to this theory, you construct a mental diagram like that on the left of Figure 6.3a, in which *St.T* is a token that stands for the possibility that Martha is in St. Tropez and *St.M* stands for the possibility that Martha is in St. Moritz. In this diagram, each row (in this case, each row has just a single token) is called a *mental model*.

Mental models   Truth tables

(a)

St.T

     St.M

Martha in St. Tropez	Martha in St. Moritz	M in St. Tropez or M in St. Moritz (not both)
T	T	F
T	F	T
F	T	T
F	F	F

(b)

P	L	
P		R

Martha in Paris	Stella in London	Ethel in Rome	If Martha then either Stella or Ethel (not all three)
T	T	T	F
T	T	F	T
T	F	T	T
T	F	F	F
F	T	T	T
F	T	F	T
F	F	T	T
F	F	F	T

(c)

P	L	-R
P	-L	R
-P	L	R
-P	L	-R
-P	-L	R
-P	-L	-R

Martha in Paris	Stella in London	Ethel in Rome	If Martha then either Stella or Ethel (not all three)
T	T	T	F
T	T	F	T
T	F	T	T
T	F	F	F
F	T	T	T
F	T	F	T
F	F	T	T
F	F	F	T

FIGURE 6.3 The correspondence between mental models (left-hand column) and truth tables (right-hand column) for premises with sentential connectives. Shaded cells in the truth tables are the ones symbolized by the tokens in the models.

The top mental model represents the case in which Martha is in St. Tropez (and implicitly not in St. Moritz), and the bottom row represents the case in which Martha is in St. Moritz (and implicitly not in St. Tropez). This representation is based on truth tables of elementary logic (see, e.g., Bergmann, Moor, & Nelson, 1980, chap. 3, for a full treatment of truth tables). The truth table corresponding to the premise of (16) appears at the right of Figure 6.3a. The four rows correspond to the four possible ways in which the statements *Martha is in St. Moritz* and *Martha is in St. Tropez* can be independently true or false, as indicated by a *T* (for true) or *F* (for false) in the first two columns. The right-most column shows which of these combinations make the entire sentence true. To get the two mental models from the truth table, omit the lines in which the entire sentence is false, omit any cells from the remaining rows that contain an *F*, and substitute symbols that stand for the statements *Martha is in St. Tropez* and *Martha is in St. Moritz* for the remaining *T*'s (the shaded entries in the table).

To determine the probability of the conclusion, you reason in the following way, according to Johnson-Laird et al. (1999, p. 69):

> Individuals should construct models of the true possibilities on the basis of the premises (the truth principle). In the absence of contrary evidence, individuals should assume that the models represent equally probable alternatives (the equiprobability principle), and they should infer that the probability of an event, *A*, equals the proportion of models in which *A* occurs (the proportionality principle):
>
> $$P(A \mid Premises) = \frac{n_A}{n},$$
>
> where P(*A* | *premises*) is the conditional probability of *A* given the premises, n_A is the number of models of the premises in which *A* occurs, and *n* is the number of models of the premises. The twist in this prediction is that equiprobability applies to mental models, and mental models represent only what is true within the true possibilities.

The phrase "true possibilities" in this passage does not mean possibilities that are true, but instead possibilities that are consistent with the premises (i.e., the rows of the truth table in which the entire set of premises is true). In the present example, there are two such possibilities, corresponding to the two mental models in Figure 6.3a. Since we know nothing further about the relative likelihood of these two possibilities, people will assume they are equally probable, according to Johnson-Laird et al.'s equiprobability principle. So people will calculate the probability of the conclusion of (16) by counting the number of models in the diagram in which Martha is in St. Tropez (there's just one of them) and dividing by the total number of models (the two rows of the diagram at the left), which yields a probability of ½.

Johnson-Laird (1994, p. 201) explicitly identifies the strength of an inference with the same proportion n_A/n just discussed: The psychological strength of an argument is equal to Pr(Conclusion | Premises), when calculated over mental diagrams. For example, the strength of Argument (16) is also ½. To tie up this package, Johnson-Laird also proposes that an argument is an entailment just in case Pr(Conclusion | Premises) = 1. So we seem to have a unified theory based on Pr(Conclusion | Premises) that is quite similar to the one we envisioned earlier (see Section 6.3.1.1), but with the "twist" that everything is calculated over mental diagrams.

Mistakes in calculating probabilities.   The twist is important to Johnson-Laird et al. (1999) because they use it to explain some departures between people's judgments about the probability of conclusions and the dictates of probability theory. First, people may err when they assume that each represented possibility (each row of a diagram like that at the left of Figure 6.3a) is equally probable. (This assumption is related to debates about the Principle of Indifference in probability theory; see Hájek, 2007.) Nothing guarantees that Martha is as likely to be in St. Tropez as in St. Moritz. The right answer to the question about the conclusion of (16) might be that the premises simply don't determine its probability.

The more important reason for the discrepancy between people's judgments and true probability, however, is that, according to Johnson-Laird et al., people sometimes fail to represent all the logical possibilities that the premises imply. Unless the rows of the diagram are exclusive and exhaustive, we won't get the right answers if we use the procedure outlined in the passage quoted earlier. In the case of (16), the rows of Figure 6.3a are exclusive and exhaustive under the interpretation that Johnson-Laird et al. assign them: They represent all the ways and only the ways in which the premise is true, corresponding exactly to the "true" rows in the truth table. But for some complex arguments, Johnson-Laird et al. believe people overlook some possibilities. For example, according to Johnson-Laird et al., people represent the premise of (17) in terms of the two rows at the left of Figure 6.3b:

(17)   If Martha is in Paris, then either Stella is in London or Ethel is in Rome, but not all three.

Stella is in London and Ethel is in Rome.

In the figure, P stands for Martha is in Paris, L for Stella is in London, and R for Ethel is in Rome. The truth table at the right of the figure shows that the premise of (17) is true in six different situations (the six rows with T's in the right-most column). Two of these are cases in which (a) Martha is in Paris and Stella is in London (second row), and (b) Martha is in Paris and Ethel is in Rome (third row). The remaining four are those situations in which Martha is not in Paris (rows 4–8), since according to classical logic a conditional sentence is true if its antecedent (*if* part) is false. In the mental-model representation at the left of the figure, however, these four latter possibilities do not appear. This time Johnson-Laird et al. leave out not only the rows of the table in which the premise is false, but also some of those in which the premise is true. In neither of the two remaining mental models, shown in Figure 6.3b, are both Stella in London and Ethel in Rome, so Johnson-Laird et al. predict that people will judge the probability of the conclusion to be 0. A little over half the participants in Johnson-Laird et al.'s experiment went along with this prediction. (The semantics of the conditional is a matter of dispute, and most theorists doubt whether the *if* of ordinary language is correctly captured by classical logic's material conditional. Let's go along with this analysis temporarily, however, for the sake of illustrating Johnson-Laird et al.'s approach. For debate about the meaning of *if*, see, e.g., Edgington, 2007, and Stalnaker, 1975, 2005).

Some people do attend to all the possibilities inherent in the premises, so how can the theory explain their performance? Johnson-Laird et al. make room for a mental representation that is closer to the truth table, and they call this the set of *explicit* mental models. The explicit models for the premise of (17) are the ones at the left of Figure 6.3c. The top row shows the possibility in which Martha is in Paris (P), Stella is in

London (L), and Ethel is *not* in Rome (-R); the second row represents Martha in Paris (P), Stella *not* in London (-L), and Ethel in Rome (R); and so on. According to Johnson-Laird et al., people normally represent a premise like the one in (17) in terms of the two possibilities in Figure 6.3b. The information missing in Figure 6.3b (but present in 6.3c) is supposed to reside in "mental footnotes," whose structure Johnson-Laird et al. do not explicate. People are supposed to forget these "footnotes" rapidly, but if they happen to remember them, they can use them to construct explicit models and revise their probability estimates. Notice that each row that does appear in Figure 6.3b has only some of the information filled in. Here, the fact that Ethel is not in Rome (-R) is suppressed in the first row, and Stella is not in London (-L) is suppressed in the second (compare Figure 6.3b to the first two rows of 6.3c).[7]

Diagrams and conditional probabilities.   Not all arguments are as obliging as (16) and (17) in specifying the possibilities in the premises that are relevant to the conclusion. If you want to know the likelihood that Geritol cures cancer given the results of some clinical trials, you might consider *Pr*(Geritol cures cancer | Results …), where "Results … " is an abbreviation for the data. But how would you compute this conditional probability using the diagrammatic procedure? Perhaps you could form one row in your mental diagram that symbolizes the results and Geritol curing cancer (R-G) and another row with the results and Geritol not curing cancer (R-G), but you surely wouldn't estimate the probability of Geritol curing cancer (given the results) as .5 on this basis. Johnson-Laird et al. allow you to assign unequal probabilities to the rows of the diagram in cases where you have knowledge of the subject matter, but where do these unequal probabilities come from?

Johnson-Laird et al. (1999) acknowledge that their theory describes only what they call "extensional" reasoning with probabilities, which they define as "inferring the probability of an event from the different possible ways in which it could occur." They distinguish this type of reasoning from "nonextensional" reasoning, "which relies on some relevant heuristic, index, or evidence" (p. 63). They also believe that extensional reasoning is deductive (i.e., based on an entailment), whereas nonextensional reasoning is inductive. So they would probably regard the Geritol case as nonextensional since it depends on evidence.

Granting the distinction, we will have to look elsewhere for a theory of nonextensional reasoning. For the same reason, we may have to qualify the idea that mental-model theory is a unitary approach, since it doesn't account for inductive reasoning. We'll bear this exception in mind in evaluating the theory, but first we need to see how this approach handles other types of inference.

6.3.2.2 Mental Models for Entailments

Johnson-Laird originally designed his theory as an account of how people solve categorical syllogisms, so we might expect mental models to be more at home in the realm of entailments than in that of probabilities. In fact, we could use the models of Figure 6.3 to handle entailments on Johnson-Laird's (1994) view, since the premises of an argument will entail a conclusion if that conclusion is true in each row of the premises' diagram. Johnson-Laird, Byrne, and Schaeken (1992) take just this approach. To compare this approach to the rational-probabilistic model, however, we need to look at categorical syllogisms, and for these arguments, Johnson-Laird adopts a very different type of diagrammatic representation. A mental model for a categorical premise (*All . . . , Some . . . , No . . . , or Some . . . not . . .*) is typically a set of rows, not a single row as in Figure 6.3, and instead of standing for an entire atomic statement or proposition (e.g., *Martha is in St. Moritz*), the individual symbols (and the individual rows) stand for particular individuals (e.g., Martha). Figure 6.4 gives a number of examples, with the mental models appearing within boxes at the right.

Mental models for syllogisms.   Figure 6.4a shows how the theory represents the four categorical statements (which you can compare to the Euler circles in Figure 6.2a). For example, the representation for *All Volleyball League members are Bridge Club members* contains two rows, each representing an individual Volleyball League member (*v*) who is also in the Bridge Club (*b*). The brackets around the *v*'s indicate that you can't add any more Volleyball League members to the representation (hence, no Volleyball League members are not also in the Bridge Club). Absence of brackets around the *b*'s means that you could add more Bridge Club members (but they couldn't be members of the Volleyball League). Bucciarelli and

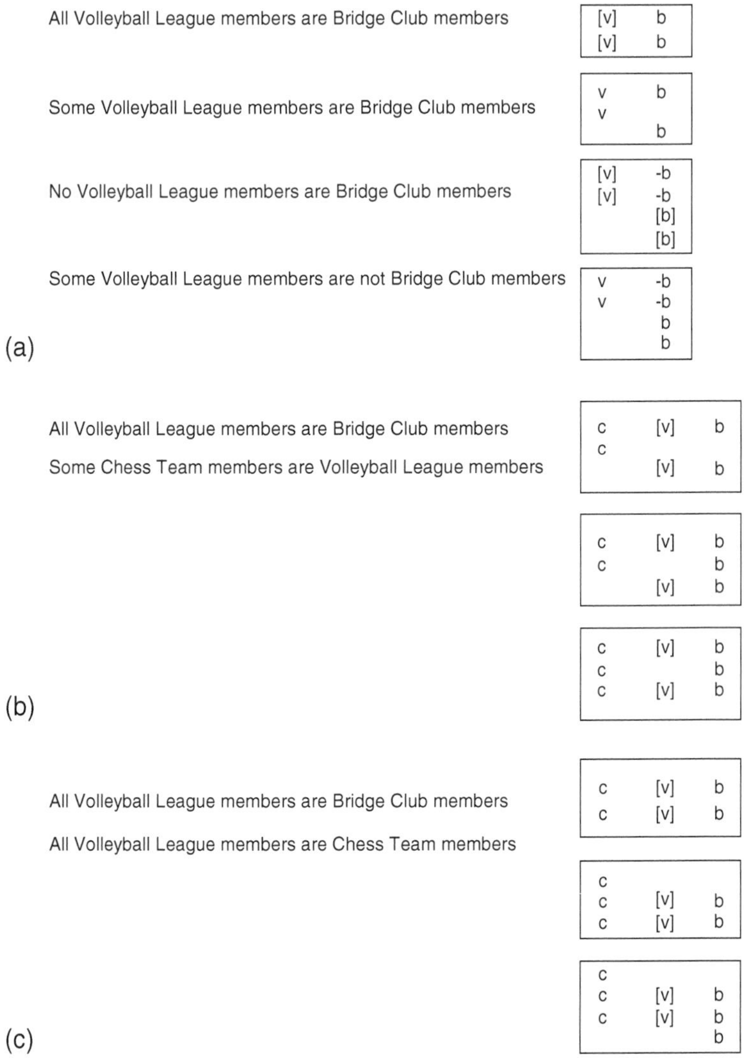

All Volleyball League members are Bridge Club members

[v]	b
[v]	b

Some Volleyball League members are Bridge Club members

v	b
v	
	b

No Volleyball League members are Bridge Club members

[v]	-b
[v]	-b
	[b]
	[b]

Some Volleyball League members are not Bridge Club members

v	-b
v	-b
	b
	b

(a)

All Volleyball League members are Bridge Club members

Some Chess Team members are Volleyball League members

c	[v]	b
c		
	[v]	b

c	[v]	b
c		b
	[v]	b

c	[v]	b
c		b
c	[v]	b

(b)

All Volleyball League members are Bridge Club members

All Volleyball League members are Chess Team members

c	[v]	b
c	[v]	b

c		
c	[v]	b
c	[v]	b

c		
c	[v]	b
c	[v]	b
		b

(c)

FIGURE 6.4 Mental models for categorical syllogisms. Panel a shows models for individual categorical statements. Panel b lists composite models for syllogism (11), and Panel c composite models for syllogism (6).

Johnson-Laird (1999) express the view that "reasoners do not adopt a fixed interpretation for each sort of syllogistic premise, but instead their interpretations vary in ways that are not entirely predictable" (p. 298). So we should interpret these diagrams as one possible representation among many. Bucciarelli and Johnson-Laird do not appear to doubt, however, that all representations that people use for syllogisms contain symbols for individuals, configured in a way that is consistent with the premises.

To decide whether a syllogism entails its conclusion (or to produce a conclusion from the premises), people are supposed to combine the two models for the premises into a composite model. They then draw candidate conclusions that hold in the composite. Finally, they attempt to refute the candidate conclusion by revising the composite. If a conclusion holds in all the composite models of the premises (original plus revisions), then that conclusion follows; if no categorical conclusion holds in all composite models, then nothing follows.

Let's try out this scheme with some of the examples we encountered earlier. Figure 6.4b shows a composite representations for the premises of syllogism (11), repeated below:

(11)   All Volleyball League members are Bridge Club members.
        Some Chess Team members are Volleyball League members.

        Some Chess Team members are Bridge Club members.

In the first composite model, the conclusion *Some Chess Team members are Bridge Club members* holds (as do a number of other possibilities such as *Some Chess Team members are not Bridge Club members*). The first row of the mental model denotes a joint member of the Chess Team and the Bridge Club (and the Volleyball League). So the conclusion of (11) is potentially correct. We can form further composite models of the premises, for example, by adding more Chess Team members and more Bridge Club members, as Figure 6.4b also shows (see the second and third models). These models rule out conclusions like *Some Chess Team members are not Bridge Club members*. However, these further models do not refute the conclusion of (11), and the theory predicts that people should think it valid.

As a second example, let's reconsider (6):

(6)   All Volleyball League members are Bridge Club members.
All Volleyball League members are Chess Team members.

Some Chess Team members are Bridge Club members.

The first composite model in Figure 6.4c supports (6)'s conclusion, as well as some stronger possibilities (e.g., *All Bridge Club members are Chess Team members*). Again, we can add further Bridge Club or Chess Team members to get the other models in Figure 6.4c. But while these rule out the stronger possibilities, they leave the conclusion of (6) intact. Syllogism (6), then, must also be correct, according to this procedure.

The predictions from this theory applied originally to a task in which participants received just the premises of a syllogism and were asked to produce on their own a categorical conclusion that followed (or to respond "no conclusion follows"). Syllogisms whose first composite model suggested a conclusion that further models could not refute were deemed "one-model" problems. Syllogisms whose first composite model suggested a conclusion that could be refuted were "two" or "three-model" problems. Some of these multiple-model problems have valid conclusions; others have no valid conclusion. The theory's main empirical hypothesis depends on this classification: One-model problems should be easier than multiple-model problems. According to Bucciarelli and Johnson-Laird's (1999) classification, for example, syllogism (11) is a one-model problem. This is because the theory predicts that people will draw from the first composite model in Figure 6.4b the conclusion *Some Chess Team members are Bridge Club members*, and this conclusion is immune to refutation. Syllogism (6), however, is a multiple-model problem. People are supposed to draw the conclusion *All Chess Team members are Bridge Club members* from the initial composite model in Figure 6.4c, but this is a possibility that later models contradict, leaving *Some Chess Team members are Bridge Club members* as the revised conclusion. (The latter, correct conclusion is also consistent with the initial model, but is not supposed to be among those that people extract from that model.)

Thus, which syllogisms are one-model problems and which are multiple-model problems depends critically on which conclusion people extract from a model and on the sequence in which they construct the composite models. With these assumptions in place, however, the theory predicts that participants should have an easier time producing the designated conclusions from one-model premises than from multiple-model premises. The participants' working-memory limitations may keep them from considering more than a single mental model, and if so, they will come up with the wrong conclusion for the multiple-model items (see Ford, 1995, pp. 7–8, for a critique of Johnson-Laird's assumptions about syllogism (6), and Rips, 1986, for related criticism). Bucciarelli and Johnson-Laird (1999, p. 299) note that in their experiments "participants differed . . . in how they went about searching for alternative models"; however, they claim that "the general principle governing the difficulty of syllogisms is straightforward: those syllogisms for which the valid conclusion depends on one model are easier than those for which the valid conclusion depends on more than one model. This difference survives the great variety of strategies and interpretations that our experiments have demonstrated" (Bucciarelli & Johnson-Laird, 1999, p. 301).[8]

Questions about syllogism models.   Bucciarelli and Johnson-Laird (1999) are right that the problems they classify as one-model syllogisms are typically easier than the multiple-model syllogisms. For example, when problems (6) and (11) are presented to participants under instructions to decide whether the conclusion follows from the premises (Rips, 1994), 80% agree with the conclusion of (11) (the one model problem), but only 45% agree with (6) (the multiple-model problem); see, also, Evans, Handley, Harper, and Johnson-Laird (1999). But can mental-model theory successfully explain why this is true? In this task, participants don't have to volunteer conclusions on their own; they merely have to check conclusions they read. The conclusions to both (6) and (11) are present in the initial composite model, as we have seen in Figures 6.4b and 6.4c, and subsequent models don't refute them. So how can mental-model theory predict a difference between them? We noted earlier that syllogism (6) is one of those whose conclusion depends on the implicature from *All* to *Some* in (5a); so perhaps the relatively poor performance on this item is due to participants' hesitation about this inference. However, the deficiency here is a general one that applies to all "multiple model" problems that have a correct categorical conclusion (and where participants see the conclusion presented along with the premises).

All such conclusions must be present in the initial composite model. To explain why participants often make errors on these problems, we may need to invoke a bias against conclusions with quantifiers that don't match premise quantifiers (a factor that we discussed during our earlier trip through syllogismland) or some further possibility.

Some research also suggests that people don't spontaneously use diagrams like those in Figure 6.4 when they have to solve syllogisms with pencil and paper. Ford (1995) analyzed participants as they were thinking aloud and drawing diagrams while solving syllogisms. Based on these data, Ford identified two groups of participants with characteristic diagrams and error patterns. One group used Euler circles (similar to those in Figure 6.2, but often with verbal tags), presumably because they had learned this technique in school. Another group used a substitution strategy, supplemented by arrows, equal signs, and overwriting to indicate substituted terms. In the case of (11), for example, these participants realized that the second premise guarantees the existence of a Chess Team member who's on the Volleyball League. They then substituted this person as an instance of the generalization in the first premise: This comember of the Chess Team and Volleyball League must be in the Bridge Club. So some Chess Team members are Bridge Club members, as the conclusion affirms (see Polk & Newell, 1995, for further evidence of this strategy, and Stenning & Yule, 1997, for a theoretical analysis). According to Ford (1995, p. 19), neither group of participants used a system like that of Figure 6.4. Similarly, Bucciarelli and Johnson-Laird (1999) report use of Euler circles, of arrows and equal signs, and other idiosyncratic symbols; however, only two of 40 participants in their Experiments 1 and 2 "used individual tokens to represent different sorts of individuals."[9] In general, mental-model theory does not seem to predict when people will use one representation rather than another.

Participants' overt procedures could be the result of their tacitly manipulating individual tokens in mental diagrams, even in the case of Ford's substitution strategy. As Stenning and Yule (1997) point out, however, results from the usual syllogism tasks don't differentiate diagrammatic from nondiagrammatic (sentential) approaches in this situation. Representations of either type are compatible with the data, as long as they are able to describe individuals who are eligible for substitution. This equivalence between diagrammatic and sentential representations is especially obvious in Polk and Newell's (1995) version of mental models (see Note 8), which include special markers in the diagrams to indicate linguistic facts, such as which terms originated from the grammatical subjects of the premises.

6.3.2.3 Mental Models for Modals

Each mental model for a set of statements is supposed to represent a possible way in which these statements could be true. So people should be able to use mental models to evaluate or to produce judgments about what's necessary and what's possible relative to these statements. In the case of syllogism (6), for example, Figure 6.4c shows that the statement *All Chess Team members are Bridge Club members* is true in at least one of the mental models for these premises, as are the conclusions *All Bridge Club members are Chess Team members*, *Some Chess Team members are not Bridge Club members*, and *Some Bridge Club members are not Chess Team members*. All these statements *might* be true if the premises of (6) are true. In addition, the statements *Some Chess Team members are Bridge Club members* and *Some Bridge Club members are Chess Team members* are true in all mental models of the premises, and they *must* therefore be true if the premises are. This distinction among statements leads Bell and Johnson-Laird (1998) to claim that "the model theory offers a unified account of reasoning about what is necessary, probable, and possible" (p. 50).

Evidence exists that people can make sensible judgments about the concepts of necessity and possibility. For example, Osherson (1976) showed that 89% of high school students correctly concluded from *It is possible that the white light is not dim* that *It is not necessary that the white light is dim.* Likewise, 95% correctly endorsed the argument from *It is necessary that both the red light is off and the purple light is blinking* to *It is necessary that the red light is off and it is necessary that the purple light is blinking.* Of course, the percentage of correct responses falls off for inferences that are more complex, but people seem to recognize a core set of such inferences as intuitively correct.

The current mental-model account of "what is necessary," however, does not go beyond what other theories of deductive reasoning provide. Although mental-model theory might be extended to reason with the concept of necessity, it doesn't do so in current incarnations. What the theory does is distinguish between conclusions that follow validly from certain premises and those that don't, just as most other deduction theories do. In deductively correct arguments, it is necessarily the case that if the premises are true, then so is the conclusion, and mental models can sanction such decisions. The premises and conclusions in question, however, do not include the logical operators *necessary* and *possible*. (See, e.g., Fitting, 1983, for modal logic systems that *do* include these operators, and Osherson, 1976, for a psychological approach.) For example, mental-model theory (unlike modal logic) does not allow us to go from a statement of the form *It is necessary that both P and Q* to one of the form *It is necessary that P.*[10]

A more interesting aspect of the mental-models approach is its treatment of possibility. When a potential conclusion is true in at least one model of the premises, then it is possible that if the premises are true then so is the conclusion. The theory does not reason with the concept of possibility any more than it reasons with the concept of necessity; in particular, it doesn't handle the sorts of inferences with the operator *possible* that one gets with modal logics and with psychological theories based on them. In addition, as Evans et al. (1999) point out, other deduction theories can yield the same decisions about possibility, at least for syllogisms and for arguments based on propositional operators (e.g., *and, or, not,* and *if . . . then*). These theories, which we will examine in Section 6.4.3, can establish that it is possible that *if premises then conclusion*, provided that there is no proof from the premises to the negation of the conclusion. However, mental models do this in a way that is less roundabout and perhaps more general: It is enough to show that the conclusion appears in at least one model of the premises.

We saw that the mental-model approach to probability leaves open how people determine probabilities in "nonextensional" cases, for example, those involving evidence. We can also ask, in a similar way, what determines possibilities in mental models. For simple arguments like syllogisms and propositional problems, a finite set of models suffices to determine validity, but for even slightly more general problems involving both quantifiers (e.g., *all, some, no*) and propositional operators (e.g., *and, or, not, if*)—for example, arguments in predicate logic—finite models won't suffice. For languages with these logical resources (including all natural languages), deductive correctness depends on an infinite number of logical models. Likewise, whether a statement in such languages is logically possible depends on whether the statement is true in at least one model among this infinity. This is a nonextensional issue in the traditional sense, and mental models are unlikely to be any more useful here than in determining "nonextensional" probabilities. In order to decide which statements are possible via mental models, we need to know which of the infinite number of potential models are available as mental ones, and no current theory of mental models is able to provide this information.

6.3.2.4 Summary of Diagrammatic Theories

For many people, the attractiveness of diagrammatic theories is their ability to symbolize concrete possibilities. People sometimes find it helpful to focus on a specific situation when reasoning about abstract matters. In the context of probabilistic reasoning, diagrams can sometimes represent each of a set of states, and this can facilitate calculating the probabilities of statements associated with these states. Students in introductory probability classes do much the same thing in computing probabilities over a sample space. In the context of deductive reasoning, diagrams can sometimes represent all logically possible situations compatible with a set of premises, and this can help determine whether a conclusion holds in each of these situations. Students in introductory logic classes do much the same thing in using truth tables to determine deductive correctness. Since diagrams are handy in both these contexts, diagrams are reasonable candidates for a unitary theory.

Diagrams, however, are not the only way to enumerate possibilities; you can list them in other notational formats. This provides an entry point for theorists to prove equivalence theorems for diagrammatic and linguistic models (Stenning & Yule, 1997). Moreover, evidence seems to be accumulating that people don't spontaneously use diagrams for syllogisms—at least not the sort of diagrams that play a role in current theories. The diagrams that some people do use—Euler circles—are arguably the result of special training in school. And for easy problems, such as (11), people seem to have no intuitive need to resort to diagrams of any type. This, of course, does not mean that diagrams are never useful, or that people don't sometimes employ them overtly or covertly. What's in doubt is the mandatory use of diagrams in all forms of reasoning—the idea that diagrams offer "a unified account of reasoning about what is necessary, probable, and possible."

These considerations also raise the point that mental diagrams depend on a system for interpreting them. A diagram of a square to the left of a rectangle might represent the proposition that there is a square to the left of a rectangle, or it might represent the proposition that there is both a square and a rectangle (as in Figure 6.3), or it might represent the proposition that some square is a rectangle (as in Figure 6.4), and so on. One trouble in evaluating diagrammatic theories is that the system that governs the representations—the semantics of the representation—is not spelled out in enough detail to assess the diagram's expressive abilities and liabilities (see Rips, 1986).

Suppose we leave diagrams aside and attend simply to the idea that people somehow represent lists of possibilities in reasoning. This sort of analysis by cases is likely to be among the strategies people employ not only in reasoning, but also in related endeavors such as planning, problem solving, and decision making (Kolodner, 1993). The issue before us, however, is whether such an approach can provide the basis for a unitary theory of reasoning. Do people always reason by cases? Mental-models theory is committed to a positive answer. Even in the domain of deduction, however, recent evidence suggests that people make crucial use of generalities, not just cases (e.g., Rips, 2000). If so, current case-based theories are incomplete at best.

Finally, as unitary theories, mental models fall prey to the same counterexamples that the rational-probabilistic theory does. If you determine the conditional probability Pr(Conclusion | Premises) by counting the number of premise models in which the conclusion is true (Johnson-Laird et al., 1999) and you also determine the validity of an argument by checking whether all the premise models contain the conclusion, then those arguments in which Pr(Conclusion | Premises) = 1 will be the same as those declared valid. The argument in (15), however, is one in which Pr(Conclusion | Premises) = 1 but which is clearly not deductively correct. You could try to salvage mental models as a unitary theory by supposing that the set of mental models people use to determine conditional probabilities is different from the one they use in deciding about validity. But you would then face the issue of determining which models are relevant for logical assessments and which for probability assessments, and this distinction makes it harder to maintain mental models as a unitary approach.

6.3.3 Other Unitary Theories

Rational-probabilistic and diagrammatic theories seem to be the only unitary theories that psychologists have advocated and elaborated. But this doesn't mean these are the only reasonable options. One alternative is to conceive of reasoning within a broader framework of justified changes in belief. These changes could include those based on entailments, as well as those based on weaker inference relations (e.g., statistical or causal ones). Within such a framework, you could then study the properties common to all forms of justified belief change. These properties might include a set of heuristics people follow in changing their beliefs or, perhaps, a set of more formal properties. This point of view is common among epistemologists and artificial intelligence researchers (e.g., Gärdenfors, 1988; Harman, 1986; I. Levi, 1996). However, corresponding empirical work in cognitive psychology is scarce (but see Elio & Pelletier, 1997; Revlis & Hayes, 1972).

You could also view research on "informal reasoning" as a start on a unified theory. Such research explores people's ability to construct and evaluate argumentation, usually pro or con some controversial issue, such as why children fail in school (e.g., Baron, 1991; Brem & Rips, 2000; Hahn & Oaksford, 2007; Kuhn, 1991; Mercier & Sperber, in press; Perkins, Farady, & Bushey, 1991; Resnick, Salmon, Zeitz, Wathen, & Holowchak, 1993; Rips, 1998; Stanovich & West, 1997; Voss & Means, 1991). Research in this tradition has documented difficulties people have in arguing in a fair and open-minded fashion—for example, in taking proper account of both sides of an issue or in properly distinguishing between evidence and unsupported explanation. These types of difficulty do not arise in tasks in which participants evaluate arguments (e.g., syllogisms) for deductive correctness, and for this reason investigators in both psychology and philosophy have sometimes seen this endeavor as part of a study of "informal reasoning" that's antithetical to "formal reasoning" or logic. An alternative perspective, however, would understand deductive reasoning as a special case of general argumentation strategies. For example, Toulmin's (1958) theory of informal reasoning could be seen as a generalization of formal arguments of the type: *All A are B; x is an A; therefore, x is a B.*

These avenues are worth exploring. Psychological theories, however, have not worked out this approach in enough detail to provide evidence for a unitary view. We therefore won't pursue this approach here, but will move on to other theories that take definite stands on our key issues.

6.4 Partitioning Theories

We come to new conclusions in an enormous variety of endeavors, from practical questions of legal responsibility to theoretical cases of which scientific model best accounts for physical phenomena. Perhaps one psychological process handles all such inferences, but then again we don't have any clear success stories on the unitary front. We've seen that unitary theories framed in terms of probabilities or in terms of case-based, diagrammatic reasoning can account for the data from some reasoning experiments. But they must be supplemented in various ways—usually by appealing to heuristics or pragmatics—in order to handle the full range of inferences. A new unitary theory based on belief change, nonmonotonic reasoning, or informal reasoning may do better, but let's consider the possibility that we can make more sense of reasoning by assuming that several types of mental mechanisms are responsible for its manifestations.

Nobody doubts that we reason differently about, say, legal matters and scientific ones. Legal reasoning makes use of a body of precedent and doctrine that's crucial to its conclusions and that's irrelevant to conclusions about scientific theories. The issue in this chapter, though, is whether reasoning about these domains also involves different mental mechanisms people use in reaching the conclusions. Posing the problem in this way raises well-known difficulties in assigning cognitive effects to process versus representation. You can usually explain the same effect in terms of either special-purpose representations or special-purpose processes. But we can't escape this indeterminacy in the present case. The thesis of the partitioning theories we review here is that important processing differences exist that we can't plausibly credit to the content of the representations these processes use. Failing to find evidence for process differences means giving up on partitioning approaches.

6.4.1 Domain Specific Theories

One way to divide human knowledge is by its subject matter. Some of it is about Abelian groups; some about darning needles; and some about the Dewey Decimal system. You might also suppose that those who are knowledgeable about such matters mentally organize this knowledge in ways that make it easier to use. Experts on darning needles may have elaborate long-term symbolic frameworks or connectionist clusterings that somehow specify the needles' types and properties. If so, then knowledge of darning needles has a psychological reflex in these experts; darning-needle mavens aren't just "situated" in the causal nexus of darning needles, according to this story. You could even say that such fans have a mini-theory of darning needles like those we discussed in Chapters 4 and 5. Still, no one would claim that a mental theory of darning needles was of much fundamental importance to cognitive psychology, apart from exemplifying one field of expertise among zillions of others. (For studies of similar domains, see, e.g., Chase & Simon, 1973, on chess; Chi & Koeske, 1983, on dinosaurs; and Voss, Vesonder, & Spilich, 1980, on baseball; of course, these investigators use these domains to make larger points about the organization of knowledge.)

Maybe there are collections of thoughts, however, that do have special cognitive status. Although knowledge of darning needles isn't one of them, you could make the case for knowledge of language, mechanics of objects, measurement and number, psychological properties of people, and a few others. To make such a case, you could argue that these systems incorporate innate, domain-specific principles that "define the entities covered by the domain and support reasoning about those entities" (Carey & Spelke, 1994, p. 169). A mental theory of darning needles doesn't support reasoning in any interesting way, though of course you can reason about darning needles, just as you can reason about anything else. Beliefs about darning needles supply information for inferences. But reasoning about darning needles does not differ in any cognitively important way from reasoning about Victorian oyster forks. So the question is: Do internal theories of mechanics or number or psychology drive reasoning in a manner that internal theories of darning needles don't? Or, to put it another way, do internal theories of mechanics or number or psychology do more than furnish beliefs that are grist for independently defined general reasoning mechanisms?

6.4.1.1 Social-Regulation Theories

Some well-known theories of domain-specific reasoning emerged in the 1980s with proposals by Cheng and Holyoak (1985) and Cosmides (1989; Fiddick, Cosmides, & Tooby, 2000). These theories claimed that people ordinarily reason by means of mental mechanisms that are practical in their orientation. In their everyday dealings, people have to cope with problems involving permission and obligation (according to Cheng & Holyoak), social exchange and hazard management (according to Cosmides), and other domains that are relevant to their goals; hence, they've learned or evolved specialized rules or mechanisms for handling such situations. These rules do not necessarily produce entailments, and they don't supplement domain-general rules but typically supplant them. According to these theories, domain-general rules either don't exist or operate only as a backup when the more practical rules fail.

Cheng and Holyoak, for example, proposed the rules in (18) as those that govern situations involving permission:

(18)   a. If the action is to be taken, then the precondition must be satisfied.
       b. If the action is not to be taken, then the precondition need not be satisfied.
       c. If the precondition is satisfied, then the action may be taken.
       d. If the precondition is not satisfied, then the action must not be taken.

The items in (18) correspond to a set of mental procedures that a permission-based situation triggers and that direct people to satisfy the appropriate precondition or take the associated action. If you're trying to get a soda from a soda machine, you first have to deposit the right amount of money; but once you've deposited it, you're entitled to the soda. Although triggering one rule triggers the others, the rules do not necessarily entail one another, as Cheng and Holyoak note. For example,

(18c) doesn't follow from (18a): In situations where more than one precondition is necessary, taking an action will require satisfying one of the preconditions (in fact, all of them); but it doesn't follow that if that precondition is satisfied, then the action may be taken. If you're trying to withdraw money from an ATM, you first have to insert your card; but inserting your card doesn't necessarily entitle you to the money. You also have to know your PIN, have the appropriate balance in your account, and so on. (The theory suggests that people don't appreciate this fact, which may lead you to question the formulation in (18). The appendix to Chapter 3 discusses research on necessary and sufficient conditions that is relevant to this point. But let's ignore this issue here in order to see where this type of theory leads.)

The debate between the Cheng-Holyoak and Cosmides proposals centers on whether the data are best explained by the permission rules in (18) or by mechanisms that are specialized for detecting cheating in social contexts. For our purposes, however, we can treat them together, since they have far more in common than either has with the other theories that we have examined, and I will use *social-regulation theory* to refer to both. Nearly all the evidence in favor of these theories comes from variations on a single experimental set up, one due to Peter Wason (1966) and known as the *selection task*. In standard versions of this task, participants inspect four cards whose face-up sides show (in one variation) the characters E, K, 4, and 7, one symbol per card. Participants are told that each card contains a letter on one side and a numeral on the other. The participants' task is "to name those cards, and only those cards, which need to be turned over to determine whether the [following] rule is true or false": *If the card has a vowel on one side, it has an even number on the other.* On the usual interpretation of the selection task, the correct response is to designate the E card and the 7 card as the ones to check. An odd number on the reverse of the E card would violate the rule, as would a vowel on the reverse of the 7 card. Other combinations are consistent with the rule. But although most participants think to check the E card (and many also check the 4 card), few check the 7 card.

What occasioned the social-regulation theory was evidence for improved performance on the selection task with change in wording. Griggs and Cox (1982, Experiment 3) framed the problem as a regulation about drinking—*If a person is drinking beer, then the person must be over*

19—and told participants that the cards represented individual people in a bar, showing on one side a person's age and on the other what that person was drinking. Instead of the E, K, 4, and 7 cards, participants instead saw analogous cards showing *beer, coke,* 22, and 16. In this version, as many as 70% of participants chose the correct *beer* and 16 cards, up from about 10% in the standard version. According to the permission-rule hypothesis (Cheng & Holyoak, 1985), this increase in performance is due to the problem's content triggering the permission rules in (18), with (18a) motivating the choice of the *beer* card, and (18d) the 16 card. Rules (18b)–(18c) establish that the *coke* and 22 cards need not be checked. According to the cheater-detection theory (Cosmides, 1989; Cosmides & Tooby, 1994), good performance is due to the drinking regulation triggering an innate cheater detector, which in turn singles out the beer drinker and the 16-year-old as potential rule-breakers. On both accounts, poor performance in the original version is due to the unavailability (or short-circuiting) of abstract logic rules for handling arbitrary conditionals.

6.4.1.2 Questions about Social Regulations

Subsequent analysis of the selection task during the 1990s, however, has questioned whether the results provide evidence for mechanisms specialized for social regulations. First, as a number of investigators have pointed out, the logical features of the standard task differ from those of the social-regulation versions (see, e.g., Manktelow & Over, 1991). The if-then "rule" in the standard task (e.g., *If vowel, then even number*) is a regularity—a universal generalization of the form: *For all x, if x is a card and x has a vowel on one side, then x has an even number on the other.* But the "rule" in the permission versions (*If a person is drinking beer, then the person must be over* 19) is a true regulation. Moreover, what these conditional regulations require is that the consequent of the conditional holds (i.e., being over 19) when the antecedent holds (drinking beer). The form of the regulation is not *Obligatory(If p then q)*, but *If p then Obligatory(q)* (as Fodor, 2000, has pointed out).[11] Because regulations make the consequent obligatory, participants are motivated to check the card in which the consequent is false (the 16 card) when they must decide if the rule holds.

Second, several experiments have demonstrated good performance on the selection task with content from a variety of domains, quite apart from social regulations (Ahn & Graham, 1999; Almor & Sloman, 1996; Sperber, Cara, & Girotto, 1995; Sperber & Girotto, 2002). In some of these experiments, what seems to be crucial is clarifying that the antecedent of the conditional "rule" is sufficient (but not necessary) for its consequent. Therefore, when an instance embodies the antecedent but not the consequent, it violates or disconfirms the rule. If this is correct, then domain general mechanisms for handling necessity and sufficiency can account for good performance. For example, Almor and Sloman (1996) used the rule *If a large object is stored, then a large container must be used*, in a context in which participants were to verify whether this rule was true of cards specifying the size of object/container combinations. Almor and Sloman hypothesize that participants know, based on previous experience, that large objects must typically be stored in large containers, while small objects may be stored in either large or small containers. This background knowledge, together with the use of *must* in the rule's consequent, makes salient the sufficiency and nonnecessity of the antecedent. For this item, about 50% of participants made correct choices (large object, small container), approximately the same percentage as for a similarly constructed permission rule. The use of *must* to emphasize strong (modal) sufficiency may be on a par with the implicit *ought* (or *obligatory*) of social regulations. A potential question about these experiments is whether to attribute the result to enhanced reasoning (based on clarification of the conditional relation) or simply to participants reading off the answers from their background knowledge. Once background knowledge clarifies the fact that there should be no instances in which the antecedent is true and the consequent false (e.g., that large objects won't fit in small containers), then participants may have an easy time spotting the correct answer (see Sperber et al., 1995; Sperber & Girotto, 2002). In this respect, however, the new studies may be in no worse position than some of the original experiments supporting social regulations.

Indicative conditional sentences, such as the original vowel-even rule, seem to express sufficiency in at least the weak (material) sense that the consequent is not false when the antecedent is true. It's a flat contradiction to claim both (a) if there is a vowel on one side of this sheet of paper, there is an even number on the other, and (b) there is a vowel on one side and no even number on the other. So why do participants appear to need help in recognizing the sufficiency of the selection-task rule? Sperber et al. (1995) make the case that because the standard rule is an implicit generalization (All vowel cards have even numbers), it leads participants to infer that cards must exist that have a vowel on one side and an even number on the other. This is the implicature in (5a) that we discussed in connection with syllogisms. This implicature causes participants to check the vowel card (to see if it has an even number) and the even card (to see if it has a vowel), producing "incorrect" responses. (These are incorrect according to the standard interpretation, but if the rule did in fact entail the existence of cards with both a vowel and an even number, then demonstrating that no such cards exist would correctly disconfirm the rule.) Sperber et al. (1995) show that rigging the context of the selection problem to deemphasize these antecedent-and-consequent instances (and to emphasize the contradictory nature of antecedent-and-no-consequent cases) greatly increases correct performance on the task. No social regulations are necessary for improved performance.

6.4.1.3 Are Social Regulations Algorithms?

In order for content manipulations to affect the selection task, participants must have specific information about the concepts that frame the task. Phrasing the problem in terms of preconditions or cheating won't help unless participants understand these concepts. The issue for social-regulation theories isn't, however, whether people have this knowledge—obviously, they do. The question is whether this knowledge is associated with special purpose reasoning procedures: algorithms for dealing with social regulations. Merely showing that people can make use of domain specific knowledge to recognize violations or cheating does not establish the existence of these algorithms (much less their credentials as innate parts of cognitive architecture, as is claimed by some social-regulation theorists). You can also detect darning needles based on your knowledge of this concept, but few theorists suppose you have innate darning-needle detectors. The issue here is similar to the one we encountered in dealing with claims for perceptual causality in Chapter 3. (For critical assessments of the evolutionary claims of Cosmides and colleagues from the standpoint of biology and philosophy, see Buller, 2005, Lloyd, 1999, and Richardson, 1996.)

What's required, then, to show that the content-based information constitutes an algorithm or reasoning procedure? The social-regulation idea seems to have been that because social regulations dominate purely logical operations in the selection task, they must be at least as efficient and algorithmic. This argument is at best indirect, since importance, salience, and other factors could equally well explain why social regulations affect responses; algorithms are only one potential reason why participants' responses depend on the problem's framing. The argument looks even less persuasive in the current landscape, since we now have evidence that linguistic-pragmatic factors divert responses from those based solely on the conditional form of the rule. More direct evidence for algorithms probably requires process-oriented experiments. But, at present, there seem to be no direct measures of processing efficiency for social regulations and no comparisons of efficiency to inferences based on other types of content.

Social-regulations theorists could take the view that the relevant rules are content-specific but not procedural. For example, they could take the precondition–action rules in (18) to be mental representations of conditional sentences without any algorithmic properties of their own. Then to apply these conditionals in specific cases, people would presumably use general-purpose procedures that would recognize that an action is (or is not) to be taken or that a precondition is (or is not) satisfied and then instantiate the corresponding representation of the conditional's consequent. Because these conditionals are relatively specific in their content, the general-purpose mechanism might grant them precedence over other applicable, but more abstract, conditionals. This way of viewing social-regulation theories, however, turns them into unitary rather than partitioning theories (in our terminology), since it gives up the possibility that social regulations are distinct inference procedures, and I doubt that proponents of these theories would be willing to bite this particular bullet. As just noted, a domain-general procedure would have to recognize that (for example) an action needs to be taken, recognize that long-term memory contains the rule "If the action is to be taken, then the precondition must be satisfied," and then conclude that the precondition must be satisfied. But this procedure is itself an example of an abstract inference rule (modus ponens), which social regulations are supposed to eclipse (see the quotation from Cosmides, 1989, in the next section).

6.4.1.3 Summary of Domain Specific Theories

Cognitively special domains of knowledge could exist, even if reasoning mechanisms are constant from one domain to the next. Domains could consist of proprietary information, they could be encapsulated (i.e., unaffected by information from other domains), they could be innate and universal, and they could be productive (i.e., capable of producing infinitely many new pieces of information) without incorporating reasoning mechanisms that differ from those of their fellow domains. The domain-specific theories we are considering here, however, are partitioning theories of reasoning, and as such, they *are* committed to distinctive reasoning mechanisms. Social-regulation theories assume that people possess reasoning procedures that are specialized for dealing with permission and obligation or with social contracts, and they assume that these procedures *don't* carry over to mechanics, biology, and other domains.

People may have developed distinctive procedures for dealing with special domain-specific concepts, but current evidence for such procedures is thin. Evidence for social-regulation theory comes almost exclusively from the selection task. Moreover, recent approaches suggest alternative explanations for the benefits that permissions or contracts confer in that paradigm. Perhaps, approaches based on mental modal logic (Osherson, 1976) might be more successful, but investigators haven't explored them in enough detail to warrant strong empirical conclusions.

Moreover, social-regulation theory has an additional burden of proof. These theories claim not only that there are domain-specific mechanisms, but also no domain-general ones exist (or that domain-general principles play only a backup role in everyday reasoning). For example, according to Cosmides (1989), social-regulation theories "agree that people lack a 'mental logic' . . . . In other words, they agree that the innate architecture of the human mind does not include a set of algorithms that instantiate the rules of inference of the propositional calculus" (pp. 234–235).[12] Again, evidence is supposed to come from the selection task—from participants' poor performance in the task's standard versions. As we've just noted, however, Sperber et al. (1995) suggest the participants' choices in the standard task may be due to domain general entailments or implicatures that eclipse the presumed correct answers. In addition, the confines of the selection task are simply too narrow for a sensible assessment of domain-general procedures.[13]

There are many simple entailments that give participants little difficulty (see, e.g., Braine, Reiser, & Rumain, 1984; Braine et al., 1995; Rips, 1994; E. E. Smith, Langston, & Nisbett, 1992). Nearly all participants, for example, recognize as deductively correct the argument from a premise of the form *p AND q* to the conclusion *p*, where *p* and *q* are statements with arbitrary content (e.g., *There's an X and there's a Y on the blackboard; therefore, there's an X on the blackboard*). To explain such findings on the basis of domain-specific mechanisms would require duplicating the procedure for each domain.

This point is connected to a more general one. Domain-specific theories have documented reasoning procedures within a very small number of domains. This is perfectly reasonable, especially if the total number of cognitive domains is small. But by definition, such theories can't claim that the procedures from one domain will generalize to others. To assure us that we can make scientific progress by studying one domain at a time, these theories need to provide evidence—not just that the total number of domains is finite—but that the domains exhaustively categorize types of reasoning. At present, no convincing evidence exists to back this hypothesis.

6.4.2 *Induction/Deduction Theories*

This chapter began by pointing out the difference between entailments and statistical or causal implications. Entailments logically guarantee the truth of the supported statement (granted the truth of the supporting ones), and they form the subject matter of deductive logic. Statistical and causal implications can increase the likelihood that the supported statement is true (granted the truth of the supporting statements), and these implications form the subject matter of the study of induction. This line of thinking suggests a partitioning theory in which the main split is between deductive reasoning and inductive reasoning.

340 Lines of Thought

One reason for adopting such a theory is that attempts to reduce one form of argument evaluation to the other have been unsuccessful for what look to be principled reasons (Osherson et al., 1986; Rips, 2001b, 2001c). For example, one possibility for reduction is to treat what seem to be inductive arguments as a type of deductive argument in which some of the background premises have been suppressed—an *enthymeme,* as these incomplete arguments are usually called. Supply the missing background, the idea goes, and what you get is a deductive argument that you can evaluate like any other. For example, the inductively strong argument from (3b) to (3c), which we considered earlier, can be turned into a deductively correct one by adding a second premise. Argument (19a) is the original enthymematic form, and (19b) the revised version:

> (19)   a. Seal-blubber sherbet revolted Miriam.
>   --
>   Miriam didn't want seconds on seal-blubber sherbet.
>
>   b. Seal-blubber sherbet revolted Miriam.
>   If something revolts Miriam, she doesn't want seconds.
>   --
>   Miriam didn't want seconds on seal-blubber sherbet.

The trouble, as Osherson et al. (1986) show, is that without some restrictions on the missing premises, any argument—even an obviously worthless one—can be turned into a deductively valid argument, and no clear restrictions on importing premises correctly distinguish the worthless from the well-founded. For example, we could reasonably require that the missing premise be a believable one, since this would rule out an inference from *Grass is green* to *Whales are birds* based on the "missing premise" *If grass is green then whales are birds*. But as Osherson et al. point out, a missing premise of the form "If premises then conclusion" will be believable only if the inference from the premises to the conclusion is inductively strong. Hence, the believability requirement on missing premises merely restates the problem rather than solving it. The question of which conditionals are believable is no clearer than the question of which inductive inferences are strong.

The opposite strategy of trying to explain deductive correctness as just an extreme case of inductive strength is equally unpromising in view of counterexamples, such as the argument about π in (15) above (see Rips, 2001c). For these reasons, we should consider the possibility that inductive reasoning and deductive reasoning are two distinct psychological processes.

6.4.2.1 Evidence in Favor of a Dual Theory

Some recent support for this view comes from brain imaging data (Goel, Gold, Kapur, & Houle, 1997; Osherson et al., 1998; L. M. Parsons & Osherson, 2001). These studies ask participants during the imaging sessions to evaluate a set of arguments. On some trials, the participants must decide for each argument whether the premises entail the conclusion; on others, they must decide whether the premises make the conclusion more plausible or probable. The findings from these experiments appear to agree that the inductive task activates brain regions of the prefrontal cortex that are important in knowledge representation and storage. The studies differ about the regions that support deductive reasoning, though all experiments exhibit dissociations between the two tasks.

Similar cognitive evidence for a dissociation comes from an experiment (Rips, 2001b) in which participants also judged arguments (in separate conditions) either for deductive correctness or inductive support and in which the arguments varied orthogonally in terms of their logical validity and their causal coherence. For example, one set of arguments appears in (20). Here arguments (20a) and (20b) are deductively correct, whereas arguments (20c) and (20d) are not. However, (20a) and (20c) describe a course of events that is causally plausible, while the events in (20b) and (20d) are causally unlikely.

(20)   a. If car X10 runs into a brick wall, it will stop.
          Car X10 runs into a brick wall.
          _____
          Car X10 will stop.

        b. If car X10 runs into a brick wall, it will speed up.
           Car X10 runs into a brick wall.
           _____
           Car X10 will speed up.

        c. Car X10 runs into a brick wall.
           _____
           Car X10 will stop.

d. Car X10 runs into a brick wall.

Car X10 will speed up.

Suppose that just one system of reasoning exists that evaluates these arguments on a single continuum of merit (e.g., suppose that a probabilistic system determines the goodness of the arguments using Pr(Conclusion | Premises)). This system could adopt different thresholds in judging deductive correctness and inductive support, using a higher criterion for the former than the latter. But because the arguments fall along the system's single evaluative continuum, judgments of deductive correctness and judgments of inductive support should preserve the same relative ordering among the arguments. For example, if Argument (20c) is judged to have more inductive support than (20b), then (20c) should also be more likely to be judged deductively correct than (20b). By contrast, if two or more systems govern reasoning, as the induction/deduction theory contends, then people might switch the order of the arguments in the two tasks. For example, they may judge Argument (20b) more likely to be deductively correct than (20c) but judge (20c) to have more inductive support than (20b).

The results of this study appear in Figure 6.5 and exhibit the interaction that the induction/deduction theory predicts: When their task was to decide whether the conclusion logically followed, participants' responses depended largely on the validity of the arguments (e.g., arguments (20a)–(20b) received many more positive responses than (20c)–(20d)). However, when the task was to decide if the premises made the conclusion stronger, responses reflected both validity and causal consistency (e.g., arguments (20a)–(20c) received more positive responses than (20d)). (Validity should influence inductive judgments, because validity means that the conclusion receives maximum support when the premises are true; see Section 6.3.1.3.)

This evidence does not show that induction and deduction aren't sometimes mutually relevant or useful. Especially when you can interpret the premises and conclusion of an argument in more than one way, you may need to use induction to reason to an interpretation and then to use deduction to check for entailments among the interpreted statements (see Stenning & van Lambalgen, 2008, for a proposal along these lines). This will be especially true if interpretation involves deeper

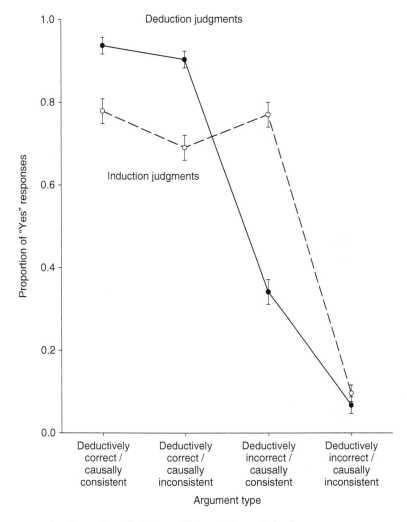

FIGURE 6.5 Proportion of trials on which participants judged arguments deductively correct (solid line) or inductively strong (dotted line). Each point represents 240 observations. Error bars show ±1 standard deviation of the proportion.

"representations about" the content that I discussed in Chapter 5. Complex problems could involve cyclical use of these processes, and if so, it might be hard to untangle their relative contributions. The claim of induction/deduction theories, however, is that these types of reasoning are distinct processes, not that they can't talk to each other. The difference in processes should be observable in situations where sentence interpretation is unproblematic, as it probably is in (20). (For related dissociations, see Heit & Rotello, 2010; Rotello & Heit, 2009.)

6.4.2.2 The Deduction Component

These results suggest a deduction component that is sensitive to the logical and mathematical aspects of an argument and a separate induction component that depends on knowledge of statistical, causal, and other aspects of scientific and everyday evidence. To handle the deduction component, we could use mental proof rules. (See Braine & O'Brien, 1998, and Rips, 1994, for proposals along these lines.) In the case of (20), for example, we might consider the rule in (21), a version of the *modus ponens* rule of classical logic:

(21)   IF P(n) THEN Q(n), P(n) ⊢ Q(n).

In this rule, P and Q stand for predicates, and n for a name. The turnstile "⊢" indicates that the sentence on the right is logically derivable from the sentences on the left. Applied to (20a), for example, $P(n)$ will be Runs_into_a_brick_wall(X10), and $Q(n)$ will be Stop(X10). The rule permits us to deduce the sentence on the right side of the turnstile, provided we have the two sentences on the left. The two premises of (20a) correspond to the two left-hand components of (21), and this rule therefore licenses the conclusion of (20a). The same rule also applies to (20b), with $Q(n)$ this time representing Speed-up(X10).

Inference rules of a similar sort can deal with more complex arguments. For example, the three rules in (22) allow us to show the deductive correctness of some of the syllogisms we considered earlier:

(22)   a. IF P(x) THEN Q(x), P(a) ⊢ Q(a).
        b. P(a) AND Q(a) ⊢ P(a).
        c. P(a), Q(a) ⊢ P(a) AND Q(a).

Here, P and Q stand for predicates, as before, x is a universal variable (everything), and a an indefinite variable (something). Thus, (22a) is a generalized version of (21), stating that if anything that has P also has Q and something has P, then that something has Q. Similarly, (22b) states that if something has both P and Q, then it has P, and (22c) that if something has P and it also has Q, then it has both P and Q.

To use the rules in (22) to show that syllogism (11) is correct, we can express the syllogism as shown in (23):

(23)   IF Volleyball_league_member(x) THEN Bridge_club_
member(x).
(I.e., All Volleyball League members are Bridge Club members.)
Chess_team_member(a) AND Volleyball_league_member(a).
(I.e., Some Chess Team member is a Volleyball League member.)

Chess_team_member(b) AND Bridge_club_member(b).
(I.e., Some Chess Team member is a Bridge Club member.)

The conclusion of this syllogism asserts that someone is both a Chess Team member and a Bridge Club member; so the conclusion follows if we can show that such an individual must exist. According to (22c), we can prove this if we can show of such an individual that he or she is a Chess Team member and (separately) a Bridge Club member. Figure 6.6a illustrates the beginning of such a proof. The two premises appear at the top of the figure. The conclusion appears at the bottom with a question mark to indicate that we seek to show it to be true. The two parts of the conclusion, connected to it by arrows, also appear with question marks, since rule (22c) requires that we prove each of these parts separately. The first part, *Chess_team_member(b)?*, asks whether someone is a member of the Chess Team, and it is easy to see there is. We know from the second premise (at the left of the figure) that someone (individual a) is both a member of the Chess Team and the Volleyball League; so by rule (22b), a is a Chess Team member. Figure 6.6b indicates this step, splitting apart the second premise via rule (22b) and identifying the Chess Team member of the conclusion with that of the second premise.

To complete the proof, we need to show that this same Chess Team member a is also in the Bridge Club.[14] We don't have any direct information

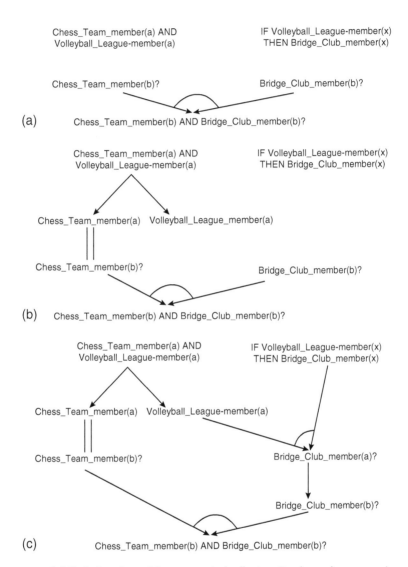

Chess_Team_member(a) AND
Volleyball_League-member(a)

IF Volleyball_League-member(x)
THEN Bridge_Club_member(x)

Chess_Team_member(b)?   Bridge_Club_member(b)?

(a)   Chess_Team_member(b) AND Bridge_Club_member(b)?

Chess_Team_member(a) AND
Volleyball_League-member(a)

IF Volleyball_League-member(x)
THEN Bridge_Club_member(x)

Chess_Team_member(a)   Volleyball_League_member(a)

Chess_Team_member(b)?   Bridge_Club_member(b)?

(b)   Chess_Team_member(b) AND Bridge_Club_member(b)?

Chess_Team_member(a) AND
Volleyball_League-member(a)

IF Volleyball_League-member(x)
THEN Bridge_Club_member(x)

Chess_Team_member(a)   Volleyball_League-member(a)

Chess_Team_member(b)?   Bridge_Club_member(a)?

Bridge_Club_member(b)?

(c)   Chess_Team_member(b) AND Bridge_Club_member(b)?

FIGURE 6.6 Rule-based proof for a categorical syllogism. Panels a–c show successive stages of the proof of syllogism (11), based on the rules in (22).

about *a*'s Bridge Club membership, but we do know from the first premise that all Volleyball League members are also in the Bridge Club. Since person *a* is in the Volleyball League (by premise 2), we can deduce that *a* is in the Bridge Club by rule (22a). This last step, shown in Figure 6.6c, makes sense of the substitution strategy that we discussed earlier (see the section *Questions about syllogism models*).

A very similar proof exists for syllogism (6) above; however, that proof depends on the presence of the implicature in (5a)—in this case from *All Volleyball League members are Chess Team members* to *Some Volleyball League members are Chess Team members*. In general, a theory based on rules like these is comparable in predictive accuracy on syllogisms to the other theories discussed in the first part of this chapter. In addition, it can handle arguments that contain any mix of connectives (IF, AND, OR, and NOT) and quantifiers (ALL and SOME). Thus, it approaches classical predicate logic in its scope, unlike the rational-probabilistic and diagrammatic theories (see Rips, 1994, for the details of this theory, including an explicit model for syllogisms). This isn't to say, however, that human deduction is an implemented version of classical logic. Although we can expect some overlap between inferences that are valid in classical logic and those that people find intuitively acceptable, plenty of evidence suggests differences, especially in the case of conditional statements (see Evans & Over, 2004, for a review of the psychological evidence, and Bennett, 2003, for a review of philosophical theories of conditionals). Logicians have also constructed many rival varieties of logic, some of which may provide better fits to human inference than does classical logic.

Finding candidate theories for the deduction half of a dual induction/deduction system is not a difficult task. The much stickier issue is to specify the inductive component. We could try to build such a component around probability theory, but we then run into the computational feasibility issues I mentioned earlier. We could also try to model the induction component on philosophical theories of belief-change, but many of these (e.g., Gärdenfors, 1988; I. Levi, 1996) rely on idealizations (e.g., possible worlds or belief states that are closed under entailment) that psychologists are unlikely to swallow as parts of a plausible cognitive theory.

6.4.2.3 Summary of Induction/Deduction Theory

Common sense, as well as neurological and cognitive evidence, suggests that inductive and deductive reasoning have some incompatible features. Inductive reasoning is knowledge intensive, relying on information about how things work, whereas deductive reasoning depends on formal relations that abstract over content. You could potentially explain these forms of reasoning as positions along a continuum, with inductive reasoning more closely tied to empirical matters and deductive reasoning less closely tied. But dissociations, such as those associated with the arguments in (20), create difficulties for a continuity theory of this sort, at least for one in which arguments are associated with a single value along a dimension of argument "strength." These theories can't predict reversals, such as those in Figure 6.5, in which people judge argument A as having more inductive warrant than argument B, but also view B as deductively valid and A as invalid. Such evidence suggests that unitary theories can't be right and that important distinctions exist among our reasoning abilities.

I illustrated the deductive component of this type of partitioning theory using mental rules, such as those in (22), but other theories of deduction could serve this function. For example, you could take mental models as the basis of the deduction component of an induction/deduction theory. To do this, however, would require rethinking the claim that mental models can handle deduction and probabilistic reasoning in a uniform way. Mental rules, however, are consistent with an abrupt separation between induction and deduction. Because they depend on the form of the sentences to which they apply, they work well with entailments but not with inductive inferences.

In the view of some researchers, mental rules have the liability of a doubtful psychological pedigree. Logic rules are all very well for logicians in their attempts to formalize mathematics, these researchers claim, but positing them as part of a cognitive account of inference is ad hoc. If these rules are parts of our mental life, why did it take the likes of Aristotle, Frege, and Russell to formulate them? One answer is that some logic rules—in particular, those governing instantiation and generalization—may be a fundamental part of our cognitive abilities (Rips, 1994, and Chapter 2 of this book). All symbolic cognitive systems presuppose the ability to bind variables to specific instances, and therefore provide direct motivation for such rules. Other rules may arise as special cases, adaptations, or elaborations of these. Of course, tacitly using these rules is one thing and formalizing them is another. Consciously describing and clarifying rule systems is a difficult matter. The fact that it takes skilled mathematicians to do this isn't any more surprising than the fact that it takes skilled linguists to formalize the syntactic rules that even three-year olds use.

6.4.3 Two-System Theories

We've seen that one difficulty with domain-specific theories (as partitioning theories of reasoning) is lack of evidence that reasoning *processes* differ from domain to domain. Although people's performance may shift with domain, the shift may be due to knowledge distinctive to the domain rather than to distinctive forms of reasoning. This problem is endemic because content is what defines a cognitive domain, not process. This suggests that if you want to partition reasoning abilities, you should start with the abilities, rather than with the content on which they operate. We've just considered one possibility along the lines—that types of reasoning divide into deductive and inductive varieties—but many other divisions are possible. Maybe reasoning sometimes takes place by symbol manipulation (via inference rules such as those in (21) or (22) or via diagrams such as those in Figure 6.4), while at other times reasoning takes place by brute association (via connectionist mechanisms). Alternatively, reasoning may sometimes occur through explicit, methodical, controlled means and sometimes through implicit, automatic ones. Or, perhaps, reasoning can take place either in an analytic mode or in a holistic, dialectical one (which Peng & Nisbett, 1999, assert to be characteristic of Western and Eastern reasoners, respectively). These possibilities differ in detail, and other variations on this theme exist as well (see Stanovich, 1999, Table 5.1, for a catalog of these proposals), but they nevertheless seem to be based on a common intuition (see Rips, 1990). Let's call them *two-system theories* for convenience.

Although the intuition behind two-system theories is compelling, evidence for them isn't easy to obtain. How can we tell whether we're dealing with two qualitatively distinct modes of reasoning rather than one type of reasoning operating at two (quantitatively different) levels of efficiency? If participants sometimes get the correct answers in evaluating syllogisms and sometimes get the wrong answers, that's surely not compelling evidence that they are using a rule-based (analytic, methodical, ...) process in the first case and an associative (intuitive, heuristic, ...) process in the second. Instead, level of performance could be due to level of attention, interest, working-memory resources, and probably many other factors. Participants who've been shanghaied from Psychology 100 to fulfill a course requirement don't always train their full mental powers on the tasks experimenters set for them.

One source of evidence for two systems might be stable individual differences. Perhaps some people are good system 1 reasoners and poor system 2 reasoners, whereas other people have the opposite pattern of abilities. In fact, performance on some of the tasks we have looked at correlates with some of the others and with general ability measures such as SAT scores. Table 6.1 (from Stanovich & West, 1998) shows relatively small but significant correlations among scores on the selection task (with arbitrary content), syllogisms (in which the truth of the conclusion is misleading), a task in which participants evaluated the strength of informal arguments, and a composite score of "cognitive ability" based on the SAT, Ravens Progressive Matrices, and the Nelson-Denny reading comprehension test. (You'll be pleased to learn that not every item in the psychologists' bag of tricks correlates with every other. For example, Stanovich & West, 1998, found no significant correlations between SAT scores or syllogism scores and accuracy on certain problems involving probabilities. This helps eliminate the possibility that

TABLE 6.1.   Correlations Among Reasoning Tests and Tests of Cognitive Abilities (from Stanovich & West, 1998, Experiment 1).

Tasks	Cognitive abilities	Syllogisms	Selection task	Argument evaluation
1 Cognitive abilities	--			
2 Syllogisms	.496	--		
3 Selection task	.328	.363	--	
4 Argument evaluation	.334	.340	.310	--

"Cognitive abilities" is a composite score based on SATs, Nelson-Denny reading comprehension, and Ravens Progressive Matrices. All correlations are significant at $p < .0001$ ($n = 197$).

general background factors, such as the participants' health, upbringing, or socioeconomic status, are responsible for the correlations.)

To explain these correlations, Stanovich (1999) contends that correct solutions on all the tasks in Table 6.1 depend on a process that abstracts over the problem's context and content. Correct evaluation of a syllogism, for example, involves thinking about the form of the argument and dismissing the misleading cues that the conclusion's content might supply. This abstraction or "decontextualizing" ability is pitted against a context-bound reasoning system that is attuned to concrete features of the problem, to conversational implicatures, such as (5), and to background knowledge about the problem's content. The context-bound/decontextualized distinction is therefore closely allied to the rule-based/association-based distinction we have just discussed. According to Stanovich, the cognitive tasks in Table 6.1 are representative of those in which context-bound reasoning produces mistakes, and he terms the tendency to depend too much on the context-bound system the "fundamental computational bias." People who do well on SATs, reading comprehension tests, and nonverbal intelligence tests, however, are those who are skilled at decontextualizing and at working at an abstract level. Thus, the two-systems view predicts the pattern of positive correlations displayed in the table.

How strong is the correlational evidence in Table 6.1 for two systems? An obvious alternative to two systems is one system: Maybe we have just one reasoning system—a system that runs better in some people than in others. High-octane reasoners outperform others on general cognitive ability tests, such as the SAT, and, unsurprisingly, also do better at evaluating arguments, solving the selection task, and so on. This suffices to explain the small correlations in the table. So why do we need a second, context-bound type of reasoning? Of course, we must explain why people make the mistakes they do within particular experiments, since the pattern of errors is sometimes systematic. But is it necessary to suppose that a single context-bound reasoning ability causes the errors in all these tasks? Suppose instead that the one-system view is correct. Then we might expect mistakes on different tasks to be due to poor performance of the single system, coupled with a variety of error tendencies—associative interference in some cases, biased guessing in others, special-purpose heuristics in still others, and many more. (Indeed, some two-system theorists acknowledge this variety; see Evans, 2003.) In order to defend the two-system view from this one-system alternative, we first need justification for considering error tendencies as instances of *reasoning*. (E.g., if associative interference misleads participants, is this a case of their reasoning to a wrong answer?) And, second, we need justification for bundling error tendencies together as a single system (Bedford, 1997; Keren & Schul, 2009).

A look at individual differences is valuable in highlighting the demands of reasoning tasks. Stanovich and colleagues' research, in particular, has been helpful in showing that the experimenter-approved "correct" answers in many tasks are nonarbitrary: Participants who get the designated answer on the selection task also tend to get the designated answer on syllogism tests, among others, and they also score higher on tests of cognitive ability like the SAT (Stanovich, 1999). Individual differences can also help identify common components of tasks, in line with traditional psychometric research. To obtain evidence for two systems of reasoning on this basis, however, we need not just a single pattern of high versus low scorers, but two orthogonal patterns—good and bad contextual reasoners, as well as good and bad decontextual reasoners. The assumption in the literature is that everyone is a good contextual reasoner, since contextual reasoning is primitive, perhaps for evolutionary reasons. Maybe so. But if this is the case, then evidence based on individual differences will be of no help in finding out about contextual reasoning, since there are no individual differences to be had.

6.5 Concluding Comments

One idea that's common to unitary and partitioning theories is that participants don't always classify reasoning tasks in the way experimenters do. An experimenter may view a task as calling for straightforward deductive-mathematical reasoning, whereas a participant may view it as an occasion for causal or probabilistic reasoning. If so, then the participant's answer will probably differ from the answer that the experimenter deems correct. Unitary and partitioning theories disagree, however, in how to diagnose this situation. For a unitary theorist, the experimenter is making unreasonable demands when she tries to get the participant to perform according to a standard that doesn't fall within the unitary purview. If all human reasoning is probabilistic, for example, then asking the poor participant to determine whether the conclusion of a syllogism logically follows is like asking him or her to balance upside-down on one pinky. People are just not built that way, and the result is likely to be slapstick. Only rigorous instruction and plenty of practice will allow people to perform skilled acrobatics, and the same is true of skilled acts of deduction, according to this view. Likewise, if you think that all human reasoning is naturally deductive, then certain sorts of probabilistic problems (e.g., "nonextensional" ones) will be out for a participant who hasn't the benefit of formal training in probability theory. Such a participant will have to resort to heuristics and other second-class methods, taking some mental pratfalls along the way.

Partitioning theorists have the option of viewing the participant's difficulties as confusions rather than incapacities. Ordinary folk might have at least a rudimentary capacity for different sorts of reasoning, but they may not always recognize which sort is appropriate in a specific experiment. Which confusions are possible depend on what sort of partitioner you are. Two-system theorists tend to believe that surface features of a reasoning task trigger automatic (or—take your pick—contextual, holistic, associationist, or implicit) processes when what the experimenter requires is controlled (decontextualized, analytic, rule-based, explicit) processes. The two-system view is similar to the unitary views in that both explain nominal errors as due to psychological mechanisms that don't correspond to logic or probability theory. However, two-system theorists tend to view the automatic system as a legitimate form of reasoning with its own advantages—not just a makeshift. For example, some proponents claim that the automatic system is one that evolution has built for optimal decision-making in everyday social settings. It is more robust, more flexible, more tolerant of contradiction, more attuned to the perceptual and social environment, and so on. What we don't have is any idea of how it works.

Partitioning theorists of the domain-specific variety take an even more sanguine view of these context-bound processes. In fact, the context-bound processes are what they partition according to the sphere of information in which they reside. One system of reasoning might be allotted to dealing with causation, another for regulations, maybe another for measurement, and so on. Aside from these goal-bound domains, however, little reasoning may be in evidence (unless, of course, specific schooling has dunned an individual into using techniques such as logic and probability theory). Theorists of this stripe therefore have to explain away evidence for domain-general inferences or, perhaps, explain them as the coevolution of the same principles in several domains.

The evidence we've reviewed seems to me to suggest that partitioning theories have an advantage simply by virtue of their pluralism. Attempts to build general theories of reasoning solely on a probabilistic basis or solely on a deductive basis end up having to make room for heuristics (or similar mechanisms) to take up the slack. No strong reason exists for excluding deductive reasoning as a genuine part of human thinking and ditto for inductive reasoning. In each case, people are able to recognize as correct simple inferences that are difficult to explain through other mechanisms. For the same reason, we should view skeptically claims by some domain-specific theorists that the only inferences people can perform are ones that are tightly bound to particular content areas. This isn't to deny inference procedures that are specialized for particular domains or associative processes that affect reasoning performance.

The induction/deduction theory is consistent with the existence of empirical dissociations (Section 6.4.2) and with the theoretical distinction between probability and deductive validity. It has a deduction component that's reasonably well specified, with some supporting empirical evidence. Its links with instantiation and generalization give it a clear motivation within a general cognitive framework. The main difficulty with the theory is the one it shares with two-system views: The second, inductive component is simply stipulated. Making sense of inductive reasoning may be among cognitive science's most difficult problems. The puzzle is just where you'd predict it to be, but unfortunately, that doesn't make it any easier.

NOTES

This chapter draws heavily on Rips (2001b, 2001c, 2002). Thanks to Douglas Medin, Mike Oaksford, Dan Osherson, and Keith Stenning for very helpful remarks on an earlier version of the chapter.

1. *Inference* and *reasoning* are interchangeable terms in this chapter.

2. One omission from the chapter is a discussion of research on analogical reasoning. Investigators in this area have adopted methods and pursued issues that diverge from the emphasis on belief-strengthening relations between statements. This may be a welcome change, but the shift makes it difficult to integrate analogical theories with other approaches. (For perspectives on analogical reasoning, see, for example, Gentner & Markman, 1997, and Holyoak & Thagard, 1995.)

3. This is not intended as a criticism of Grice's theory. Grice was concerned about what sentences convey in the context of conversations and not with what people mentally infer from previously-drawn implicatures. However, these considerations point to limits on use of implicature in psychological theories of reasoning. (For a related notion of *reasonable inference* relative to a conversational context, see Stalnaker, 1975.)

4. The definition of Pr(Conclusion | Premises) might suggest that the conditional probability is less fundamental than the other probabilities represented there: Pr(Premises), Pr(Conclusion), and Pr(Premises and Conclusion). Theoretically, however, Pr(Premises and Conclusion) and Pr(Conclusion | Premises) are very much on a par. Neither of them can be reduced to Pr(Premises) and Pr(Conclusion), except in (the same) special cases, and either one can be defined in terms of the other.

5. One reaction that sometimes occurs in discussions of this material is puzzlement about why anyone would suppose that people's assessment of confidence or likelihood should conform to a seemingly artificial system, such as formal probability theory. (Much the same reaction comes up for the relation between people's deductive inferences and formal logic.) From this point of view, the departures from probability theory that are evident in Kahneman and Tversky's work seem completely unsurprising. Perhaps one way to restore the importance of these findings is to note that standard probability theory rests on assumptions that are extremely simple. For example, suppose we have a set of sentences such that if S and T are sentences in the set, then so is: *It is not the case that S, It is not the case that T,* and *S or T.* Then a function on these sentences, Pr, obeys classical probability theory provided only that it meets three conditions:

(a) $Pr(S) \geq 0$ for all sentences S;
(b) if S is a tautology (e.g., *either T or not T*), then $Pr(S) = 1$; and
(c) if it is impossible for S and T to be simultaneously true, then $Pr(S \text{ or } T) = Pr(S) + Pr(T)$.

In other words, Pr assigns to each sentence a number greater than or equal to 0, assigns 1 to sentences that are necessarily true, and assigns to disjunctions the sum of the probabilities of the disjuncts if the disjuncts are logically independent. Given the intuitive appeal and simplicity of these conditions, departures from probability theory in people's actual judgments may seem more intriguing.

6. Gilbert Harman suggested this example. A similar one appears in Priest (1999). See, also, Carnap's (1950) discussion of "almost L-true sentences."

7. Johnson-Laird et al. (1992) refer to the suppressed information as "false components" on an analogy to the F's in the truth table. However, it is true rather than false, for example, that Ethel is not in Rome (−R) in the possibility represented by the first mental model in Figures 6.3b and 6.3c. You might suppose that what Johnson-Laird et al. are doing is systematically eliminating symbols containing negatives (e.g., −L or −R), but this is not the case. If the premise had been, for example, *If Martha is not in Paris, then either Stella is in London or Ethel is in Rome, but not all three*, then the models in Figure 6.3b would have −P in place of P. A more accurate description of Johnson-Laird et al.'s practice is this: (a) If an atomic proposition (e.g., *Martha is in Paris*) is not directly negated in the original sentence, and this proposition has the value T in a row of the truth table that makes the original sentence true, then a corresponding token (e.g., P) appears in the mental model; (b) if an atomic proposition is directly negated (e.g., *Martha is not in Paris*) in the original sentence, and the *unnegated* proposition has the value F in a row of the truth table that makes the original sentence true, then a corresponding *negated* token (e.g., −P) appears in the mental model. The effect of this policy is to include tokens for atomic propositions or their negations that the original sentence mentions explicitly. It is interesting to speculate how much of the predictive power of the theory is based solely on representing information contained in the surface structure of the sentences of the argument and suppressing the rest. Could reasoning mistakes be due to people ignoring propositions that the surface structure fails to highlight?

8. In a related theory, Polk and Newell (1995) proposed that people translate the premises of syllogisms into representations similar to those of Figure 6.4 and read off conclusions from them; however, the diagrams take no active part in the reasoning process. In particular, people never revise composite models in order to test conclusions. Instead, if the initial composite model fails to support a categorical conclusion, people try reencoding one or more of the premises in an alternative way. This process may eventually lead to a conclusion, or if not, to a "no conclusion follows" response. Polk and Newell contend that all reasoning is a matter of encoding, reencoding, or decoding: "The claim is simply that the most important cognitive processes in deduction are the same ones that are used in language comprehension and generation" (Polk & Newell, 1995, p. 235). Most theories of reasoning, including Bucciarelli and Johnson-Laird's, do some of their inferential work in transforming natural language into an underlying representation. But Polk and Newell (1995) are clearly at the extreme of this continuum in banishing processes that transform one underlying representation into another. Some of the reencoding processes they envision, though, include representing *Some A are B* as if it were *Some B are A* and representing *No A are B* as *No B are A*. People probably don't perform such transformations in immediately comprehending such sentences, and the model doesn't undertake them unless it

reaches an impasse. It seems fair to say that Polk and Newell's theory does have processes that are dedicated to reasoning, but processes that are restricted to those running between natural language and diagrams. The theory appears to capture many of the regularities found in experiments in which participants must produce conclusions to syllogistic premises. Polk and Newell also provide an account of individual differences in these experiments, which most other theories have not attempted.

9. If participants are given a set of cut out shapes that represent individuals—for example, members of the Chess Team—and are told to use them to construct a picture of the premises, then they do so (Bucciarelli & Johnson-Laird, 1999, Experiments 3 & 4).

10. This gap is obscured in presentations of mental-model theory because of the way the authors frame their stimulus items. For example, Evans et al. (1999, p. 1500) asked their participants to make decisions like the following one:

GIVEN THAT
 Some T are P
 No P are G
IS IT NECESSARY THAT

	YES	NO
All T are G	☐	☐
Some T are G	☐	☐
No T are G	☐	☐
Some T are not G	☐	☐

The last of these potential conclusions follows validly from the premises, but it is not necessarily true (true in all possible worlds or situations), even when the premises are true. To see this, suppose that T stands for teachers, P for plutocrats, and G for garbage collectors. Although *Some teachers are not garbage collectors* follows from the above syllogism, this is certainly not a necessary truth. Who knows? In some possible Marxist worlds, all teachers might be required to double as garbage collectors. Moreover, even if some teachers are plutocrats and no plutocrats are garbage collectors (as might be), it still wouldn't be true in all possible worlds that some teachers are not garbage collectors. What the deductive correctness of the syllogism does show is that it is necessarily true that: If some T are P and no P are G, then some T are not G. But this is simply another way of expressing the validity of the syllogism.

11. Griggs and Cox (1982) used the conditional *If a person is drinking beer, then the person must be over* 19 *years of age,* which suggests the representation *If beer than Obligatory(over* 19), on Fodor's (2000) parsing. This means, though, that if Calvin is a 16-year-old who is drinking a bottle of beer, he would then be obligated to be over 19. However, deontic theories usually require that an obligatory action be one that it is possible for the agent to carry out, and voluntarily changing one's age is not a possible action. As Fodor also notes, "there's nothing much

that he can do about how old he is (in, alas, either direction)" (p. 103). This could be an argument that the logical form of the conditional is actually *Obligatory* (*If beer then over* 19), after all. But a better solution—one that accords both with Fodor's hypothesis and with the requirement on obligatory actions—is to assume that people interpret the conditional as *If under* 19 *then Obligatory(no beer),* which does seem to capture the intended meaning and also highlights the beer drinker and the 16-year-old. (I'm grateful to Daniel Osherson for pointing out this issue.)

12. In more recent work, however, Fiddick et al. (2000, p. 65) concede the existence of some algorithms that instantiate the rules of inference of propositional calculus—for example, modus ponens. (See (24) and (25a) for statements of this rule.)

13. The selection task is one of cognitive psychologists' favorite paradigms, and nearly every theory of reasoning has had something to say about it. For a view of the selection task from the rational-probabilistic perspective, see Oaksford and Chater (1994). For the mental models perspective, see Johnson-Laird and Byrne (1991).

14. To produce the correct inference, the deduction system must ensure that when the individual variable *b* is bound to individual *a* in determining that someone is on the Chess Team, the same individual *a* must be in the Bridge Club. Otherwise, the system could err in deciding that someone is on the Chess Team and the Bridge Club on the grounds that Fred is on the Chess Team and Mary is in the Bridge Club. Figure 6.6c illustrates this restriction in substituting the subgoal *Bridge_Club_member(a)?* for *Bridge_Club_member(b)?* on the right side of the diagram. In the system described here, this substitution is carried out by the rule for And Introduction, the counterpart of (22c). See Rips (1994) for full details.

7

Conclusions: Cognitive Structure

During the course of the book, we've looked at domains where our knowledge of how things could be or must be goes beyond our knowledge of how things are. These domains include both traditionally a priori areas, such as logic and math, and, perhaps more surprisingly, traditionally a posteriori areas, such as the causal workings of individual objects and natural kinds. In both types of domains, we've seen that our cognitive abilities rely on top-down support from structures and rules that are unlikely to come from perception or imagery, general learning (heuristics or analogy or bootstrapping or statistical abstraction), embodiment in the world or in culture, or other empirical and inductive sources of information. We haven't eliminated all possible theories along these lines, but we've seen enough to make it reasonable to seek alternatives.

Nativist views about such matters typically make psychologists break out in hives. Most psychologists recognize that something has to be innate in order for learning to be possible at all, but they prefer minimalistic assumptions about what this something might be. However, explicitly modal thinking—thinking about nonactual possibilities—makes it difficult to craft a plausible nonnativist theory because, by definition, no empirical traces of such possibilities exist. You could try relying on similarity to actual states. But aside from the usual problems of circularity in dealing with similarity (Goodman, 1970), which we noticed in Chapter 1 of this book, similarity in the context of possibilities presents special difficulties. For example, the question of whether a logical or mathematical system is possible would seem to depend on internal properties, such as logical consistency, and not on external relations, such as similarity to known systems. Since the problem of explaining modal thinking takes its extreme form in logic and mathematics, let's begin with these domains and then see whether related considerations apply to causal necessity and possibility.

7.1 Origins of Deduction and Mathematics

The elementary deduction rules that we looked at in Chapter 6—rules such as And Elimination ("P and Q" entails "P") and Modus Ponens ("If P then Q" and "P" entail "Q")—express relations that are necessarily true, true in all states of affairs and not just in those we inhabit. But if so, how do we have access to these truths, given our limited experience and limited information-processing abilities?

This issue is important in the present context because such rules seem cut off from normal means of belief acquisition. Normal acquisition of belief is inductive in nature. Evidence we gather about Hope suggests she's gone out with Fred rather than Ed, and this confirms (or is best explained by) the hypothesis that she has found a new boyfriend. Likewise, a particular spatial or temporal pattern of sunspots may suggest that one hypothesis about the origin of sunspots is correct and another incorrect. If one of the unified approaches to reasoning (described in Chapter 6) were right, then we could regard our knowledge of deductively correct arguments as due to this same type of inductive belief attainment. For example, if an argument were deductively correct whenever Pr(Conclusion | Premises) $= 1$, then perhaps we could understand knowledge of deductive correctness in terms of whatever processes are responsible for normal changes in probability.[1] But by treating deduction as unique, the deduction/induction approach, which seemed in Chapter 6 to make the best sense of people's reasoning, leaves itself stranded. We can't easily fall back on inductive belief formation to explain knowledge of deduction principles.

Of course, we do sometimes learn new deductive reasoning skills by inductive methods, for example, when we enroll in logic and math courses. We might learn techniques like truth tables or Euler diagrams, for instance, as ways of determining the validity of certain arguments, as we've seen in our discussion of diagrammatic theories in the previous chapter. But the ability to learn these techniques depends on prior knowledge of deduction principles that these methods overlay. We are able to understand why truth tables and Euler diagrams produce correct answers because we see that they connect to information that we already have about the logical behavior of concepts such as *and*, *if*, and *all*. As many theorists have pointed out, we can't explain how people acquire logical information without presupposing core logical abilities (see, e.g., Fodor, 1975).The present issue is how an induction/deduction theory accounts for this underlying logical knowledge.

This issue, being psychological, is descriptive rather than normative. In asking how we happen to know necessary truths of logic, we're not asking how we are able to justify our logical resources as correct, though this is a clearly important philosophical issue (and perhaps one to which a psychological account can contribute). Instead, we're asking how our mental logical resources came to be. So, in principle, it might be sufficient to say that logical rules, such as And Elimination and Modus Ponens, are simply innate aspects of our cognitive architecture. If the best theory of our reasoning abilities says that people make use of necessary logical principles like these and if no normal (inductive) learning mechanism could account for their acquisition, then innateness seems the only option. I think this is, in fact, the right answer, but psychologists are sometimes unhappy stopping the inquiry at this point. For example, Elman et al. (1996) complain that "calling a behavior innate does very little to explain the mechanism by which that behavior comes to be inevitable. So there is little explanatory power in the term." A search for an explanatory mechanism then leads psychologists to biological or evolutionary levels of analysis. If normal learning can't account for the presence of such logical rules, then they must be the product of the species' evolutionary history or a causal consequence of its biological make up. This is the impetus behind the social exchange approach, reviewed in Section 6.4.1. Let's call this issue the *etiology* question.

However, psychological questions about knowledge of logical rules might take another form. In looking for an explanation, we might be asking why we have just these logical principles and not others (or none at all). Why, for example, do people have the Modus Ponens rule and not some contrary rule such as Modus Shmonens (Rips, 1994): "If P then Q" and "P" entail "Not Q"? This way of framing the question is fishing for some merit that Modus Ponens has (and that Modus Shmonens doesn't) that would make it clear why we ended up with the logical principle we happen to possess. This is a question about the psychological *superiority* of certain logical principles. If we could find an answer to the superiority question, then we might be a step closer to answering the etiology question. Superiority of Modus Ponens over Modus Shmonens, for example, would provide a reason why some psychological, biological, or evolutionary mechanism might have favored the former over the latter and thus explain how it came about. Adaptationist explanations in evolutionary psychology or sociobiology use a form of superiority—namely, fitness—to explain etiology.

Etiology doesn't require superiority, however. Two rules or two systems of rules might exist that are incompatible but equivalent on any evaluative measure. Then any account of why we have one rather than the other would have to depend on factors like historical accident or side effects of other more fundamental processes.

7.1.1 Etiology Without Superiority

The most obvious form of an etiology-without-superiority explanation is convention. We certainly don't insist that the sequence of steps that constitute the tango is inherently superior to some other pattern of steps it might have contained. (There could be inferior tango steps, of course, that no one could execute or that are aesthetically unappealing, but there are certainly potential tango steps that are just as good as the usual ones.) So the question of what explains why the tango contains just this pattern is partly a historical or sociological story about its development. Along the same lines, then, you might hold that we shouldn't try to explain our logical rules by invoking some inherent merit that they have over other potential rule systems; instead, they're just a matter of convention.

As a philosophical theory of the justification of logic, however, conventionalism has run into well-known problems. Quine (1936) pointed out that logical conventions have to be abstract in order to explain how they can apply to an infinite number of distinct statements. Modus ponens, for example, applies to *all* statements that have the form *If P then Q* and *P*. But applying these abstract forms to particular cases—instantiating them—depends on using the logical principles that conventionalism is supposed to explain. If we have to invoke further rules to explain the latter ones, we're faced with an infinite regress. In a psychological context, conventionalism seems to fare no better. Logic and math rules can't be cultural conventions that we learn in the way we learn dance steps, since this would run into the problems about normal learning we've already encountered. If normal learning isn't responsible, though, in what sense could the relevant rules be conventions? Perhaps people engage in a primitive type of learning of conventions that doesn't require basic logical abilities, such as instantiation and recursion, but would such a system be capable of learning even simple logic rules?

If learning is not available to explain the availability of logic rules, then the temptation is to try a different, noncognitive level of analysis, presumably a biological one. In the case of an etiology-without-superiority thesis, the mechanism we appeal to must select logic rules in an arbitrary way or as a secondary effect of a more basic process. Since attributing logic rules to arbitrary selection is tantamount to giving up on explaining the rules (and with conventionalism set aside), we need to think about the possibility that logic is a side effect of other biologically or evolutionarily determined choices. And here it seems we have an obvious candidate for a primary process. No one denies a close connection between logic and language, especially the connection between logic rules and the linguistic meaning of logical constants, such as *if*, *and*, *not*, *some*, *all*, and so on. (For one theory of this connection, see Dummett, 1975.) Moreover, linguists have given well-known reasons for supposing that basic language mechanisms are innate. And although you might want to give a deeper account of why language is innate in order to satisfy questions like that of Elman et al. (1996), quoted earlier, nevertheless for our purposes we can piggyback on any such theory. So a possible account of where logic rules come from is that they come from the meanings of logical words in natural language, and these meanings are, in turn, determined by whatever factors are responsible for language itself. This idea parallels, in some ways, the language-based theories of numbers that we met in Chapter 2.

A proponent of the idea that logic is a consequence of language would presumably not claim that logic is a consequence of learning a natural language. Natural languages vary somewhat in the operators they include, just as logical languages can vary in their operators. But no evidence exists to suggest that speakers of different languages vary in their logical abilities. Moreover, infants may well possess the same underlying logical resources as adults, despite not knowing their native language. Instead, the more reasonable position is that what's innate is the universal basis of natural language (universal grammar), that universal grammar provides a language of thought, and that the language of thought embeds rules governing some base set of logical operators. This position leaves it partially open exactly which set of rules we have innately. For example, whether these rules include ones for *and* and *not*, or instead ones for *neither . . . nor* is an empirical question, since these two options have the same logical expressiveness. What's important is that an innate language of thought supports our fundamental logical abilities, whatever these may be.

One immediate objection to this theory of the origin of logic, however, is that it confuses innateness of grammar and innateness of word meaning. We have good reasons to suppose that universal syntactic mechanisms are innate, but the meaning of words is another, more controversial matter. Few people think the meanings of general terms like *cribbage* or *pastrami* are innate. So unless we can make the case that language necessitates the meaning of *if* but doesn't necessitate the meaning of *pastrami*, then we need to call off the project of explaining logic rules based on linguistic ones.

Arguing for logical terms as intrinsic to language, however, might not be an impossible task. Specific closed-class lexical items, including the connectives and determiners that play key logical roles, may be crucial to syntax in a way that open-class items (e.g., particular nouns, verbs, and adjectives) are not. Of course, language depends crucially on nouns and verbs, especially for semantic and pragmatic purposes. But the grammatical structure of a sentence depends more tightly on *if, and, not, all, each,* and so on, than on nouns and verbs (see, e.g., Chierchia & McConnell-Ginet, 1990, for an introduction to contemporary theories of the syntax-semantics relation). Current research in generative grammar suggests some interplay between syntax and logic, even to the extent of having deductive relations determine which syntactic configurations are possible (Fox, 2000).[2] So perhaps deduction rules provide the meaning of logical concepts, logical concepts are part of universal grammar, and universal grammar is innate for independent reasons. The details of this piggybacking story obviously need a more careful formulation. In particular, we would need to account for evidence that deductive reasoning and language may draw on separate brain regions (L. Parson & Osherson, 2001). But let's consider it a possibility on at least a temporary basis while we examine a more direct attempt to explain logical rules.

7.1.2 *Etiology via Superiority*

Do rules of logic possess a direct advantage that could explain their role in our innate mental apparatus? One obvious benefit that logic rules confer is preserving the truth of the premises of an argument. Because logic rules license only entailments, they can't take us from true premises to false conclusions. Inductive inferences are, by definition, not invariably truth-preserving. Assuming that humans find it useful to keep track of what's true, they should find it helpful to have logic rules that guarantee that the conclusion of an inference is true if the premises are. This does not mean that blindly drawing conclusions based on such rules is a good idea. Some such conclusions may be trivial, irrelevant, or may contradict more firmly held beliefs (as Harman, 1986, has argued). Nevertheless, entailments are surely useful on some occasions, for example, to simplify or to systematize our beliefs and observations (see Skyrms, 2000). So perhaps logic rules are the result of cognitive mechanisms underlying truth preservation.

Logic rules are useful, not only for making or evaluating individual inferences, but also for directing other cognitive operations. Systems of logic rules can carry out the same set of operations as standard production-system theories of cognition (e.g., J. R. Anderson, 1993; Newell, 1990), mostly due to logic rules' ability to bind variables. Computer languages like LISP and PROLOG have similar abilities. Thus, logic-based systems can provide an operating system for cognition that can implement all the usual search and comparison methods that underlie higher mental processes (see Rips, 1994 [chap. 8] and 1995a, for a sketch of such a system). This advantage seems so compelling that it's surprising that psychologists have usually ignored it. The fact that most studies of deduction have used artificial stimulus domains, such as syllogisms or selection-task variations, probably accounts for the common feeling that deductive reasoning is a peripheral skill with few ties to other mental activities. People's lackluster performance in some of these tasks may also have convinced psychologists that deduction isn't reliable enough to play a more general cognitive role. These error tendencies can yield important information about our deductive abilities, but they no more show that deduction is generally unreliable than speech errors show that language processing is unreliable. Basic inferences, such as And Introduction or

Modus Ponens, yield virtually errorless performance in contexts where no interfering factors operate (e.g., the sentences involved aren't so long that they tax working memory and the inferences don't have to be combined into lengthy derivations).

These advantages for logic rules—their ability to preserve truth and to direct other cognitive components—do not show that other forms of reasoning are second-class. Recall that the induction/deduction theory of Chapter 6 explicitly recognizes a distinct set of operations devoted to causal and probabilistic inference. (These could include social-regulation rules, which proponents usually claim to be nondeductive in nature.) This induction/deduction distinction is not undermined even if logic rules operate as executive mechanisms, as we noted at the beginning of Section 6.3. However, the advantages of logic rules as executive processes do provide a reason for their existence, a reason that could help explain why we might have developed such rules innately. These advantages do not amount to an evolutionary explanation of deduction. Such explanations inhabit a scientific limbo because we lack the historical evidence to confirm them (Lewontin, 1998). No mental fossils exist to help us sort matters out. What we do have is a way of viewing logic rules that may make them seem nonarbitrary parts of cognitive architecture.

7.1.3 Roots of Logical Powers

We've considered the possibility that people come to possess logic rules as a side effect of language and also the possibility that logic rules arose on their own merits. But these two possibilities aren't mutually exclusive. On the one hand, suppose we have certain primitive cognitive operations, such as instantiation and generalization, that have a logical character and that stand as prerequisites for nearly all forms of mental activities. Some connectionist theories, it is true, attempt to sidestep instantiation, but the result of doing so is to introduce difficulties (the "binding problem") that appear to threaten that enterprise. If we assume instantiation and generalization as fundamental, then we can view some of the quantificational parts of language (determiners such as *each* and *some* and adverbials such as *always* or *sometimes*) as reflections of these operations. On the other hand, natural language quantifiers may motivate the appearance of related logical expressions. For example, a close connection exists between *all* and *and*, and between *some* and *or*. (All x have property P if and only if x_1 has P and x_2 has P and . . . ; similarly, some x has P if and only if x_1 has P or x_2 has P or . . .) In this way, quantificational language creates the need for additional logic operators and rules that stand as special cases of more general quantificational ones.

The idea that quantifiers precede propositional connectives in the explanation of human thinking may seem backward. Quantifiers and their related apparatus (variables and constants) have wider expressive possibilities and require more complex rules, at least in standard formulations. So you might think quantifiers would be more difficult to acquire than connectives, both ontogenetically and phylogenetically. Based on the equivalence in the previous paragraph, for example, *all* and *some* seem to presuppose infinite conjunctions or disjunctions. (See, also, the reconstruction that Quine, 1974, gives of learning the meaning of logical-scientific idioms.) But we're not trying to explain how people learn logical rules from scratch or how these rules evolved from simpler systems through incremental refinement, since no account along those lines is likely to succeed. Instead, we're attempting to understand what factors contribute to their status in the cognitive system, and for these purposes, we have no need to suppose that simpler parts have to precede more complex ones. What does matter is the causal centrality of these rules among other cognitive components. From this perspective, the links to instantiation and generalization make the presence of logic rules seem no more mysterious than the presence of perceptual or linguistic abilities in people's mental framework.

We considered a similar top-down approach to mathematical knowledge at the end of Chapter 2. However, we do not need to view mathematical knowledge as based solely on logical knowledge. Reductions of this sort, although not out of the question, have not met with obvious success in the history and philosophy of math (see Note 16 in Chapter 2). Logical and mathematical abilities share some underlying cognitive mechanisms, such as generalization, recursion, and instantiation. But mathematics may depend on other sources, both innate and learned.

7.2 Origins of Causal Knowledge

Chapters 1 and 4 argued that knowledge of objects and kinds depends on causal information: Causal forces tie together object stages over time, and similarly, causal forces account for the cohesion of natural kinds. The general picture is that a cloud of causal forces is responsible for the existence of independent objects and that commonalities among these forces group the objects into kinds. In both cases, we are sensitive to causal equilibria, but at different levels of abstraction. Chapter 3 suggested that we have abstract schemas representing this knowledge of cause. So a unifying thesis is that we have causal schemas for the sorts of equilibrium conditions that support our beliefs about individuals and kinds.

Causal schemas, although they're based on empirical knowledge of specific objects and kinds, nevertheless support modal notions of what might or must happen to such things. These modal notions could underwrite impressions that kinds or individuals have certain of their properties essentially. But even if we reject psychological essentialism about objects and kinds, as I've urged in these chapters, we do retain the idea that many of their properties would persist in nonactual situations. I've argued that causal schemas do not depend purely on (conditional) probabilities of events, but instead depend on functional specifications, where the functions themselves are parasitic on causal laws. This goes along with the fact that causal laws, but not conditional probabilities, are stable across situations. It's the causal laws that ground our modal notions in these domains (see Section 3.2.1.3).

A parallel exists between these conclusions about causal knowledge and the ones we drew earlier about logical-mathematical thought. We seem to have in both cases general organizing principles—rules of logic and math, laws for causal systems—and these principles lend structure to our thoughts about the relevant domains. For the deductive domains, the structures will be specific math or logic systems, such as the natural numbers. For causal systems, the structures will be schemas of certain sorts, perhaps resembling qualitative specifications of functional dependencies.

7.2.1 Innate Causal Knowledge

But although we can reasonably conclude that the general principles underlying logic and math derive from innate mental resources for instantiation, recursion, and so forth, the case is less clear for knowledge of causal laws. Do people have innate concepts corresponding to familiar causal principles, such as those of Newtonian mechanics? For one thing, although such laws make some events or interactions causally necessary, they are not themselves true in all possible situations. That the physics of our universe obeys certain laws is a contingent matter. The availability of rival physical systems, each self-consistent, is a reminder that causal laws could be other than how each system portrays them. This is the difference between merely causally necessary statements and logically necessary ones. If we suppose some such physical system is innate and fixes our thinking about causal matters, then how are we able to learn or to understand rival systems? We would seem to be stuck in the innate system, with no way to learn our way out.

However, we shouldn't proceed too quickly here. Rival systems also exist in logic and math—for example, rival modal logics and rival geometries (e.g., Euclidean vs. hyperbolic)—that seem to offer an analogy to rival physical systems. If we had, say, Euclidean geometry as an innate system, wouldn't it be impossible for us to learn systems like hyperbolic geometry, which is obviously not the case? To defend innate knowledge of geometry, we might naturally go to a more abstract level, claiming that some of our geometric knowledge is innate but that this innate knowledge is only partial, insufficient to differentiate rival geometric systems. For example, perhaps we have innate knowledge of "absolute" geometry, which is neutral between Euclidean and non-Euclidean theories (Ryan, 1986).[3] This move would parallel the principles-and-parameters idea in linguistics (Chomsky & Lasnik, 1993): As hinted earlier (Section 7.1.1), infants start with universal grammar, which specifies a framework for all languages, but allows for the setting of particular parameters to yield the grammar of any specific language. We might similarly have innate knowledge of math and logic that is abstract in the same sense as universal grammar and permits parameter settings for more specific systems.[4]

This type of move appeals to innateness at a more abstract level than the rival systems in question, and it is consistent with the stance I've taken earlier in this chapter. The claim is that only some of our logical abilities are fixed and that others are filled in through learning. Taking this tack with respect to causal knowledge would mean claiming that what we have innately are abstract causal rules or principles, which we can elaborate in order to understand specific causal systems (see Bullock, Gelman, & Baillargeon, 1982, for a related point of view).

A second way to square innate causal principles with the variety of possible causal laws is to claim that, although we start with specific causal principles, we can transcend these innate principles through radical conceptual change (see Carey, 2009, for theories of children's concepts of objects and number that involve such change). The innate causal principles stay with us, but they don't limit our learning of new principles, even conflicting ones, since we can bootstrap our way to new causal concepts. Perhaps by combining conceptual primitives from several different innate systems (not all of them causal), we are able to think about causal laws that we couldn't initially formulate within our innate causal theories. But although some such route might be possible, I think we can safely say that such proposals are beset by difficulties. Chapter 2 traces the problems for such a theory within the domain of numbers, and I see no reason to think that the prospects are any better for causal knowledge.[5]

However, one fact about causal cognition that may seem to favor the second (radical change) route over the first (abstraction) route is that people's causal knowledge often displays some gross errors, as shown in McCloskey's (1983a, 1983b) and Clement's (1983) studies of intuitive physics among adults. For example, many college students (22% in McCloskey's sample) apparently believe that if a ball rolls off a cliff, it will continue to have horizontal velocity for a short time but then begin to fall straight down, like Wile E. Coyote running off a mesa. You could make the case that such errors result from an innate naïve physics that traps us in a set of incorrect causal concepts. In other words, if our innate causal ideas are quite specific and error-prone, rather than being abstract schemas on a par with universal grammar, then the only way to avoid the errors is to bootstrap our way out.

Should we regard the intuitive physics errors as reflecting an innate causal theory? Perhaps the errors are the result of conscious (and incorrect) rationalizations when we're faced with problems for which we don't have conscious knowledge. If I'm asked about the trajectory of an object that rolls off a cliff, I may not have detailed enough knowledge of the relevant physical principles to derive the right answer. My innate causal principles may be at too abstract a level to allow me to do this, and I may have to make something up that sounds good to the investigator, but which actually reveals my ignorance. This would help explain better performance on these problems when participants actually witness the motion paths of objects in computer animations than when they have to draw them (Kaiser, Proffitt, & Anderson, 1985). McCloskey (1983b), however, makes the case that these errors are very deep-seated and are similar to the impetus theories of the fourteenth–sixteenth centuries. So the errors aren't simply unsystematic rationales.

But even if intuitive physics is systematic, that doesn't mean that it's innate. We might regard these error tendencies as natural misconceptions prompted by simplicity, representativeness, and other heuristics in our thinking. In terms of the abstraction (principles-and-parameters) route we've been considering, we might suppose that the abstract rules leave open lower-level details that get filled in by default as the result of natural but incorrect conjectures. As we learn more about physics, we revise these details to bring our theories in better line with the physical facts. If so, then we have no need for radical conceptual change, but only normal learning to correct the default misrepresentations. Although mistakes about causal matters may be widespread, they don't seem as stubborn as ordinary visual illusions. Perceptual illusions persist, despite our knowledge of their true nature, and this argues that they're supported by fairly low-level perceptual processes or modules that are hardwired and non-negotiable. But intuitive physics doesn't persist in the same way. Once we've learned that a projectile dropped from a moving vehicle continues to move horizontally, instead of plummeting straight down, we're not likely to make the same mistake again. That suggests that naïve physics is not part of people's cognitive architecture, even though we may be predisposed to accept it.

7.2.2 Knowledge of Objects and Kinds

I'm maintaining that our thinking about certain causal properties of objects and natural kinds is robust across possible changes in situations, including counterfactual situations. I'm also claiming that what give these thoughts their authority are ideas about the causal interactions in which objects and kinds take part, shaping them to be what they are. However, the previous section suggests that innate beliefs about causal necessity are likely to be fairly abstract ones, more abstract than the beliefs that compose intuitive physics, for example. One question might therefore be whether these beliefs about causal necessity are too abstract to ground beliefs about objects and kinds.

This question comes up naturally in the context of psychological essentialism. Psychological essentialists about biological kinds (e.g., S. A. Gelman, 2003; Medin & Ortony, 1989) think that these essentialist beliefs are illusory in something like the way that intuitive physics is. Not only do ordinary people have "placeholders" rather than descriptive notions about cow essence, but also no essence-of-cow actually exists that could correctly fill the position of those placeholders. Shouldn't we say, then, that essentialist beliefs are like the beliefs of intuitive physics in being natural defaults within a more abstract causal framework? But if we embrace such a view, we may no longer be in a position to claim that innate causal schemas are sufficient to account for our modal thinking about objects and kinds. Essentialism is modal to the core. An essential property, by definition, is one that an object *must* have to retain its existence and identity. If we don't get essentialism from fundamental features of our cognitive make up, where do such modal ideas come from?

I argued in Chapter 4 that psychological essentialism may be wrong in ascribing to people the belief that just a single essential property is responsible for all a biological kind's typical properties. Similarly, I argued in Chapter 1 that psychological sortalism may be wrong in ascribing to people the belief that objects' essential properties are inherited from concepts of kinds. We're more likely to believe that clusters of causal forces hold objects together over the course of their existence and that we abstract some of these forces as supplying the nature of kinds. This account is not as naïve as essentialism. In fact, it stands a chance of being true. So the present theory is in a different dialectical position than sortalism, essentialism, and naïve physics. If the cluster-of-causes theory is innate, then no drastic revisions may be required to account for correct ideas about objects and biological kinds. The theory also supports modal notions, since it's backed by schemas of causal configurations that are stable across settings. Nevertheless, if what's innate in our causal thinking is so abstract that it's unable to distinguish between essentialism and the interactive view, then innate causal schemas may not reach down far enough to be responsible for our modal intuitions about how objects and kinds operate. We have exactly the same problem we had before (i.e., in connection with essentialism) in accounting for these intuitions. Moreover, good reasons may exist for going abstract and making room for both essentialism and interactionism in people's thinking. Essentialism might be the right theory for some natural kinds, particularly chemical kinds, even if it's the wrong theory for biology (Sober, 1980). Having atomic number 80 would seem to be essential for mercury, for example.

But I think you can make a case that starting out with an innate interactive theory of causal transactions allows enough flexibility to accommodate plausible variations in theories. The interactive view and the essentialist view are related in an asymmetric way. If you start with an interactive theory of kinds, you shouldn't find it difficult to treat, as a special case, kinds that have just a single important cause. Whereas if you start with an essentialist view, the change to an interactive one would seem to involve a more radical conceptual reorganization. Given the choice between an interactionist and an essentialist view as a starting point, the interactionist theory would seem to provide a simpler account of later learning, as I suggested at the end of Chapter 4.

Suppose, then, that we're innately disposed to think of causes as interacting (and mutually supporting each other) within certain regions—relatively independent causal systems. A living thing or a mechanical device embodies such a system, which accounts for its stability over time and its resistance to accidents. Equilibrium systems of causal forces are natural ways of preserving a system's properties over time, as fans of connectionism are fond of pointing out. We needn't credit kids as having innate knowledge of the particular causes that inhabit these systems or with numerical information (e.g., conditional probabilities) associated with the causes. Clearly, adults' knowledge of objects and kinds differ from those of children, and any theory of kinds has to accommodate this increase in knowledge. A nativist version of a causal interaction theory simply provides a framework, with later learning filling in the details of the specific causes that operate within a given causal system. Similarly, we've already raised doubts about whether even adults have quantitative information of about cause-effect relations, except in special cases. What's important is that kids have structural information about the nature of interacting causes that can ground further knowledge of a more detailed sort.

Time for a summary. Section 7.1 argued that there are innate aspects of the cognitive operating system that include processes like recursion and instantiation, and these underlie the necessity of logical and mathematical thought. Section 7.2 raised the issue of whether one can legitimately take a similar position with respect to causal systems. What if we're born with an idea of interactive causal systems that shapes our notions of objects and kinds? One objection to this view is that knowledge of causal laws can't easily be innate if we can conceive of incompatible systems of laws—incompatible physical systems, say. To handle this problem, we could opt for: (a) innate abstract schemas, which we can complete in different ways, or (b) innate specific schemas, plus conceptual restructuring. At first sight, findings on intuitive physics and essentialism might seem to favor (b) over (a). But we can regard these latter notions as the result of completing our causal schemas in natural but incorrect ways, commitments which we can then undo by ordinary learning and problem solving.

7.3 A Role for Nonperceptual Structure in Cognition

In this final chapter, we've looked at the problem of where we get our beliefs about the possibility or necessity of certain states of affairs. But the conclusions we've reached about these matters come along with some implications about how to pursue higher-level cognition. Most cognitive psychologists in this area probably reject traditional empiricist theories, which view all mental life as constructed from elementary sense data. Probably few investigators these days see knowledge of kinds, causes, or numbers as reducible to raw sense impressions. Yet much of the field still views perceptual processes as foundational for the rest of cognition. As I mentioned in the Preface, every cognition textbook starts with basic perceptual operations, advances to short-term or working memory, and then proceeds to higher-level skills, such as decision-making, reasoning, and problem-solving. And many sophisticated investigators whose theories have little else in common—Fodor (1983, 2000) and Rumelhart (1992), for example—give perception a special place among other cognitive abilities.

Why privilege perception? One reason is that we know quite a lot about it, so it provides a model for how to do cognitive psychology. If we can view an issue in higher cognition as reducible (or at least analogous) to an issue in perception, and if we know how the perceptual system solves this problem, then we might hope that a similar solution will work at the higher level. You could also argue that we know more about perception than about higher cognition because it's easier to study: Perception is more self-contained and less subject to effects of context, beliefs, values, and other diffuse influences. Less self-contained processes, such as concept fixation or reasoning or decision-making or problem solving, are difficult to study because psychologists find it hard to identify the stable properties of these systems (if, indeed, any stable properties exist). Apart from behaviorists, psychologists don't deny that people engage in such mental processes, and they reserve chapters for them at the back of the book. But many probably doubt that we can learn anything important about them, even with the aid of technical breakthroughs in imaging.

A second reason for an emphasis on perception might be its availability. Nonhuman animals and human infants can perceive the world around them, whereas they regularly fail with even simple math or reasoning tasks. Likewise, nonhuman animals and human infants can often act effectively on their environment. Given these perceptual and motor skills, infants might advance to more complex cognitive levels by building on the already-developed ones. Of course, they may not be able to get very far with *only* perceptual or motor abilities, for reasons that are analogous to the impossibility of reducing cognition to sensation. Theorists may need to add to the mix certain conceptual primitives, such as the concept CAUSE, or they may have to factor in the effects of language or culture. Nevertheless, one strategy for understanding adult cognition is to view it as based on more easily available perceptual or motor abilities and to look for traces of these abilities in higher-level thinking. If this is right, you might expect to see effects of visual or motoric imagery, psychophysical effects, and perception-like illusions or heuristics even in reasoning and decision making, and quite often you do.

Perception may be the part of cognitive psychology that's easiest to investigate, that has yielded the most detailed knowledge, and that's most easily available to cognizers. As a model for theorizing, we can legitimately look to perception for analogies, just as we can look to biology or physics or other scientific fields. But we run into problems in understanding higher-level cognition if we let perception-envy keep us from seeing what's distinctive to these higher-level domains of thought. (Calling these domains "higher-level" may itself be misleading if it suggests that they rest on "lower-level" perceptual ones.) Nearly every chapter of this book furnishes examples of how overreliance on perceptual models in cognitive theories can lead to deficiencies. Take knowledge of numbers. If we insist that the concept of natural number necessarily develops out of perceptual skills in tracking or enumerating objects, then we're stuck with having to tell a very complex—I would claim, implausible—story about how radical conceptual change transforms these immature concepts into adult notions of natural numbers, with their unique initial number and infinite extent. Chapter 2 argues that a more reasonable theory starts with knowledge of possible sequences and then selects among those sequences the one that best matches the natural numbers' inherent structure. Both routes to number knowledge end up positing complex innate mechanisms—innate object trackers, set extractors, and bootstrapping devices in the first case and innate knowledge of sequences in the second. In fact, the first route must also posit innate knowledge of certain sequences in order to explain how children are able to learn the initial count list. What could favor the indirectness of the first route, then, other than the idea that number knowledge must begin with the perceptual impression of objects' cardinality?

Even the notion of object itself may be distorted if we think of it merely as an extension of familiar objects of perception. If we think this way, we're tempted to view our concepts of objects as based on spatiotemporal properties, such as spatial separation from their background or coherent movement, that allow us to track them perceptually, or on qualitative properties, such as shape, that permit us to recognize them over the short term. A perception-centered notion of objects is going to miss the fact that many things we easily acknowledge as physical objects—houses, telephone poles, lakes—don't move coherently and aren't separated from their background, as we noted in Chapter 1. Similarly, recognition of objects—that is, recognition that something is the same object we've previously encountered—is not always secured simply by noting similarity of qualitative properties. Especially for objects we care about, qualitative or perceptual similarity isn't enough to guarantee identity. Otherwise, clever imposters would succeed in becoming the people they imitate. Perceptual and spatiotemporal information is certainly helpful in carving out and identifying objects, but it is simply too shallow to capture what we take to be definitive about these concepts. In much the same way, theories of natural-kind concepts that are based on perceptual similarity are far too flimsy to explain how we think about these categories with their intricate causal connections (see Chapter 4 in this book and Rips, 1989).

Much the same tendency to model cognition on perception appears in the sorts of diagrammatic theories of reasoning that we met in Chapter 6. External diagrams are useful tools because they are often able to summarize and to highlight facts in a way that makes them easy to remember. A good diagram embodies constraints that can guide problem solving. Mental diagrams have these same advantages, and they appeal to psychologists as explanations of reasoning and problem solving because of these properties (Larkin & Simon, 1987). But thinking of reasoning as inspecting and manipulating mental diagrams can lead investigators to overlook the mental processes that inform the diagrams. Diagrams that we've learned in school and have simply internalized can be useful in their place, as are mental Euler circles or Venn diagrams. Yet as we noticed in Chapter 6, these diagrams would make no sense to us as reasoning tools if they didn't graft onto preexisting concepts of the subject matter (e.g., sets in the case of Euler circles). In addition, mental manipulation of these diagrams in solving problems usually has to be guided by further restrictions in order to ensure correct answers. This is clearly the case, for example, in the diagrams that constitute mental models (e.g., Johnson-Laird & Byrne, 1991). Spelling out which manipulations are legal and which illegal takes us beyond the perceptual aspects of the diagram and into deeper considerations about the nature of the represented domain.

Whatever advantages perception has as a model for other forms of thought, it also has the disadvantage of leading us to overlook the complexities of cognition. Because our percepts seem simply given—because we don't usually have conscious access to the inferences that produce them—we can mistake their immediacy for explanatory grounding. This immediacy can fool us into believing that once we've identified perception-like elements in our thinking about objects, numbers, causes, kinds, or reasons, then we're done. I have argued, though, that in all these domains we need to look beyond perception for adequate psychological theories. Our thoughts about these domains depend on our ability to contemplate possible states of affairs that leave no perceptual evidence. Our knowledge of these dependencies means that correct theories must appeal to arrangements of abstract, internal structures.

NOTES

Thanks to Winston Chang and Eyal Sagi for astute comments on an earlier version of this chapter.

1. Or could we? If we change our beliefs by standard methods of conditionalization, then the probabilities of particular beliefs will change as we come to accept others, but the conditional probabilities themselves remain fixed (Kaplan, 1996). So if Pr(Conclusion | Premises) is our measure of argument strength, then standard methods of learning by conditionalization will leave it untouched. We can't change Pr(Conclusion | Premises) < 1 to Pr(Conclusion | Premises) = 1 in this manner, and we would need some other method to learn that an argument was stronger than we initially supposed.

2. And, of course, in older "generative semantic" theories, the relation between logic and natural language was even closer. See, for example, Lakoff (1970).

3. See also Asmuth (2010) for psychological implications of rival geometries and Dehaene, Izard, Pica, and Spelke (2006) for evidence of innate geometrical intuitions.

4. Another route to accommodating rival systems by way of abstraction takes a cue from early Putnam (1967). Perhaps what's innate is not the set of axioms of a particular logic or mathematics, but instead conditionals along the lines of *If such-and-such axioms are the case then so-and-so theorems follow.*

5. A third possibility here would be to suppose that we have innate and specific causal schemas that are potentially erroneous and which we're stuck with, but later learning about objects and kinds takes place on a different innate foundation, which allows an end run around the incorrect system. This is similar to what's suggested in Chapter 2: We may have innate magnitude mechanisms that are approximate and error-prone, but we also develop true number systems on a different, structural basis. Although the magnitude system persists into adulthood, yielding merely ballpark estimates, we're still able to obtain correct numerical information by means of the second system. In the present case, however, a multiple system view is not only relatively unparsimonious but also unnecessary for reasons that we're about to examine.

References

Abbott, B. (1997). A note on the nature of "water." *Mind, 106,* 311–319.

Ahn, W. (1998). Why are different features central for natural kinds and artifacts?: The role of causal status in determining feature centrality. *Cognition, 69,* 135–178.

Ahn, W., & Dennis, M. J. (2001). Dissociations between categorization and similarity judgement: Differential effects of causal status on feature weights. In U. Hahn & M. Ramscar (Eds.), *Similarity and categorization* (pp. 87–107). Oxford: Oxford University Press.

Ahn, W., & Graham, L. M. (1999). The impact of necessity and sufficiency in the Wason four-card selection task. *Psychological Science, 10,* 237–242.

Ahn, W., Kalish, C. W., Medin, D. L., & Gelman, S. A. (1995). The role of covariation versus mechanism information in causal attribution. *Cognition, 54,* 299–352.

Ahn, W., & Kim, N. (2000). The causal status effect in categorization: An overview. *Psychology of Learning and Motivation, 40,* 23–65.

Alexander, J., & Weinberg, J. M. (2007). Analytic epistemology and experimental philosophy. *Philosophy Compass, 2,* 56-80.

Alloy, L. B., & Tabachnik, N. (1984). Assessment of covariation by humans and animals. *Psychological Review, 91,* 112–148.

Almor, A., & Sloman, S. A. (1996). Is deontic reasoning special? *Psychological Review, 103,* 374–380.

Anderson, J. A. (1998). Learning arithmetic with a neural network: Seven times seven is about fifty. In D. N. Osherson (Series Ed.), and D. Scarborough & S. Sternberg (Eds.), *An invitation to cognitive science: Methods, models, and conceptual issues* (Vol. 4, pp. 255–300). Cambridge, MA: MIT Press.

Anderson, J. R. (1977). Memory for information about individuals. *Memory and Cognition, 5*, 430–442.

Anderson, J. R. (1983). *The architecture of cognition*. Cambridge, MA: Harvard University Press.

Anderson, J. R. (1993). *Rules of the mind*. Hillsdale, NJ: Erlbaum.

Anderson, J. R., & Hastie, R. (1974). Individuation and reference in memory: Proper names and definite descriptions. *Cognitive Psychology, 6*, 495–514.

Anderson, J. R., & Lebiere, C. (1998). *Atomic components of thought*. Mahwah, NJ: Erlbaum.

Anderson, R. C. (1990). Inferences about word meanings. In A. C. Graesser & G. H. Bower (Eds.), *Inferences and text comprehension*. Orlando, FL: Academic Press.

Anisfeld, M., & Knapp, M. (1968). Association, synonymity, and directionality in false recognition. *Journal of Experimental Psychology, 77*, 171–179.

Armstrong, D. M. (1980). Identity through time. In P. van Inwagen (Ed.), *Time and cause* (pp. 67–78). Dordrecht, Holland: Reidel.

Armstrong, S. L., Gleitman, L. R., & Gleitman, H. (1983). What some concepts might not be. *Cognition, 13*, 263–308.

Asher, H. B. (1983). *Causal modeling* (2nd ed.). Newbury Park, CA: Sage.

Asmuth, J. (2010). The role of structure in learning non-Euclidean geometry. *Dissertation Abstracts International: Section B. Science and Engineering, 70*(12).

Atran, S. (1995). Classifying nature across cultures. In E. E. Smith & D. N. Osherson (Eds.), *Thinking* (2nd ed., pp. 131–174). Cambridge, MA: MIT Press.

Atran, S. (1998). Folk biology and the anthropology of science: Cognitive universals and cultural particulars. *Behavioral and Brain Sciences, 21*, 547–609.

Au, T. K. (1983). Chinese and English counterfactuals: The Sapir-Whorf hypothesis revisited. *Cognition, 15*, 155-187.

Ayers, M. (1997). Is *physical object* a sortal? A reply to Xu. *Mind and Language, 12*, 393–405.

Banks, W. P., Fujii, M., & Kayra-Stuart, F. (1976). Semantic congruity effects in comparative judgments of magnitudes of digits. *Journal of Experimental Psychology: Human Perception and Performance, 2*, 435–447.

Bar-Hillel, M. A., & Falk, R. (1982). Some teasers concerning conditional probabilities. *Cognition, 11*, 109–122.

Baron, J. (1991). Beliefs about thinking. In J. F. Voss, D. N. Perkins, & J. W. Segal (Eds.), *Informal reasoning and education* (pp. 169–186). Hillsdale, NJ: Erlbaum.

Baroody, A. J., & Gannon, K. E. (1984). The development of the commutativity principle and economical addition strategies. *Cognition and Instruction, 1*, 321–339.

Baroody, A. J., Wilkins, J. L. M., & Tiilikainen, S. (2003). The development of children's understanding of additive commutativity: From protoquantitative concept to general concept? In A. J. Baroody & A. Dowker (Eds.), *The development of arithmetic concepts and skills* (pp. 127–160). Mahwah, NJ: Erlbaum.

Barry, D. (2003, July 19). He conned the society crowd but died alone. *New York Times*, pp. A1, B3.

Barsalou, L. W. (1985). Ideals, central tendency, and frequency of instantiation as determinants of graded structure in categories. *Journal of Experimental Psychology: Learning, Memory, and Cognition, 11*, 629–654.

Barsalou, L. W. (1987). The instability of graded structure: Implications for the nature of concepts. In U. Neisser (Ed.), *Concepts and conceptual development*. Cambridge, UK: Cambridge University Press.

Bartels, D. M., & Rips, L. J. (2010). Psychological connectedness and intertemporal choice. *Journal of Experimental Psychology: General, 139*, 49-69.

Barth, H., Kanwisher, N., & Spelke, E. (2003). The construction of large number representations in adults. *Cognition, 86*, 201–221.

Barth, H., La Mont, K., Lipton, J., Dehaene, S., Kanwisher, N., & Spelke, E. (2006). Non-symbolic arithmetic in adults and young children. *Cognition, 98*, 199–222.

Barton, M. E., & Komatsu, L. K. (1989). Defining features of natural kinds and artifacts. *Journal of Psycholinguistic Research, 18*, 433–447.

Bates, D. M., & Watts, D. G. (1988). *Nonlinear regression analysis and its applications.* New York: Wiley.

Bauer, L. (1983). *English word formation.* Cambridge, UK: Cambridge University Press.

Bedford, F. L. (1997). False categories in cognition: The not-the-liver fallacy. *Cognition, 64*, 231–248.

Begg, I., & Harris, G. (1982). On the interpretation of syllogisms. *Journal of Verbal Learning and Verbal Behavior, 21*, 595–520.

Bell, V. A., & Johnson-Laird, P. N. (1998). A model theory of modal reasoning. *Cognitive Science, 22*, 25–51.

Bemis, D. K., Franconeri, S. L., & Alvarez, G. A. (2008). *Rapid enumeration is based on a segmented visual scene.* Manuscript submitted for publication.

Benacerraf, P. (1973). Mathematical truth. *Journal of Philosophy, 70*, 661–680.

Bennett, J. F. (2003). *A philosophical guide to conditionals.* Oxford: Oxford University Press.

Bergmann, M., Moor, J., & Nelson, J. (1980). *The logic book.* New York: Random House.

Bergmann, M., Moor, J., & Nelson, J. (2008). *The logic book* (5th ed.). New York: McGraw-Hill.

Beth, E. W., & Piaget, J. (1966). *Mathematical epistemology and psychology* (W. Mays, Trans.). Dordrecht, Holland: Reidel.

Biederman, I. (1987). Recognition by components: A theory of human image understanding. *Psychological Review, 94*, 115–147.

Bjork, R. A. (1978). The updating of human memory. *Psychology of Learning and Motivation, 12,* 235–259.

Blaisdell, A. P., Sawa, K., Leising, K. J., & Waldmann, M. R. (2006). Causal reasoning in rats. *Science, 311,* 1020–1022.

Bloch, M. E. F. (1998). *How we think they think: Anthropological approaches to cognition, memory, and literacy.* Boulder, CO: Westview.

Block, N. (1985). Advertisement for a semantics for psychology. In P. A. French, T. E. Uehling, Jr., & H. K. Wettstein (Eds.), *Midwest studies in philosophy, X.* Minneapolis: University of Minnesota Press.

Blok, S., Newman, G., & Rips, L. J. (2005). Individuals and their concepts. In W-k. Ahn, R. L. Goldstone, B. C. Love, A. B. Markman, & P. Wolff (Eds.), *Categorization inside and outside the lab.* Washington, DC: American Psychological Association.

Blok, S. V., Newman, G. E., & Rips, L. J. (2007). Out of sorts? Remedies for theories of object concepts: A reply to Rhemtulla and Xu. *Psychological Review, 114,* 1096–1102.

Bloom, A. (1981). *The linguistic shaping of thought: A study in the impact of language and thinking in China and the West.* Hillsdale, NJ: Erlbaum.

Bloom, P. (1994). Generativity within language and other cognitive domains. *Cognition, 51,* 177–189.

Bloom, P. (1996). Intention, history, and artifact concepts. *Cognition, 60,* 1–29.

Bloom, P. (2000). *How children learn the meaning of words.* Cambridge, MA: MIT Press.

Bobrow, D. G., & Winograd, T. (1977). An overview of KRL: a knowledge representation language. *Cognitive Science, 1,* 3-46.

Bonatti, L., Frot, E., Zangl, R., & Mehler, J. (2002). The human first hypothesis: identification of conspecifics and individuation of objects in the young infant. *Cognitive Psychology, 44,* 388–426.

Boroditsky, L. (2001). Does language shape thought?: Mandarin and English speakers' conceptions of time. *Cognitive Psychology, 43,* 1-22.

Bower, G. H., & Glass, A. L. (1976). Structural units and the redintegrative power of picture fragments. *Journal of Experimental Psychology: Human Learning and Memory, 2,* 456–466.

Boyd, R. (1999). Homeostasis, species, and higher taxa. In R. A. Wilson (Ed.), *Species: New interdisciplinary essays* (pp. 141–185). Cambridge, MA: MIT Press.

Brachman, R. J., & Schmolze, J. G. (1985). An overview of kl-one knowledge representation system. *Cognitive Science, 9,* 171–216.

Braine, M. D. S., & O'Brien, D. P. (1998). *Mental logic.* Mahwah, NJ: Erlbaum.

Braine, M. D. S., O'Brien, D. P., Noveck, I. A., Samuels, M., Lea, R. B., Fisch, S. M., et al. (1995). Predicting intermediate and multiple conclusions in propositional logic inference problems. *Journal of Experimental Psychology: General, 124,* 263–292.

Braine, M. D. S., Reiser, B. J., & Rumain, B. (1984). Some empirical justification for a theory of natural propositional logic. In G. H. Bower (Ed.), *Psychology of learning and motivation* (Vol. 18, pp. 313–371). New York: Academic Press.

Braisby, N., Franks, B., & Hampton, J. (1996). Essentialism, word use, and concepts. *Cognition, 59,* 247–274.

Brandom, R. (1988). Inference, expression, and induction. *Philosophical Studies, 54,* 257–285.

Brandom, R. (1994). *Making it explicit.* Cambridge, MA: Harvard University Press.

Brem, S. K., & Rips, L. J. (2000). Evidence and explanation in informal argument. *Cognitive Science, 24,* 573–604.

Brown, R. (1958). How shall a thing be called? *Psychological Review, 65,* 14–21.

Bryant, P., Christie, C., & Rendu, A. (1999). Children's understanding of the relation between addition and subtraction: Inversion, identity, and decomposition. *Journal of Experimental Child Psychology, 74,* 194–212.

Bucciarelli, M., & Johnson-Laird, P. N. (1999). Strategies in syllogistic reasoning. *Cognitive Science, 23,* 247–304.

Buckley, P. B., & Gillman, C. B. (1974). Comparison of digits and dot patterns. *Journal of Experimental Psychology: Human Perception and Performance, 103,* 1131–1136.

Buller, D. J. (2005). *Adapting minds: Evolutionary psychology and the persistent quest for human nature.* Cambridge, MA: MIT Press.

Bullock, M., Gelman, R., & Baillargeon, R. (1982). The development of causal reasoning. In W. J. Friedman (Ed.), *The developmental psychology of time* (pp. 209–254). New York: Academic Press.

Burge, T. (1979). Individualism and the mental. In P. A. French, T. E. Uehling, & H. K. Wettstein (Eds.), *Midwest studies in philosophy, IV.* Minneapolis: University of Minnesota Press.

Burge, T. (1999). Comprehension and interpretation. In L. E. Hahn (Ed.), *The philosophy of Donald Davidson* (pp. 229–250). Chicago: Open Court.

Burks, A. W. (1977). *Chance, cause, reason.* Chicago: University of Chicago Press.

Burstein, M. H., Collins, A., & Baker, M. (1991). Plausible generalization: Extending a model of human plausible reasoning. *Journal of the Learning Sciences, 1,* 319–359.

Busemeyer, J. R. (1991). Intuitive statistical estimation. In N. H. Anderson (Ed.), *Contributions to information integration theory* (Vol. 1, pp. 187–215). Hillsdale, NJ: Erlbaum.

Byrne, R. M. (1989). Suppressing valid inferences with conditionals. *Cognition, 31,* 61–83.

Byrne, R. M. J., Espino, O., & Santamaria, C. (1999). Counterexamples and the suppression of inferences. *Journal of Memory and Language, 40,* 347–373.

Canobi, K. H., Reeve, R. A., & Pattison, P. A. (2002). Young children's understanding of addition concepts. *Educational Psychology, 22,* 513–532.

Caramazza, A., Grober, E., Garvey, C., & Yates, J. (1977). Comprehension of anaphoric pronouns. *Journal of Verbal Learning and Verbal Behavior, 16,* 601–609.

Carey, S. (1985). *Conceptual change in childhood.* Cambridge, MA: MIT Press.

Carey, S. (1995a). Continuity and discontinuity in cognitive development. In D. N. Osherson (Series Ed.) and E. E. Smith & D. N. Osherson (Vol. Eds.), *Invitation to cognitive science: Vol. 3. Thinking* (2nd ed., pp. 101–129). Cambridge, MA: MIT Press.

Carey, S. (1995b). On the origins of causal understanding. In D. Sperber, D. Premack, & A. J. Premack (Eds.), *Causal cognition* (pp. 268–302). Oxford, UK: Oxford University Press.

Carey, S. (2001). Cognitive foundations of arithmetic: Evolution and ontogenesis. *Mind and Language, 16,* 37–55.

Carey, S. (2004). Bootstrapping and the origins of concepts. *Daedalus, 133,* 59–68.

Carey, S. (2009). *The origin of concepts.* Oxford: Oxford University Press.

Carey, S., & Sarnecka, B. W. (2006). The development of human conceptual representations: A case study. In Y. Munakata & M. H. Johnson (Eds.), *Attention and performance XXI: Processes of change in brain and cognitive development* (pp. 473–496). Oxford: Oxford University Press.

Carey, S., & Spelke, E. (1994). Domain-specific knowledge and conceptual change. In L. A. Hirschfeld & S. A. Gelman (Eds.), *Mapping the mind* (pp. 169–200). Cambridge, UK: Cambridge University Press.

Carey, S., & Xu, F. (1999). Sortals and kinds. In R. Jackendoff, P. Bloom, & K. Wynn (Eds.), *Language, logic, and concepts* (pp. 311–335). Cambridge, MA: MIT Press.

Carey, S., & Xu, F. (2001). Infants' knowledge of objects: Beyond object files and object tracking. *Cognition, 80,* 179–213.

Carlson, G. N. (1982). Generic terms and generic sentences. *Journal of Philosophical Logic, 11,* 145–181.

Carnap, R. (1950). *Logical foundations of probability.* Chicago: University of Chicago Press.

Carston, R. (1998). Informativeness, relevance, and scalar implicature. In R. Carston & S. Uchida (Eds.), *Relevance theory: Applications and implications* (pp. 179–236). Amsterdam: John Benjamins.

Cartwright, N. (2001). What is wrong with Bayes nets? *Monist, 84,* 242–264.

Cartwright, N. (2002). Against modularity, the causal Markov condition, and any link between the two. *British Journal for the Philosophy of Science, 53,* 411–453.

Chan, S-f. F. (2000). Formal logic and dialectical thinking are not incongruent. *American Psychologist., 55,* 1063-1064.

Chapman, G. B., & Robbins, S. J. (1990). Cue interaction in human contingency judgment. *Memory and Cognition, 18,* 537–545.

Chapman, L. J. (1967). Illusory correlation in observational report. *Journal of Verbal Learning and Verbal Behavior, 6,* 151–155.

Chapman, L. J., & Chapman, J. P. (1967). Genesis of popular but erroneous psychodiagnostic observations. *Journal of Abnormal Psychology, 72,* 193–204.

Chase, W. G., & Simon, H. A. (1973). Perception in chess. *Cognitive Psychology, 4,* 55–81.

Chater, N., & Oaksford, M. (1999). The probability heuristics model of syllogistic reasoning. *Cognitive Psychology, 38,* 191–258.

Chen, J-Y. (2007). Do Chinese and English speakers think about time differently? Failure of replicating Boroditsky (2001). *Cognition, 104,* 427-436.

Cheng, P. W. (1997). From covariation to causation: A causal power theory. *Psychological Review, 104,* 367–405.

Cheng, P. W. (1985). Pictures of ghosts: A critique of Alfred Bloom's *The Linguistic Shaping of Thought. American Anthropologist, 87,* 917–922.

Cheng, P. W., & Holyoak, K. J. (1985). Pragmatic reasoning schemas. *Cognitive Psychology, 17,* 391–416.

Cheng, P. W., & Novick, L. R. (1990). A probabilistic contrast model of causal induction. *Journal of Personality and Social Psychology, 58,* 545–567.

Cheng, P. W., & Novick, L. R. (1992). Covariation in natural causal induction. *Psychological Review, 99,* 365–382.

Cheng, P. W., & Novick, L. R. (2005). Constraints and nonconstraints in causal learning. *Psychological Review, 112,* 694–707.

Cherniak, C. (1986). *Minimal rationality.* Cambridge, MA: MIT Press.

Chi, M. T. H., & Koeske, R. D. (1983). Network representation of a child's dinosaur knowledge. *Developmental Psychology, 19,* 29-39.

Chierchia, G., & McConnell-Ginet, S. (1990). *Meaning and grammar.* Cambridge, MA: MIT Press.

Chomsky, N. (1957). *Syntactic structures.* The Hague: Mouton.

Chomsky, N. (1965). *Aspects of a theory of syntax.* Cambridge, MA: MIT Press.

Chomsky, N. (1988). *Language and problems of knowledge.* Cambridge, MA: MIT Press.

Chomsky, N., & Lasnik, H. (1993). The theory of principles and parameters. In J. Jacobs, A. von Stechow, W. Sternefeld, & T. Vennemann (Eds.), *Syntax: An international handbook of contemporary research.* Berlin: De Gruyter.

Chrisomalis, S. (2004). A cognitive typology for numerical notation. *Cambridge Archaeological Journal, 14,* 37–52.

Church, R. M., & Broadbent, H. A. (1990). Alternative representations of time, number, and rate. *Cognition, 37,* 55–81.

Clark, H. H. (1974). *Semantics and comprehension.* The Hague: Mouton.

Clark, H. H. (1983). Making sense of nonce sense. In G. B. Flores d'Arcais & R. J. Jarvella (Eds.), *The process of language understanding.* New York: Wiley.

Clearfield, M. W., & Mix, K. S. (1999). Number versus contour length in infants' discrimination of small visual sets. *Psychological Science, 10,* 408–411.

Clement, J. (1983). A conceptual model discussed by Galileo and used intuitively by physics students. In D. Gentner & A. L. Stevens (Eds.), *Mental models* (pp. 325–340). Hillsdale, NJ: Erlbaum.

Cliff, N. (1983). Some cautions concerning the application of causal modeling methods. *Multivariate Behavior Research, 18,* 115–128.

Cohen, L. B., & Oakes, L. M. (1993). How infants perceive a simple causal event. *Developmental Psychology, 29,* 421–433.

Coley, J. D., Medin, D. L., & Atran, S. (1998). Does rank have its privilege? Inductive inferences within folkbiological taxonomies. *Cognition, 64,* 73–112.

Coley, J. D., Medin, D. L., Proffitt, J. B., Lynch, E., & Atran, S. (1999). Inductive reasoning in folkbiological thought. In D. L. Medin & S. Atran (Eds.), *Folkbiology* (pp. 205–232). Cambridge, MA: MIT Press.

Collins, A., & Michalski, R. (1989). The logic of plausible reasoning: A core theory. *Cognitive Science, 13,* 1–49.

Collins, J., Hall, N., & Paul, L. A. (2004). *Causation and counterfactuals.* Cambridge, MA: MIT Press.

Conrad, F., Brown, N. R., & Cashman, E. R. (1998). Strategies for estimating behavioral frequency in survey interviews. *Memory, 6,* 339–366.

Cook, T. D., & Campbell, D. T. (1979). *Quasi-experimentation.* Chicago: Rand-McNally.

Cordes, S., & Gelman, R. (2005). The young numerical mind: When does it count? In J. Campbell (Ed.), *Handbook of mathematical cognition* (pp. 127–142). New York: Psychology Press.

Cordes, S., Gelman, R., Gallistel, C. R., & Whalen, J. (2001). Variability signatures distinguish verbal from nonverbal counting for both large and small numbers. *Psychonomic Bulletin and Review, 8,* 698–707.

Cosmides, L. (1989). The logic of social exhange: Has natural selection shaped how humans reason? *Cognition, 31,* 187–276.

Cosmides, L., & Tooby, J. (1994). Beyond intuition and instinct blindness: Toward an evolutionarily rigorous cognitive science. *Cognition, 50,* 41–77.

Cowan, R. (2003). Does it all add up? Changes in children's knowledge of addition combinations, strategies, and principles. In A. J. Baroody & A. Dowker (Eds.), *The development of arithmetic concepts and skills* (pp. 35–74). Mahwah, NJ: Erlbaum.

Cowan, R., & Renton, M. (1996). Do they know what they are doing? Children's use of economical addition strategies and knowledge of commutativity. *Educational Psychology, 16,* 407–420.

Cummins, D. D., Lubart, T., Alksnis, O., & Rist, R. (1991). Conditional reasoning and causation. *Memory and Cognition, 19,* 274–282.

Darden, L., & Maull, N. (1977). Interfield theories. *Philosophy of Science, 44,* 43–64.

Davis, N. Z. (1983). *The return of Martin Guerre*. Cambridge, MA: Harvard University Press.

Davis, P. J., & Hersh, R. (1980). *The mathematical experience*. Boston: Birkhäuser.

De Neys, W., Schaeken, W., & D'Ydewalle, G. (2003). Inference suppression and semantic memory retrieval: Every counterexample counts. *Memory and Cognition, 31*, 581–595.

Dedekind, R. (1963). *Essays on the theory of numbers: The nature and meaning of numbers*. New York: Dover. (Original work published 1888)

Dehaene, S. (1997). *The number sense*. Oxford: Oxford University Press.

Dehaene, S., & Changeux, J. P. (1993). Development of elementary numerical abilities: A neuronal model. *Journal of Cognitive Neuroscience, 5*, 390–407.

Dehaene, S., Izard, V., Pica, P., & Spelke, E. (2006). Core knowledge of geometry in an Amazonian indigene group. *Science, 311*, 381–384.

Dehaene, S., Spelke, E., Pinel, P., Stanescu, R., & Tsivkin, S. (1999). Sources of mathematical thinking: Behavioral and brain-imaging evidence. *Science, 284*, 970–974.

Dehghani, M., Iliev, R., & Kaufmann, S. (2007). Effects of fact mutability in the interpretation of counterfactuals. *Proceedings of the Cognitive Science Society, 29*, 941–946.

DeJong, G. (1988). An introduction to explanation-based learning. In H. E. Shrobe (Ed.), *Exploring artificial intelligence*. Los Altos, CA: Morgan Kaufmann.

DeSoto, C. B., London, M., & Handel, S. (1965). Social reasoning and spatial paralogic. *Journal of Personality and Social Psychology, 2*, 513–521.

Dickstein, L. S. (1978). The effect of figure on syllogistic reasoning. *Memory and Cognition, 6*, 76–83.

Diesendruck, G., & Gelman, S. A. (1999). Domain differences in absolute judgments of category membership. *Psychonomic Bulletin and Review, 6*, 338–346.

diSessa, A. A. (2000). *Changing minds: Computers, learning, and literacy*. Cambridge, MA: MIT Press.

Downing, P. (1977). On the creation and use of English compound nouns. *Language, 53*, 810–842.

Dowty, D. R. (1979). *Word meaning and Montague grammar*. Dordrecht, Holland: Reidel.

Dummett, M. (1973). *Frege: Philosophy of language*. Cambridge, MA: Harvard University Press.

Dummett, M. (1975). The justification of deduction. *Proceedings of the British Academy, 59*, 201–232.

Dummett, M. (1991). *Frege: Philosophy of mathematics*. Cambridge, MA: Harvard University Press.

Dupré, J. (1993). *The disorder of things: Metaphysical foundations of the disunity of science*. Cambridge, MA: Harvard University Press.

Edgington, D. (2007). Conditionals. In E. N. Zalta (Ed.), *The Stanford encyclopedia of philosophy*. Stanford, CA: Metaphysics Research Lab, Center for the Study of Language and Information, Stanford University. Retrieved from http://plato.stanford.edu/archives/entries/conditionals

Einhorn, H. J., & Hogarth, R. M. (1986). Judging probable cause. *Psychological Bulletin, 99*, 3–19.

Elio, R., & Pelletier, F. J. (1997). Belief change as propositional update. *Cognitive Science, 21*, 419–460.

Ellis, B. (1996). Natural kinds and natural kind reasoning. In P. J. Riggs (Ed.), *Natural kinds, laws of nature, and scientific methodology* (pp. 11–28). Dordrecht, Holland: Kluwer Academic.

Elman, J. L., Bates, E. A., Johnson, M. H., Karmiloff-Smith, A., Parisi, D., & Plunkett, K. (1996). *Rethinking innateness*. Cambridge, MA: MIT Press.

Elmes, D. G., Kantowitz, B. H., & Roediger, H. L., III. (1999). *Research methods in psychology*. Pacific Grove, CA: Brooks/Cole.

Enderton, H. B. (1977). *Elements of set theory*. New York: Academic Press.

Erickson, J. R. (1974). A set analysis theory of behavior in formal syllogistic reasoning tasks. In R. L. Solso (Ed.), *Theories in cognitive psychology* (pp. 305–329). Potomac, MD: Erlbaum.

Evans, J. St. B. T. (2003). In two minds: Dual-process accounts of reasoning. *Trends in Cognitive Sciences, 7*, 454–459.

Evans, J. St. B. T., & Frankish, K. (2009). *In two minds: Dual processes and beyond*. Oxford: Oxford University Press.

Evans, J. St. B. T., Handley, S. J., Harper, C. N. J., & Johnson-Laird, P. N. (1999). Reasoning about necessity and possibility. *Journal of Experimental Psychology: Learning, Memory, and Cognition, 25*, 1495–1513.

Evans, J. St. B. T., & Over, D. (2004). *If*. Oxford: Oxford University Press.

Ewert, J.-P. (1974). The neural basis of visually guided behavior. *Scientific American, 230*, 34–42.

Falk, R. (1992). A closer look at the probabilities of the notorious three prisoners. *Cognition, 43*, 197–223.

Farrell, J. E., & Shepard, R. N. (1981). Shape, orientation, and apparent rotational motion. *Journal of Experimental Psychology: Human Perception and Performance, 7*, 477–486.

Feigenson, L. (2005). A double dissociation in infants' representation of object arrays. *Cognition, 95*, B37–B48.

Feigenson, L., & Carey, S. (2003). Tracking individuals via object files: Evidence from infants' manual search. *Developmental Science, 6*, 568–584.

Feigenson, L., & Carey, S. (2005). On the limits of infants' quantification of small object arrays. *Cognition, 97*, 295–313.

Feigenson, L., Carey, S., & Hauser, M. (2002). The representations underlying infants' choice of more: Object files versus analog magnitudes. *Psychological Science, 13*, 150–156.

Feigenson, L., Carey, S., & Spelke, E. (2002). Infants' discrimination of number vs. continuous extent. *Cognitive Psychology, 44,* 33–66.

Feigenson, L., Dehaene, S., & Spelke, E. (2004). Core systems of number. *Trends in Cognitive Sciences, 8,* 307–314.

Feigenson, L., & Halberda, J. (2004). Infants chunk object arrays into sets of individuals. *Cognition, 9,* 173–190.

Fiddick, L., Cosmides, L., & Tooby, J. (2000). No interpretation without representation. *Cognition, 77,* 1–79.

Field, H. H. (1977). Logic, meaning, and conceptual role. *Journal of Philosophy, 74,* 379–409.

Fillmore, C. J. (1978). On the organization of semantic information in the lexicon. In D. Farkas, W. M. Jacobsen, & K. W. Todrys (Eds.), *Papers from the parasession on the lexicon.* Chicago: Chicago Linguistic Society.

Fitelson, B. (1999). The plurality of Bayesian measures of confirmation and the problem of measure sensitivity. *Philosophy of Science, 66,* S362–S378.

Fitting, M. (1983). *Proof methods for modal and intuitionistic logics.* Dordrecht, Holland: Reidel.

Fodor, J. (1974). Special sciences. *Synthese, 28,* 77–115.

Fodor, J. (1975). *The language of thought.* New York: Crowell.

Fodor, J. (1981). The present status of the innateness controversy. In *Representations* (pp. 257–316). Cambridge, MA: MIT Press.

Fodor, J. (1983). *Modularity of mind: An essay on faculty psychology.* Cambridge, MA: MIT Press.

Fodor, J. (1994). Concepts: A pot-boiler. *Cognition, 50,* 95–113.

Fodor, J. A. (1998). *Concepts: Where cognitive science went wrong.* Oxford: Oxford University Press.

Fodor, J. (2000). *The mind doesn't work that way.* Cambridge, MA: MIT Press.

Fodor, J. (2003). *Hume variations.* Oxford: Oxford University Press.

Fodor, J. (2008). *LOT2: The language of thought revisited.* Oxford: Oxford University Press.

Fodor, J. A., Garrett, M. F., Walker, E. C. T., & Parkes, C. H. (1980). Against definition. *Cognition, 8,* 263–367.

Fodor, J., & Lepore, E. (1991). Why meaning (probably) isn't conceptual role. *Mind and Language, 6,* 328–343.

Fodor, J., & Lepore, E. (1992). *Holism: A shopper's guide.* Oxford: Blackwell.

Ford, M. (1995). Two modes of mental representation and problem solution in syllogistic reasoning. *Cognition, 54,* 1–71.

Fox, D. (2000). *Economy and semantic interpretation.* Cambridge, MA: MIT Press.

Franks, B. (1995). Sense generation: A "quasi-classical" approach to concepts and concept combination. *Cognitive Science, 19,* 441–505.

Frege, G. (1970). On sense and reference. In P. Geach & M. Black (Eds.), *Translations from the philosophical writings of Gottlob Frege.* Oxford: Blackwell. (Original work published 1892)

Frege, G. (1974). *The foundations of arithmetic* (J. L. Austin, Trans.). Oxford: Blackwell. (Original work published 1884)

Freud, S. (1961). *The future of an illusion* (J. Strachey, Trans.). New York: Norton. (Original work published 1927)

Fuson, K. C. (1988). *Children's counting and concepts of number.* New York: Springer-Verlag.

Gagné, C. L., & Shoben, E. J. (1997). Influence of thematic relations on the comprehension of modifier-head combination. *Journal of Experimental Psychology: Learning, Memory, and Cognition, 23,* 71–87.

Gallistel, C. R., & Gelman, R. (1992). Preverbal and verbal counting and computation. *Cognition, 44,* 43–74.

Gallistel, C. R., Gelman, R., & Cordes, S. (2006). The cultural and evolutionary history of the real numbers. In S. C. Levinson & P. Jaisson (Eds.), *Evolution and culture* (pp. 247–274). Cambridge, MA: MIT Press.

Gao, F., Levine, S. C., & Huttenlocher, J. (2000). What do infants know about continuous quantity? *Journal of Experimental Child Psychology, 77,* 20–29.

Gärdenfors, P. (1988). *Knowledge in flux.* Cambridge, UK: Cambridge University Press.

Gardner, M. (1958). *Logic machines and diagrams.* New York: McGraw-Hill.

Gelman, R. (1972). The nature and development of early number concepts. *Advances in Child Development and Behavior, 7,* 115–167.

Gelman, R., & Butterworth, B. (2005). Number and language: How are they related? *Trends in Cognitive Sciences, 9,* 6–10.

Gelman, R., & Gallistel, C. R. (1978). *The child's understanding of number.* Cambridge, MA: Harvard University Press.

Gelman, R., & Greeno, J. G. (1989). On the nature of competence: Principles for understanding in a domain. In L. B. Resnick (Ed.), *Knowing, learning, and instruction* (pp. 125–186). Hillsdale, NJ: Erlbaum.

Gelman, S. A. (1988). The development of induction within natural kind and artifact categories. *Cognitive Psychology, 20,* 65–95.

Gelman, S. A. (2003). *The essential child: Origins of essentialism in everyday thought.* Oxford: Oxford University Press.

Gelman, S. A., & Coley, J. D. (1990). The importance of knowing a dodo is a bird. *Developmental Psychology, 26,* 796–804.

Gelman, S. A., & Hirschfeld, L. A. (1999). How biological is essentialism? In D. L. Medin & S. Atran (Eds.), *Folkbiology* (pp. 403–446). Cambridge, MA: MIT Press.

Gelman, S. A., & Markman, E. M. (1986). Categories and induction in young children. *Cognition, 23,* 183–209.

Gelman, S. A., & O'Reilly, A. W. (1988). Children's inductive inferences within superordinate categories: The role of language and category structure. *Child Development, 59,* 876–887.

Gelman, S. A., & Wellman, H. M. (1991). Insides and essences: Early understanding of the non-obvious. *Cognition, 38,* 213–244.

Gentner, D. (1983). Structure mapping: A theoretical framework for analogy. *Cognitive Science, 7,* 155–170.

Gentner, D., & Markman, A. B. (1997). Structural alignment in analogy and similarity. *American Psychologist, 52,* 45–56.

Giaquinto, M. (2002). *The search for certainty: A philosophical account of foundations of mathematics.* Oxford: Oxford University Press.

Gigerenzer, G. (1991). From tools to theories: A heuristic of discovery in cognitive psychology. *Psychological Review, 98,* 254–267.

Gigerenzer, G. (2000). *Adaptive thinking.* Oxford: Oxford University Press.

Ginsberg, M. L. (1987). Introduction. In M. L. Ginsberg (Ed.), *Readings in nonmonotonic reasoning* (pp. 1–23). Los Altos, CA: Morgan Kaufmann.

Gleitman, L. R., & Gleitman, H. (1970). *Phrase and paraphrase.* New York: W. W. Norton.

Glymour, C. (2001). *The mind's arrows: Bayes nets and graphical causal models in psychology.* Cambridge, MA: MIT Press.

Godfrey-Smith, P. (2003). Goodman's problem and scientific methodology. *Journal of Philosophy, 100,* 573–590.

Goel, V., Gold, B., Kapur, S., & Houle, S. (1997). The seats of reason? An imagining study of deductive and inductive reasoning. *NeuroReport, 8,* 1305–1310.

Goodman, N. (1955). *Fact, fiction, and forecast.* Cambridge, MA: Bobbs-Merrill.

Goodman, N. (1970). Seven strictures on similarity. In L. Foster & J. W. Swanson (Eds.), *Experience and theory.* Amherst: University of Massachusetts Press.

Gopnik, A., Glymour, C., Sobel, D. M., Schulz, L., Kushnir, T., & Danks, D. (2004). A theory of causal learning in children: Causal maps and Bayes nets. *Psychological Review, 111,* 3–32.

Gordon, P. (2004). Numerical cognition without words: Evidence from Amazonia. *Science, 306,* 496–499.

Grann, D. (2008, August 11). The chameleon: The many lives of Frédéric Bourdin. *The New Yorker, 84,* 66–79.

Gray, K. C., & Smith, E. E. (1997). The role of instance retrieval in understanding complex concepts. *Memory and Cognition, 23,* 665–674.

Gregory, R. L. (1978). *Eye and brain* (3rd ed.). New York: McGraw-Hill.

Grene, M. (1963). *A portrait of Aristotle.* London: Faber and Faber.

Grice, H. P. (1989). Logic and conversation. In *Studies in the way of words* (pp. 22–143). Cambridge MA: Harvard University Press.

Griggs, R. A., & Cox, J. R. (1982). The elusive thematic-materials effect in Wason's selection task. *British Journal of Psychology, 73,* 407–420.

Grinstead, J., MacSwan, J., Curtiss, S., & Gelman, R. (2005). *The independence of language and number.* Manuscript submitted for publication.

Gutheil, G., Bloom, P., Valderrama, N., & Freedman, R. (2004). The role of historical intuitions in children's and adults' naming of artifacts. *Cognition, 91,* 23–42.

Gutheil, G., & Gelman, S. A. (1997). Children's use of sample size and diversity information with basic-level categories. *Journal of Experimental Child Psychology, 64,* 159–174.

Gutheil, G., & Rosengren, K. S. (1996). A rose by any other name: Preschoolers' understanding of individual identity across name and appearance changes. *British Journal of Developmental Psychology, 14,* 477–498.

Gvozdanović, J. (1992). *Indo-European numerals.* Berlin: Mouton de Gruyter.

Hadamard, J. (1945). *The mathematician's mind: The psychology of invention in the mathematical field.* Princeton, NJ: Princeton University Press.

Hadjichristidis, C., Sloman, S., Stevenson, R., & Over, D. (2004). Feature centrality and property induction. *Cognitive Science, 28,* 45–74.

Hahn, U., & Oaksford, M. (2007). The rationality of informal argumentation: A Bayesian approach to reasoning fallacies. *Psychological Review, 114,* 704–732.

Hájek, A. (2007). Interpretations of probability. In E. N. Zalta (Ed.), *The Stanford encyclopedia of philosophy.* Stanford, CA: Metaphysics Research Lab, Center for the Study of Language and Information, Stanford University. Retrieved from http://plato.stanford.edu/entries/probability-interpret

Halberda, J., Sires, S. F., & Feigenson, L. (2006). Multiple spatially overlapping sets can be enumerated in parallel. *Psychological Science, 17,* 572–576.

Halff, H. M., Ortony, A., & Anderson, R. C. (1976). A context-sensitive representation of word meanings. *Memory and Cognition, 4,* 378–383.

Hall, D. G. (1998). Continuity and the persistence of objects: When the whole is greater than the sum of the parts. *Cognitive Psychology, 37,* 28–59.

Hall, D. G., Lee, S. C., & Bélanger, J. (2001). Young children's use of syntactic cues to learn proper names and count nouns. *Developmental Psychology, 37,* 298–307.

Hall, D. G., Waxman, S. R., Brédart, S., & Nicolay, A.-C. (2003). Preschoolers' use of form class cues to learn descriptive proper names. *Child Development, 74,* 1547–1560.

Hamilton, A. G. (1982). *Numbers, sets, and axioms.* Cambridge, UK: Cambridge University Press.

Hamilton, W. R. (1969). *Elements of quaternions.* New York: Chelsea. (Original work published 1866)

Hampton, J. A. (1979). Polymorphous concepts in semantic memory. *Journal of Verbal Learning and Verbal Behavior, 18,* 441–461.

Hampton, J. A. (1987). Inheritance of attributes in natural concept conjunctions. *Memory and Cognition, 15,* 55–71.

Hampton, J. A. (1988). Overextension of conjunctive concepts: Evidence for a unitary model of concept typicality and class inclusion. *Journal of Experimental Psychology: Learning, Memory, and Cognition, 14,* 12–32.

Hampton, J. A. (1995a). Similarity-based categorization: The development of prototype theory. *Psychologica Belgica, 35,* 103–125.

Hampton, J. A. (1995b). Testing the prototype theory of concepts. *Journal of Memory and Language, 34,* 686–708.

Hanlon, C. (1988). The emergence of set-relational quantifiers in early childhood. In F. S. Kessel (Ed.), *The development of language and language researchers: Essays in honor of Roger Brown* (pp. 65–78). Hillsdale, NJ: Erlbaum.

Harman, G. (1965). The inference to the best explanation. *Philosophical Review, 74,* 88–95.

Harman, G. (1986). *Change in view: Principles of reasoning.* Cambridge, MA: MIT Press.

Harper, W. (1989). Consilience and natural kind reasoning. In J. R. Brown & J. Mittelstrass (Eds.), *An intimate relation* (pp. 115–152). Dordrecht, Holland: Kluwer.

Hartnett, P. M. (1991). *The development of mathematical insight: From one, two, three to infinity.* Unpublished doctoral dissertation, University of Pennsylvania, Philadelphia.

Hastie, R., Schroeder, C., & Weber, R. (1990). Creating complex social conjunction categories from simple categories. *Bulletin of the Psychonomic Society, 28,* 242–247.

Hauser, M. D., Chomsky, N., & Fitch, W. T. (2002). The faculty of language: What is it, who has it, and how did it evolve? *Science, 298,* 1569–1579.

Hausman, D. M., & Woodward, J. (1999). Independence, invariance, and the causal Markov condition. *British Journal for the Philosophy of Science, 50,* 521–583.

Hayes, P. J. (1979). The logic of frames. In D. Metzing (Ed.), *Frame conceptions and text understanding.* Berlin: de Gruyter.

Heider, F., & Simmel, M. (1944). An experimental study of apparent behavior. *American Journal of Psychology, 57,* 243–259.

Heit, E. (1998). A Bayesian analysis of some forms of inductive reasoning. In M. Oaksford & N. Chater (Eds.), *Rational models of cognition* (pp. 248–274). Oxford: Oxford University Press.

Heit, E. (2000). Properties of inductive reasoning. *Psychonomic Bulletin and Review, 7,* 569–592.

Heit, E., & Rotello, C. M. (2010). Relations between inductive reasoning and deductive reasoning. *Journal of Experimental Psychology: Learning, Memory, and Cognition, 36,* 805-812.

Heit, E., & Rubinstein, J. (1994). Similarity and property effects in inductive reasoning. *Journal of Experimental Psychology: Learning, Memory, and Cognition, 20,* 411–422.

Hempel, C. G. (1965). *Aspects of scientific explanations.* New York: Free Press.

Hespos, S. J., Dora, B., Rips, L. J., & Christie, S. (in press). Infants make quantity discriminations for substances *Child Development.*

Hiddleston, E. (2005). A causal theory of counterfactuals. *Nous, 39,* 632–657.

Hilbert, D. (1983). On the infinite (E. Putnam & G. J. Massey, Trans.). In P. Benacerraf & H. Putnam (Eds.), *Philosophy of mathematics* (2nd ed., pp. 183–201). Cambridge, UK: Cambridge University Press. (Original work published 1926)

Hilbert, D. (1996). The new grounding of mathematics: First report (W. Ewald, Trans.). In W. B. Ewald (Ed.), *From Kant to Hilbert* (Vol. 2, pp. 1117–1134). Oxford: Oxford University Press. (Original work published 1922)

Hilton, D. J. (1988). Logic and causal attribution. In D. J. Hilton (Ed.), *Contemporary science and natural explanation: Commonsense conceptions of causality* (pp. 33–65). New York: New York University Press.

Hilton, D. J. (1990). Conversational processes and causal explanation. *Psychological Bulletin, 107,* 65–81.

Hilton, D. J., Jaspars, J. M. F., & Clarke, D. D. (1990). Pragmatic conditional reasoning. *Journal of Pragmatics, 14,* 791–812.

Hintzman, D. L. (1986). "Schema abstraction" in a multiple-trace memory model. *Psychological Review, 93,* 411–428.

Hirsch, E. (1982). *The concept of identity.* Oxford: Oxford University Press.

Hirsch, E. (1997). Basic objects: A reply to Xu. *Mind and Language, 12,* 406–412.

Ho, D. Y. F. (2000). Dialectical thinking: Neither Eastern nor Western. *American Psychologist, 55,* 1064-1065.

Hobbes, T. (1839–1845). De corpore. In W. Molesworth (Ed.), *The English works of Thomas Hobbes* (Vol. 1). London: John Bohn.

Hodes, H. T. (1984). Logicism and the ontological commitments of arithmetic. *Journal of Philosophy, 81,* 123–149.

Holyoak, K. J., & Thagard, P. (1995). *Mental leaps.* Cambridge, MA: MIT Press.

Hood, B. M., & Bloom, P. (2008). Children prefer certain individuals over perfect duplicates. *Cognition, 106,* 455–462.

Horn, L. R. (1989). *A natural history of negation.* Chicago: University of Chicago Press.

Horty, J. F., Thomason, R. H., & Touretzky, D. S. (1987). A skeptical theory of inheritance in nonmonotonic semantic networks. *Proceedings of the Sixth National Conference on Artificial Intelligence,* 358–363.

Houdé, O., & Tzourio-Mazoyer, N. (2003). Neural foundations of logical and mathematical cognition. *Nature Neuroscience, 4,* 507–514.

Hume, D. (1967). *A treatise of human nature* (L. A. Selby-Bigge, Ed.). Oxford: Oxford University Press. (Original work published 1739)

Huntley-Fenner, G., Carey, S., & Solimando, A. (2002). Objects are individuals but stuff doesn't count: Perceived rigidity and cohesiveness influence infants' representations of small groups of discrete entities. *Cognition, 85,* 203–221.

Hurford, J. R. (1975). *The linguistic theory of numerals.* Cambridge, UK: Cambridge University Press.

Hurford, J. R. (1987). *Language and number: The emergence of a cognitive system.* Oxford: Blackwell.

Huttenlocher, J., & Hedges, L. V. (1994). Combining graded categories: Membership and typicality. *Psychological Review, 101,* 157–165.

Inagaki, K., & Hatano, G. (1993). Young children's understanding of the mind-body distinction. *Child Development, 64,* 1534–1549.

Intriligator, J., & Cavanagh, P. (2001). The spatial resolution of visual attention. *Cognitive Psychology, 43,* 171–216.

Jackendoff, R. (1990). *Semantic structures.* Cambridge, MA: MIT Press.

January, D., & Kako, E. (2007). Re-evaluating evidence for linguistic relativity: Reply to Boroditsky (2001). *Cognition, 104,* 417–426.

Jeshion, R. (2010). Singular thought: acquaintance, semantic instrumentalism, and cognitivism. In R. Jeshion (Ed.), *New Essays on Singular Thought* (pp. 105-140). Oxford, UK: Oxford University Press.

Johnson, C. N. (1990). If you had my brain, where would I be? Children's understanding of the brain and identity. *Child Development, 61,* 962–972.

Johnson, C., & Keil, F. C. (2000). Explanatory knowledge and conceptual combination. In F. C. Keil & R. A. Wilson (Eds.), *Explanation and cognition* (pp. 327–359). Cambridge, MA: MIT Press.

Johnson, S. C., & Carey, S. (1998). Knowledge enrichment and conceptual change in folk biology: Evidence from people with Williams syndrome. *Cognitive Psychology, 37,* 156–200.

Johnson-Laird, P. N. (1987). The mental representation of the meaning of words. *Cognition, 25,* 189–211.

Johnson-Laird, P. N. (1994). Mental models and probabilistic thinking. *Cognition, 50,* 189–209.

Johnson-Laird, P. N., & Byrne, R. M. J. (1991). *Deduction.* Hillsdale, NJ: Erlbaum.

Johnson-Laird, P. N., Byrne, R. M. J., & Schaeken, W. (1992). Propositional reasoning by model. *Psychological Review, 99,* 418–439.

Johnson-Laird, P. N., Legrenzi, P., Girotto, V., Legrenzi, V., & Caverni, J.-P. (1999). Naive probability: A mental model theory of extensional reasoning. *Psychological Review, 106,* 62–88.

Jones, G. V. (1982). Stacks not fuzzy sets: An ordinal basis of prototype theory of concepts. *Cognition, 12,* 281–290.

Just, M. A., & Carpenter, P. A. (1971). Comprehension of negation with quantification. *Journal of Verbal Learning and Verbal Behavior, 10,* 244–253.

Just, M. A., & Carpenter, P. A. (1987). *The psychology of reading and language comprehension.* Boston: Allyn and Bacon.

Kahneman, D., & Miller, D. T. (1986). Norm theory: Comparing reality to its alternatives. *Psychological Review, 93,* 136–153.

Kahneman, D., Treisman, A., & Gibbs, B. J. (1992). The reviewing of object files: Object-specific integration of information. *Cognitive Psychology, 24,* 175–219.

Kaiser, M. K., Proffitt, D. R., & Anderson, K. (1985). Judgments of natural and anomalous trajectories in the presence and absence of motion. *Journal of Experimental Psychology: Learning, Memory, and Cognition, 11,* 795–803.

Kalish, C. W. (1995). Essentialism and graded membership in animal and artifact categories. *Memory and Cognition, 23,* 335–349.

Kamp, H., & Partee, B. (1995). Prototype theory and compositionality. *Cognition, 57,* 129–191.

Kaplan, M. (1996). Decision theory as philosophy. Cambridge, UK: Cambridge University Press.

Kaye, R. (1991). *Models of Peano arithmetic.* Oxford: Oxford University Press.

Keil, F. C. (1989). *Concepts, kinds, and cognitive development.* Cambridge, MA: MIT Press.

Keil, F. C. (1995). The growth of causal understanding of natural kinds. In D. Sperber, D. Premack, & A. J. Premack (Eds.), *Causal cognition* (pp. 234–262). Oxford: Oxford University Press.

Keil, F. C., Smith, W. C., Simons, D. J., & Levin, D. T. (1998). Two dogmas of conceptual empiricism: Implications for hybrid models of the structure of knowledge. *Cognition, 65,* 103–135.

Kelley, H. H. (1967). Attribution theory in social psychology. In D. Levine (Ed.), *Nebraska symposium on motivation* (Vol. 15, pp. 192–241). Lincoln: University of Nebraska Press.

Kemp, C., & Tenenbaum, J. B. (2009). Structured statistical models of inductive reasoning. *Psychological Review, 116,* 20–58.

Keren, G., & Schul, Y. (2009). Two is not always better than one: A critical evaluation of two-system theories. *Perspectives on Psychological Science, 4,* 533-550.

Kintsch, W. (1974). *The representation of meaning in memory.* Hillsdale, NJ: Erlbaum.

Kintsch, W. (1988). The role of knowledge in discourse comprehension: A construction-integration model. *Psychological Review, 95,* 163–182.

Klahr, D., & Wallace, J. G. (1976). *Cognitive development: An information-processing view.* Hillsdale, NJ: Erlbaum.

Klem, L. (1995). Path analysis. In L. G. Grimm & P. R. Yarnold (Eds.), *Reading and understanding multivariate statistics* (pp. 65–97). Washington, DC: American Psychological Association.

Knuth, D. E. (1974). *Surreal numbers.* Reading, MA: Addison-Wesley.

Kobayashi, T., Hiraki, K., Mugitani, R., & Hasegawa, T. (2004). Baby arithmetic: One object plus one tone. *Cognition, 91,* B23–B34.

Kolodner, J. L. (1993). *Case-based reasoning.* San Mateo, CA: Morgan Kaufmann.

Komatsu, L. (1992). Recent views of conceptual structure. *Psychological Bulletin, 112,* 500–526.

Kornblith, H. (1993). *Inductive inference and its natural ground.* Cambridge, MA: MIT Press.

Koslowski, B. (1996). *Theory and evidence: The development of scientific reasoning.* Cambridge, MA: MIT Press.

Kotovsky, L., & Baillargeon, R. (2000). Reasoning about collisions involving inert objects in 7.5-month-old infants. *Developmental Science, 3,* 344–359.

Krifka, M., Pelletier, F. J., Carlson, G. N., ter Meulen, A., Chierchia, G., & Link, G. (1995). Genericity: An introduction. In G. N. Carlson & F. J. Pelletier (Eds.), *The generic book* (pp. 1–124). Chicago: University of Chicago Press.

Kripke, S. A. (1972). *Naming and necessity*. Cambridge, MA: Harvard University Press.

Kuhlmeier, V. A., Bloom, P., & Wynn, K. (2004). Do 5 month old infants see humans as material objects? *Cognition, 94*, 95–103.

Kuhn, D. (1991). *The skills of argument*. Cambridge, UK: Cambridge University Press.

Kunda, Z., Miller, D. T., & Claire, T. (1990). Combining social concepts: The role of causal reasoning. *Cognitive Science, 14*, 551–577.

Kyburg, H. (1983). Recent work in inductive logic. In K. G. Lucey & T. R. Machan (Eds.), *Recent work in philosophy* (pp. 87–150). Totowa, NJ: Rowman & Allanheld.

Lagnado, D. A., & Sloman, S. (2005). The advantage of timely intervention. *Journal of Experimental Psychology: Learning, Memory, and Cognition, 30*, 856–876.

Lakoff, G. (1970). Linguistics and natural logic. *Synthese, 22*, 151–271.

Lakoff, G. (1987). *Women, fire, and dangerous things*. Chicago: University of Chicago Press.

Lakoff, G., & Núñez, R. E. (2000). *Where mathematics comes from: How the embodied mind brings mathematics into being*. New York: Basic Books.

Larkin, J. H., & Simon, H. A. (1987). Why a diagram is (sometimes) worth a thousand words. *Cognitive Science, 11*, 65–99.

Lassaline, M. E. (1996). Structural alignment in induction and similarity. *Journal of Experimental Psychology: Learning, Memory, and Cognition, 22*, 754–770.

Laurence, S., & Margolis, E. (1999). Concepts and cognitive science. In E. Margolis & S. Laurence (Eds.), *Concepts: Core readings* (pp. 3–81). Cambridge, MA: MIT Press.

Laurence, S., & Margolis, E. (2005). Number and natural language. In P. Carruthers, S. Laurence, & S. Stich (Eds.), *The innate mind: Structure and content* (pp. 216–235). Oxford: Oxford University Press.

Lave, J. (1988). *Cognition in practice: Mind, mathematics, and culture in everyday life*. Cambridge, UK: Cambridge University Press.

Lawlor, K. (2001). *New thoughts about old things: Cognitive policies as the ground of singular concepts*. New York: Garland.

Le Corre, M., & Carey, S. (2007). One, two, three, four, nothing more: An investigation of the conceptual sources of the verbal counting principles. *Cognition, 105*, 395–438.

Le Corre, M., Van de Walle, G., Brannon, E. M., & Carey, S. (2006). Revisiting the competence/performance debate in the acquisition of counting principles. *Cognitive Psychology, 52*, 130–169.

Lee, Y-T. (2000). What is missing in Chinese-Western dialectical reasoning. *American Psychologist, 55*, 1065-1067.

Leslie, A. M. (1984). Spatiotemporal continuity and the perception of causality in infants. *Perception, 13*, 287–305.

Leslie, A. M. (1986). Getting development off the ground: Modularity and the infant's perception of causality. In P. V. Geert (Ed.), *Theory building in development* (pp. 405 – 437). Amsterdam: Elsevier, North-Holland.

Leslie, A. M., Friedman, O., & German, T. P. (2004). Core mechanisms in "theory of mind." *Trends in Cognitive Sciences, 8*, 528–533.

Leslie, A. M., Gallistel, C. R., & Gelman, R. (2007). Where integers come from. In P. Carruthers, S. Laurence, & S. Stich (Eds.), *The innate mind: Foundations and future* (pp. 109–138). Oxford: Oxford University Press.

Leslie, A. M., & Keeble, S. (1987). Do six-month-olds perceive causality? *Cognition, 25*, 265–288.

Leslie, S.-J. (2008). Generics: Cognition and acquisition. *Philosophical Review, 117*, 1–47.

Levi, I. (1996). *For the sake of the argument.* Cambridge, UK: Cambridge University Press.

Levi, J. N. (1978). *The syntax and semantics of complex nominals.* New York: Academic Press.

Lewis, D. (1973a). Causation. *Journal of Philosophy, 70*, 556–567.

Lewis, D. (1973b). *Counterfactuals.* Cambridge, MA: Harvard University Press.

Lewis, D. (1979). Counterfactual dependence and time's arrow. *Noûs, 13*, 455–476.

Lewis, D. (1983). Survival and identity. In *Philosophical papers* (Vol. 1, pp. 55–77). Oxford: Oxford University Press.

Lewis, D. (1986). Causal explanation. In *Philosophical papers* (Vol. 2, pp. 214–240). Oxford: Oxford University Press.

Lewontin, R. C. (1998). The evolution of cognition: Questions we will never answer. In D. Scarborough & S. Sternberg (Eds.), *An invitation to cognitive science: Vol. 4. Methods, models, and conceptual issues* (pp. 107–132). Cambridge, MA: MIT Press.

Liittschwager, J. C. (1995). Children's reasoning about identity across transformation. *Dissertation Abstracts International, 55*(10), 4623B. (University Microfilms No. AAC95-08399)

Lipton, J. S., & Spelke, E. S. (2003). Origins of number sense: Large number discrimination in human infants. *Psychological Science, 14*, 396–401.

Liu, L. G. (1985). Reasoning counterfactually in Chinese: Are there any obstacles? *Cognition, 21*, 239-270.

Lloyd, E. A. (1999). Evolutionary psychology: The burdens of proof. *Biology and Philosophy, 14*, 211–233.

Locke, J. (1975). *An essay concerning human understanding* (P. H. Nidditch, Ed.). Oxford: Clarendon Press. (Original work published 1690)

Loehlin, J. C. (1992). *Latent variable models: An introduction to factor, path, and structural analysis* (2nd ed.). Hillsdale, NJ: Erlbaum.

Lombrozo, T. (2009). Explanation and categorization: How "why?" informs "what?" *Cognition, 110,* 248–253.

Lopez, A., Atran, S., Coley, J. D., Medin, D. L., & Smith, E. E. (1997). The tree of life: Universal and cultural features of folkbiological taxonomies and inductions. *Cognitive Psychology, 32,* 251–295.

Loux, M. J. (1991). *Primary ousia: An essay on Aristotle's Metaphysics Z and H.* Ithaca, NY: Cornell University Press.

Lovejoy, A. O. (1936). *The great chain of being: A study of the history of an idea.* Cambridge, MA: Harvard University Press.

Lowe, E. J. (1989). What is a criterion of identity? *Philosophical Quarterly, 39,* 1–21.

Luhmann, C. C., & Ahn, W. k. (2005). The meaning and computation of causal power: Comment on Cheng (1997) and Novick and Cheng (2004). *Psychological Review, 112,* 685–693.

Lynch, E. B., Coley, J. D., & Medin, D. L. (2000). Tall is typical: Central tendency, ideal dimensions, and graded category structure among tree experts and novices. *Memory and Cognition, 28,* 41–50.

Macaulay, D. (1988). *The way things work.* Boston: Houghton Mifflin.

MacGregor, M., & Stacey, K. (1997). Students' understanding of algebraic notations: 11–15. *Educational Studies in Mathematics, 33,* 1–19.

Mackie, P. (2006). *How things might have been: Individuals, kinds, and essential properties.* Oxford: Oxford University Press.

Macnamara, J. (1986). *A border dispute: The place of logic in psychology.* Cambridge, MA: MIT Press.

Malt, B. C. (1990). Features and beliefs in the mental representations of categories. *Journal of Memory and Language, 29,* 289–315.

Malt, B. C. (1994). Water is not H_2O. *Cognitive Psychology, 27,* 41–70.

Mandler, J. M., & McDonough, L. (1998). Studies in inductive inference in infancy. *Cognitive Psychology, 37,* 60–97.

Manktelow, K. I., & Over, D. E. (1991). Social roles and utilities in reasoning with deontic conditionals. *Cognition, 39,* 85–105.

Margolis, E., & Laurence, S. (2008). How to learn the natural numbers: Inductive inference and the acquisition of number concepts. *Cognition, 106,* 924–939.

Markman, E. M. (1989). *Categorization and naming in children: Problems of induction.* Cambridge, MA: MIT Press.

Markovits, H. (1984). Awareness of the "possible" as a mediator of formal thinking in conditional reasoning problems. *British Journal of Psychology, 75,* 367–376.

Marsh, J. K., & Ahn, W. (2006). The role of causal status versus inter-feature links in feature weighting. *Proceedings of the 26th Annual Conference of the Cognitive Science Society* (pp. 561–566). Mahwah, NJ: Erlbaum.

Matz, M. (1982). Towards a process model for high school algebra errors. In D. Sleeman & J. S. Brown (Eds.), *Intelligent tutoring systems* (pp. 25–50). London: Academic Press.

McCarthy, J., & Hayes, P. (1969). Some philosophical problems from the standpoint of artificial intelligence. In B. Meltzer & D. Michie (Eds.), *Machine intelligence 4* (pp. 463–502). Edinburgh: Edinburgh University Press.

McCawley, J. D. (1968). Lexical insertion in a transformational grammar without deep structure. In *Papers from the 4th regional meeting, Chicago Linguistics Society* (pp. 71–80). Chicago: Chicago Linguistics Society.

McCloskey, M. (1983a). Intuitive physics. *Scientific American, 24,* 122–130.

McCloskey, M. (1983b). Naïve theories of motion. In D. Gentner & A. L. Stevens (Eds.), *Mental models* (pp. 299–324). Hillsdale, NJ: Erlbaum.

McCloskey, M., & Glucksberg, S. (1978). Natural categories: Well-defined or fuzzy sets? *Memory and Cognition, 6,* 462–472.

McCloskey, M., & Lindemann, A. M. (1992). MATHNET: Preliminary results from a distributed model of arithmetic fact retrieval. In J. I. D. Campbell (Ed.), *The nature and origins of mathematical skills* (pp. 365–409). Amsterdam: North-Holland.

McDonald, J., Samuels, M., & Rispoli, J. (1996). A hypothesis-assessment model of categorical argument strength. *Cognition, 59,* 199–217.

McGee, V. (1997). How we learn mathematical language. *Philosophical Review, 106,* 35–68.

McNamara, T. P., & Miller, D. L. (1989). Attributes of theories of meaning. *Psychological Bulletin, 106,* 355–376.

McNamara, T. P., & Sternberg, R. J. (1983). Mental models of word meaning. *Journal of Verbal Learning and Verbal Behavior, 22,* 449–474.

McNeill, W. H. (2001). What if Pizarro had not found potatoes in Peru? In R. Cowley (Ed.), *What if? 2* (pp. 415–427). New York: Berkley Books.

Medin, D. L. (1989). Concepts and conceptual structure. *American Psychologist, 44,* 1469–1481.

Medin, D. L., Goldstone, R. L., & Markman, A. B. (1995). Comparison and choice: Relations between similarity processes and decision process. *Psychonomic Bulletin and Review, 2,* 1–19.

Medin, D. L., Lynch, E. B., Coley, J. D., & Atran, S. (1997). Categorization and reasoning among tree experts. *Cognitive Psychology, 32,* 49–96.

Medin, D. L., & Ortony, A. (1989). Psychological essentialism. In S. Vosniadou & A. Ortony (Eds.), *Similarity and analogical reasoning* (pp. 179–195). Cambridge, UK: Cambridge University Press.

Medin, D. L., & Rips, L. J. (2005). Concepts and categories: Memory, meaning, and metaphysics. In K. J. Holyoak & R. G. Morrison (Eds.), *The Cambridge handbook of thinking and reasoning* (pp. 37–72). Cambridge, UK: Cambridge University Press.

Medin, D. L., & Schaffer, M. M. (1978). Context theory of classification learning. *Psychological Review, 85,* 207–238.

Medin, D. L., & Shoben, E. J. (1988). Context and structure in conceptual combination. *Cognitive Psychology, 20,* 158–190.

Medin, D. L., & Waxman, S. R. (2007). Interpreting asymmetries of projection in children's inductive reasoning. In A. Feeney & E. Heit (Eds.), *Inductive reasoning* (pp. 55–80). New York: Cambridge University Press.

Mendelson, E. (1964). *Introduction to mathematical logic.* New York: Van Nostrand.

Mercier, H., & Sperber, D. (in press). Why do humans reason? Arguments for an argumentative theory. *Behavioral and Brain Sciences.*

Michotte, A. (1963). *The perception of causality.* New York: Basic Books.

Mill, J. S. (1868). *An examination of Sir William Hamilton's philosophy, and of the principle philosophical questions discussed in his writings.* Boston: W.V. Spencer.

Mill, J. S. (1874). *A system of logic* (8th ed.). New York: Harper & Brothers.

Miller, G. A., & Johnson-Laird, P. N. (1976). *Language and perception.* Cambridge, MA: Harvard University Press.

Miller, K. F., & Stigler, J. W. (1987). Counting in Chinese: Cultural variation in a basic cognitive skill. *Cognitive Development, 2,* 279–305.

Minsky, M. (1975). A framework for representing knowledge. In P. H. Winston (Ed.), *The psychology of computer vision* (pp. 211-277). New York: McGraw-Hill.

Mix, K. S., Huttenlocher, J., & Levine, S. C. (2002a). Multiple cues for quantification in infancy: Is number one of them? *Psychological Bulletin, 128,* 278–294.

Mix, K. S., Huttenlocher, J., & Levine, S. C. (2002b). *Quantitative development in infancy and early childhood.* Oxford: Oxford University Press.

Moyer, R. S., & Landauer, T. K. (1967). Time required for judgments of numerical inequality. *Nature, 215,* 1519–1520.

Munsell, J. (1854). *Cases of personal identity.* Albany, NY: J. Munsell.

Murphy, G. L. (1988). Comprehending complex concepts. *Cognitive Science, 12,* 529–562.

Murphy, G. L. (2002). *The big book of concepts.* Cambridge, MA: MIT Press.

Murphy, G. L., & Medin, D. L. (1985). The role of theories in conceptual coherence. *Psychological Review, 92,* 289–316.

Musolino, J. (2004). The semantics and acquisition of number words: Integrating linguistic and developmental perspectives. *Cognition, 93,* 1–41.

Newell, A. (1990). *Unified theories of cognition.* Cambridge, MA: Harvard University Press.

Newell, A., & Simon, H. A. (1972). *Human problem solving.* Englewood Cliffs, NJ: Prentice-Hall.

Newstead, S. E. (1995). Gricean implicatures and syllogistic reasoning. *Journal of Memory and Language, 34,* 644–664.

Newstead, S. E., & Griggs, R. A. (1983). Drawing inferences from quantified statements: A study of the square of opposition. *Journal of Verbal Learning and Verbal Behavior, 22,* 535–546.

Nichols, S., & Bruno, M. (2010). Intuitions about personal identity: An empirical study. *Philosophical Psychology, 23,* 293-312.

Nisbett, R. E., Krantz, D. H., Jepson, C., & Kunda, Z. (1983). The use of statistical heuristics in everyday inductive reasoning. *Psychological Review, 90,* 339–363.

Nisbett, R. E., Peng, K., Choi, I., & Norenzayan, A. (2001). Culture and systems of thought: Holistic versus analytic cognition. *Psychological Review, 108,* 291–310.

Nisbett, R. E., & Ross, L. (1980). *Human inference.* Englewood Cliffs, NJ: Prentice-Hall.

Nisbett, R. E., & Wilson, T. D. (1977). Telling more than we can know: Verbal reports on mental processes. *Psychological Review, 84,* 231-259.

Noles, N. S., & Bloom, P. (2006, May). *The ship of Theseus: Concepts and identity.* Poster presented at the Association for Psychological Science, New York.

Noonan, H. W. (1985). The closest continuer theory of identity. *Inquiry, 28,* 195–229.

Nosofsky, R. M. (1986). Attention, similarity, and the identification-categorization relationship. *Journal of Experimental Psychology: General, 115,* 39–57.

Novick, L. R., & Cheng, P. W. (2004). Assessing interactive causal power. *Psychological Review, 111,* 455–485.

Nozick, R. (1981). *Philosophical explanations.* Cambridge, MA: Harvard University Press.

Oakes, L. M. (1994). The development of infants' use of continuity cues in their perception of causality. *Developmental Psychology, 30,* 869–879.

Oaksford, M., & Chater, N. (1994). A rational analysis of the selection task as optimal data selection. *Psychological Review, 101,* 608–631.

Oaksford, M., & Chater, N. (1998). *Rationality in an uncertain world.* Hove, UK: Psychology Press.

Oaksford, M., & Chater, N. (2003). Conditional probability and the cognitive science of conditional reasoning. *Mind and Language, 18,* 359–379.

Oaksford, M., & Chater, N. (2007). *Bayesian rationality: The probabilistic approach to human reasoning.* Oxford: Oxford University Press.

Oden, G. C. (1984). *Everything is a good example of something, and other endorsements of the adequacy of a fuzzy theory of concepts* (Tech. Rep. No. 21). Madison: University of Wisconsin, Wisconsin Human Information Processing Program.

Osherson, D. N. (1976). *Logical abilities in children: Vol 4. Reasoning and concepts.* Hillsdale, NJ: Erlbaum.

Osherson, D., Perani, D., Cappa, S., Schnur, T., Grassi, F., & Fazio, F. (1998). Distinct brain loci in deductive versus probabilistic reasoning. *Neuropsychologica, 36,* 369–376.

Osherson, D. N., & Smith, E. E. (1981). On the adequacy of prototype theory as a theory of concepts. *Cognition, 11,* 35–58.

Osherson, D. N., & Smith, E. E. (1982). Gradeness and conceptual combination. *Cognition, 12,* 299–318.

Osherson, D. N., & Smith, E. E. (1997). On typicality and vagueness. *Cognition,* *64,* 189-206.

Osherson, D. N., Smith, E. E., Myers, T. S., Shafir, E., & Stob, M. (1994). Extrapolating human probability judgment. *Theory and Decision, 36,* 103–129.

Osherson, D. N., Smith, E. E., & Shafir, E. B. (1986). Some origins of belief. *Cognition, 24,* 197–224.

Osherson, D. N., Smith, E. E., Shafir, E., Gualtierotti, A., & Biolsi, K. (1995). A source of Bayesian priors. *Cognitive Science, 19,* 377–405.

Osherson, D. N., Smith, E. E., Wilkie, O., Lopez, A., & Shafir, E. (1990). Category-based induction. *Psychological Review, 97,* 185–200.

Oshima-Takane, Y. (1999). The learning of first and second person pronouns in English. In R. Jackendoff, P. Bloom, & K. Wynn (Eds.), *Language, logic, and concepts* (pp. 373–409). Cambridge, MA: MIT Press.

Parfit, D. (1984). *Reasons and persons.* Oxford: Oxford University Press.

Parkman, J. M. (1971). Temporal aspects of digit and letter inequality judgments. *Journal of Experimental Psychology, 91,* 191–205.

Parsons, C. (2008). *Mathematical thought and its objects.* Cambridge, UK: Cambridge University Press.

Parsons, L. M., & Osherson, D. (2001). New evidence for distinct right and left brain systems for deductive versus probabilistic reasoning. *Cerebral Cortex, 11,* 954–965.

Parsons, T. (1990). *Events in the semantics of English: A study in subatomic semantics.* Cambridge, MA: MIT Press.

Pearl, J. (1988). *Probabilistic reasoning in intelligent systems: Networks of plausible inference.* San Mateo, CA: Morgan Kaufmann.

Pearl, J. (2000). *Causality.* Cambridge, UK: Cambridge University Press.

Pelham, B. W., & Blanton, H. (2003). *Conducting research in psychology* (2nd ed). Belmont, CA: Wadsworth/Thomson.

Peng, K., & Nisbett, R. E. (1999). Culture, dialectics, and reasoning about contradiction. *American Psychologist, 54,* 741–754.

Perkins, D. N., Farady, M., & Bushey, B. (1991). Everyday reasoning and the roots of intelligence. In J. F. Voss, D. N. Perkins, & J. W. Segal (Eds.), *Informal reasoning and education* (pp. 83–105). Hillsdale, NJ: Erlbaum.

Perry, J. (1972). Can the self divide? *Journal of Philosophy, 69,* 463–488.

Perry, J. (2001). *Knowledge, possibility, and consciousness.* Cambridge, MA: MIT Press.

Peterson, M. A. (2001). Object perception. In E. B. Goldstein (Ed.), *Blackwell handbook of perception* (pp. 168–203). Oxford: Blackwell.

Piaget, J. (1970). *Genetic epistemology* (E. Duckworth, Trans.). New York: Columbia University Press.

Pica, P., Lemer, C., Izard, V., & Dehaene, S. (2004). Exact and approximate arithmetic in an Amazonian indigene group. *Science, 306,* 499–503.

Polk, T. A., & Newell, A. (1995). Deduction as verbal reasoning. *Psychological Review, 102,* 533–566.

Pollard, P. (1982). Human reasoning: Some possible effects of availability. *Cognition, 12,* 65–96.

Pollmann, T. (2003). Some principles involved in the acquisition of number words. *Language Acquisition, 11,* 1–31.

Posner, M. I. (Ed.). (1989). *Foundations of cognitive science.* Cambridge, MA: MIT Press.

Posner, M. I., & Keele, S. W. (1968). On the genesis of abstract ideas. *Journal of Experimental Psychology, 77,* 353–363.

Posner, M. I., & Keele, S. W. (1970). Retention of abstract ideas. *Journal of Experimental Psychology, 83,* 304–308.

Potter, M. C., & Faulconer, B. A. (1979). Understanding noun phrases. *Journal of Verbal Learning and Verbal Behavior, 18,* 509–522.

Prasada, S., & Dillingham, E. M. (2006). Principled and statistical connections in common sense conception. *Cognition, 99,* 73–112.

Priest, G. (1999). Validity. In A. C. Varzi (Ed.), *The nature of logic* (pp. 183–206). Stanford, CA: CSLI Publications.

Proffitt, D. R., & Kaiser, M. K. (1995). Perceiving events. In W. Epstein & S. Rogers (Eds.), *Perception of space and motion* (pp. 227–261). San Diego, CA: Academic Press.

Proffitt, J. B., Coley, J. D., & Medin, D. L. (2000). Expertise and category-based induction. *Journal of Experimental Psychology: Learning, Memory, and Cognition, 26,* 811–828.

Putnam, H. (1967). Mathematics without foundations. *Journal of Philosophy, 64,* 5–22.

Putnam, H. (1971). *Philosophy of logic.* New York: Harper.

Putnam, H. (1975). The meaning of "meaning." In K. Gunderson (Ed.), *Minnesota studies in the philosophy of science, VII.* Minneapolis: University of Minnesota Press.

Putnam, H. (1988). *Representation and reality.* Cambridge, MA: MIT Press.

Putnam, H. (1990). Is water necessarily H2O? In J. Conant (Ed.), *Realism with a human face* (pp. 54–79). Cambridge, MA: Harvard University Press.

Pylyshyn, Z. (2001). Visual indexes, preconceptual objects, and situated vision. *Cognition, 80,* 127–158.

Quine, W. V. (1936). Truth by convention. In O. H. Lee (Ed.), *Philosophical essays for A. N. Whitehead.* New York: Longmans.

Quine, W. V. (1960). *Word and object.* Cambridge, MA: MIT Press.

Quine, W. V. (1969). Natural kinds. In *Ontological relativity and other essays* (pp. 114–138). New York: Columbia University Press.

Quine, W. V. (1974). *The roots of reference.* La Salle, IL: Open Court.

Rabb, T. K. (2001). If Charles I had not left Whitehall, August 1641. In R. Cowley (Ed.), *What if? 2* (pp. 122–133). New York: Berkley Books.

Ramsey, F. P. (1990). General propositions and causality. In D. H. Mellor (Ed.), *Philosophical papers* (pp. 145–163). Cambridge, UK: Cambridge University Press. (Original work published 1929)

Rasmussen, C., Ho, E., & Bisanz, J. (2003). Use of the mathematical principle of inversion in young children. *Journal of Experimental Child Psychology, 85,* 89–102.

Reed, S. K. (1972). Pattern recognition and categorization. *Cognitive Psychology, 3,* 382–407.

Rehder, B. (2006a). Human deviations from normative causal reasoning. *Proceedings of the Cognitive Science Society* (p. 2596). Mahwah, NJ: Erlbaum.

Rehder, B. (2006b). When similarity and causality compete in category-based property generalization. *Memory and Cognition, 34,* 3–16.

Rehder, B., & Burnett, R. C. (2005). Feature inference and the causal structure of categories. *Cognitive Psychology, 50,* 264–314.

Rehder, B., & Hastie, R. (2001). Causal knowledge and categories: The effects of causal beliefs on categorization, induction, and similarity. *Journal of Experimental Psychology: General, 130,* 323–360.

Reiter, R. (1980). A logic for default reasoning. *Artificial Intelligence, 13,* 81–132.

Reiter, R., & Criscuolo, G. (1981). On interacting defaults. *Proceedings of the Seventh International Joint Conference on Artificial Intelligence,* 270–276.

Rescorla, R. A., & Wagner, A. R. (1972). A theory of Pavlovian conditioning: Variations in the effectiveness of reinforcement and nonreinforcement. In A. H. Black & W. F. Prokasy (Eds.), *Classical conditioning II: Current research and theory.* New York: Appleton-Century Crofts.

Resnick, L. B. (1992). From protoquantities to operators: Building mathematical competence on a foundation of everyday knowledge. In G. Leinhardt, R. Putnam, & R. A. Hattrup (Eds.), *Analysis of arithmetic for mathematics teaching* (pp. 373–429). Hillsdale, NJ: Erlbaum.

Resnick, L. B., Salmon, M., Zeitz, C. M., Warthen, S. H., & Holowchak, M. (1993). Reasoning in conversation. *Cognition and Instruction, 11,* 347-364.

Resnik, M. D. (1992). Proof as a source of truth. In M. Detlefsen (Ed.), *Proof and knowledge in mathematics* (pp. 6–32). London: Routledge.

Resnik, M. D. (1997). *Mathematics as a science of patterns.* Oxford: Oxford University Press.

Revlis, R., & Hayes, J. R. (1972). The primacy of generalities in hypothetical reasoning. *Cognitive Psychology, 3,* 268–290.

Rey, G. (1983). Concepts and stereotypes. *Cognition, 15,* 237–262.

Rhemtulla, M. (2005). *Proper names do not allow identity maintenance within the basic level.* Unpublished master's thesis, University of British Columbia, British Columbia, Canada.

Rhemtulla, M, & Hall, D. G. (2009). Basic-level kinds and object persistence. *Memory and Cognition, 37,* 292-301.

Richardson, R. C. (1996). The prospects for an evolutionary psychology: Human language and human reasoning. *Minds and Machines, 6,* 541–557.

Rips, L. J. (1975). Inductive judgments about natural categories. *Journal of Verbal Learning and Verbal Behavior, 14,* 665–681.

Rips, L. J. (1983). Cognitive processes in propositional reasoning. *Psychological Review, 90,* 38–71.

Rips, L. J. (1986). Mental muddles. In M. Brand & R. M. Harnish (Eds.), *The representation of knowledge and belief* (pp. 258–286). Tucson: University of Arizona Press.

Rips, L. J. (1989). Similarity, typicality, and categorization. In S. Vosniadou & A. Ortony (Eds.), *Similarity and analogical reasoning* (pp. 21–59). Cambridge, UK: Cambridge University Press.

Rips, L. J. (1990). Reasoning. *Annual Review of Psychology, 41,* 321–353.

Rips, L. J. (1991). Similarity and the structure of categories. In D. J. Napoli & J. A. Kegl (Eds.), *Bridges between psychology and linguistics: A Swarthmore festschrift for Lila Gleitman.* Hillsdale, NJ: Erlbaum.

Rips, L. J. (1994). *The psychology of proof: Deductive reasoning in human thinking.* Cambridge, MA: MIT Press.

Rips, L. J. (1995a). Deduction and cognition. In D. N. Osherson & E. E. Smith (Eds.), *Invitation to cognitive science* (Vol. 3, pp. 297–343). Cambridge, MA: MIT Press.

Rips, L. J. (1995b). The current status of research on concept combination. *Mind and Language, 10,* 72–104.

Rips, L. J. (1998). Reasoning and conversation. *Psychological Review, 105,* 411–441.

Rips, L. J. (2000). The cognitive nature of instantiation. *Journal of Memory and Language, 43,* 20–43.

Rips, L. J. (2001a). Necessity and natural categories. *Psychological Bulletin, 127,* 827–852.

Rips, L. J. (2001b). Two kinds of reasoning. *Psychological Science, 12,* 129–134.

Rips, L. J. (2001c). Reasoning imperialism. In R. Elio (Ed.), *Common sense, reasoning, and rationality* (pp. 215–235). Oxford: Oxford University Press.

Rips, L. J. (2002). Reasoning. In H. F. Pashler (Series Ed.) and D. L. Medin (Vol. Ed.), *Stevens' handbook of experimental psychology: Vol. 2. Cognition* (3rd ed., pp. 363–411). New York: Wiley.

Rips, L. J. (2008). Causal thinking. In J. E. Adler & L. J. Rips (Eds.), *Reasoning: Studies of human inference and its foundation.* Cambridge, UK: Cambridge University Press.

Rips, L. J. (2010a). *Causation from perception.* Perspectives on Psychological Science, in press.

Rips, L. J. (2010b). Two causal theories of counterfactual conditionals. *Cognitive Science, 34,* 175-221.

Rips, L. J., & Asmuth, J. (2007). Mathematical induction and induction in mathematics. In A. Feeney & E. Heit (Eds.), *Induction* (pp. 248–268). Cambridge, UK: Cambridge University Press.

Rips, L. J., Asmuth, J., & Bloomfield, A. (2006). Giving the boot to the bootstrap: How not to learn the natural numbers. *Cognition, 101*, B51–B60.

Rips, L. J., Asmuth, J., & Bloomfield, A. (2008). Do children learn the integers by induction? *Cognition, 106*, 940–951.

Rips, L. J., Blok, S., & Newman, G. (2006). Tracing the identity of objects. *Psychological Review, 113*, 1–30.

Rips, L. J., Bloomfield, A., & Asmuth, J. (2008). From numerical concepts to concepts of numbers. *Behavioral and Brain Sciences, 31*, 623–642.

Rips, L. J., & Collins, A. (1993). Categories and resemblance. *Journal of Experimental Psychology: General, 122*, 468–486.

Rips, L. J., & Conrad, F. G. (1989). Folk psychology of mental activities. *Psychological Review, 96*, 187–207.

Roelofs, A. (1996). Computational models of lemma retrieval. In T. Dijkstra & K. De Smedt (Eds.), *Computational psycholinguistics: AI and connectionist models of human language processing* (pp. 308–327). London: Taylor & Francis.

Roese, N. (1997). Counterfactual thinking. *Psychological Bulletin, 121*, 133–148.

Rosch, E. (1978). Principles of categorization. In E. Rosch & B. B. Lloyd (Eds.), *Cognition and categorization* (pp. 27–48). Hillsdale, NJ: Erlbaum.

Rosch, E., & Mervis, C. B. (1975). Family resemblance: Studies in the internal structure of natural categories. *Cognitive Psychology, 7*, 573–605.

Rosch, E. H., Mervis, C. B., Gray, W. D., Johnson, D. M., & Boyes-Braem, P. (1976). Basic objects in natural categories. *Cognitive Psychology, 8*, 382–439.

Rosenberg, R. D., & Carey, S. (2009). Infants' representations of material entities. In B. M. Hood & L.R. Santos (Eds.), *The origins of object knowledge* (pp. 165–188). Oxford: Oxford University Press.

Rosengren, K. S., Gelman, S. A., Kalish, C. W., & McCormick, M. (1991). As time goes by: Children's early understanding of growth in animals. *Child Development, 62*, 1302–1320.

Roser, M. E., Fugelsang, J. A., Dunbar, K. A., Corballis, P. M., & Gazzaniga, M. S. (2005). Dissociating processes supporting causal perception and causal inference in the brain. *Neuropsychology, 19*, 591–602.

Ross, B. H., & Murphy, G. L. (1999). Food for thought: Crossclassification and category organization in a complex real-world domain. *Cognitive Psychology, 38*, 495–553.

Rossor, M. N., Warrington, E. K., & Cipolotti, L. (1995). The isolation of calculation skills. *Journal of Neurology, 242*, 78–81.

Rotello, C. M., & Heit, E. (2009). Modeling the effects of argument length and validity on inductive and deductive reasoning. *Journal of Experimental Psychology: Learning, Memory, and Cognition, 35*, 1317-1330.

Roth, E. M., & Mervis, C. B. (1983). Fuzzy set theory and class inclusion relations in semantic categories. *Journal of Verbal Learning and Verbal Behavior, 22,* 509–525.

Rozenblit, L., & Keil, F. (2002). The misunderstood limits of folk science: An illusion of explanatory depth. *Cognitive Science, 26,* 521–562.

Rudolph, U., & Försterling, F. (1997). The psychological causality implicit in verbs: A review. *Psychological Bulletin, 121,* 192–218.

Rumelhart, D. E. (1975). Notes on a schema for stories. In D. G. Bobrow & A. Collins (Eds.), *Representation and understanding* (pp. 211–236). New York: Academic Press.

Rumelhart, D. E. (1992). Toward a microstructural account of human reasoning. In S. I. Davis (Ed.), *Connectionism: Theory and practice* (pp. 69–83). Oxford: Oxford University Press.

Rumelhart, D. E., & Norman, D. A. (1988). Representation in memory. In R. C. Atkinson, R. J. Herrnstein, G. Lindzey, & R. D. Luce (Eds.), *Stevens' handbook of experimental psychology.* New York: Wiley.

Russell, B. (1919). *Introduction to mathematical philosophy.* New York: Dover.

Ryan, P. J. (1986). *Euclidean and non-Euclidean geometry: An analytic approach.* Cambridge, UK: Cambridge University Press.

Sadock, J. M. (1984). The poly-redundant lexicon. In D. Testen, V. Mishra, & J. Drogo (Eds.), *Papers from the Parasession on Lexical Semantics.* Chicago: Chicago Linguistic Society.

Saxe, G. B. (1988). Candy selling and math learning. *Educational Researcher, 17,* 14-21.

Saxe, R., & Carey, S. (2006). The perception of causality in infancy. *Acta Psychologica, 123,* 144–165.

Schaeffer, B., Eggleston, V. H., & Scott, J. L. (1974). Number development in young children. *Cognitive Psychology, 6,* 357–379.

Schank, R. C., & Abelson, R. P. (1977). *Scripts, plans, goals, and understanding.* Hillsdale, NJ: Erlbaum.

Schank, R. C., & Riesbeck, C. K. (1981). *Inside computer understanding.* Hillsdale, NJ: Erlbaum.

Schank, R. C., Collins, G. C., & Hunter, L. E. (1986). Transcending inductive category formation in learning. *Behavioral and Brain Sciences, 9,* 639–686.

Schellenberg, E. G. (2005). Music and cognitive abilities. *Current Directions in Psychological Science, 14,* 317–320.

Schlottmann, A. (2000). Is perception of causality modular? *Trends in Cognitive Sciences, 4,* 441–442.

Schlottmann, A., & Shanks, D. (1992). Evidence for a distinction between judged and perceived causality. *Quarterly Journal of Experimental Psychology, 44A,* 321–342.

Scholl, B. J., & Leslie, A. M. (1999). Explaining the infant's object concept: Beyond the perception/cognition dichotomy. In E. Lepore & Z. Pylyshyn (Eds.), *What is cognitive science?* (pp. 26–73). Oxford: Blackwell.

Scholl, B. J., & Tremoulet, P. (2000). Perceptual causality and animacy. *Trends in Cognitive Sciences, 4,* 299–309.

Schwartz, R. (1995). Is mathematical competence innate? *Philosophy of Science, 62,* 227–240.

Scribner, S. (1984). Studying working intelligence. In B. Rogoff & J. Lave (Eds.), *Everyday cognition: Its development and social context* (pp. 9–40). Cambridge, MA: Harvard Press.

Sells, S. B. (1936). The atmosphere effect: An experimental study of reasoning. *Archives of Psychology, 29,* 1–72.

Shafir, E., Simonson, I., & Tversky, A. (1993). Reason-based choice. *Cognition, 49,* 11–36.

Shafto, P., & Coley, J. D. (2003). Development of categorization and reasoning in the natural world: Novices to experts, naive similarity to ecological knowledge. *Journal of Experimental Psychology: Learning, Memory, and Cognition 29,* 641–649.

Shafto, P., Kemp, C., Bonawitz, E. B., Coley, J. D., & Tenenbaum, J. B. (2008). Inductive reasoning about causally transmitted properties. *Cognition, 109,* 175–192.

Shanks, D. R., & Dickinson, A. (1987). Associative accounts of causality judgment. *Psychology of Learning and Motivation, 21,* 229–261.

Shapiro, S. (1997). *Philosophy of mathematics.* Oxford: Oxford University Press.

Shiffrar, M. (2001). Movement and event perception. In E. B. Goldstein (Ed.), *Blackwell handbook of perception* (pp. 237–271). Oxford: Blackwell.

Shimojo, S., & Ichikawa, S. (1989). Intuitive reasoning about probability: Theoretical and experimental analyses of the "problem of three prisoners." *Cognition, 32,* 1–24.

Shipley, E. F. (1993). Categories, hierarchies, and induction. *Psychology of Learning and Motivation, 30,* 265–301.

Shoemaker, S. (1979). Identity, properties, and causality. *Midwest Studies in Philosophy, 4,* 321–342.

Siegler, R. S., & Ramani, G. B. (2009). Playing linear number board games — but not circular ones — improves low-income preschoolers' numerical understanding. *Journal of Educational Psychology, 101,* 545–560.

Simon, H. A. (1953). Causal ordering and identifiability. In W. C. Hood & T. C. Koopmans (Eds.), *Studies in econometric method* (pp. 49–74). New York: Wiley.

Simons, D. J., & Keil, F. C. (1995). An abstract to concrete shift in the development of biological thought: The *insides* story. *Cognition, 56,* 129–163.

Simons, D. J., & Levin, D. T. (1998). Failure to detect changes to people during a real-world interaction. *Psychonomic Bulletin and Review, 5,* 644–649.

Simpson, E. H. (1951). The interpretation of interaction in contingency tables. *Journal of the Royal Statistical Society, Series B, 13,* 238–241.

Skyrms, B. (2000). Evolution of inference. In T. Kohler & G. Gumerman (Eds.), *Dynamics in human and primate societies* (pp. 77–88). Oxford: Oxford University Press.

Sloman, S. A. (1993). Feature-based induction. *Cognitive Psychology, 25,* 231–280.

Sloman, S. A. (1994). When explanations compete: The role of explanatory coherence on judgments of likelihood. *Cognition, 52,* 1–21.

Sloman, S.A. (1996a). The empirical case for two systems of reasoning. *Psychological Bulletin, 119,* 3–22.

Sloman, S. A. (1996b). The probative value of simultaneous contradictory belief. *Psychological Bulletin, 119,* 27–30.

Sloman, S. A. (1997). Explanatory coherence and the induction of properties. *Thinking and Reasoning, 3,* 81–110.

Sloman, S. A. (2005). *Causal models: How people think about the world and its alternatives.* Oxford: Oxford University Press.

Sloman, S.A., & Ahn, W-K. (1999). Feature centrality: Naming versus imagining. *Memory and Cognition, 27,* 526–537.

Sloman, S.A., & Lagnado, D.A. (2005). Do we "do"? *Cognitive Science, 29,* 5–39.

Sloman, S.A., Love, B. C., & Ahn,W.-K. (1998). Feature centrality and conceptual coherence. *Cognitive Science, 22,* 189–228.

Sloman, S.A., & Malt, B. (2003). Artifacts are not ascribed essences, nor are they treated as belonging to kinds. *Language and Cognitive Processes, 18,* 563–582.

Sloman, S. A., & Rips, L. J. (1998). Similarity as an explanatory construct. *Cognition, 65,* 87–101.

Sloutsky, V. M., & Fisher, A. V. (2004). Induction and categorization in young children: A similarity-based model. *Journal of Experimental Psychology: General, 133,* 166–188.

Smith, E. E., & Gray, K. C. (1995). The role of instance retrieval in understanding complex concepts. *Memory and Cognition, 23,* 665-675.

Smith, E. E., Langston, C., & Nisbett, R. (1992). The case for rules in reasoning. *Cognitive Science, 16,* 1–40.

Smith, E. E., & Medin, D. L. (1981). *Categories and concepts.* Cambridge, MA: Harvard University Press.

Smith, E. E., & Osherson, D. N. (1984). Conceptual combination with prototype concepts. *Cognitive Science, 8,* 337–361.

Smith, E. E., & Osherson, D. N. (Eds.). (1995). *Thinking.* Cambridge, MA: MIT Press.

Smith, E. E., Osherson, D. N., Rips, L. J., & Keane, M. (1988). Combining prototypes: A selective modification model. *Cognitive Science, 12,* 485–527.

Smith, E. E., Shafir, E., & Osherson, D. (1993). Similarity, plausibility, and judgments of probability. *Cognition, 49,* 67–96.

Smith, E. E., Shoben, E. J., & Rips, L. J. (1974). Structure and process in semantic memory: A featural model for semantic decisions. *Psychological Review, 81,* 214–241.

Smith, E. E., & Sloman, S. A. (1994). Similarity- versus rule-based categorization. *Memory and Cognition, 22,* 377–386.

Smith, L. (2002). *Reasoning by mathematical induction in children's arithmetic.* Amsterdam: Pergamon.

Smith, R. H., Hilton, D. J., Kim, S. H., & Garonzik, R. (1992). Knowledge-based causal inference: Norms and the usefulness of distinctiveness. *British Journal of Social Psychology, 31,* 239–248.

Sober, E. (1980). Evolution, population thinking, and essentialism. *Philosophy of Science, 47,* 350–383.

Solomon, G. E. A., Johnson, S. C., Zaitchik, D., & Carey, S. (1996). Like father, like son: Young children's understanding of how and why offspring resemble their parents. *Child Development, 67,* 151–171.

Sontag, S. (1992). *The volcano lover: A romance.* New York: Farrar Straus Giroux.

Sophian, C., Harley, H., & Manos Martin, C. S. (1995). Relational and representational aspects of early number development. *Cognition and Instruction, 13,* 253–268.

Sorrentino, C. M. (2001). Children and adults represent proper names as referring to unique individuals. *Developmental Science, 4,* 399–407.

Spelke, E. S. (1990). Principles of object perception. *Cognitive Science, 14,* 29–56.

Spelke, E. S. (2000). Core knowledge. *American Psychologist, 55,* 1233–1243.

Spelke, E. S. (2003). What makes us smart? Core knowledge and natural language. In D. Gentner & S. Goldin-Meadow (Eds.), *Language in mind* (pp. 277–311). Cambridge, MA: MIT Press.

Spelke, E. S., Breinlinger, K., Macomber, J., & Jacobson, K. (1992). Origins of knowledge. *Psychological Review, 99,* 605–632.

Spelke, E. S., Gutheil, G., & Van de Walle, G. (1995). The development of object perception. In D. N. Osherson (Series Ed.) and S. M. Kosslyn & D. N. Osherson (Vol. Eds.), *Invitation to cognitive science: Vol. 2. Visual cognition* (2nd ed., pp. 297–330). Cambridge, MA: MIT Press.

Spelke, E. S., Kestenbaum, R., Simons, D. J., & Wein, D. (1995). Spatiotemporal continuity, smoothness of motion, and object identity in infancy. *British Journal of Developmental Psychology, 13,* 113–142.

Spelke, E. S., & Tsivkin, S. (2001). Language and number: A bilingual training study. *Cognition, 78,* 45–88.

Spellman, B. A. (1996). Conditionalizing causality. *Psychology of Learning and Motivation, 34,* 167–206.

Sperber, D. (1985). Anthropology and psychology: Toward an epidemiology of representations. *Man, 20,* 73–89.

Sperber, D., Cara, F., & Girotto, V. (1995). Relevance theory explains the selection task. *Cognition, 57,* 31–95.

Sperber, D., & Girotto, V. (2002). Use or misuse of the selection task: rejoinder to Fiddick, Cosmides, and Tooby. *Cognition, 85,* 277–290.

Sperber, D., & Wilson, D. (1986). *Relevance: Communication and cognition.* Cambridge, MA: Harvard University Press.

Spirtes, P., Glymour, C., & Scheines, R. (2000). *Causation, prediction, and search* (2nd ed.). Cambridge, MA: MIT Press.

Springer, K. (1996). Young children's understanding of a biological basis for parent-offspring relations. *Child Development, 67,* 2841–2856.

Springer, K., & Keil, F. C. (1989). On the development of biologically specific beliefs: The case of inheritance. *Child Development, 60,* 637–648.

Springer, K., & Murphy, G. L. (1992). Feature availability in conceptual combination. *Psychological Science, 3,* 111–117.

Stalnaker, R. (1968). A theory of conditionals. In N. Rescher (Ed.), *Studies in logical theory* (pp. 98–112). Oxford: Blackwell.

Stalnaker, R. (1975). Indicative conditionals. *Philosophia, 5,* 269–286.

Stalnaker, R. (2005). Conditional assertions and conditional propositions. *MIT Working Papers in Linguistics and Philosophy, 51.*

Stanovich, K. E. (1999). *Who is rational?* Mahwah, NJ: Erlbaum.

Stanovich, K. E., & West, R. F. (1997). Reasoning independently of prior belief and individual differences in actively open-minded thinking. *Journal of Educational Psychology, 89,* 342–357.

Stanovich, K. E., & West, R. F. (1998). Individual differences in rational thought. *Journal of Experimental Psychology: General, 127,* 161–188.

Starkey, P., & Gelman, R. (1982). The development of addition and subtraction abilities prior to formal schooling in arithmetic. In T. P. Carpenter, J. M. Moser, & T. A. Romberg (Eds.), *Addition and subtraction: A cognitive perspective* (pp. 99–116). Hillsdale, NJ: Erlbaum.

Staudenmayer, H. (1975). Understanding conditional reasoning with meaningful propositions. In R. J. Falmagne (Ed.), *Reasoning: Representation and process in children and adults* (pp. 55–79). Hillsdale, NJ: Erlbaum.

Stenning, K., & van Lambalgen, M. (2008). Interpretation, representation, and deductive reasoning. In J. Adler & L. J. Rips (Eds.), *Reasoning: Studies of human inference and its foundations.* Cambridge, UK: Cambridge University Press.

Stenning, K., & Yule, P. (1997). Image and language in human reasoning: A syllogistic illustration. *Cognitive Psychology, 34,* 109–159.

Sternberg, R. J. (1982). Natural, unnatural, and supernatural concepts. *Cognitive Psychology, 14,* 451–488.

Sternberg, R. J., Chawarski, M. C., & Allbritton, D. W. (1998). If you changed your name and appearance to those of Elvis Presley, who would you be? Historical features in categorization. *American Journal of Psychology, 111,* 327–351.

Sternberg, R. J., & Gastel, J. (1989). If dancers ate their shoes: Inductive reasoning with factual and counterfactual premises. *Memory and Cognition, 17,* 1–10.

Steyvers, M., Tenenbaum, J. B., Wagenmakers, E., & Blum, B. (2003). Inferring causal networks from observation and interventions. *Cognitive Science, 27,* 453–489.

Stone, J. V. (1998). Object recognition using spatiotemporal signatures. *Vision Research, 38,* 947–951.

Strawson, P. F. (1959). *Individuals: An essay in descriptive metaphysics.* London: Routledge.

Strevens, M. (2000). The essentialist aspect of naive theories. *Cognition, 74,* 149–175.

Sturges, P. (1985). *Five screenplays by Preston Sturges* (B. Henderson, Ed.). Berkeley: University of California Press.

Sun, R. (1995). Robust reasoning: Integrating rule-based and similarity-based reasoning. *Artificial Intelligence, 75,* 241–295.

Swinney, D. (1979). Lexical access during sentence comprehension: (Re) consideration of context effects. *Journal of Verbal Learning and Verbal Behavior, 18,* 645–659.

Swinney, D., Love, T., Walenski, M., & Smith, E. E. (2007). Conceptual combination during sentence comprehension: Evidence for compositional processes. *Psychological Science, 18,* 397–400.

Tally, S. (2000). *Almost America.* New York: HarperCollins.

Talmy, L. (1988). Force dynamics in language and cognition. *Cognitive Science, 12,* 49–100.

Tenenbaum, J. B., Griffiths, T. L., & Niyogi, S. (2007). Intuitive theories as grammars for causal inference. In A. Gopnik & L. Schulz (Eds.), *Causal learning: Psychology, philosophy, and computation* (pp. 301–322). Oxford: Oxford University Press.

Tentori, K., Crupi, V., Bonini, N., & Osherson, D. (2007). Comparison of confirmation measures. *Cognition, 103,* 107–119.

Thagard, P. (1988). *A computational philosophy of science.* Cambridge, MA: MIT Press.

Thagard, P. (1997). Coherent and creative conceptual combinations. In T. B. Ward, S. M. Smith, & J. Viad (Eds.), *Creative thought: An investigation of conceptual structures and processes* (pp. 129–141). Washington, DC: American Psychological Association.

Thagard, P., & Nisbett, R. E. (1982). Variability and confirmation. *Philosophical Studies, 42,* 379–394.

Thompson, V. A. (1994). Interpretational factors in conditional reasoning. *Memory and Cognition, 22,* 742–758.

Toulmin, S. E. (1958). *The uses of argument.* Cambridge, UK: Cambridge University Press.

Tourangeau, R., & Rips, L. J. (1991). Interpreting and evaluating metaphors. *Journal of Memory and Language, 30,* 452–472.

Touretzky, D. S. (1984). Implicit ordering of defaults in inheritance systems. *Proceedings of the Fifth National Conference on Artificial Intelligence,* 322–325.

Trabasso, T., & Sperry, L. (1985). Causal relatedness and importance of story events. *Journal of Memory and Language, 24,* 595–611.

Trabasso, T., & Van den Broek, P. (1985). Causal thinking and the representation of narrative events. *Journal of Memory and Language, 24,* 612–630.

Tufte, E. (2006). *Beautiful evidence.* Cheshire, CT: Graphics Press.

Tversky, A. (1969). The intransitivity of preferences. *Psychological Review, 76,* 31–48.

Tversky, A. (1977). Features of similarity. *Psychological Review, 84,* 327–352.

Tversky, A., & Kahneman, D. (1974). Judgment under uncertainty: Heuristics and biases. *Science, 185,* 1124–1131.

Tversky, A., & Kahneman, D. (1980). Causal schemas in judgments under uncertainty. In M. Fishbein (Ed.), *Progress in social psychology* (Vol. 1, pp. 49–72). Hillsdale, NJ: Erlbaum.

Tversky, B. (in press). Visualizing thought. *Topics in Cognitive Science.*

Tversky, B., & Hemenway, K. (1984). Objects, parts, and categories. *Journal of Experimental Psychology: General, 113,* 169–193.

Ullman, S. (1979). *The interpretation of visual motion.* Cambridge, MA: MIT Press.

Van de Walle, G. A., Carey, S., & Prevor, M. (2000). Bases for object individuation in infancy: Evidence from manual search. *Journal of Cognition and Development, 1,* 249–280.

Van Fraassen, B. C. (1980). *The scientific image.* Oxford: Oxford University Press.

vanMarle, K. L. (2004). *Infants' understanding of number: The relationship between discrete and continuous quantity.* Unpublished doctoral dissertation, Yale University, New Haven, CT.

vanMarle, K., Aw, J., McKrink, K., & Santos, L. R. (2006). How capuchin monkeys (cebus apella) quantify objects and substances. *Journal of Comparative Psychology, 120,* 416–426.

Varley, R. A., Klessinger, N. J. C., Romanowski, C. A. J., & Siegal, M. (2005). Agrammatic but numerate. *Proceedings of the National Academy of Science, 102,* 3519–3524.

Vilette, B. (2002). Do young children grasp the inverse relationship between addition and subtraction? Evidence against early arithmetic. *Cognitive Development, 17,* 1365–1383.

Voss, J. F., & Means, M. L. (1991). Learning to reason via instruction in argumentation. *Learning and Instruction, 1,* 337–350.

Voss, J. F., Vesonder, G. T., & Spilich, G. J. (1980). Text generation and recall by high knowledge and low knowledge individuals. *Journal of Verbal Learning and Verbal Behavior, 19,* 651-667.

Waldmann, M. R. (1996). Knowledge-based causal induction. *Psychology of Learning and Motivation, 34,* 47–88.

Waldmann, M. R., & Hagmayer, Y. (2001). Estimating causal strength: The role of structural knowledge and processing effort. *Cognition, 82,* 27–58.

Waldmann, M. R., & Hagmayer, Y. (2005). Seeing versus doing: two modes of accessing causal knowledge. *Journal of Experimental Psychology: Learning, Memory, and Cognition, 31,* 216–227.

Walsh, C., & Sloman, S. (2007). Updating beliefs with causal models: Violations of screening off. In M. A. Gluck, J. R. Anderson, & S. M. Kosslyn (Eds.), *Memory and mind: A festschrift for Gordon H. Bower* (pp. 345-357). New York: Erlbaum.

Wason, P. C. (1966). Reasoning. In B. M. Foss (Ed.), *New horizons in psychology* (pp. 135–151). Harmondsworth, UK: Penguin.

Wasserman, E. A., Kao, S. F., Van Hamme, L. J., Katagiri, M., & Young, M. E. (1996). Causation and association. *Psychology of Learning and Motivation, 34,* 207–264.

Waxman, S. R., Lynch, E. B., Casey, K. L., & Baer, L. (1997). Setters and samoyeds: The emergence of subordinate level categories as a basis for inductive inference in preschool-age children. *Developmental Psychology, 33,* 1074–1090.

Wellman, H. M. (1990). *The child's theory of mind.* Cambridge, MA: MIT Press.

Wellman, H., & Miller, K. F. (1986). Thinking about nothing: Development of the concepts of zero. *British Journal of Developmental Psychology, 4,* 31–42.

Wetherick, N. E. (1989). Psychology and syllogistic reasoning. *Philosophical Psychology, 2,* 111–124.

Wetherick, N. E., & Gilhooly, K. J. (1990). Syllogistic reasoning: Effects of premise order. In K. J. Gilhooly, M. T. G. Keane, R. H. Logie, & G. Erdos (Eds.), *Lines of thinking* (Vol. 1, pp. 99–108). New York: Wiley.

Whalen, J., Gallistel, C. R., & Gelman, R. (1999). Nonverbal counting in humans: The psychophysics of number representation. *Psychological Science, 10,* 130–137.

White, P. A. (2005). The power PC theory and causal powers: Comments on Cheng (1997) and Novick and Cheng (2004). *Psychological Review, 112,* 675–684.

Wiese, H. (2003). Iconic and non-iconic stages in number development: The role of language. *Trends in Cognitive Sciences, 7,* 385–390.

Wiggins, D. (1980). *Sameness and substance.* Cambridge, MA: Harvard University Press.

Wiggins, D. (1997). Sortal concepts: A reply to Xu. *Mind and Language, 12,* 413–421.

Wiggins, D. (2001). *Sameness and substance renewed.* Cambridge, UK: Cambridge University Press.

Wilcox, T., & Baillargeon, R. (1998). Object individuation in infancy: The use of featural information in reasoning about occlusion events. *Cognitive Psychology, 37,* 97–155.

Williams, B. (1982, February 18). Cosmic philosopher. *New York Review of Books, 29,* 32–34.

Williamson, T. (2007). *The philosophy of philosophy.* Oxford: Blackwell.

Wilson, R. A. (1999). Realism, essence, and kind: Resuscitating species essentialism? In R. A. Wilson (Ed.), *Species: New interdisciplinary essays* (pp. 187–207). Cambridge, MA: MIT Press.

Wisniewski, E. J. (1997). When concepts combine. *Psychonomic Bulletin and Review, 4,* 167–183.

Wolff, P., Klettke, B., Ventura, T., & Song, G. (2005). Expressing causation in English and other languages. In W.-k. Ahn, R. L. Goldstone, B. C. Love, A. B. Markman, & P. Wolff (Eds.), *Categorization inside and outside the laboratory* (pp. 29–48). Washington, DC American Psychological Association.

Wood, J. N., Hauser, M. D., Glynn, D. D., & Barner, D. (2008). Free-ranging rhesus monkeys spontaneously individuate and enumerate small numbers of non-solid portions. *Cognition, 106,* 207–221.

Wood, J. N., & Spelke, E. S. (2005). Chronometric studies of numerical cognition in five-month-old infants. *Cognition, 97,* 23–39.

Woodworth, R. S. (1938). *Experimental psychology.* New York: Henry Holt.

Woodworth, R. S., & Sells, S. B. (1935). An atmosphere effect in formal syllogistic reasoning. *Journal of Experimental Psychology, 18,* 451–460.

Wright, S. (1960). Path coefficients and path regressions: Alternative or complementary concepts. *Biometrics, 16,* 189–202.

Wynn, K. (1992a). Children's acquisition of the number words and the counting system. *Cognitive Psychology, 24,* 220–251.

Wynn, K. (1992b). Evidence against empiricist accounts of the origins of numerical knowledge. *Mind and Language, 7,* 315–332.

Wynn, K. (1996). Infants' individuation and enumeration of actions. *Psychological Science, 7,* 164–169.

Wynn, K., Bloom, P. & Chiang, W.-C. (2002). Enumeration of collective entities by 5-month-old infants. *Cognition, 83,* B55–B62.

Xu, F. (1997). From Lot's wife to a pillar of salt: Evidence that *physical object* is a sortal concept. *Mind and Language, 12,* 365–392.

Xu, F. (2002). The role of language in acquiring object kind concepts in infancy. *Cognition, 85,* 223-250.

Xu, F. (2003a). The development of object individuation in infancy. In J. Fagen & H. Hayne (Eds.), *Progress in infancy research* (Vol. 3, pp. 159–192). Mahwah, NJ: Erlbaum.

Xu, F. (2003b). Numerosity discrimination in infants: Evidence for two systems of representation. *Cognition, 89,* B15–B25.

Xu, F., & Arriaga, R. I. (2007). Number discrimination in 10-month-old infants. *British Journal of Developmental Psychology, 25,* 103–108.

Xu, F., & Baker, A. (2005). Object individuation in 10-month-old infants using a simplified manual search method. *Journal of Cognition and Development, 6,* 307-323.

Xu, F., & Carey, S. (1996). Infants' metaphysics: The case of numerical identity. *Cognitive Psychology, 30,* 111–153.

Xu, F., Carey, S., & Quint, N. (2004). The emergence of kind-based object individuation in infancy. *Cognitive Psychology, 49,* 155–190.

Xu, F., & Spelke, E. S. (2000). Large number discrimination in 6-month-old infants. *Cognition, 74,* B1–B11.

Xu, F., Spelke, E. S., & Goddard, S. (2005). Number sense in human infants. *Developmental Science, 8,* 88–101.

Yeh, W., & Rips, L. J. (1992). [Emergent properties for familiar and unfamiliar adjective-noun combinations.] Unpublished raw data.

Young, A. W., Hay, D. C., & Ellis, A. W. (1985). The faces that launched a thousand slips: Everyday difficulties and errors in recognizing people. *British Journal of Psychology, 76,* 495–523.

Zadeh, L. A. (1965). Fuzzy sets. *Information and Control, 8,* 338–353.

Zadeh, L. A. (1982). A note on prototype theory and fuzzy sets. *Cognition, 12,* 291–297.

Zhang, J., & Norman, D. A. (1995). A representational analysis of numeration systems. *Cognition, 57,* 271–295.

Author Index

Abbott, B., 216
Abelson, R. P., 119, 151
Ahn, W. K., 22, 119, 140, 145, 172, 173, 178n12, 217, 218, 219, 245n11, 253, 335
Alexander, J., x
Allbritton, D. W., 18
Alloy, L. B., 141
Almor, A., 335
Alvarez, G. A., 113n4
Anderson, J. A., xxiv
Anderson, J. R., vii, 38, 89, 117n16, 300, 365
Anderson, K., 371
Anderson, R. C., 286n9, 287n9
Anisfeld, M., 8
Armstrong, D. M., 10, 19
Armstrong, S. L., 267, 268
Arriaga, R. I., 70, 71
Asher, H. B., 138
Asmuth, J., 84, 104, 111, 378n3
Atran, S., 152, 193, 194, 202, 205, 210, 227, 230, 243n3
Au, T. K., xi

Aw, J., 112n3
Ayers, M., 53n6

Baer, L., 186
Baillargeon, R., 53n7, 129, 130, 131, 152, 370
Baker, A., 53n7
Baker, M., 197
Banks, W. P., 69
Bar-Hillel, M. A., 304
Barner, D., 112n3
Baron, J., 329
Baroody, A. J., 92, 94
Barry, D., 30
Barsalou, L. W., 226, 257, 272
Bartels, D. M., 41
Barth, H., 69, 71, 72, 77, 112n4, 113n4
Barton, M. E., 119, 204, 206, 215, 225, 236
Bates, D. M., 50
Bauer, L., 288n13
Bedford, F. L., 352
Begg, I., 299

Subject Index

Printed in the USA/Agawam, MA
September 5, 2014

596566.018